D1519795

Letters

THE WORKS OF SAINT AUGUSTINE

A Translation for the 21st Century

Part II – Letters

Volume 3:

Letters 156 – 210

THE WORKS OF SAINT AUGUSTINE
A Translation for the 21st Century

Letters 156 – 210
(*Epistulae*)

II/3

translation and notes by
Roland Teske, S.J.

editor
Boniface Ramsey

New City Press
Hyde Park, New York

Published in the United States by New City Press
202 Cardinal Rd., Hyde Park, New York 12538
©2004 Augustinian Heritage Institute

Library of Congress Cataloging-in-Publication Data:

Augustine, Saint, Bishop of Hippo.
    The works of Saint Augustine.
    "Augustinian Heritage Institute"
    Includes bibliographical references and indexes.
    Contents: — pt. 3, v .15. Expositions of the Psalms, 1-32
—pt. 3, v. 1. Sermons on the Old Testament, 1-19.
— pt. 3, v. 2. Sermons on the Old Testament, 20-50 — [et al.] — pt. 3,
v. 10 Sermons on various subjects, 341-400.
    1.   Theology — Early church, ca. 30-600.   I. Hill,
Edmund.   II. Rotelle, John E.   III. Augustinian
Heritage Institute.   IV. Title.
BR65.A5E53   1990   270.2   89-28878
ISBN 1-56548-055-4 (series)
ISBN 1-56548-200-X (pt. 2, v. 3)

Printed in the United States of America

To

Mary T. Clark, R.S.C.J.

A great friend, scholar, and religious

Contents

Introduction

The sixty-two letters contained in this volume were written between 414 and 422 or 423, though a number of them are virtually impossible to date with any certainty. During these years Augustine became deeply involved in the controversy on grace with Pelagius and his ally, Caelestius, both of whom had passed through North Africa shortly after the fall of Rome. Caelestius, in fact, managed to get himself condemned at a council of Carthage in 411 before moving on to the East. The controversy on grace is the explicit topic of many of the letters in this volume and lurks in the background of others. A few letters deal with the remains of the Donatist schism, which had come to its official end at the Conference of Carthage in June of 411. Still other letters are unrelated to either of these major themes.

There are ten letters to Augustine from others: Letter 156 from Hilary, a Catholic layman from Syracuse in Sicily, who asked Augustine for help with certain "Pelagian" questions that were bothering people in Sicily; Letters 158, 160, 161, and 163 from Evodius, the bishop of Uzalis, who presented Augustine with a series of questions ranging over topics from the nature of the soul to Christ's descent into hell; Letter 168 from Timasius and James, former disciples of Pelagius, who were won over by Augustine to the side of grace and presented Augustine with a copy of Pelagius' book, *Nature*, in response to which Augustine wrote *Nature and Grace*; Letters 172, 195, and 202 from Jerome, who had calmed down considerably since his earlier letters to Augustine; and Letter 198 from Hesychius, bishop of Salona in Dalmatia, who posed for Augustine a series of questions on the end of the world.

There are two letters neither to nor from Augustine: Letter 165 from Jerome to Marcellinus, the imperial commissioner, and his wife, Anapsychia, in response to Marcellinus' request to know what Jerome held on the origin of the soul, and Letter 201 from the emperors Honorius and Theodosius to Aurelius of Carthage, in which the emperors proclaim new sanctions against the Pelagians.

There are three letters from Pope Innocent in reply to letters he received from Africa on the Pelagian heresy: Letter 181 to the participants in the Council of Carthage, who had sent him Letter 175; Letter 182 to the participants in the Council of Milevis, who had sent him Letter 176; and Letter 183 to Augustine, Aurelius, and three other bishops, who had sent him Letter 177.

There are also four letters jointly written by Augustine and Alypius to various persons: Letter 170 to Maximus, a physician in the Province of Byzacena, who had recently converted from Arianism; Letter 171 to Peregrinus, Maximus' bishop, in order to check on how their letter to Maximus was received; Letter 186 to Paulinus, the bishop of Nola and a friend of Pelagius, whom Augustine and Alypius warn about the dangers of the new heresy of Pelagianism and Letter

188 to Juliana, whose daughter, Demetrias, had recently taken vows as a consecrated virgin and had received from Pelagius a letter of exhortation, which Augustine and Alypius warn places too much emphasis on the unaided strength of the human will.

The present volume contains forty letters written by Augustine alone. Four of these he calls "books" in his *Revisions*. These include Letter 166, also called *The Origin of the Soul*, and Letter 167, also called *The Opinion of James*, both addressed to Jerome. In the first of these Augustine pleads with Jerome to explain to him how one can defend the position that God creates a new soul for each infant born without endangering the most firmly founded faith in the inheritance of original sin from Adam. In the second letter Augustine does not so much consult Jerome as explain his own understanding of the opinion of James: *Whoever observes the whole law, but offends on one point, has become guilty of all* (Jas 2:10). Augustine also calls Letter 185 to Boniface a book and entitles it *The Correction of the Donatists*. In it he explains to the tribune of Africa how he should implement the imperial laws against the Donatists who have persisted in their schism after the Conference of Carthage in 411, when the schism was in principle brought to an end. Finally, there is Letter 187 to Dardanus, a Catholic layman in Italy, which in the *Revisions* Augustine calls a book and gives the title *The Presence of God*. In it Augustine explains how, though God is omnipresent, he does not dwell in every human being but only in those whom he has brought to life through his grace.

Besides the four letters that Augustine explicitly called "books" in the *Revisions*, there are other letters that can—not unreasonably—be regarded as books. In *The Deeds of Pelagius* Augustine mentions a book written for Hilary concerning various "Pelagian" propositions being taught in Sicily. This book would seem to be Letter 157, which Augustine wrote in reply to Letter 156 from Hilary. In *The City of God* 20,5,4, Augustine refers to the book-length Letter 199 to Hesychius, the bishop of Salona, and calls it *The End of the World*, though he does not speak of it as a book in the *Revisions*. Letter 197 and Letter 199, both in reply to Hesychius' questions, argue that the prophecies concerning the end of the world do not allow one to calculate the time of Christ's second coming as judge of the living and the dead.

Letters 159 to 164 and 169 represent an interesting exchange with Evodius, Augustine's friend from before his baptism and now bishop of Uzalis. In four of these letters Augustine replies to various questions posed by Evodius. In Letter 159 he tells his friend that the soul does not take a body with it when it dies and points to dreams as evidence of our being able to see with non-bodily eyes. In Letter 162 he again tells his friend that the soul does not take with it a body at death and explains that images seen in dreams are not bodily but like bodies. In Letter 164 Augustine develops a lengthy exegesis of the passage in the First Letter of Peter on Christ's preaching in the underworld to those who did not believe at the time of Noah; he also discusses the origin of Christ's soul. Finally, in Letter 169 Augustine assures Evodius that a Christian need not attain an understanding of the Trinity, which always acts as a unity; he also distinguishes between the union of the Word with the assumed man in the incarnation and the union of the Holy Spirit with the dove at Christ's baptism.

Besides the book-length Letter 185, Augustine also wrote to Boniface Letter 185A, of which we have only a fragment, and Letter 189, in which he encourages Boniface to live a life of Christian holiness and assures him that being a soldier is not incompatible with pleasing God. Augustine wrote two letters to Optatus, the bishop of Milevis. In Letter 190 Augustine explains his views on the question of the origin of the soul and argues for the centrality of the doctrine of original sin to the Catholic faith, though he admits that one can maintain creationism as long as it does not undermine that faith. In Letter 202A Augustine first explains that he will not send Optatus a copy of Letter 166 because he is still awaiting a reply from Jerome and then goes on to justify his own agnosticism with regard to the origin of souls. Augustine also wrote two letters to Sixtus, the future bishop of Rome. In Letter 191 Augustine congratulates Sixtus on having ceased to side with Pelagius and on having come to the defense of the grace of God, while warning him about those who continue to hold Pelagian beliefs. Letter 194 is a book-length letter that presents the whole Augustinian doctrine on the absolute gratuity of grace, the need for baptism, and the inscrutable judgments of God. Another pair of letters are addressed to Celestine, a deacon, who became the Bishop of Rome in 422. In Letter 192 Augustine simply returns Celestine's warm greetings. In Letter 209 Augustine explains to Celestine, who was at that time the pope, the problems he has had with Antonius, the bishop of Fussala, whose outrageous behavior has brought Augustine to the point of resigning his episcopacy. Augustine also wrote two letters to Valerius, an official at the imperial court in Ravenna. Letter 200 accompanied the first book of *Marriage and Desire*, which Augustine wrote and dedicated to Valerius. Letter 206 commended Felix, a bishop from North Africa, to Valerius.

The remaining letters were written by Augustine to various individuals. In Letter 171A to Maximus, to whom Augustine and Alypius wrote Letter 170, Augustine urges the recent convert to a greater purity of heart. Letter 173 to Donatus, a priest of the Donatist sect who had tried to kill himself rather than be forced into the Catholic Church, argues for the legitimacy of religious coercion and urges the priest to study the acts of the Conference of Carthage. Letter 173A is an answer to a number of clerics in the church of Carthage who wanted a scriptural proof of the divinity of the Holy Spirit. Letter 174 to Aurelius, the bishop of Carthage and primate of Africa, is a covering letter that accompanied the finished work, *The Trinity*.

In Letter 178 Augustine wrote to Hilary, most probably the bishop of Narbonne, in order to warn him of the dangers of the new heresy of Pelagianism.

In Letter 179 Augustine wrote to John, the bishop of Jerusalem, who had sympathized with Pelagius when Pelagius was tried in Palestine. Augustine warns John of the dangers of Pelagianism and sends him copies of Pelagius' *Nature* and his own *Nature and Grace*. In Letter 180 Augustine wrote to Oceanus, a Roman nobleman and friend of Jerome, to explain why he has problems with creationism and why he disagrees with Jerome's interpretation of Paul's rebuke to Peter in the Letter to the Galatians. In Letter 184A Augustine wrote to the monks Peter and Abraham on the importance of the baptism of infants, on the inheritance of original sin, and on the need to pray for the conversion of non-believers.

Letter 193 to Marius Mercator, a Catholic layman and author, thanks Mercator for sending him his books against the Pelagians, touches upon various Pelagian teachings, and raises the question of those found living at Christ's coming. Letter 196 to Asselicus, a bishop in Byzacena, deals with the teaching of a certain Aptus, who urged Christians to live like Jews; the letter also discusses whether a Christian should be called a Jew or an Israelite. Letter 203 to Largus, a Catholic layman, consoles him over his sufferings and encourages him to look to the world to come. In Letter 204 Augustine answers the request of Dulcitius, an imperial commissioner in charge of implementing the laws against the Donatists, for instructions on how to deal with the Donatist heretics and argues against the Donatist justification of suicide in the face of coercion. Augustine wrote Letter 205 to Consentius, a Catholic layman from the Balearic Islands, to whom he also wrote Letter 120 and to whom he dedicated the work *Against Lying*. In the present letter he principally discusses the risen body of Christ. Letter 207 to Claudius, an Italian bishop from whom Augustine had received Julian of Eclanum's *To Turbantius*, accompanied Augustine's reply to it, namely, his *Answer to Julian*. In Letter 208 Augustine wrote to Felicia, a consecrated virgin and recent convert from Donatism, to alleviate her distress over scandals in the Church, especially from its shepherds. Finally, in Letter 210 Augustine wrote to Felicity, the mother superior of the women's monastery in Hippo, in order to console her amid her tribulations and to counsel her about giving rebukes.

Letter 156

In 414 or 415 Hilary, a Catholic layman from Syracuse in Sicily, wrote to Augustine asking for instruction with regard to five propositions that were being taught by a certain unnamed individual in Sicily. In *The Deeds of Pelagius* 11, 23, Augustine mentions certain other statements besides those of Caelestius that were condemned at Carthage that "had been sent to me from Sicily." He says that these statements were upsetting the Catholic brethren there and adds, "I replied to them quite sufficiently, I believe, in the book written for Hilary." The "book written for Hilary" must refer to Letter 157, though in *The Deeds of Pelagius* Augustine mentions only three statements, and they do not perfectly match those in this letter from Hilary.

To Augustine, my holy lord and rightly and deservedly venerable bishop who are to be reverenced in every way, Hilary sends greetings.

The grace of Your Holiness, which is known to all, has persuaded my lowly self to give to some of our men who are returning from Syracuse to Hippo this letter for Your Reverence, whom I ought to praise. I ask the sovereign Trinity that, safe and sound and prospering by God's favor, you may welcome this letter of mine for your consideration, my holy and rightly and deservedly venerable lord who are to be reverenced in every way. Next I ask that you deign to be mindful of me in your holy prayers and to instruct our ignorance about what certain Christians in Syracuse are teaching. They say that human beings can be without sin and easily keep the commandments of God if they will, that an infant who was not baptized because prevented by death cannot deserve to perish because it is born without sin, that a rich man who remains in his riches cannot enter the kingdom of God unless he has sold all his possessions, and that it does not profit him if he has perhaps observed all the commandments by the use of his riches, and that one ought not to swear at all. And with regard to the Church, which church is it about which scripture says that it does not have wrinkle or spot? Is it this one in which we are now gathered, or is it that one which we hope for? But a certain man claimed that it is this church in which we now gather with people and that it can be without sin. About all these questions I ask Your Holiness with as many prayers as I can that you command that we be more clearly instructed in order that we may know how we ought to think. I pray, my holy and rightly and deservedly venerable lord who are to be reverenced in every way, that the mercy of our God may keep Your Holiness safe and sound for countless years.

Letter 157

In 414 or 415 Augustine replied to the previous letter from Hilary, who had asked Augustine a series of questions about various Pelagian teachings. Augustine begins by praising Hilary's zeal for the word of God (paragraph 1). If, Augustine points out, some people claim that they can be without sin in this life, they should be confronted with the words of Saint John, who said that they are deceiving themselves, as well as with the fact that even Daniel prayed for the forgiveness of his sins (paragraph 2). With God's help one can refrain from serious sins, but not from daily lesser sins, for which we must daily ask forgiveness (paragraph 3).

Those who claim that some persons live without sin are perhaps tolerable, but those who say that free choice is sufficient for observing the commandments, even without God's help, must be condemned (paragraph 4). With the help of God's grace free choice can perform good works, but without his help it will not attain righteousness, as the petitions of the Lord's prayer show (paragraph 5). The benefit of the law lies in its leading us to ask for the grace to fulfill what the law commands (paragraph 6). Those who reject the medicine of Christ's grace are like sick people who are so deranged that they reject the help of a doctor (paragraph 7). Our free will is freer to the extent that it is healthier, and it is healthier to the extent that it is subject to grace (paragraph 8). Without grace the law makes sin abound, but God gives his grace that we may fulfill his commandments (paragraph 9). Grace does not take away our will but helps it (paragraph 10).

The Pelagian claim that infants who die without baptism cannot be lost because they are born without sin runs counter to the words of the apostle (paragraph 11). Paul teaches that all human beings contract sin from Adam by birth, not by imitation of his sin (paragraph 12). As no one is born except under condemnation because of Adam, so no one is reborn for righteousness except through Christ (paragraph 13). The righteous men and women of the Old Testament were set free through faith in Christ who was to come, just as we are set free through faith in Christ who has come (paragraph 14). Through the law human beings became not merely sinners but transgressors, but the grace of Christ sets them free from all kinds of sin (paragraph 15). Human beings must not neglect what God commands and must not proudly presume upon their own ability to fulfill his commands (paragraph 16). The grace of the savior is able to set us free from original sin and any personal sins we have added to it (paragraph 17). The Pelagians must not impede the salvation of infants by arguing that they do not need baptism (paragraph 18). From the time of Adam sin has reigned over all, even over those who did not sin like Adam (paragraph 19). The grace of Christ brings us greater benefits than the sin of Adam brought us losses (paragraph 20). Augustine again argues that the sin we derive from Adam is not contracted by imitation of his sin (paragraph 21). Caelestius had not wanted to say anything about original sin, but in saying that infants needed to be baptized in order to be redeemed he undermined his own position (paragraph 22).

Augustine turns to Hilary's question about the Pelagian claim that the wealthy must renounce all their riches if they are to enter the kingdom of heaven. He first points out that the patriarchs were wealthy men to order to show that wealth itself does not merit condemnation (paragraph 23). Though the patriarchs did not sell all they had and give it to the poor, God called himself the God of Abraham, Isaac, and Jacob (paragraph 24). In speaking to the rich young man Jesus distinguished between the commandments and the counsels of perfection (paragraph 25). In writing to Timothy Paul instructed the rich how they ought to live, but he did not command them to give up their riches (paragraph 26). And Paul certainly did not contradict Jesus' teaching (paragraph 27). Augustine presents the Pelagian interpretation of Jesus' words about selling all one has and giving it to the poor and points out that the act of abandoning one's wealth is a gift of God (paragraphs 28 and 29). According to the Pelagian teaching Paul was deceiving those who had possessions by what he said when he wrote to Timothy (paragraph 30). Augustine examines Jesus' words about abandoning all things on account of Jesus and explains the conditions under which one must do this (paragraph 31). For a person must abandon his wife, children, parents, and everyone rather than abandon Christ (paragraph 32). So too, a Christian must prefer Christ to any external possessions (paragraph 33). Augustine explains Jesus' words about the necessity of renouncing all things in order to be his disciple (paragraph 34). He also teaches how Christians may possess what they have without preferring their possessions to Christ (paragraph 35). Christians should, nonetheless, hold their wealth in contempt rather than hold Christ in contempt (paragraph 36).

Hence, the Pelagians should cease to speak against the teaching of scripture when they exhort others to greater virtue by condemning lesser virtue (paragraph 37). Those Christians who live a life of religious poverty should not condemn other Christians who have not sold all they have and given it to the poor (paragraph 38). In the same way those who have committed themselves to lives of celibacy ought not to condemn those Christians who live in marital chastity (paragraph 39).

Finally, Augustine takes up Hilary's question about swearing and states that it is better not to swear at all than to fall into perjury, but he points out that even the apostle swore in his letters (paragraph 40). In conclusion he asks Hilary to let him know what is being said in Gaul about the Pelagian errors (paragraph 41).

Bishop Augustine, the servant of Christ and of his Church, sends greetings in the Lord to his son, Hilary.

1, 1. From your letter I learned not only of your good health, but also of your religious zeal concerning the word of God and the pious concern for your own salvation, which is in Christ Jesus our Lord. Thanking God for this, I have not postponed giving my reply.

2. If, then, you ask whether in this life anyone advances in the perfection of righteousness to the point where he lives without any sin at all, pay attention to what the apostle John said, whom the Lord especially loved among his disciples. He said, *If we say that we have no sin, we deceive ourselves, and the truth is not*

in us (1 Jn 1:8). If those, then, about whom you wrote to me, say that they are without sin, you see that they deceive themselves, and the truth is not in them. If, however, they admit that they are sinners in order that they may be able to deserve the mercy of God, let them restrain themselves from deceiving others whom they try win over to this pride. For the Lord's Prayer is necessary for all; the Lord gave it even to the rams of the flock, that is, to his own apostles in order that each would say to God, *Forgive us our debts, as we also forgive our debtors* (Mt 6:12). After all, one for whom these words in the prayer will not be necessary would have to claim to live here without sin. If the Lord foresaw that some other people of that sort were going to exist, better persons, of course, than his apostles, he would have taught them another prayer by which they would not ask that their sins be forgiven, since all their sins were already forgiven in baptism. For, if holy Daniel confessed (not before human beings as if in false humility, but before God, that is, in a prayer which he prayed to God) not only the sins of his people but also his own sins, as his truthful lips expressed this,[1] nothing else, it seems, ought to be said to these people but what the Lord commands to be said by the prophet Ezekiel to a certain proud man, *Are you wiser than Daniel?* (Ez 28:3)

3. But clearly one who is helped by the mercy and grace of God and holds himself back from the sins that are also called grievous and does not neglect to purify himself by works of mercy and by pious prayers from those sins without which no one lives here will merit to leave here without sin, though, while he lives here, he will have some sins. For, just as these sins were not lacking, so were the remedies also present by which they might be washed away. But if anyone, hearing that no one lives here without sin by means of his own choice, takes, as it were, the occasion, abandons himself to his passions and unspeakable sins, and persists in these criminal and outrageous actions until his last day, he leads an unhappy life and ends it even more unhappily, regardless of any alms that he may give.

2, 4. But these people are to be tolerated to some extent when they say that in this life there is or has been some righteous person besides the Holy of holies,[2] who had no sin at all.[3] But their claim that free choice is sufficient for a human being to fulfill the commandments of the Lord, even if one is not helped for good

---

1. See Dn 9:20.
2. See Dn 9:24, where this Hebraism seems to apply to the Messiah.
3. Before 418 Augustine granted that some people actually did live sinless lives after baptism. See *The Perfection of Human Righteousness* 21, 44, where he says of the idea that, besides Christ, some human beings are or have been without sin after baptism, "I do not believe that one should resist this idea too much, for I know that such is the view of some whose position on this matter I dare not reprehend." Canons 6 to 8 of the Council of Carthage in 418, however, clearly condemned this position. Augustine was most probably influenced by Ambrose's statements in his *Commentary on the Gospel of Luke*, which Pelagius had appealed to as evidence for human sinlessness. See *The Grace of Christ and Original Sin* 1, 42, 46-46, 51.

works by the grace of God and the gift of the Holy Spirit, is absolutely to be declared anathema and to be excoriated with every form of curse. For those who assert this are completely estranged from the grace of God, for *not knowing the righteousness of God*, as the apostle says of the Jews, *and wanting to establish their own, they are not subject to the righteousness of God* (Rom 10:3). *The fullness of the law is*, of course, *love* (Rom 13:10), and *the love of God has been poured out in our hearts* not through ourselves, nor by the powers of our own will, but *through the Holy Spirit who has been given to us* (Rom 5:5).

5. Free choice, then, is capable of good works if it is helped by God, which happens when we ask and speak humbly. But if free choice is abandoned by God's help, no matter how great is the knowledge of the law with which it excels, it will by no means have the solidity of righteousness but the bloated condition and deadly swelling of impious pride. The same Lord's Prayer teaches this. For we ask God in vain when we say, *Bring us not into temptation* (Mt 6:13), if this has been placed in our own power so that we are able to achieve this without God's help. For it says, *Bring us not into temptation*, and this is interpreted as: Do not permit us to be brought there by abandoning us. *For God is faithful*, the apostle says, *who will not permit you to be tempted beyond that which you are capable of, but will bring about a way out along with the temptation so that you are able to withstand it* (1 Cor 10:13). Why did he say that God does this if this lies in our power alone without his help?

6. For the law itself was given as a help to those who make lawful use of it[4] in order that they might know through it either what righteousness they have already received, for which they should give thanks, or what righteousness is still lacking to them, for which they should insistently ask. But for those who hear the words of the law, *You shall not desire* (Ex 20:17; Dt 5:21; 7:25; Rom 7:7; 13:9), think that it is sufficient for them to have learned this, do not believe that they are given by the help of God's grace the strength to do what was commanded, and do not ask for it, *the law has entered in so that sin might abound* (Rom 5:20), as was said of the Jews. For it is not enough that they do not fulfill the commandment of the law, *You shall not desire*, but beyond that they also are proud, and *not knowing the righteousness of God*, that is, the righteousness that God who makes the sinner righteous gives, and *wanting to establish their own*, as if it were produced by the power of their own will, *they are not subject to the righteousness of God. For the end of the law is Christ for the righteousness of everyone who believes.* (Rom 10:3-4) He, of course, came in order that, *where sin abounded* (Rom 5:20), grace might abound even more. If the Jews, *not knowing the righteousness of God* and *wanting to establish their own*, were enemies of this grace, why are these people now also its enemies if they have believed in him whom those others killed? Is it so that those Jews may

---

4. See Is 8:20 LXX; 1 Tim 1:8.

receive the reward who, after putting Christ to death, confessed their wickedness and made themselves subject to his grace once they knew it, while these present people meet with condemnation who want to believe in Christ in such a way that they try to put to death his very grace?

7. Those who believe correctly believe in him, of course, in order that they may hunger and thirst for righteousness and be satisfied by his grace. For *everyone*, as scripture says, *who calls upon the name of the Lord shall be saved* (Jl 2:32; Acts 2:21; Rom 10:13), not, of course, with the health of the body that many have, though they do not call upon the name of the Lord, but with that health of which he says, *It is not the healthy but the sick who need a physician* (Mt 9:12). And what he said afterwards explains this; he says, *I did not come to call the righteous but sinners* (Mt 9:13). He called the righteous healthy, then, and sinners sick. Let the sick person, then, not presume upon his strength, because *he will not be saved by the greatness of his power* (Ps 33:16). For, if he presumes upon it, let him watch out lest this strength not be the sort that usually belongs to the healthy but the sort that usually belongs to the insane who, when they are sick, think they are healthy to the point that they do not even seek a doctor and go on to strike him as if he were cruel and troublesome. In the same way, with their unhealthy pride these people in a certain sense strike Christ, when they maintain that the help of his grace, which is so kind, is not necessary for acting with righteousness once they are given the commandment of the law. Let them, therefore, cease to be so insane, and let them understand, to the extent that they can, that they have free choice not in order to reject help with their proud will but to call upon the Lord with a pious will.

8. For this free will will be more free to the extent that it is more healthy and more healthy to the extent that it is more subject to divine grace and mercy. For it faithfully prays and says, *Direct my journeys according to your word, and let not every iniquity have dominion over me* (Ps 119:133). For how is it free if iniquity has dominion over it? But in order that it may not have dominion over it, see whom it calls upon. For it does not say, "Direct my journeys according to free choice because no iniquity has dominion over me," but, *Direct my journeys according to your word, and let not every iniquity have dominion over me.* It prays; it does not promise. It confesses; it does not claim. It longs for full freedom; it does not boast of its own power. For not everyone who places his trust in his own strength will be saved, but everyone who calls upon the name of the Lord. *But how shall they call upon him,* the apostle asks, *in whom they have not believed?* (Rom 10:14) They who believe correctly believe, therefore, so that they may call upon him in whom they have believed and may be able to do what they have received in the commandments of the law, because faith obtains what the law commands.

9. For, in order to omit for the time being the many commandments of the law and to call to mind what the apostle chose to call to mind when the law says, *You shall not desire* (Ex 20:17), what else does it seem to command but continence with respect to illicit desires? The mind is, of course, carried by its love as if by a weight wherever it is carried; we are commanded, therefore, to take away from the weight of desire what is added to the weight of love until the former is done away with and the latter is made perfect. For *the fulfillment of the law is love* (Rom 13:10). And yet, see what scripture says about continence: *And since I knew*, it says, *that no one can be continent unless God grants this, and it is itself a mark of wisdom to know whose gift this is, I approached the Lord and entreated him* (Wis 8:21). Did it say, "And since I knew that no one can be continent except by his own free choice, and it is itself a mark of wisdom to know that this good comes from myself"? It clearly did not say this, which some people say in their folly, but what ought to be said in the truth of the holy scripture. It said, *Since I know that no one can be continent unless God grants this*. God, therefore, commands continence, and he gives continence. He commands through the law; he gives through grace; he commands through the letter; he gives through the Spirit. For without grace the law makes sin abound,[5] and without the Spirit the letter kills.[6] He commands, therefore, in order that, having tried to do what was commanded, and worn out in our weakness under the law, we would know how to ask for the help of grace and, if we are able to do any good work, we would not be ungrateful to him who helps us. The one who wrote those words also did this; for wisdom taught him whose gift this was.

10. After all, the choice of the will is not destroyed because it is helped; rather, it is helped because it is not destroyed. For one who says to God, *Be my helper* (Ps 27:9), confesses that he wants to carry out what is commanded but asks for help from him who gave the command in order that he may be able to do so. So too, since that person knew that no one could be continent unless God granted it, he approached the Lord and entreated him. He willingly approached him, of course, and he willingly entreated him, nor would he have asked unless he had a will. But if he had not asked, how much would the will be able to do? For even if the will could do something before it asked, what good does it do it unless, because of what it can do, it gives thanks to him from whom it must ask for what it cannot yet do? Hence, even one who is already continent certainly does not have continence unless the will is present. But unless the will had received it, what would the will have? *For what do you have*, he asks, *that you have not received? But if you have received, why do you boast as if you have not received?* (1 Cor 4:7) That is, why do you boast as if you have from yourself what, if you had not received, you could not have from yourself? But the apostle

---

5. See Rom 5:20
6. See 2 Cor 3:6.

said this so that *one who boasts may boast* not in himself but *in the Lord* (1 Cor 1:31 2 Cor 10:17), and so that one who does not yet have that about which he might boast might not hope for it from himself but might ask the Lord. It is, after all, better that someone have less and ask for more from God than that he have more and attribute it to himself, because it is better to rise from below than to fall from on high. For scripture says, *God resists the proud, but gives grace to the humble* (Jas 4:6). The law, therefore, teaches us what we ought to will in order that sins may abound if grace does not help us to be able to do what we will and to carry out what we are able to do. But grace will help us if we do not presume upon our own strength and do not have proud thoughts[7] but agree with the humble and give thanks for what we already can do, while petitioning God as suppliants with a longing will, supporting our prayer with fruitful works of mercy by giving in order that it may be given to us and forgiving in order that we may be forgiven.[8]

3, 11. They say that an infant who was not baptized because it was prevented by death cannot perish because it is born without sin. This is not, however, what the apostle says, and I think it better that we believe the apostle than these people. For the teacher of the nations in whom Christ spoke said, *Through one man sin entered the world, and through sin death, and in that way it was passed on to all human beings, in whom all have sinned* (Rom 5:12), and a little later he says, *For judgment comes from the one sin for condemnation, but grace comes from many sins for justification* (Rom 5:16). If these people, then, have perhaps found an infant who was not procreated as a result of the concupiscence stemming from that one man, let them say that this infant is not subject to that condemnation and does not need to be set free from that condemnation by the grace of Christ. After all, what does *from the one sin for condemnation* mean but in that sin by which Adam fell? And what does *from many sins for justification* mean but that the grace of Christ removed not only that sin by which infants are bound because they are procreated from that one man, but also the many sins that, when they are grown up, human beings add by their evil actions? And yet he says that that one sin by which the carnal offspring that take their origin from that first man are bound is sufficient for condemnation. Hence, the baptism of infants is not super-fluous; for those who are held bound to that condemnation by birth are released from the same condemnation by rebirth. For, just as no human being is found who was born in the flesh except from Adam, so there is found no human being who is reborn spiritually except from Christ. Birth in the flesh, however, is subject to that one sin and its condemnation, while spiritual rebirth causes the destruction not only of that one sin on account of which infants are baptized but of the many sins that by living badly human beings have added to that sin in

---

7. See Rom 12:16.
8. See Lk 6:37-38, 11:4.

which they were born. For this reason he goes on to say, *For if on account of the sin of one person death reigned through one person, much more will they who receive an abundance of grace and righteousness reign in life through the one Jesus Christ. Therefore, just as through the sin of one person all entered into condemnation, so through the righteousness of one all will enter the righteousness of life. For, just as through the disobedience of one man many were made sinners, so through the obedience of one man many are made righteous.* (Rom 5:17-19)

12. What will they say to these words? Or what remains for them but to claim that the apostle was mistaken? The vessel of election, the teacher of the nations, the trumpet of Christ shouts, *Judgment comes from the one for condemnation* (Rom 5:16), and these people shout back, claiming that infants, who they admit take their origin from that one man of whom the apostle speaks, do not enter into condemnation even if they have not been baptized in Christ. He says, *Judgment comes from the one for condemnation.* What does *from the one* mean but from one sin? For he continues, *But grace comes from many sins for justification.* Therefore, judgment leads to condemnation from the one sin, but from condemnation grace leads from many sins to justification. Hence, if they do not dare to resist the apostle, let them explain to us why judgment leads to condemnation from the one sin, though many human beings come to judgment who will be condemned because of many sins. Or if they think that it was said because Adam produced the beginning of sin which the rest imitated, so that in that way they are dragged from that one sin to judgment and condemnation who have committed many sins by imitating him, why is the same thing not said of grace and justification? Why is it not likewise said, "And from one sin grace leads to justification"? For many sins of human beings are found between the one that they imitated and the judgment by which the many are punished. From the one they came to many so that they are brought to judgment and condemnation from many. In the same way the same many sins stand between this one sin, in imitation of which they were committed, and grace, by which they are forgiven. For from that one sin they came to many sins in order that they might come to grace to be justified from many sins. Since, therefore, in each case, that is, in the case of judgment and in the case of grace, there is one and the same proportion with regard to what pertains to the one and to the many sins, let them tell us why he said that from one sin judgment leads to condemnation but from many sins grace leads to justification. Or let them grant that it was said in this way because in this matter there are set before us two men—Adam, from whom there comes birth in the flesh, and Christ, from whom there comes spiritual rebirth. But because the former was only a man, but the latter both God and man, this rebirth does not remove the one sin which comes from Adam in the same way that that birth bound us by that sin which comes from Adam. But for that birth the connection to the one sin is suffi-

cient for condemnation. For whatever human beings add afterward by their evil actions does not pertain to that birth but to human living. But for this rebirth it is not sufficient to remove this one sin alone that is contracted from Adam, but whatever else is added to it afterward from the wicked actions of human life. For this reason *judgment comes from the one for condemnation, but grace from many sins for justification.*

13. *For if on account of the sin of one person death reigned through one person,* from which sin infants are cleansed in baptism, *much more will those who receive an abundance of grace and righteousness reign in life through the one Jesus Christ.* They will, of course, reign much more in life because it will be the kingdom of eternal life, but death passes in them in time and will not reign for eternity. *Therefore, just as through the sin of one person all enter into condemnation,* from which condemnation infants must be set free by the sacrament of baptism, *so through the righteousness of one all will enter the righteousness of life.* Both here and there he said *all, not because all human beings come to the grace of the righteousness of Christ, since so many die separated from it for eternity, but because all who are reborn for righteousness are reborn only through Christ, just as all who are born for condemnation are born only through Adam. No one, of course, is born in that way apart from Adam; no one is reborn in this way apart from Christ. Therefore he says, all* in both cases, but he afterward says that the same *all* are also *many,* when he adds, *Just as through the disobedience of one man many were made sinners, so through the obedience of one man many are also made righteous.* Who are the *many,* but those whom he had a little before called *all?*

14. See how he stresses *one* in both cases, that is, Adam and Christ, the former for condemnation, the latter for justification, though Christ came in the flesh so long after Adam. He stresses these two in order that we might know that whoever were able to be righteous among the people of the Old Testament were also set free only through the same faith by which we too are set free, that is, faith in the incarnation of Christ, which was foretold to them as it was announced to us now that it has taken place. For this reason he mentions Christ the man, though he was also God, so that no one would think that the righteous of old could have been set free through Christ as God alone, that is, as the Word, which *was in the beginning* (Jn 1:1), not through faith in his incarnation, because of which Christ is also said to be man. This statement cannot, of course, be destroyed by which he says elsewhere, *Through one man came death, and through one man the resurrection of the dead. For, just as in Adam all die, so in Christ all will also be brought to life.* (1 Cor 15:21-22) He is, of course, speaking of the resurrection of the righteous where there is eternal life, not of the resurrection of the wicked where there will be eternal death. And for this reason he says, *They will be brought to life,* because those others will be condemned. Hence, in the old sacraments it was

commanded that the circumcision of infants take place on the eighth day,[9] because Christ, in whom the removal of carnal sin occurs, which circumcision signifies, rose on the Lord's day, which after the seventh day of the Sabbath is the eighth day. This, therefore, was also the faith of the righteous of old. For this reason the apostle also says, *Having the same spirit of faith on account of which it was written, I believed, and on this account I have spoken, we too believe, and on this account we also speak* (2 Cor 4:13; Ps 116:10). He would not say *the same spirit of faith* unless he were warning us that the righteous of old had the same spirit of faith, that is, in the incarnation of Christ. But because this was announced to them as future, while it is announced to us as already having occurred and because in the time of the Old Testament there was veiled what in the time of the New Testament is revealed, the sacraments of that faith were, for this reason, changed so that they were different in the Old Testament from the New, though the faith itself is not changed and is one.[10] For, *just as in Adam all die, so in Christ all will also be brought to life.*

15. To these words on which we are commenting he adds and says, *But the law entered in so that sin might abound* (Rom 5:20); this no longer pertains to that sin which is contracted from Adam, about which he previously said, *Death reigned through one person* (Rom 5:17). We should, of course, understand either the natural law, which is known by persons at those ages that are capable of using reason, or the written law that was given through Moses. For the law was not able to give life and set us free *from the law of sin and death* (Rom 8:2), which was contracted from Adam; rather it added increases in sin through transgression. *For, where there is no law,* the same apostle says, *there is also no transgression* (Rom 4:15). Hence, since there is also a law in the reason of a human being who already uses free choice, a law naturally written in his heart, by which he is warned that he should not do anything to anyone else that he himself does not want to suffer, all are transgressors according to this law, even those who have not received the law given through Moses. Of these the psalm said, *All the sinners of the earth have been judged to be transgressors* (Ps 119:119). For not all the sinners of the earth transgressed the law given through Moses, but still, unless they had transgressed some law, they would not be called transgressors. For *where there is no law, there is also no transgression.* Because of the transgression of the law that was given in paradise, a human being is born of Adam with *the law of sin and death,* of which it is said, *I see another law in my members that resists the law of my mind and holds me captive under the law of sin that is in my members* (Rom 7:23). Yet, unless this law afterward grows strong by a bad habit, it is conquered rather easily, but only by the grace of God. Because of the transgression of the other law, however, which is found in the use

9. See Gn 17:12 Lv 12:3.
10. The CSEL edition has *vera* ("true"), but I have followed the reading *una* ("one") in PL.

of the reason of the rational soul at the age when a human being already has the use of reason, *all the sinners of the earth* become *transgressors*. But because of the transgression of the law that was given through Moses, sin abounds much more. *For if a law were given that could bring to life, righteousness would certainly come from the law, but scripture enclosed all things under sin in order that the promise might be given to those who believe on the basis of faith in Jesus Christ* (Gal 3:21-22). These words (if you recognize them) are from the apostle. Again he says of this law, *The law was established for the sake of transgression until the offspring would come to whom the promise was made, the law given by angels through the hands of a mediator* (Gal 3:19). He mentions Christ by whose grace all are saved, whether infants *from the law of sin and death* (Rom 8:2) with which they are born, or adults who, by making bad use of the choice of their will, have transgressed the natural law of reason itself, or those who have received the law that was given through Moses and, in transgressing it, were killed by the letter.[11] But when a man transgresses the commandments of the gospel, he stinks like one who has been dead four days.[12] But on account of the grace of him who did not softly say, but shouted with a loud voice, *Lazarus, come forth* (Jn 11:43), we should not stop hoping for him.

16. *The law, therefore, entered in so that sin might abound* (Rom 5:20), either when human beings neglect what God commands or when, presuming upon their own strength, they do not implore the help of grace and add pride to their weakness. When, however, by God's calling they understand why[13] they must groan and call upon him in whom they rightly believe, saying, *Have mercy on me, God, according to your great mercy* (Ps 51:3), and, *I said, Lord, have mercy on me; heal my soul because I have sinned against you* (Ps 41:5), and, *In your righteousness bring me to life* (Ps 119:40), and, *Remove from me the way of iniquity, and by your law have mercy on me* (Ps 119:29), and, *Let not the foot of pride come to me, and let the hand of sinners not move me* (Ps 36:12), and, *Direct my journey according to your word, and let not every iniquity have dominion over me* (Ps 119:133), for *the steps of a man are directed by the Lord, and he will choose his ways* (Ps 36:23), and the many other passages that were written precisely so as to warn us that in order to fulfill what we are commanded we must ask for help from him who gave the commandments—when someone stretches out to him, therefore, and groans in that way, there will happen what follows, *Where sin abounded, grace was even more abundant* (Rom 5:20), and, *Many sins are forgiven her, because she loved much* (Lk 7:47), and the love of God is poured out in our heart,[14] as a result of which there comes about *the fulfillment of the law* (Rom 13:10), this happens not through the strength of choice that is

---

11. See 2 Cor 3:6.
12. See Jn 11:39.
13. I have followed the PL reading of *cur* ("why") rather than that in CSEL of *cui* ("to whom").
14. See Rom 5:5.

found in us but *through the Holy Spirit who has been given to us* (Rom 5:5). He, of course, knew the law who said, *For I find delight in the law of God in accord with the inner self*, and yet he added, *I see, however, another law in my members that resists the law of my mind and holds me captive under the law of sin that is in my members. Wretched man that I am! Who will set me free from the body of this death? The grace of God through Jesus Christ our Lord* (Rom 7:22-25). Why did he not say instead, "Through my free choice," if not because freedom without the grace of God is not freedom but proud rebelliousness?

17. After the apostle, therefore, said, *The law entered in so that sin might abound, but where sin abounded, grace was even more abundant*, he went on and added, *in order that, as sin reigned in death, so grace also might reign through righteousness in eternal life through Jesus Christ our Lord* (Rom 5: 20-21). But when he said, *in order that, as sin reigned in death*, he did not say, "Through one man," or, "Through the first man," or, "Through Adam," because he had already said, *The law entered in so that sin might abound*, and this abundance of sin does not pertain to the descendants propagated from the first man but to the transgressions committed in human life. To that one sin by which alone infants are held bound these transgressions were added later at an adult age because of the abundance of iniquity. But because the grace of the savior is, nonetheless, able to remove this totality, even what does not pertain to the origin of that one sin, after he had said, *So grace also might reign through righteousness in eternal life*, he added, *through Jesus Christ our Lord.*

18. And so, let no one's arguments that are brought forth against these words of the apostle keep infants from the salvation found in Christ Jesus our Lord. We must, after all, speak for them the more insofar as they cannot speak for themselves. *Through one man sin entered the world, and through sin death, and in that way it was passed on to all human beings, in whom all have sinned* (Rom 5:12). Just as they could not come into being apart from that one man, so they cannot be free from the same sin unless they are released from its guilt through the baptism of Christ. *For sin was in the world up to the law* (Rom 5:13). This was not said because from then on sin was found in no one but because what could be removed only by the spirit of grace could not be removed by the letter of the law. Lest anyone, therefore, who puts his trust in the strength, I do not say of his will but rather of his vanity, should think that the law could be enough for free choice and should mock the grace of Christ, the apostle says, *For up to the law, sin was in the world, but sin was not imputed when the law did not exist* (Rom 5:13). He did not say, "Sin did not exist," but *was not imputed*, because there did not exist a law that by its accusations made sin known, whether the law of reason in an infant or the written law in the people.

19. *But death reigned*, he says, *from Adam to Moses* (Rom 5:14), because the law given through Moses could not take away the reign of death, which only the grace of Christ took away. But see over whom it reigned; he says, *even over*

those who did not sin in the likeness of the transgression of Adam. It reigned,
therefore, even over those who did not sin. But he showed why it reigned when
he says, *in the likeness of the transgression of Adam.* For this is the better interpretation of these words, namely, that, after he had said, *Death reigned over
those who did not sin,* as if to teach us why it reigned over those who did not sin,
he added, *in the likeness of the transgression of Adam,* that is, because the likeness of the transgression of Adam was present in their members. It can also be
understood in this way: *Death reigned from Adam to Moses even over those who
did not sin in the likeness of the transgression of Adam,* because in themselves,
when they were already born but did not yet have the use of reason, which he
used when he sinned, they had not received the commandment that he transgressed but were held bound only by original sin, by which the reign of death
was dragging them to condemnation. This reign of death exists in all except
those who have been reborn by the grace of Christ and belong to his kingdom.
For, though temporal death was also propagated by original sin, it kills the body
in them but does not drag the soul to punishment, by which he wanted us to
understand the reign of death. In that way the soul renewed by grace no longer
dies in hell, that is, is not estranged, is not separated from the life of God, but the
temporal death of the body remains for the time being, even in these people who
are redeemed by the death of Christ for the exercise of their faith and the contest
of this present struggle, in which the martyrs have also done battle. But this death
too is taken away in the renewal of the body that the resurrection promises. For
there death, whose reign the grace of Christ is now destroying, will be
completely swallowed up by victory[15] so that it does not drag their souls to the
pains of hell. Some manuscripts, to be sure, do not have: *over those who have not
sinned,* but: *over those who have sinned in the likeness of the transgression of
Adam,* by which words this meaning is in no way destroyed. In accord with it, of
course, they are understood to have sinned *in the likeness of the transgression of
Adam,* in accord with the previous words, *in whom all have sinned* (Rom 5:12).
But more Greek manuscripts, from which the scripture has been translated into
Latin, have what we said.

20. But what he added concerning Adam, *who is the pattern of the one to
come* (Rom 5:14), is also not understood in one way. For either he is the pattern
of Christ by way of contrast so that, as all die in him, so all will also be brought to
life in Christ and, *as through* his *disobedience many were made sinners, so
through the obedience of Christ many were made righteous* (Rom 5:19), or he
called him the pattern of the one to come because he himself inflicted the pattern
of his death upon his descendants. The former is, nonetheless, the better interpretation, according to which he is believed to be the pattern by way of contrast,
as the apostle emphasizes. Then, so that the opposites would not be considered

---

15. See 1 Cor 15:54.

entirely equal in this pattern, he added and said, *But the gift is not like the sin; for, if on account of the sin of the one many have died, the grace and gift of God in the grace of the one man Jesus Christ has abounded much more for many* (Rom 5:15). We should not understand "for many more," since the sinful who will be condemned are many more, but "abounded more," because the pattern of death coming from Adam has power for a time over those who are redeemed by Christ, but the pattern of life through Christ will have power over them for eternity. Although, then, he says that Adam is the pattern of the one to come by way of contrast, Christ, nonetheless, benefited those who are reborn more than Adam harmed those who are born. *And the gift is not like the result of the one who sinned, for judgment comes from the one for condemnation, but grace comes from many sins for justification* (Rom 5:16). The pattern, he says, is not equal not only insofar as Adam did temporal harm to those whom Christ redeemed for eternity but also insofar as, unless they are redeemed by Christ, his descendants are handed over to condemnation because of that one sin of his, whereas Christ's redemption also removed the many sins that the abundance of sinful transgression added to that one, about which we spoke above.

21. Yield to no one regarding these words of the apostle and their sound interpretation if you wish to live for Christ and in Christ. For, if, as they say, the apostle mentioned these things in order that we might understand that sinners pertain to the first man not because we contracted sin from him by being born but because we sin by imitating him, he would have instead put the devil there, who sinned first and from whom the human race did not derive the propagation of its substance but only followed after him by imitating him. Thus the devil would be said to be the father of the wicked, just as Abraham is said to be our father because of our imitation of his faith, not because of the origin of our flesh.[16] For scripture said of the devil himself, *But those who are on his side imitate him* (Wis 2:25). Then, if the apostle mentioned the first man in this passage on account of imitation, because he was the first sinner among human beings, so that for this reason he said that all human sinners belong to him, why did he not put the saintly Abel there, who was the first righteous person among human beings, to whom all would belong by imitating his righteousness? But he put Adam there and put no one but Christ in opposition to him because, just as that man by his sin damaged his posterity, so this God-man by his righteousness saved his heritage, the former by passing on the impurity of the flesh, something the wicked devil could not do, the latter by giving the grace of the Spirit, something the righteous Abel could not do.

22. We have said much about these questions in our other works and sermons in church, because there were also among us certain persons who sowed these new seeds of their error wherever they could, some of whom the mercy of the

---

16. See Jn 8:38-39.44.

Lord healed from that disease through our ministry and that of our brothers. And I suspect that there are still some here, especially in Carthage, but they now whisper in hiding, fearing the most well-founded faith of the Church. For in the church of the same city one of them by the name of Caelestius had already deviously begun to seek the honor of the priesthood, but he was brought by the solid faith and freedom of the brothers straight to an episcopal court on account of these discourses opposed to the grace of Christ.[17] He was, however, forced to confess that infants must be baptized because they too need redemption. Although at the time he refused to say there anything more explicit about original sin, he did, nonetheless, do considerable harm to his position by the mention of redemption. After all, from what did they need to be redeemed except from the power of the devil in which they could not have been except by the bonds of sin? Or at what price are they redeemed except by the blood of Christ, of which scripture stated most clearly that it was shed for the forgiveness of sins?[18] But because he went off, having been found guilty and detested by the Church rather than corrected and subdued, I was afraid that it was perhaps he himself there who was trying to disturb your faith, and for this reason I thought I should mention his name. But it makes no difference whether it is he or others who partake of his error. For there are more than we would expect. And where they are not refuted, they win over others to their sect, and they are becoming so numerous that I do not know where they will turn up. Yet we prefer that they be healed within the framework of the Church rather than cut off from its body like incurable members, at least if the very gravity of the situation permits this. For we have to fear that more may begin to go bad if the rottenness is spared. But the mercy of our Lord, which would rather set them free from this plague, is able to do so. And it will undoubtedly do this if they faithfully pay attention to and hold what scripture says: *He who calls upon the Lord will be saved* (Jl 2:32).

4, 23. Listen now to a few points about the rich, which is the next question in your letter. For you said that those people claim, "A rich man who remains in his riches cannot enter the kingdom of God unless he has sold all his possessions, and it does not profit him if he has perhaps observed all the commandments by the use of his riches."[19] Our forefathers, Abraham, Isaac, and Jacob, who departed from this life so long ago, avoided the criticisms of these people. All these men, of course, had significant riches, as scripture, which is most reliable, testifies. He himself, *who for our sake became poor, though he was truly rich* (2 Cor 8:9), foretold in a perfectly true promise that many will come from the east and from the west and will recline in the kingdom of heaven, not above them or

---

17. See *The Deeds of Pelagius* 11, 23 for the propositions of Caelestius that were condemned at Carthage in 411 or 412 after Caelestius was accused of heresy by Paulinus of Milan.
18. See Mt 26:28.
19. Letter 156.

apart from them, but with them.[20] And although the proud *rich man who was clothed in purple and linen and feasted splendidly every day* (Lk 16:19) died and was tormented in hell, nonetheless, if he had shown pity for the poor man covered with sores who lay despised before his gate, he too would have merited mercy.[21] And if that poor man's merit was his indigence, not his righteousness, he would certainly not have been carried by the angels into the bosom of Abraham, who was rich in this life. But in order to show us that God did not reward poverty itself in the poor man and did not condemn riches in that other, but that piety in this one and impiety in the other each met with their own recompense, the torment of fire received that impious rich man while the bosom of a rich man received the pious poor man. Abraham, of course, who lived here as a rich man possessed his riches and valued them so slightly in comparison with the commandments of God that he was unwilling to offend God who commanded it, even in the sacrifice of his son whom he both hoped and desired to be the heir of his riches.[22]

24. What they say here, to be sure is that the patriarchs of old did not sell all they possessed and did not give it to the poor because the Lord had not commanded them to do this. For, when the New Testament was not yet revealed, something that had to come about only in the fullness of time, their virtue also did not have to be revealed. For God knew that by their virtue he could most easily bring this about in their hearts, since he offered to them so remarkable a testimony that, though he is the God of all the holy and righteous, he deigned to say as if of his special friends, *I am the God of Abraham and the God of Isaac and the God of Jacob; this is my name for eternity* (Ex 3:15). But afterwards *the great sacrament of piety was revealed in the flesh* (1 Tm 3:16), and the coming of Christ shone forth to call all the nations. Those patriarchs had also believed in him, but they preserved the domesticated olive tree of this faith, which was to be made manifest in its own time, in the root, as it were, of that tree, of which the apostle spoke.[23] Then Christ said to the rich man, *Go, sell all that you have, and give it to the poor, and you will have a treasure in heaven, and come follow me* (Mt 19:21).

25. If they say this, they seem to say something reasonable, but let them listen to the whole context; let them pay attention to the whole context; let them not open their ears in part and close them in part. For whom did the Lord command concerning this? That rich man, of course, who was asking advice for attaining eternal life. For he said this to the Lord, *What should I do to attain eternal life?* (Mt 19:16) But the Lord did not answer him, "If you wish to attain life, go, sell all you have," but, *If you wish to attain life, keep the commandments* (Mt 19:17).

---

20. See Mt 8:11.
21. See Lk 16:20-22.
22. See Gn 22:1-10.
23. See Rom 11:17.

When the young man said that he had kept the commandments from the law that the Lord mentioned to him and asked what was still lacking for him, he received the answer, *If you wish to be perfect, go, sell all that you have, and give it to the poor.* And in order that he would not think that he was in this way losing the things that he loved greatly, he said, *And you will have treasure in heaven.* Then he added, *And come, follow me* (Mt 19:21), in order that he would not suppose that it profits anyone, when he does this, if he does not follow Christ. But that man, of course, went off sad who saw how he had observed the commandments of the law. For I think that he replied with more arrogance than truth that he had observed them. The good teacher, nonetheless, distinguished the commandments of the law from that more excellent perfection. For he said there, *If you wish to attain life, observe the commandments,* but here he says, *If you wish to be perfect, go, sell all that you have,* and so on. Why, then, should we deny that rich people, though they lack that perfection, still attain life if they have kept the commandments and have given in order that it may be given them and have forgiven in order that it may be forgiven them?[24]

26. We believe that the apostle Paul was a minister of the New Testament when in writing to Timothy he said, *Command the rich of this world not to think proud thoughts and not to place hope in the uncertainty of riches, but in the living God who offers us all things in abundance for enjoyment. Let them do good; let them be rich in good works; let them give readily, share, and store up for themselves a good foundation for the future in order that they may obtain true life.* (1 Tm 6:17-19) With regard to this life it was said to that young man, *If you wish to attain life.* I think that in commanding these things the apostle was instructing and not deceiving the rich; he did not say, "Command the rich of this world to sell all that they have, give it to the poor, and follow the Lord," but, *not to think proud thoughts and not to place their hope in the uncertainty of riches.* It was this pride and this hope in the uncertainty of the riches by which he thought that he was happy because of his purple and linen and splendid feasts, and not the riches themselves, that brought to the torments of hell the rich man who held in contempt that poor man lying at his door.

27. Or do they perhaps, because the Lord went on to say, *Truly I say to you, a rich man will enter the kingdom of heaven with difficulty, and again I say to you, a camel will enter through the eye of a needle more easily than a rich man into the kingdom of heaven* (Mt 19:23-24), think that, even if a rich man does those things that the apostle writes the rich should be ordered to do, he cannot enter into the kingdom of heaven? What, then, does this mean? Does the apostle contradict the Lord, or do these people not know what he is saying? Let a Christian choose which of these to believe. I think that it is better that we believe that they do not know what to say than that Paul is contradicting the Lord. Next, why

---

24. See Lk 6:38.37.

do they not listen to the Lord himself as he speaks in the following verses to his disciples who were saddened over the misfortune of the rich? *What is impossible for human beings is easy for God* (Mt 19:26).

28. But this was said, the Pelagians say, because it will transpire that, once they have heard the gospel, the rich will follow the Lord after selling their inheritance and giving it to the poor and will enter the kingdom of heaven. And in that way there will come about what seemed difficult. It was not that, while remaining in possession of their riches, they would obtain true life by observing the commandments of the apostle, that is, by not thinking proud thoughts and not placing their hope in the uncertainty of riches but in the living God, doing good, giving readily, and sharing with the needy. Rather, they would fulfill these commandments of the apostle after having sold all their possessions.

29. If they say this—I know, of course, that they do say this—they do not, first of all, pay attention to how the Lord preached his grace in opposition to their teaching. For he did not say, "What seems impossible for human beings is easy for human beings if they will it," but, *What is impossible for human beings is easy for God*, showing that, when these things are done correctly, they are not done by the power of a human being but by the grace of God. Let these people, then, pay attention to this, and if they find fault with those who boast of their riches, let themselves avoid placing their trust in their own strength. For both are blamed together in the psalm, *those who place their trust in their own strength and those who boast of their riches* (Ps 49:7). Let the rich, therefore, hear, *What is impossible for human beings is easy for God*, and whether remaining in possession of their riches and doing good works with them or having sold them and distributed them in accord with the needs of the poor, let them enter the kingdom of heaven; let them attribute their goodness to the grace of God, not to their own strength. For *what is impossible for human beings is easy* not for human beings but *for God*. Let these people also hear this, and if they have already either sold all their possessions and given them to the poor or are still doing this and arranging it and in this way preparing to enter the kingdom of heaven, let them not attribute this to their own strength but to the same grace of God. For *what is impossible for human beings is easy* not for them, since they are human beings, but *for God*. The apostle also, of course, says this to them, *Work out your own salvation with fear and trembling, for it is God who produces in you both the willing and the action in accord with good will* (Phil 2:12-13). They say, to be sure, that they received from the Lord the counsel of perfection about selling their possessions in order to follow the Lord because this was added: *And come, follow me.* Why, then, do they presume upon their own will alone in these good actions that they do and not hear the Lord, whom they say they follow, upbraiding them and testifying, *Without me you can do nothing* (Jn 15:5).

30. But if the apostle said, *Command the rich of this world not to think proud thoughts and not to put their hope in the uncertainty of riches*, in order that they

would sell all that they possess and, by distributing the income from it to the needy, would do what follows: *Give readily, share, and store up for themselves a good foundation for the future* (1 Tm 6:17-19), and if he believes that they could not otherwise enter the kingdom of heaven, he deceives those whose homes he so carefully puts in order by the soundness of his teaching, when he admonishes and commands wives how they should behave toward their husbands and husbands toward their wives, children toward their parents and parents toward their children, servants toward their masters and masters toward their servants. For how could they do this without a home and without some family property?

31. Or do the words of the Lord disturb them, *Whoever leaves all his posses-sions on my account will receive a hundredfold in this world and will possess eternal life in the world to come* (Mt 19:29)? It is one thing to leave and another thing to sell. For a wife is also mentioned among the things that he commands us to leave, but no human laws permit a man to sell his wife. But the laws of Christ do not permit him to leave her *except in the case of fornication* (Mt 5:32). What, then, do those commandments mean—for they cannot be mutually contradic-tory—if not that at times there arises a moment of crisis in which one must leave either his wife or Christ—to pass over other occasions—if a wife is unhappy with her Christian husband and proposes to him a divorce either from her or from Christ? At this point what should he do but choose Christ and leave his wife in a praiseworthy fashion on account of Christ? In a case where both are Christians the Lord, of course, commanded that one should not leave his wife *except in the case of fornication*. But where either of them is a non-believer, the counsel of the apostle should be followed, namely, that, if the non-believer consents to live with the believing husband, the husband should not divorce his wife. Likewise, as well a believing wife should not dismiss her husband if he consents to live with her. *But if the one who is a non-believer*, he says, *leaves, let him leave; for the brother or sister is not subject to slavery in such matters* (1 Cor 7:12-13), that is, if the non-believer refuses to live with the believing spouse, let the believer in this case recognize his freedom so that he does not regard himself as subject to slavery, leaving the faith to avoid losing an unbelieving spouse.

32. This rule is also understood with regard to children and parents and also with regard to brothers and sisters. We should leave them all on account of Christ, when the condition is set that we should leave Christ if we want to have them with us. This, then, should also be understood with regard to house and fields; it should also be understood with regard to those things that are owned by right of purchase. After all, he does not say of these things, "Whoever sells on my account whatever it is, of course, permissible to sell," but, *Whoever leaves*. For it is possible that some authority might say to a Christian, "Either cease to be a Christian, or, if you choose to remain one, you will not have your house and possessions." But then those rich persons, who had decided to retain their riches

in order that they might merit God as their reward on the basis of good works with them, should leave them on account of Christ rather than Christ on account of them, in order that they may receive a hundredfold in this world. For the perfection of this number signifies all things. *A believer, of course, has a whole world of riches* (Prv 17:6 LXX); in this way they become *as if having nothing and possessing all things* (2 Cor 6:10). And in the future world they will possess eternal life; otherwise, if they leave Christ on account of these things, they will be cast down into eternal death.

33. Under this law and condition there stand not only those who by the excellence of their intention have embraced the counsel of perfection so that, having sold their possessions, they distribute the proceeds to the poor and bear the lighter burden of Christ with their shoulders freer from every burden of this world, but also anyone weaker and less suited to this glorious perfection who, nonetheless, remembers that he is truly a Christian when he hears the condition set before him that, unless he abandons all these things, he will abandon Christ. He will rather seize the tower *of strength from before the enemy* (Ps 61:4) because, when he was building it by his own faith, he calculated the expenses by which it could be completed,[25] that is, he approached the faith with such a spirit that he did not renounce this world only in words, for, even if he bought something, he was like someone who did not own it, and if he used the world, he was like someone who did not use it,[26] not *putting his hope in the uncertainty of riches, but in the living God* (1 Tm 6:17).

34. For everyone who renounces this world undoubtedly renounces everything that belongs to it in order to be a disciple of Christ. For, he himself, after he had first set forth the parables about the expenses necessary for the building of the tower and about preparing for war against another king,[27] added this: *One who does not renounce everything that belongs to him cannot be my disciple* (Lk 14:33). Such a person, then, should certainly also renounce his riches if he has any, either so that, not loving them at all, he may distribute all of them to the poor and be relieved of needless burdens, or so that, loving Christ more, he may transfer his hope from them to him and use them so that, freely giving and sharing them, he may store up a treasure in heaven and also be ready to leave them, like parents and children and brothers and wife, if he were faced with such a condition that, unless he left Christ, he could not have them. For, if he renounces this world in another way when he approaches the sacrament of the faith, he does what blessed Cyprian bemoaned, when he said of apostates, "They renounce the world in words alone and not in actions."[28] With regard to this sort of person it is said, when at the arrival of temptations he feared more to lose these

---

25. See Lk 14:28.
26. See 1 Cor 7:30-31.
27. See Lk 14:28-32.
28. Cyprian, Letter 7, 1.

possessions than to deny Christ, *There you see a man who began to build a building and could not complete it* (Lk 14:30). He is also the man who, when his enemy was still far off, sent envoys seeking peace; that is, when temptation is not yet attacking but still threatening and menacing him, he agrees to abandon and deny Christ in order not to lose the things that he loves more. And there are many of this sort who even suppose that the Christian religion ought to help them to increase their riches and to multiply earthly pleasures.

35. But rich Christians are not this sort of people; though they possess riches, they are not, nonetheless, possessed by them so that they prefer them to Christ. For they have renounced the world with a sincere heart so that they place no hope in such things. These men educate with sound discipline their wives and children and their whole families to hold the Christian religion; their homes, warm with hospitality, receive a righteous person in the name of a righteous person in order that they may receive the reward of the righteous.[29] They break their bread with the needy; they cloth the naked, redeem the captive,[30] and store up for themselves *a good foundation for the future in order that they might attain true life* (1 Tm 6:19). And if monetary losses have to be suffered for the faith of Christ, they place no value on their own riches; if this world threatens them with the losses of or separations from members of their family for the sake of Christ, they hate their parents, brothers, children, and wives. Finally, if they have to negotiate with an enemy over the very life of this body in order that Christ may not abandon them after they have abandoned him, they also hate their own life. With regard to all of these things they have received the commandment that they cannot otherwise be disciples of Christ.[31]

36. And yet, because they received the commandment to hate even their own lives for the sake of Christ, they do not consider that they should sell them or destroy them by laying their own hands upon themselves, but they are ready to lose them by dying for the name of Christ, lest they live as though they were dead for having denied Christ. So too, they ought to be ready, for the sake of Christ, to lose the riches that they were not ready to sell, as Christ counseled, in order that they may not be lost along with them after they have lost Christ. For this reason we have rich and most glorious persons of both sexes who have been exalted by the glory of martyrdom. Many who hesitated before to become perfect by the selling of their possessions have suddenly been made perfect by imitating the suffering of Christ, and those who by some weakness of flesh and blood spared their riches suddenly did battle against sin for the faith to the point of shedding their blood. But those who did not attain the crown of martyrdom and did not accept the great and glorious counsel about selling their possessions and yet, free

---

29. See Mt 10:41.
30. See Is 58:7; Mt 25:35.
31. See Lk 14:26-27.

from grave sins worthy of condemnation, fed the hungry Christ, gave him drink in his thirst, clothed him when he was naked, and welcomed him when he was traveling, will not, of course, sit with Christ to judge from on high, but will stand at his right hand to be judged with mercy.[32] For blessed are the merciful because God will show them mercy,[33] and *judgment will be without mercy for one who has not shown mercy, but mercy triumphs over judgment* (Jas 2:13).

37. Hence, let these people stop speaking contrary to the scriptures, and in their exhortations let them rouse people to greater goods without condemning lesser ones. Is it true, after all, that with their exhortations they can only lead people to holy virginity by condemning the bonds of marriage, since, as the apostle teaches, *Each has his own gift from God, one this gift, another that* (1 Cor 7:7)? Let them, therefore, walk in the path of perfection after having sold all their possessions and given them away in acts of mercy. But if they are truly the poor of Christ and gather riches not for themselves but for Christ, why should they punish his weaker members before they have received their seats as judges? For, if they are the sort of persons to whom the Lord says, *You shall sit upon twelve thrones, judging the twelve tribes of Israel* (Mt 19:28 and Lk 22:30), and of whom the apostle says, *Do you not know that we shall judge the angels?* (1 Cor 6:3) let them prepare themselves rather to welcome into eternal dwelling places not rich criminals but the devout rich, who made friends *by means of the mammon of iniquity* (Lk 16:9). For I suspect that some of those who spread about these ideas impudently and imprudently are supported by rich and pious Christians in their needs. For the Church has, in a sense, its own soldiers and its own officials. Hence, the apostle says, *Who ever serves as a soldier at his own expense?* (1 Cor 9:7) It has its vineyard and its cultivators; it has its flock and its pastors. Hence, he says by way of conclusion, *Who plants a vineyard and does not eat of its fruit? Who shepherds a flock and does not receive milk from it?* (1 Cor 9:7) And yet, to argue for such ideas as they argue for is not to serve as soldiers but to engage in rebellion; it is not to plant a vineyard but to uproot it; it is not to gather sheep to feed them but to separate them for the flock to lose them.

38. These people, however, who are fed and clothed by the pious services of the rich—for they do not receive things for their needs only from those who sell their possessions—are not, nonetheless, judged and condemned by the more excellent members of Christ who, thanks to their greater virtue, which the apostle commends,[34] support themselves by their own hands. In the same way these people ought not to condemn Christians of lesser merit by whose wealth they are supported but ought rather to say to them, by living well and by teaching correctly, *If we have sown spiritual goods among you, is it too much if we gather*

---

32. See Mt 25:34-40.
33. See Mt 5:7.
34. See 1 Thes 4:11; Acts 20:34.

in a natural harvest from you? (1 Cor 9:11) The servants of God, of course, who live by selling the honest work of their own hands, condemn with far less impudence the people from whom they receive nothing than those people do who are unable to work with their hands on account of some bodily weakness and condemn those from whose resources they themselves live.

39. I myself who write these words have deeply loved the perfection about which the Lord spoke when he said to the rich young man, *Go, sell all that you have, and give it to the poor, and you will have treasure in heaven, and come, follow me* (Mt 19:21), and I have done this not by my own strength but by the help of his grace. It is not true that I will receive less credit because I was not rich. For the apostles themselves who first did this were not rich either. But he abandons the whole world who abandons both what he has and what he hopes to have. I, of course, know better than any other human being how far I have made progress in this path of perfection, but God knows this better than I. And with as much energy as I can, I exhort others to this goal, and in the name of the Lord I have companions who have been persuaded to this by my ministry in such a way that, above all, we still maintain sound doctrine, and we do not judge with vain pride those who live like us, saying that it profits them nothing that they live chastely, though as married, that they govern their homes and families, and that by works of mercy they store up for themselves treasure for the next life. Otherwise, by arguing for these ideas we might be found not to be interpreters of the holy scriptures but attackers of them. I have mentioned this because, when the Pelagians are prevented from saying such things by those who have not accepted this counsel of the Lord, they reply that those people do not want to discuss these points because they are attached to their own vices and refuse to fulfill the commandments of the Lord. Now, not to mention those who, though weaker, still use riches in a religious manner, even the covetous and greedy people who use these riches badly and set their hearts of clay upon an earthly treasure are more tolerable in the Church than these people. [For it is necessary that the Church carry even these up to the end, like those nets carried bad fish to the shore.[35]] For by preaching and spreading these ideas these Pelagians want to appear great because they have sold their riches and any inheritance in accord with the commandment of the Lord, and they work to disturb and undermine by this unsound doctrine his heritage, which is spread far and wide up to the ends of the earth.

40. Hence, because I have on this occasion already said, though only briefly, what I hold about the Church of Christ in this world, that is, that it must carry within her good and bad people until the end of this world, for you asked this too among your other questions, I shall finally conclude this lengthy letter.

---

35. See Mt 13:47-48.

But avoid swearing an oath as much as possible. One does better, of course, not to swear to the truth than by the habit of swearing to fall into perjury often and always come close to perjury. But those people—to the extent that I have heard some of them—have no idea at all what it is to swear. For they think that they do not swear when they have on their lips, *God knows* (2 Cor 11:31; 12:2), *God is my witness* (Rom 1:9; Phil 1:8) and, *I call God as witness to my soul* (2 Cor 1:23), because one does not say, "by God," and because such expressions are found in the apostle Paul. But against them that expression, which they admit is an oath, is also found there in the apostle where he says, *I die every day, brothers; I swear by the boast about you that I have in Christ Jesus our Lord* (1 Cor 15:31). For in the Greek manuscripts this is certainly found to be an oath so that no one should understand in the Latin language that *by the boast about you* was said in the same way as *by my coming to you again* (Phil 1:26) and many other expressions in which there is said, "by something," and there is no oath. But it is not the case that an oath ought to be a joke for us because the apostle, a man most solid in the truth, swore in his letter. For we act much more safely, as I said, if, to the extent it is up to us, we never swear so that *yes, yes; no, no* (Mt 5:37, Jas 5:12) is on our lips, as the Lord admonishes, not because it is a sin to swear to the truth but because it is a very grave sin to swear falsely, and one falls more quickly into this who becomes used to swearing.

41. You see now what I think. Better people—not those whose view I already know must be rejected, but others who can do so with truth—may explain these points better. For I am more ready to learn than to teach, and you will bestow a great benefit upon me if you do not allow me to be ignorant of what the holy brethren there say against the empty chatter of these people. May you live correctly and happily in the Lord, my most beloved son.

Letter 158

In 414 or 415 Evodius, the bishop of Uzalis and Augustine's friend of long standing, wrote to Augustine. Evodius tells Augustine of the exemplary life and the pious death of a young man who had become close to Evodius (paragraphs 1 and 2). He tells Augustine of the dream of a widow that the young man was taken from his grave to heaven (paragraph 3). He acknowledges how during this life the body is a hindrance to the soul (paragraph 4) and asks whether after death the soul is completely without a body (paragraph 5). Evodius expresses his conviction that the soul does not entirely lack a body after death and points to biblical evidence that the dead still have a body (paragraph 6). He tells Augustine that he thinks that the soul will be much more alert after death, but he also expresses a worry that death will be like a deep sleep (paragraph 7). Furthermore, he wonders whether, if the soul is entirely without a body, it will also be entirely without any senses (paragraph 8).

Evodius also asks Augustine about various dead persons who have appeared to him and spoken with him (paragraph 9). He recounts how the young boy whom he had mentioned earlier was seen in a vision at the time of his death and how in another vision he appeared and said that he had come for his father, who then died within a few days (paragraph 10). Evodius again expresses his idea that the soul cannot be entirely without a body but enjoys a great freedom when it is delivered from this present body (paragraph 11). Finally, Evodius asks Augustine to explain to him the many different ways in which "wisdom" is used in the scriptures (paragraph 12).

To my lord and venerably most beloved brother and fellow priest, Augustine, and to the brothers who are with you, Evodius and the brothers who are with me send greetings in the Lord.

1. I ask payment of the debt you owe me for the letter I sent you. I first wanted to learn what I asked and afterwards to ask for this. But let me tell you, because you are so kind, what it is that makes me impatient so that I am in a hurry to know this as well, if it is possible in this life. I had with me a certain boy, a scribe, the son of the priest Armenus of Memlonitanis. God rescued him through my lowly self when he was already drowning in the world—for he was acting as secretary to an advocate of the proconsul. He was, of course, as a boy is at that age, eager and somewhat restless, but with the approach of maturity—for he completed his twenty-second year—a moral seriousness and watchfulness made him attractive because of his good life, so that it is quite a delight to remember him. He was, however, meticulous with notes and worked quite hard at writing; he had also come to enjoy reading to the point that he used to urge me on in my slowness to read at night. For he himself would read to me for some time at night when everything had fallen silent, and he did not want to pass over a passage if he had

40

not understood it, and he repeated it a third and fourth time and did not let it go unless what he was seeking had become clear to him. I began to regard him not as a boy and a scribe but as a rather close and dear friend. For his stories brought me delight.

2. He also desired *to be dissolved and to be with Christ* (Phil 1:23), and this prayer was granted him. For he was ill for sixteen days in the home of his parents, and by the power of his memory[1] he spoke about the scriptures during almost the whole illness. But when he began to be near the end of life, he sang in the hearing of all, *My soul longs for and hastens to the courts of God* (Ps 84:3), and after this he again sang, *You have anointed my head with oil and how wonderful is your cup which inebriates me!* (Ps 23:5) With that he was occupied; with this consolation he found joy. Then, when he began to be released, he began to sign himself on the forehead so that his hand went down in that way to his mouth, which he desired to sign for himself, though *the interior self*, which was also *renewed from day to day* (2 Cor 4:16), had already left its house of clay. Such great joy increased within me that I think that, having left his own body, he has entered into my soul and is there offering me a certain brightness by his presence. It cannot be said that I am rejoicing too much over his deliverance and security. For I showed him no slight concern, fearing for the age of the youth, inasmuch as I took care to ask of him whether he had perhaps been defiled by contact with a woman; he assured me that he was free from such defilement, so that our joy was increased even more. He was, therefore, set free. We gave him an altogether honorable funeral worthy of such a soul. For during three days we praised the Lord with hymns over his tomb and offered on the third day the mysteries of our redemption.

3. But now, after two days, a certain good widow, Urbica of Figentes, who said that she was a widow for twelve years, a servant of God, had a dream of this sort. She sees a certain deacon who had died four years previously, with servants and handmaids of God, virgins and widows, prepare a palace. It was, however, decorated so that the splendor of the place shone and the whole place was thought to be silver. When she asked with great curiosity for whom this palace was being prepared, the deacon replied that it was being prepared for the boy who was taken yesterday, the son of the priest. And in the same palace there appeared an old man clothed in white who ordered two men in white to go and take the body from the tomb and raise it up to heaven. After the body was taken from the tomb and lifted up to heaven, she said, branches of virgin roses—for closed buds are usually called that—sprang up from the same tomb.

4. I have recounted what happened. Now be so good as to listen to my question and teach me what I ask. The journeying of this soul forces me to ask such

---

1. I have followed the reading in PL of *memoriae vi* ("by the power of his memory") instead of that in CSEL of *memor sui* ("mindful of himself").

questions. When we are in the body, our interior sense is active in accord with the quickness of our desire and is more vigilant and more fervent to the extent that we are more desirous, and yet it seems probable that we are slowed down by the impediment of the body. But who could recount all that the mind suffers from the body? Among these crowds of troubles coming from suggestions, temptations, needs, and various disasters, the mind does not abandon its courage; it resists, conquers and is at times conquered. Still, because it is mindful of itself, once awakened by such labors, it becomes more agile and attentive, breaks certain knots of sinfulness, and passes on to better things. Your Holiness graciously understands what I say. When, therefore, we are in this life, we are impeded by such needs, and still, as scripture says, *We more than conquer through him who has loved us* (Rom 8:37). What are we when we leave the body and escape every burden and sin that suddenly comes upon us?

5. And I ask first whether there is a body that does not abandon the incorporeal reality, that is, the substance of the soul, when it leaves this earthly body, that is, either an airy or an ethereal body, if it is perhaps one of the four elements. For, since the soul is incorporeal, if it lacks all body, there is now one soul for all. And where will that rich man dressed in purple and the afflicted Lazarus be? Also how will they be distinguished by their merits so that the one has punishment and the other joy if one soul has been formed from all incorporeal souls, at least if those things are not described in figurative language? It is, however, certain that, if things are contained in places, they are contained in bodies, as that rich man is in flames and the other in the bosom of Abraham.[2] If these are places, they are bodies, and incorporeal souls are in bodies. Or if punishments and rewards are found in the consciousness of each, whatever this one soul that has been formed out of the many souls is, it is afflicted and rejoices in the one substance that has been put together, it seems, from many souls. Or if it is said that the incorporeal soul is like one reality and that memory, will, and understanding are in it, all these faculties are incorporeal and have a proper part for their functions, and yet one does not interfere with the other. Somehow or other I think one can reply that punishments follow upon some and rewards follow upon others in the one substance put together from many souls.

6. Or if it is not so, if each soul has another body when it no longer has this solid body, what prevents the soul from always animating some body, or how does it effect its passage if there is any region to which it must go? For even the angels themselves cannot be said to be many if they are not counted by the number of their bodies. As the Truth himself says in the gospel, *I could have asked my Father, and he would have sent me twelve legions of angels* (Mt 26:53). Secondly, it is agreed that Samuel was seen in the body when he was

2. See Lk 16:19-22.

raised up at the request of Saul,[3] and it is evident according to the gospel that Moses, whose body was buried, came to the Lord on the mountain in a body, when they stood there together.[4] And yet, even in the apocryphal books and in the secret writings of Moses, writings that lack authority, when he ascended the mountain to die, the power of the body brings it about that what was committed to the earth was one thing, while what went along with the accompanying angel was something else. But it does not move me enough to prefer an opinion from apocryphal writings to those previous ones that are well established. One must see, therefore, and investigate, either by authority or by reason, the question posed. It is, however, said that the future resurrection shows that the soul will have been without any body. But it does not pose a serious objection since those angels, who are also invisible, chose to appear and to be seen with bodies, and whatever was the disposition of the bodies worthy of their spirits, they nonetheless appeared to Abraham[5] and to Tobit.[6] Thus it is possible that there will be the resurrection of this flesh, which we do well to believe will take place, and yet that the soul will be restored to the body in such a way that it is found never to have lacked a body. For, since a body is composed of four elements, it seems to lose one, namely, warmth, when the soul is seen to depart from this body. After all, the earthly element remains, and liquid is not absent, nor is the element of the cold substance lacking. Only warmth is taken from it, which the soul itself perhaps takes with it if it moves from one place to another. This is what I would say for the time being about the body.

7. It also seems to me that if, when it is located in the living body, as I already said, it uses the vigorous intention of the mind, how much more quick, thriving, earnest, fervent, vigorous and intent it will be once it has been set free and how much more capable and better it becomes since, even when it was located in the body, it enjoyed such power. When the body has been laid aside, like a cloud that has been wiped away, having become wholly clear and located in peace without temptation, it will see what it has desired and embrace what it has loved. It will also recall friends and recognize those whom it has sent on ahead and those whom it has left behind. Perhaps it is so; I do not know; I ask in order to learn. But I worry a great deal whether the soul goes into a kind of somnolent state so that it is as it is when it is present in the body and sleeps, as if it were buried and living only in hope, otherwise doing nothing, knowing nothing, especially if it is touched by no dream. This idea is very frightening and makes it seem that the soul is dead.

8. I also ask this: If the soul will be found to have a body, will it be without any sense? Surely, if the need for smelling cannot be attributed to it, nor of tasting or

---

3. See 1 Sm 28:14.
4. See Mt 17:3.
5. See Gn 18:1.
6. See Tb 12:15.

touching, I wonder whether there remains the need for seeing and hearing. For why is it that the demons are said to hear not only in all whom they torment—for there is a question even about these—but also when they appear in bodies of their own. Concerning sight, however, how do they pass from place to place if they have a body and if they lack sight to guide them? Don't you think that all human souls, when they depart from bodies, are such that they have some body and are not without some sense? Why is it that persons who are awake or walking about see many of the dead entering homes, as they have been accustomed to, either during the day or during the night? I have heard this more than once, and there is the fact that it is said that at a certain moment of the night disturbances and prayers are made in places where bodies are buried, especially in basilicas. For I remember that I heard this from more than one person. A certain holy priest bears witness to this vision: he saw a large number of such persons coming out of a baptistry with bright bodies and afterward heard prayers in the middle of the church. All these events, then, support our inquiry. Or if they are just stories, it is strange. I would, nonetheless, like to know something about this since the dead come, pay visits, and are seen outside of dreams.

9. From this another question arises. For I am not now concerned about an image that an uneducated heart forms for itself; I am speaking about visitations, in the way that an angel appeared to Joseph in a dream[7] and as many people have received visitations. In that way, then, our friends whom we have sent on ahead sometimes come; they appear in a dream and speak. For I remember that I saw Profuturus and Privatus and Servilus, holy men from the monastery, whom I remember went on ahead, and they spoke to me, and things happened as they said. Or if there is some better spirit who assumes their shape and visits the mind, he knows to whom all things lie bare from the very top of the head. If, then, the Lord will deign, through reason, to say something to Your Holiness on all these topics, I ask that you be so good as to make me a partaker of this knowledge. But I did not want to pass this over, for it may perhaps pertain to my inquiry.

10. The boy himself whom we are discussing departed and was seen somehow at the time at which he was released from the body. For his fellow student and reader, with whom he was assisting me and who had already been taken from the body eight months before, was seen in a dream to have come. When he was asked by the one who saw him then why he had come, he said, "I have come to guide my friend from here." And so it happened. For in the very house there appeared to an old man who was almost awake a man carrying in his hand a laurel and a document. But where that youth was seen, it also happened that after the death of the boy his father, the priest, withdrew to the monastery with Bishop Theasius for the sake of finding consolation. But the third day after the boy's death the same boy was seen to enter the monastery and was asked by a

---

7. See Mt 1:20.

certain brother in a dream whether he knew that he was dead. He said that he knew. He was asked whether he was welcomed by God. And with great gratitude he replied that he had been. And when he was asked the reason why he had come, he then said, "I was sent to deliver my father." The one to whom these things were shown woke up and recounted them. It reached the ear of Bishop Theasius. He was upset and scolded the man who said this lest this story readily come to the ear of the priest and he be disturbed by such a report. Why should I go on longer? Perhaps four days after this visitation, when the priest was speaking, he noticed a slight fever. There was no danger; the doctor was not there to assure them that there was absolutely no worry. But the priest died as soon as he lay down in bed. And I do not pass over in silence that, on the very day on which the boy died, he asked his father for a sign of peace; he asked three times and with each embrace he said to his father, "Father, let us give thanks to God." And he forced his father to say it as well along with him, as if exhorting him to leave this life along with him. For between the two deaths seven days intervened. What is one to make of such strange events? Who will teach us with great reliability about such hidden causes? The turmoil of my heart is poured out to you in the time of my trouble. God's providence in the death of the boy and of his father is evident since not even two swallows fall to the earth apart from the will of the Father.[8]

11. That event, I believe, shows, then, that the soul cannot be completely without a body because God is the only one who is always without a body. But the setting aside of the great burden of the body shows, I think, how much more alert the soul will be after its passing. For then, set free from so great a bond in action and thought, I think, it appears more excellent, and all that spiritual rest shows that it is free from all emotions and errors but does not make it feeble, lazy, apparently sluggish, and entrapped. It is, of course, enough for it to enjoy the freedom that it has acquired when it is removed from the world and its body. For you wisely said that the intellect will be fed by it and will put its spiritual mouth to the fountain of life. For one time, when I was still living in the monastery, I saw Brother Servilus in a dream after his death. He said that we labor to come to understanding through reason, but that he and those like him abide in the delight of contemplation itself.

12. I ask also that you show me in how many ways wisdom is spoken of. For example, God is wisdom, and the soul is wise with wisdom, just as it is also called light. So too, there is the wisdom of Bezahel who made the tabernacle or the vessel for oil.[9] And there is the wisdom of Solomon[10] and any other wisdom there is. How do these differ from one another? And is that one wisdom eternal with the Father to be understood on the same different levels as there are said to

---

8. See Mt 10:29.
9. See Ex 31:2.
10. See 1 Kgs 4:30; Mt 12:42.

be different gifts of the Holy Spirit, *who apportions to each his own gifts as he wills* (1 Cor 7:12,11)? Or, with the exception of that wisdom that alone was not made, are these instances of wisdom made, and do they have their own substance? Or were they caused and did they receive their name from the definition of the work? I have many questions. May the Lord give you the grace to find the answers and the wisdom to dictate them and to write to us quickly. I have written without skill or eloquence, but since you are so kind as to understand what I am asking, I beg you by Christ the Lord to correct me on these points and to teach me what you understand that I want to know.

Letter 159

In 414 or 415 Augustine replied to the previous letter from Evodius. Augustine tells his friend and fellow bishop that he cannot find the other letter from Evodius and that a full answer to Letter 158 would take much time and energy. His brief answer is that the soul does not leave the body with a body (paragraph 1). He refers Evodius to his long discussion of the kinds of visions in *The Literal Meaning of Genesis* (paragraph 2). He tells Evodius of the experience of a well-known doctor living in Carthage whose dream convinced him that there is a life after death in which we will be able to see with non-bodily eyes (paragraphs 3 and 4). Furthermore, each person can withdraw into himself and ponder and distinguish the images of things that are produced in his mind (paragraph 5).

To my most blessed lord and venerable and lovable brother and fellow priest, Evodius, and to the brothers with you, Augustine and the brothers with me send greetings in the Lord.

1. This brother, a servant of God by the name of Barbarus, has long since been living in Hippo as a fervent and zealous hearer of the word of God. He desired a letter from us to Your Holiness by which we would commend him to you in the Lord and express to you through him our dutiful greeting. But to reply to the letter of Your Holiness in which you set forth immense questions would involve much hard work even for those who are at leisure and are endowed much more than we are with an ability to speak and a keenness of understanding. Of the two letters from you in which you ask many and important questions, one somehow or other has become lost and could not be found though I searched for it for a long time, but the other that I found has a most tender commendation of a good servant of God and chaste youth, stating how he left this life and the testimonies of the brothers' visions that were able to make known to you his merit. Then on this occasion you propose and examine a most obscure question concerning the soul, namely, whether it leaves the body with some body by which it can be carried to bodily places or contained in bodily places. The treatment of this matter, if it can be brought to the point of clarity by such persons as we are, demands a most diligent care and effort and, for this reason, a mind at leisure from these present occupations. But if you wish to listen briefly to my opinion, I do not in any way think that the soul leaves the body with a body.

2. How those visions and predictions of the future come about, let him try to explain who knows the power by which such marvelous images of things are produced in each mind when it thinks. For we see and clearly discern that there come to be in the mind countless images of many visible things and of things pertaining to the other senses of the body. It is now of no concern with what order or disorder they come to be, but only *that* they come to be, which is something

that is evident. But let anyone who can explain by what power or how they come to be—all these things are surely daily and constant occurrences—dare also to presume to determine something about those extremely rare visions. I, however, dare less to do so to the extent that I am less able to explain how that takes place which we also constantly experience in our life in our own selves, when awake and asleep. For, when I dictate this letter to you, I see you in my mind, though you are, of course, absent and unaware of this, and I imagine how you can be touched by these words in accord with the knowledge I have of you. And I could not grasp or search out how that is produced in my mind, certain as I was, nonetheless, that it is not produced by bodily masses or by bodily qualities, though something very much like a body is produced. For the time being accept this as something dictated by a busy and hurried man. But in the twelfth book of those I wrote on Genesis,[1] this question is closely examined, and that discussion is filled with many examples of things that have been experienced and reported in a way that deserves belief. You will judge what we were able to do or what we accomplished in them when you read them, if the Lord deigns to grant that I may now publish those books that have been suitably corrected to the extent that I could do so and not hold up the expectation of many brothers by a long discussion.

3. I shall, however, briefly recount one story for you to ponder. Our brother, Gennadius, is a man known to almost all and a physician most dear to us; he now lives at Carthage, and he excelled in the practice of his art in Rome. You knew him as a religious man and one most kind, with unstinting mercy and a most ready spirit for the care of the poor. He doubted, nonetheless, at one point, as he recently told us, when he was still a youth and was most dedicated to these acts of almsgiving, whether there was any life after death. Because God would in no way abandon this man's mind and works of mercy, there appeared to him in a dream a striking youth worthy of being noticed, and he said to him, "Follow me," and when he followed him he came to a certain city where he began to hear from the right side sounds of the sweetest singing beyond the usual and familiar sweetness. Then that youth said to the man intent upon knowing what this was that they were the hymns of the blessed and the saints. But what he reported that he saw on the left side I do not remember well enough. He woke up; the dream vanished, and he thought about that youth as much as about the dream.

4. But on another night, see, the same youth again appeared to him and asked whether he recognized him. This man answered that he recognized him well and clearly. Then he asked from where he knew him. Nor did he fail to remember what this same man replied, and he recounted the whole vision and the hymns of the saints that he had come to hear under his guidance and the ease with which he recalled them as fresh to his mind. At this point that youth asked him whether he had seen the things that he had recounted in a dream or when awake. He replied,

---

1. See *The Literal Meaning of Genesis* 12, 6, 15-22. 61.

"In a dream." The youth said, "You recall well; it is true; you saw them in a dream. But even now you know that you are seeing this in a dream." When the man heard this, he believed that it was so, and he affirmed it with his reply. Then the youth who was teaching the man went on to ask, "Where is your body now?" He replied, "In my bedroom." "Do you know," the other asked, "that in that body your eyes are closed, shut, and idle and that you are seeing nothing with those eyes?" He answered, "I know." Then the youth asked, "What, then, are these eyes by which you see me?" Not finding what he might reply to this, he was silent. As he hesitated, the youth disclosed to him what he was trying to teach him by these questions and went on to say, "Just as those eyes of your flesh are now indeed idle in the body that is asleep and lying in bed and are doing nothing, and yet there are these eyes by which you see me and enjoy this present vision, so, when you are dead and the eyes of your flesh are doing nothing, there will be present in you the life by which you live and the consciousness by which you are aware. Be careful from now on not to doubt that life remains after death." That trustworthy man says that in that way the doubt about this matter was taken from him. Who taught him but God in his providence and mercy?

5. Someone might say that by that story we have not resolved but complicated the question about so important an issue. But a person is free to believe these words or not, and everyone has himself into whom he may withdraw for this most profound question. A human being both awakes and goes to sleep daily, and he thinks. Let him say if he can how there come to be things like shapes, like qualities, like the motions of bodies, yet without bodily material. But if he cannot say, why is he in a rush to pronounce a definitive judgment, as it were, about things that are most rare and unprecedented, since he does not resolve constant and daily questions? Although it is true that I cannot explain in words how images like bodies come about without a body, I do nonetheless know that they are not produced by a body. I wish I knew how those things are differentiated that are seen at times through the spirit and that are thought to be seen through the body or how the visions of those people are distinguished whom error or impiety deludes when many events are recounted like the visions of pious and holy people! If I had wanted to mention examples, time would run out on me rather than the supply of examples. Mindful of us, may you prosper in the mercy of the Lord, my most blessed lord and venerable and loveable brother.

Letter 160

In 414 or 415 Evodius, the bishop of Uzalis, again wrote to Augustine in an attempt to speak about the relation between the Father and the Son. He begins by touching upon the relation between eternal reason for all things and God (paragraph 1). Evodius wonders whether, since reason proves that God exists, reason is prior to God (paragraph 2). Reason cannot be prior to God nor God prior to reason. Evodius links reason with the Son of God, whom God begets and who in turn reveals God (paragraph 3). As he continues the arduous and very difficult task of his theological reflections, Evodius wonders whether the Father is wordless without the Son (paragraph 4).

1. That is perfect reason which offers knowledge of all things and especially of eternal things that will be grasped by the intellect. Reason itself teaches that it is eternal and must be eternal. That is eternal which neither begins nor ceases, neither changes nor varies. Reason must be eternal not merely because it teaches and proves eternal truths but much more because eternity itself cannot be without reason. And I think eternity would not exist if reason itself were not eternal. Second, reason itself demonstrates that God exists or must have existed and that it cannot be otherwise than that God exists. Whether there were those who knew this or not, since God, nonetheless, is eternal, we should not doubt that reason is eternal, which aims to prove the necessary existence of God and thus to show that it is coeternal to him.

2. There are, however, certain things whose existence reason demands so that reason must be prior, and there follows the occurrence of that which reason showed would ensue. For example, when the world was made, reason knew that the world would be made. Reason, therefore, is prior to the world. Those things, therefore, which reason knew were going to come followed afterward so that reason was first and the production of the world afterward. Now then, since reason shows that God exists or that it is necessary that God exist, which one shall we put before the other? Reason before God, as we put reason before the world, or God before reason, without which it can in no way be proved that God exists? For, if God's being is eternal and reason is eternal, reason, then, is either God or belongs to God, as reason itself teaches. But if it is God, reason has shown that God is reason and that they can be coeval and coeternal to each other. But if this reason is a likeness of God, it shows that reason likewise belongs to God, and this will be coeval and coeternal. Reason itself shows that it is impossible that God be in such a way unless God exists. If this reason should be taken away—and this is wicked to say—God will not exist if reason does not show that God exists necessarily. God, therefore, exists when there is the reason for God to

exist. Because, then, God exists, reason certainly exists, which has taught that he exists.

3. What, then, if we can say this, is first in God: reason or God? But God will not exist unless reason exists, which teaches that God must exist. Reason also will not exist unless God will exist. Nothing, therefore, is first and last in God. This divine nature, therefore, has somehow or other both reason and God simultaneously. One, however, is the source of the other. Either reason is the source of God or God is the source of reason. Perhaps, however, reason and God may be said to be a subject or to be in a subject. God and reason might be one in the other. It is good, however, if God generates reason because reason reveals that God exists. God, however, is understood by reason as the Son is understood by the Father, and reason is understood by God as the Father is understood by the Son. For reason itself is also God with God. For God was not at some time without reason, or reason without God. For God exists if reason exists, and the Son exists if the Father exists so that, if, as was said, reason were taken away, something that it is impious to say, God himself does not exist. For through his reason there is the action and operation of God's existence. Let us repeat the same points. If reason did not exist, God did not exist, and if God does not exist, reason did not. Reason, therefore, and God are something everlasting, and God and reason are in a similar way something everlasting. The connection and union, however, of reason to God and of God to reason, of the Father to the Son and of the Son to the Father, furnish to each other, so to speak, principles and causes for existing, because the one cannot be without the other. Words fail us, and we say something or other in order not to remain silent. But should we say that God is the origin of reason or that reason is the origin of God? For there cannot be fruit without the root, nor is the root anything without the fruit. A likeness is drawn in order that we may have a sign of some understanding of God. For even in the grain of wheat there lives a principle of life that does not allow it to remain sterile. But again, if there were not the grain of wheat from which it might produce this, the principle would not exist.

4. Since, therefore, reason, which is God, shows either that God is reason or that reason is God, showing that the one is somehow the other, the Father is not revealed except through the Son, and the Son is not revealed except through the Father. Thus the Father remains as it were in silence when one comes to the Father through the Son, and the Son remains as it were in silence when one comes to the Son through the Father. Thus the one is somehow hidden when the other is revealed. And yet, in revealing himself the one also reveals the other, nor can the one be known so that the other remains hidden, because he says, *The one who has seen me has also seen the Father* (Jn 14:9), and, *No one comes to the Father except through me* (Jn 14:6), and, *No one comes to me unless the Father draws him* (Jn 6:44). We have entered upon an arduous and very difficult task of understanding something about God, though we do not understand. And yet, just

as all the things that exist are not understood and are not knowable without some form, neither—and even more so—is anything known without the Son, that is, without reason. How so? Was the Father ever wordless[1] without reason? Who would dare to say this? We must, therefore, know by reason that God, who is one from one or one in one, is at the same time one, because God is one, and it is necessary that there be present in him that love which reason itself teaches and God commands that we should always have and show.

---

1. Evodius uses *alogus*, which means either wordless or irrational.

Letter 161

In 414 or 415 Evodius wrote to Augustine about what Augustine had written to Volusian in Letter 137, namely, that if, in regard to Christ's conception and birth, a reason is sought, it will not be a source of wonder, and if an example is demanded, it will not be singular. Evodius first argues that a reason or explanation cannot be given for the conception of any being (paragraph 1). Furthermore, he points to examples of virginal conceptions found in nature (paragraph 2). Finally, he applies Augustine's statement to the question raised in Letter 92 to Italica about Christ's seeing the substance of God with his bodily eyes (paragraph 3).

To my holy and venerable lord and most beloved brother and fellow priest, Augustine, and to the brothers with him, Evodius and the brothers who are with me send greetings in the Lord.

1. By means of Jobinus, who had been sent to the Marcian estate, I already asked one question in the letter I sent concerning reason and God,[1] and I still have not merited a reply to this. But because we had in our hands and read the letters of Your Holiness, the one to the illustrious man, Volusian,[2] and the other to Italica, an illustrious lady in Christ,[3] I noticed that, in the former letter on the carnal conception in the Virgin of the Lord Jesus Christ our God, you said concerning that birth, "If a reason is sought, it will not be a source of wonder; if an example is demanded, it will not be singular,"[4] and it seemed that something like this could be said of every birth of a human being or of any living being or seed. For, if the reason for it is sought, it will not be found, and it will, of course, still be a source of wonder. And if an example is demanded, it will still be singular since nothing like it is found in examples. For no offspring of a male and a female or of any conception can ever be explained by reason, since its formation is in secret. Nor will any reason be found for seeds springing up from the earth, which first decay and afterward bear fruit. And it is a source of wonder as well that a single worm without any parent, if this is required for singularity, is found complete, formed by a virginal conception, within an apple. For this reason I think it was said by way of example, *I am a worm and no man* (Ps 22:7). I do not, then, know what reason can be given concerning conceptions whether from couples or from individuals. It is not with regard to the conception of the

---

1. See Letter 160.
2. That is, Letter 137.
3. That is, Letter 92.
4. See Letter 137, 2, 8.

Virgin alone, then, that no reason is given; rather, I think no reason can be given with regard to any conception.

2. But if an example is demanded, look, mares are said to bring forth their young, after being impregnated by the wind, and chickens after being impregnated by ashes and ducks by water, and some other animals are said to bring forth their young without male seed. Certainly, if they do not give birth without loss of virginity, they can nonetheless conceive without intercourse. How, then, can you say, "If an example is demanded, it will not be singular," since so many examples can be produced? Everyone knows that certain living beings are born within the bodies not only of females but also in those of males, I mean inside them. Does seed cause the conception even in that case? See the examples, see the miracles concerning which a reason is in no way given. Or, if it is replied to this that nothing of the sort ever happened in a human virgin, there are nonetheless examples in the natures of other things because they come to be and are conceived without seeds, and no reason can ever be given for these. And in generation one can still find something like this that brings forth its offspring without violating the integrity of its nature. For I often hear that a female spider brings forth in a wondrous manner without any conception from a male or any corruption from birth all those threads from which it is accustomed to weave its webs, and it does this in accord with its nature and shows that this was granted to it alone quite singularly. If this, then, is also questioned, is it not a great source of wonder, though examples of similar things can in no sense be given? For I suspect that these events came along first by way of example precisely in order that those persons who did not believe that a virgin could conceive would be convinced by these examples that it is indeed a source of wonder, but it will, nonetheless, not be singular. For all the works of God are reasons for wonder because they were produced with wisdom. If, then, we are faced with this objection, what shall we reply?

3. It also troubles me very deeply that anyone can say that the substance of the glorified body of the Lord can see the substance of God. For you said in the letter to Italica that it cannot, and this is certain. For, when we begin to give a reason why it cannot, we may receive this objection: If, because something wondrous and singular took place in that conception and birth, they do not want us to look for a reason or an example, because this was something granted to him alone, then, just as a reason is not given concerning his conception and birth, but it is something singular found in him alone, so a reason should not be given nor an example sought concerning his vision, but he alone is singularly allowed to see the substance of the divinity by his body. But if it will be said in reply that a reason can be given, namely, that it is not permitted to gaze upon something incorporeal by way of something corporeal, I fear that it may be said in reply that his conception can be explained by reason and supported by examples. For either reason will fail in human beings, and examples will cease, and they will

maintain that the Only-Begotten could see God with his body, or, if a reason is given for this, it will follow that a reason can be given by some extremely wise persons for both that conception and the consequent birth. I ask, then, what answer might be given them. Now, I am not sowing the seeds of disputes; rather, I am asking how one might reply to those who are insidious. I still believe in the Virgin's conceiving and giving birth, as I have always believed, and I have somehow by reason concluded that God cannot be seen by a body, however glorified. I think that we must address people who are accustomed either to stir up unrest by their questions or to devote themselves with a burning desire to learning. Pray for us. May the peace and love of Christ make Your Holiness mindful of us, my holy lord and venerably most blessed brother.

Letter 162

In 414 or 415 Augustine wrote to Evodius in order to reply to the questions the bishop of Uzalis had asked him in Letters 159, 160, and 161. Augustine first of all explains why he had not written an answer to Evodius' earlier letter (paragraph 1). He also tells Evodius that some of his questions have been dealt with in works he has not yet published and that Evodius could have figured out the answers to some of his questions from works of Augustine that Evodius has (paragraph 2). Augustine assures Evodius that, when the soul leaves the body, it does not take with it something bodily (paragraph 3). He explains that images seen in dreams are not bodily but like bodies (paragraph 4), and he discusses the images that we form at will as well as those that are caused in us by some external factor (paragraph 5).

Augustine then turns to an explanation of his statement to Volusian in Letter 137 about miracles (paragraph 6) and explains why different things arouse wonder (paragraph 7). He deals with Evodius' attempt to apply the statement from Letter 137 to the question of the Son's seeing the Father with bodily eyes (paragraph 8). In closing, he insists that God cannot be seen with the eyes of the body (paragraph 9).

To my blessed and venerable brother and holy fellow bishop, Evodius, and to the brothers with you, Augustine and the brothers with me send greetings in the Lord.

1. You ask many questions of a very busy man and, what is worse, you think that I should rush in dictating those ideas which are so difficult that, even if they are dictated or written with great care, they can scarcely be presented to the intellect even of persons as capable as you yourself are. In addition there is the fact that we must bear in mind that it is not only you and persons like you who are going to read what we write, but there are of course also those persons who are endowed with a mind that is less sharp and less well trained but who are carried along by a desire to know our writings, whether with a friendly or a hostile intention, so that they can by no means be kept from them. You see how much care in writing one who ponders these questions ought to have, especially concerning topics so great that even great minds struggle with them. If, however, when I have some task in hand, I must let go of it and postpone it in order to reply instead to those questions that arise later, what will happen if other even later questions arise when I am replying to these? Do you want me to take up the most recent ones while omitting the others and always put first those that arise later, so that it turns out that I finish only those ones subsequent to which no further question arises when they are being written? It would be very difficult for me if this should happen, but I do not think that this is what you want. I ought, then, not to

have interrupted other works when your questions came along, just as I ought not to interrupt yours if some others burst in upon us in turn. And still I do not permit myself to observe this norm of justice. For, see, I have set aside what I was working on in order to answer you with an admonition, and I have turned my mind to this letter from another important project.

2. It would, however, have been easy to send back to you by letter this excuse, which is, I think, a valid one, but it is not so easy to reply to your questions, and I think that in these works that now hold my full attention there will be certain passages where I will handle the very questions that you ask, if the Lord grants his help. Many of the questions that you just sent me have also already been resolved in the books that I have not published, either *The Trinity* or *Genesis*.[1] And yet, if you reread those books that you have known for a long time or that, unless I am mistaken, you once did know (for you may have forgotten those books I wrote when you were conferring and holding a discussion with me, either *The Magnitude of the Soul* or *Free Will*), you will find the means to resolve your doubts without my effort. But you will have to use some hard work in thinking, in order to draw the consequences from these points that were brought to a clear and certain understanding in them. You also have in the book *True Religion* points that, if you would recall and carefully examine them, would never lead you to think that God is forced to exist by reason or that reasoning makes it necessary that God exist. For if, regarding the nature of numbers, which we certainly use every day, we say, "Seven and three ought to be ten," we speak somewhat carelessly. For it is not true that they ought to be ten but that they are ten. We have, then, in my opinion already sufficiently discussed in those books I mentioned the things about which we correctly say that they ought to be, whether they already are or with an eye to their coming to be. For a human being ought to be wise; if he is wise, he ought to remain such, but if he is not yet wise, he ought to become such. God, however, ought not to be wise, but is wise.

3. Also, as for those points concerning visions that I recently wrote to you, you mention that they were stated with subtlety but that they entangled you in greater questions; rethink them again and again and ponder them with more care. Let your attention not move on but dwell on them, and from them you will perhaps somehow or other conjecture how the soul is present or absent. It lingers, of course, over those visions in dreams when it is far from the awareness and the activity of seeing that it bestows on the eyes when it is awake. But if, as occurs when we sleep, a greater force increases this absence of the soul from the eyes, that is, from the lights, so to speak, of the body, so that the whole of the soul is withdrawn from them, this state amounts to death. The soul, then, does not depart along with some body from the sense of seeing to what is seen in dreams—unless perhaps we are going to suppose that those bodily things that

---

1. That is, *The Literal Meaning of Genesis*.

are seen in dreams and we ourselves are carried here and there and back and forth with some body, which is something that I think you do not believe. So too, if the soul is completely withdrawn and absent, as happens in death, it should not be thought to carry off from the body some body with itself. For, if it did carry off some body, it would also, when we are asleep and it departs from the eyes insofar as it leaves them, take with it bodily eyes, though more subtle ones, but it does not do that. Yet it takes with itself certain eyes very similar to bodily eyes, though not bodily ones, by which it sees in dreams objects very much like bodies but not themselves bodily.

4. But if someone contends that even the visions seen in dreams that appear most like bodies are only bodily, he may think that he says something. Nor is this slowness of mind readily overcome. It is, of course, typical of many people who are not just average in intelligence that they pay too little attention to how much those images of bodies can do that are produced in the spirit and are absolutely not bodies. But when they are forced to look at them, if they correctly turn to them and discover that they are not bodies, but very similar to bodies, they still cannot immediately give an account of their causes and of how they come about, nor of the nature by which they exist, nor of the subject in which they inhere. They cannot explain whether they are produced in the mind like letters of ink on parchment, in which case each of them is a substance, that is, the parchment and the ink, or like a seal in wax or like any shape of which the wax is a subject and the shape in the subject, or whether they are produced in our spirit in both ways, at times this way, at other times that way.

5. For it is not just a problem that we think of those things that are far from the senses of the body and are found in our memory or that we ourselves produce, arrange, increase, diminish, and vary as we please in posture, apparel, motion, and countless qualities and forms. Of this sort are perhaps also those images by which we are deceived when sleeping, when we are not being warned by God, except that we produce the former images willingly but are affected by the latter apart from our choosing. Not only are these images disturbing that one not absurdly thinks are produced in the mind by the mind itself, though the causes remain quite hidden by which this image rather than that is made to come before the eyes of the mind, but there is also what the prophet says, *And the angel who was speaking in me said to me* (Zec 1:9). For we should not believe that words came externally to the bodily ears of the prophet when he says, *who was speaking in me*, not "to me." Were the words produced from the spirit like bodily words, the sort we produce when silently within ourselves we run through many items from memory and often even when singing, but brought forth by the angel, words which he saw were suggested to him in marvelous ways by someone other than he was? And there are the words in the gospel, *Behold, an angel of the Lord appeared to him in a dream, saying* (Mt 1:20). For how did even the body of an angel appear to eyes that were closed? Angels appeared to Abraham, of course,

when he was awake, so that he also felt them by touch when he washed their feet.[2] Or did a spirit appear to the spirit of the sleeping man with some form like a body, just as we ourselves see ourselves move through places with such a shape when we are dreaming in a far different manner than our members that are lying in bed?

6. These things are disturbing and are sources of wonder because they have a more hidden cause than one human being can see or convey to another. For these things are causes of wonder when the reason for any event is hidden or the same event is not familiar because it is singular or rare. Concerning a hidden reason, therefore, in the letter that you mention having read, I said when I was replying to those who deny that we should believe that the Virgin gave birth to Christ and remained a virgin, "If a reason is sought, it will not be a source of wonder." For I did not say this because the event lacks a reason but because it is hidden from those for whom God willed that this be a source of wonder. But concerning the other reason for wonder, that is, because something unusual has occurred, it was written of the Lord that he wondered at the faith of the centurion.[3] For no reason for any event could have been hidden from him, but his wonder was mentioned there as praise for the man whose equal had not been found in the Hebrew people. Hence, this wonder was sufficiently explained when the Lord said, *Truly I say to you, I have not found such great faith in Israel* (Mt 8:10; Lk 7:9).

7. But with regard to what I added in the same letter, "If an example is demanded, it will not be singular," you thought, though in vain, that you found examples, as it were, from the worm that comes to be in an apple and the spider that brings forth the thread of its web with its body intact, as it were. For some examples are cleverly produced on account of a certain likeness, some more remote and others more apt, but only Christ was born of a virgin. Hence, you now understand, I think, why I stated this without an example. All the things, then, that God does, whether usual or unusual, have their correct and blameless causes and reasons. But when these causes and reasons are hidden, we wonder at what happens, but when they are evident, we say that events happen in an orderly or suitable manner and that we should not be surprised that they happened since reason demanded that they happen. Or if we are surprised, we wonder in awe at something unexpected or in praise of something excellent. That centurion was praised by this latter kind of wonder. Nor should one find fault with the sentence which stated, "If a reason is sought, it will not be a source of wonder," because it is another kind of wonder when the reason is evident to the one who wonders. After all, we do not criticize the statement that says, *God tempts no one* (Jas 1:13), because there is another kind of temptation on account of which scripture also correctly said, *The Lord your God is tempting you* (Dt 13:3).

---

2. See Gen 18:4.
3. See Mt 8:10, Lk 7:9.

8. Nor should anyone suppose that he can correctly say that the Son sees the Father with bodily eyes and not rather as the Father sees the Son, on the grounds that, when those who think this fail to give a reason, they too can say, "If a reason is sought, it will not be a source of wonder." For this was said not because there is no reason but because it is hidden. But anyone who undertakes to refute those holding this opinion ought to demonstrate that there is no reason not for that miracle but for that error. For, just as there is no reason why the nature of God dies or is corrupted or sins and, when we say that God cannot do this, we do not take anything from his power but praise his eternity and truth, so, when we say that he cannot be seen by bodily eyes, the reason is not hidden but obvious to those who understand well. For it is clear that God is not a body, that only something which is seen at some distance in space can be seen by bodily eyes, and that it is only a body and a substance that is smaller in a part than in the whole. And to believe this of God ought to be unthinkable, even for these people who cannot yet understand this.

9. The reason for different changes in speed and slowness in the motions of bodies and of bodily qualities is hidden from us. For this reason there is the great multitude of all the visible wonders. Yet it is not hidden, is it, that there are bodies, that we have a body, that there is no body, however small, which does not occupy an area of space in accord with its size, and that in the space that it occupies it is not whole everywhere but smaller in a part than in the whole? Since these points are not hidden we need to draw some conclusions from them—which it would take too much time to do now—in order to show that the reason is not hidden, but that there is no reason at all why one should believe or be able to understand that God can be seen by bodily eyes. For he is whole everywhere and is not spread out through areas of space by a bodily mass because of which he would necessarily have to consist of larger and smaller parts. I would say more on this if I had taken up this topic in this letter. Without realizing it I have gone on at such length in it that I have almost forgotten my tasks and have perhaps done enough, something that I was not thinking of, for the sake of you who, once admonished by a few words, can think of many things that are pertinent, but not also for the sake of those into whose hands these writings can come with some benefit, if they are discussed more carefully and at greater length. But human beings have a hard time in learning when they cannot understand brief explanations and do not like to read long ones. They likewise have a hard time in teaching who without any benefit bring a few points to the minds of the slow and many to the minds of the lazy. Send me as well a copy of that letter that has become lost and cannot be found here. May you be rightly hale and hearty in the Lord and mindful of us.

Letter 163

In 414 or 415 Evodius wrote to Augustine, proposing several questions concerning the origin of the soul of Christ and concerning the spirits to whom he preached when he descended into hell.

Bishop Evodius to Bishop Augustine.

Some time ago I sent to Your Holiness one question concerning reason and God[1]—I think that it was by means of Jobinus, who serves the servants of God—and another concerning the body of the savior,[2] about which some think that it sees the substance of God. I now pose a third question: Does the rational soul that the savior assumed along with his body correspond to one of those opinions that are proposed when one asks about the origin of the soul, if any can be upheld by the truth, or, though it is rational, will it nonetheless not come to be in accord with these sorts of origin that are attributed to the human soul? I ask a fourth question: What spirits are those about which Peter testifies in his Letter concerning the Lord when he says, *He was put to death in the flesh, but brought to life in the spirit, and in that spirit he also preached to those spirits that were in prison* (1 Pt 3:18-19), and so on? He adds that those spirits were in hell and that Christ descended there and brought the good news to all and by grace set all free from darkness and punishments, so that from the time of the Lord's resurrection we await the judgment while hell is meanwhile empty. I desire to know what Your Holiness thinks on this matter.

---

1. See Letter 160.
2. See Letter 161.

Letter 164

In 414 or 415 Augustine wrote to Evodius to answer the latter's questions in Letter 163 concerning the Lord's preaching to the dead according to the First Letter of Peter. Augustine begins by admitting that he finds the passage difficult (paragraph 1). His first difficulty has to do with the identity of the unbelievers to whom Christ preached in hell (paragraph 2). His second difficulty concerns Christ's loosening the pains of hell (paragraph 3). He tell Evodius that, if Christ descended into hell to empty it of everyone, one can perhaps hope for the salvation of the great poets and philosophers of the pagan world (paragraph 4). If, however, Christ did empty hell, as Evodius suggested, there are still problems, which Augustine points out (paragraph 5). The Church does, of course, believe that Christ released Adam, the patriarchs, and the prophets of the Old Testament from the pains of hell (paragraph 6).

A third difficulty concerns the bosom of Abraham into which the poor Lazarus was received, for it does not seem to be a part of hell (paragraph 7). So too, Augustine wonders how Christ promised the good thief that he would be with him in paradise on the day of his death if Christ descended into hell to preach to the spirits who were there (paragraph 8). Furthermore, Augustine wonders how Christ can be *the firstborn from the dead* (Rv 1:5) if others rose from the tomb at his death (paragraph 9). The whole passage from the First Letter of Peter is deeply puzzling (paragraph 10).

Augustine presents his own interpretation of the passage according to which the dead to whom Christ preached are not those who have left their bodies (paragraph 11). If Christ descended to hell to preach the gospel to those who had no chance to hear it while they were alive, there are others who did not have a chance to hear the gospel after Christ's resurrection (paragraph 12). Furthermore, it is absurd to suppose that people who died without any belief in Christ could come to believe in him in hell and be saved (paragraph 13).

Augustine distinguishes matters of certain faith from other matters that remain uncertain and that pose problems (paragraph 14). He suggests that those who did not believe at the time of Noah symbolize those who do not now believe the gospel and that those who were saved through the ark symbolized those who are saved through baptism (paragraph 15). In that case one need not interpret the Letter of Peter in the sense that Christ preached the gospel to the souls in hell in order to make them believers (paragraph 16). Though in the days of Noah Christ had not yet come in the flesh, the Son of God spoke to human beings from the beginning of the world (paragraph 17). Before Christ came in the flesh, he came in the spirit and appeared and spoke to those he wanted to (paragraph 18).

Augustine turns to the question about the origin of Christ's soul and suggests that he could have created a soul for himself as he created a soul for Adam, but he insists that Christ's soul did not contract original sin since he was born of a virgin (paragraph 19). Christ's soul was both immortal and free from all sin (paragraph

20). He suggests that the dead to whom Peter said that the gospel was preached are those who were dead in their sins, but not those who died a bodily death (paragraph 21). In closing, Augustine hopes that his explanation will satisfy Evodius and claims that he has replied sufficiently to Evodius' questions (paragraph 22).

To Evodius, most blessed lord, brother, and fellow bishop, Augustine sends greetings in the Lord.

1, 1. The question that you proposed to me from the Letter of the apostle Peter—namely, how the words should be interpreted that seem to refer to hell—always disturbs us very deeply. And so I turn back to you the same question in order that, if you yourself can, or if you can find someone who can, you may remove and end my doubt about it. But if I can do so first because the Lord shall have granted this and if I can share it with you, I will not deprive Your Benevolence of it. But now I shall indicate what points bother me about it in order that in relation to them you yourself may either ponder these words of the apostle or consult someone suitable whom you may find.

2. After he said that Christ was put to death in the flesh but brought to life in the spirit, he immediately added in the same sentence that he went and preached *to the spirits who were held in prison* (1 Pt 3:19), the spirits who *were once unbelievers in the days when the patience of God was still waiting, in the days of Noah, when the ark was being constructed, in which a few, that is, eight souls, were saved through water* (1 Pt 3:20). Then he went on and said, *Now baptism also saves you by a similar form* (1 Pt 3:21). The problem, therefore, is this: If, when he died, the Lord preached in hell to the spirits held in prison, what good did they alone merit who were unbelievers when the ark was being constructed? For after the time of Noah so many thousands from so many nations died up to the passion of Christ whom he could have found in hell. I do not, of course, mean those who believed in God like the prophets and patriarchs of the family of Abraham or like Noah and his whole household who were earlier saved through water, except perhaps for one son who was afterward rejected.[1] So too there were others apart from the family of Jacob who believed in God, such as Job, such as the city of Nineveh and any others there were, whether they are found in the scriptures or are unknown in the human race. Rather, I mean those many thousands of human beings who, not knowing God and given to the worship of demons or idols from the time of Noah to the passion of Christ, left this life and whom Christ found in hell. How was it that he did not preach to them but only to those who were unbelievers in the days of Noah when the ark was being constructed? Or if he preached to all of them, why did Peter mention only those, while passing over so countless a multitude of the others?

---

1. See Gn 9:20-25.

2, 3. It is clear enough that the Lord, having been put to death in the flesh, entered into hell. For one cannot contradict either the prophecy that said, *For you will not leave my soul in hell* (Ps 16:10), which the same Peter explains in the Acts of the Apostles lest anyone dare to interpret it otherwise,[2] or the words of the same Peter by which he said that Jesus loosened the pains of hell *in which it was not possible that he be held* (Acts 2:24). Who, then, save an unbeliever, would deny that Christ was in hell? But if it poses a problem how we should interpret his having loosened the pains of hell—for he had not begun to be in them as if in bonds and thus loosened them as if he had loosened chains by which he had been bound—it is easy to understand that he loosened them in the way that the snares of hunters can be loosened so that they do not hold anything, not because they *did* hold anything. It can also be understood in the sense that we believe that he loosened those pains by which he himself was not held but by which others were held who he knew were to be set free.

4. But it is rash to state who these might be. For, if we say that absolutely all who were found there were then set free, who will not rejoice if we could show this, especially for the sake of certain persons who have become well known to us by their literary work and whose eloquence and natural talent we admire? I do not mean only the poets and orators who showed by many passages of their works that those same false gods of the nations are to be scorned and laughed at and who have at times even confessed the one God, though they worshiped those objects of superstition along with the rest, but also those who said these things not in poetry or oratory but in philosophy. There are many others as well whose writings we do not have, but in the writings of the former people we have learned that their lives were praiseworthy in some fashion. For, apart from the worship of God in which they were mistaken, since they worshiped the useless gods that had to be publicly worshiped and served the creature rather than the creator, they are proposed not only to citizens but even to enemies as rightly deserving imitation in their other practices of frugality, self-control, chastity, sobriety, contempt of death for the safety of the fatherland, and keeping faith. When, of course, all these are not referred to the end of correct and true piety but to the empty conceit of human praise and glory, they themselves become empty in a sense and are rendered sterile. Nonetheless, they cause delight by a certain gift of soul so that we would want those in whom these virtues are found, either especially or along with others, to be set free from the torments of hell, if human sentiment did not differ from the justice of the creator.

5. Since this is so, if the savior released everyone from there and, as you wrote in your request, emptied hell in order that from then on people would await the last judgment, here you have the things that with good reason disturb me in regard to this issue and that often occur to me as I now ponder this question:

---

2. See Acts 2:27.

First, by what authority is this view defended? For what scripture says happened at the death of Christ, *when he loosened the pains of hell* (Acts 2:24), can be understood to pertain to him, because he loosened them to this extent, that is, he made them ineffective so that he himself was not held by them, especially since there follows, *in which it was not possible that he be held* (Acts 2:24). Otherwise, if one asks for the reason why he wanted to come to hell, where he would find pains by which he could absolutely not have been held who was, as scripture says, *free among the dead* (Ps 88:6) and in whom the prince and leader of death did not find anything[3] that deserved punishment, the words of scripture, *when he loosened the pains of hell* (Acts 2:24), could be interpreted in reference to certain persons whom he judged worthy of this deliverance rather than to everyone. Then he would not be thought to have descended there uselessly without benefiting any of them who were held imprisoned there, and it would not follow that what the divine mercy and justice granted to certain persons must be thought to have been granted to all.

3, 6. Almost the whole Church agrees concerning that first man, the father of the human race, that Christ released him, and we should not suppose that the Church has believed this in vain, from whatever source this has been handed down, even if the authority of the canonical scriptures is not explicitly brought forth on this subject. And yet that statement in the Book of Wisdom, *This* [wisdom] *preserved the man who was made first, the father of the human race, when he was created alone, and it led him away from his sin and gave him the power of governing all things* (Wis 10:1-2), seems to be more in favor of this view than of any other interpretation. Certain persons add that this benefit was also granted to the saints of old, Abel, Seth, Noah and his family, Abraham, Isaac, Jacob, and the other patriarchs and prophets, namely, that, when the Lord descended into hell, they were released from those pains.

7. But I do not see how we are to understand that Abraham was in those pains when that holy poor man was taken up into his bosom; those who can may perhaps explain it. But I do not know whether there is anyone who does not think it absurd that only two men, that is, Abraham and Lazarus, were in that bosom of remarkable peace before the Lord descended into hell and that it was said to the rich man of those two alone, *Between you and us a great chasm has been established so that those who will cannot pass from here to you nor come here from there* (Lk 16:26). But if more than two were there, who would dare to say that the patriarchs and prophets were not there when in scripture such a remarkable testimony is offered to their righteousness and piety? I do not yet understood, therefore, what he gave them when he loosened the pains of hell which did not bind them, especially since I could not find anywhere in the scriptures that hell was referred to in a positive sense. But even if we never read this in the divine author

---

3. See Jn 14:30.

ities, we certainly should not believe that that bosom of Abraham, that is, that dwelling place of secret rest, is a part of hell. And yet in the very words of that great teacher, where he reports that Abraham said, *Between you and us a great chasm has been established*, it is quite clear, I think, that the bosom of that great happiness is not a particular part and a section, as it were, of hell. For what is a great chasm but a certain gap that separates very much those areas between which it not merely exists but exists firmly? Hence, if scripture had said that, after Christ died, he had come to that bosom of Abraham without mentioning hell and its pains, I wonder whether anyone would dare to say that he descended into hell.

8. But because clear testimonies mention both hell and its pains, no reason comes to mind why the savior should be believed to have gone there except to save people from those pains. But I still ask whether he judged worthy of that benefit all those whom he found there or only certain persons. I do not doubt that he was in hell and that he gave this benefit to people situated in those pains. Hence, I have not yet found what he bestowed on those righteous people who were in the bosom of Abraham when he descended into hell, for I do not see that he ever withdrew from them in terms of the beatific presence of his divinity. In the same way, on the very day on which he died, he promised the thief that he would be with him in paradise when he was on the point of descending to loosen the pains of hell. Even before, then, he was certainly in paradise and in the bosom of Abraham by his beatifying wisdom and in hell by his power of judgment. For where is the divinity surrounded by any place? Scripture nonetheless clearly states that in terms of the creature that he took on at a given moment in order to become man while remaining God, that is, in terms of his soul, he was in hell. For it was both announced beforehand by the prophet and sufficiently explained through the apostle's interpretation, where it says, *You will not leave my soul in hell* (Ps 16:10; Acts 2:27).

9. I know that some people think that the death of Christ the Lord already provided the righteous with a resurrection like that which is promised us in the end, because scripture says that, at the earthquake, when rocks were split and tombs were opened at his passion, many bodies of the righteous rose and appeared with him in the holy city when he rose. If, of course, they did not again set aside their bodies and fall asleep, one would have to see how we should understand that Christ is *the firstborn from the dead* (Col 1:18; Rev 1:5) if so many preceded him in that resurrection. But if they answer that this was said by way of anticipation, so that the tombs are indeed understood to have been opened by that earthquake when Christ hung upon the cross, while the bodies of the righteous did not rise then, but after he had first risen, though this was added at that point, as I said, by way of anticipation, then we could believe without any ambiguity that Christ is *the firstborn from the dead* and that it was immediately granted to those righteous people to rise into eternal incorruption and immor-

tality after he went first. But there still remains a problem that troubles me, namely, how Peter could have said that his flesh did not see corruption. To be sure, he said this with complete truth since he stated that it was not David but Christ who was foretold by that prophecy. But he added concerning David that his tomb is in their midst, and he certainly did not convince them of this if his body was no longer in it. After all, if he had risen before soon after his death and his flesh had not seen corruption, that tomb could still remain. But it seems difficult to think that David was not included in that resurrection of the righteous if the eternal resurrection was already given to them. For Christ is so often and with such great clarity and honor commended as having come as his descendant. It is said to the Hebrews concerning the righteous people of old that they foresaw better things for us *so that they would not be made perfect without us* (Heb 11:40). That statement is also undermined if they already attained that incorruption of resurrection that is promised to us who will be made perfect in the end.

4, 10. You see, therefore, how obscure it is that Peter chose to mention only those people locked in prison to whom the gospel was preached, *who were unbelievers in the days of Noah when the ark was being constructed* (1 Pt 3:20), and you see what disturbs me so that I do not dare to affirm anything about this. Added to this is the fact that, when the apostle said, *Baptism also saved you by a similar form, not the removal of dirt from the flesh, but the plea of a good conscience to God through the resurrection of Jesus Christ who at the right hand of God is devouring death so that we might become heirs of eternal life. He has entered into the heavens, with the angels and principalities and powers subject to himself*, he immediately added, *Since Christ, therefore, suffered in the flesh, arm yourselves with the same knowledge. For one who has suffered in the flesh has ceased from sin in order to live in the flesh for the time that remains, not by human desires, but by the will of God.* (1 Pt 3:21-4:2) Then he added, *For the past time spent in doing the will of human beings is sufficient; they live in passions and desires and drunkenness and feasting and drinking bouts and the forbidden worship of idols. They are surprised that you do not join them in the same disgrace of dissoluteness, and they speak abuse of you who will give an account to him who is ready to judge the living and the dead.* (1 Pt 4:3-5) He adds to these words, *On this account the gospel was preached even to the dead in order that they might be judged in the flesh like human beings, but might live in the spirit like God* (1 Pt 4:6).

11. Who is not moved by this profundity? He says that the gospel was preached to the dead. If indeed we understand them to be persons who have left the body, they will, I think, be those of whom he said above, *who were unbelievers in the days of Noah*, or surely all those whom Christ found in hell. What, then, does this mean: *in order that they might be judged in the flesh like human beings, but might live in the spirit like God*? How are they judged in the flesh

which they do not have if they are in hell or which they have not yet received even if they have been released from the pains of hell? For even if, as you say in posing your question, hell was emptied, we need not believe that all who were there at that time also rose in the flesh or that those who rose and appeared with the Lord received flesh in order that they might be judged in it like human beings. Nor do I see how this can be applied to those *who were unbelievers in the days of Noah.* For scripture does not say that they were alive in the flesh, nor can we believe that the pains of hell were loosened in order that those who were set free from them might receive flesh in order to undergo punishment. What, then, does this mean: *in order that they might be judged in the flesh like human beings, but might live in the spirit like God?* Was it perhaps granted to those whom Christ found in hell to be brought to life in the spirit by the gospel, though they were going to be judged in the flesh at the future resurrection in order that they might pass into the kingdom of God through some punishment of the flesh? If that is so, why is this said only of those who formerly did not believe in the days of Noah and not of the others whom Christ's visit found there, that is, that they came back to life in the spirit by the preaching of the gospel and afterward were going to be sentenced in the flesh to a passing punishment? But if we interpret this of everyone, the question remains why Peter mentioned only those *who were then unbelievers when the ark was being constructed.*

12. It is also disturbing that the people who try to give an account of this matter say that, when Christ descended into hell to the people whom he found there, those places of punishment were like prisons that had been emptied out, for they had not heard the gospel, which was not yet preached in the whole world when they were living, and they had just reasons why they did not believe what was not proclaimed to them. They say that from then on people have no excuse if they reject the preaching of the gospel that is widely known and spread through all the nations. And so they claim that, after those prisons were emptied at that time, there now remains a just judgment by which the contemptuous and unbelieving are punished even with eternal fire, nor do they who say this notice that all who have left this life even after the resurrection of Christ, before the gospel reached them, can have this excuse. For it is not true that, even after the Lord has returned from hell, no one is permitted to go to hell without hearing the gospel. After all, so many die throughout the whole world before this proclamation reaches them, all of whom will have the excuse that is said to have been taken from those to whom the Lord is said to have preached in hell when he came there, because they had not heard the gospel before.

13. Or perhaps one might say that even those who have died or are dying after the resurrection of the Lord without the gospel's having as yet been proclaimed to them could have heard or can hear the gospel in hell in order that they might believe there what is to be believed about the truth of Christ and might have the forgiveness and salvation that those merited to whom Christ proclaimed it there.

For, just because Christ ascended from hell, all word of him was not necessarily wiped out. After all, he ascended from here into heaven and those who believed in him were still saved by the preaching of him. He was indeed exalted, and he was given the name *which is above every name, so that at his name every knee might bend*, not only *of those in heaven and on earth*, but also *of those under the earth* (Phil 2:9-10). But if we admit this opinion by which one can suppose that human beings who did not believe when they were alive can believe in Christ in hell, who would put up with the absurdities and contradictions to the faith that follow? First, we would seem to mourn for no reason those who leave the body without this grace, and we would for no reason take care and constantly urge that human beings receive it before they die so that they not be punished with everlasting death. Or, if only those people uselessly and fruitlessly believe in hell who refused to believe the gospel when it was proclaimed to them here, but believing benefits those who did not reject here what they could not have heard, something else even more absurd results, namely, that the gospel should not be preached here. For all people are certainly going to die, and they ought to come to hell without any guilt for having rejected the gospel so that it may be of benefit for them when they believe there. But to think that is a mark of impious folly.

5, 14. Hence, let us hold most firmly what the faith supported by the most well-founded authority has: *Christ has died according to the scriptures and was buried, and he rose on the third day according to the scriptures* (1 Cor 15:3-4), and the other things that were written about him with the truth that is witnessed to most strongly. Among these there is also the fact that he was in hell and that, after he loosened the pains of hell by which it was not possible that he be held and from which he is also correctly understood to have released and set free those whom he willed to, he received back the body that he had left on the cross and that was placed in the tomb. But because you see what disturbs me in the question that you proposed concerning the words of the apostle Peter and because, if they are more carefully examined, other things can perhaps be disturbing, let us investigate them either by pondering them by ourselves or by consulting those whom it is worthwhile to consult and whom we can.

15. Consider, now, whether everything that the apostle Peter says concerning the spirits locked in prison who in the days of Noah did not believe does not have to do with hell at all but rather with those times whose form he compared to these times. That action was, of course, the form of things to come so that the people who now do not believe the gospel when the Church is being built in all the nations are understood to be like those who did not believe at the time when the ark was being constructed. But those who have believed and are saved through baptism are compared to those who were saved then in the same ark through the water. For this reason he says, *And baptism also saves you by a similar form* (1 Pt 3:21). Let us also adapt the other things concerning those who did not believe to this likeness of form and not suppose that the gospel was preached or is even still

being preached in hell to produce believers and to set them free, as if the Church were established there too.

16. Those people, then, seem to have been attracted to the interpretation that disturbs you; they believed that Peter held this idea because he said that the gospel was preached to the spirits locked in prison, as if the spirits cannot be understood to be souls that existed at that time in the flesh and were enclosed in the darkness of ignorance as though in a prison. From such a prison he who says, *Lead my soul out of prison in order that it may confess your name* (Ps 142:8), desires to be set free. Elsewhere it is called the shadow of death from which they are set free, certainly not in hell, but here, of whom scripture says, *For those who sat in the shadow of death a light has arisen* (Is 9:2). But what was preached to those people in the days of Noah was in vain, since they did not believe, although the patience of God waited for them through all the years when the same ark was being constructed—for its construction was also in some way preaching—just as people like them do not believe now who under the same form are enclosed by the darkness of ignorance as by a prison. They see to no purpose that the Church is being constructed in the whole world while the judgment threatens like the flood by which all the unbelievers at that time perished. The Lord certainly says, *Just as it was in the days of Noah, so it will be in the days of the Son of Man. They ate; they drank; they married; they were given in marriage, until Noah entered the ark; the flood came and destroyed them all.* (Lk 17:26-27; Mt 24:37-39). But because that action also signified something in the future, the flood then signified baptism for believers and punishment for unbelievers, just as in the figure that was not one of an action but only of words, namely, what was written about the rock that signified Christ, two things were announced: for unbelievers a stumbling block and for believers a building.[4] But at times in the same figure, whether an action or words, two things also signify a single thing, as the timbers that were fitted into the framework of the ark signified believers, and the eight souls who were rescued in the same ark signified the same believers. In the same way in that gospel parable concerning the sheepfold, Christ himself is both the shepherd and the gate.[5]

6, 17. Do not let this fact—that the apostle Peter said that the same Christ preached to those locked in prison who formerly did not believe in the days of Noah[6]—keep you from this interpretation. We ought not to think that it should not be understood in this way because Christ had not yet come at that time. For he had not come in the flesh, as he came when *after this he was seen on the earth, and he lived with the sons of men* (Bar 3:38). But from the beginning of the human race, either in order to rebuke sinners like Cain and earlier like Adam and

---

4. See Ps 118:22, Is 28:16, Dn 2:34.45, Zec 3:3, and Mt 21:44.
5. See Jn 10:1-2.
6. See 1 Pt 3:19.

his wife, or to console the good, or to admonish both so that some might believe for their salvation and others not believe for their punishment, he came, not, to be sure, in the flesh but in the spirit, in suitable visions speaking to whom he willed and as he willed. But as for my saying that "he came in the spirit," the Son himself in the substance of his divinity is, of course, a spirit, because he is not a body. But what does the Son do without the Holy Spirit or without the Father since all the works of the Trinity are inseparable?

18. The very words of scripture with which we are dealing also indicate this well enough, I think, to those who pay careful attention. *For Christ*, it says, *died for our sins once, the just one for the unjust, in order to bring us to God. He was put to death in the flesh, but brought to life in the spirit, in which he went and also preached to the spirits who were held in prison, who were formerly unbelievers in the days when the patience of God was still waiting, in the days of Noah, when the ark was being constructed.* (1 Pt 3:18-20) Now, as I think, the order of the words is noteworthy: *Christ put to death in the flesh, but brought to life in the spirit.* And in that spirit he went and also preached to those spirits who were once unbelievers in the days of Noah, for before he came in the flesh to die for us—something he did once—he often used to come in the spirit to those to whom he wanted, admonishing them by visions, as he wanted, in the spirit, of course, the very spirit in which he was also brought to life after he had been put to death in the flesh in his Passion. For what does it mean that he was brought to life in the spirit but that the same flesh in which alone he was put to death rose by the live-giving spirit?

7, 19. For who would dare to say that Jesus died in his soul, that is, in the spirit that belongs to the man? For the death of the soul is nothing but sin, from which he was absolutely immune, although he was put to death for us in the flesh. For, if the souls of all human beings come from the one that was breathed into the first human being, through whom *sin entered the world, and through sin death, and in that way it was passed on to all human beings, in whom all have sinned* (Rom 5:12), the soul of Christ did not come from there, since he had absolutely no sin, neither original nor personal, on account of which he might seem to deserve death. It was of course on our behalf that he, in whom the prince of the world and the lord of death found nothing,[7] did away with the death that he did not deserve. For it involves no contradiction that he who created the soul for the first human being also created a soul for himself. Or, if his soul also came from that soul, he purified it in assuming it so that, when he came to us, he was born of the Virgin without any sin that he either committed or inherited. But if souls are not propagated from that one, and only the flesh contracts original sin from Adam, the Son of God created a soul for himself as he creates souls for the others, yet he did not unite it with sinful flesh but with *the likeness of sinful flesh* (Rom 8:3). For of

---

7. See Jn 14:30; 12:31; Heb 2:14.

course he took from the Virgin the true substance of flesh, but not sinful flesh, because it was not sown or conceived by concupiscence of the flesh, though it was, to be sure, mortal and changeable over the course of time, exactly like sinful flesh, but without sin.

20. And for this reason, whichever opinion on the soul is true, none of which I as yet dare rashly to affirm, except to repudiate that one by which individual souls are believed to be stuffed into individual bodies in accord with the merits of some previous actions of theirs, it is certain that the soul of Christ is not only immortal in accord with the nature of the others but also is not put to death by any sin or punished by any condemnation—the two reasons why a soul can be understood to die; and so Christ could not be said to be *brought to life in the spirit* in accord with this death. He was, of course, brought to life in the way in which he was put to death. This, then, was said of the flesh, for the flesh came back to life when the soul returned, since it had died when the soul left. He was said to have been *put to death in the flesh,* therefore, because he died only according to the flesh, *but brought to life in the spirit* because, by the work of that spirit in which he went and preached to those to whom he willed, the flesh, in which he now comes to human beings, was also brought to life and rose.

21. Hence, with regard to what was later said of the unbelievers *who will render an account to him who is ready to judge the living and the dead* (1 Pt 4:5), it does not follow that we should understand here those dead who have left the body. It is possible, after all, that he called unbelievers dead, that is, dead in their soul, the sort of people of whom it is said, *Let the dead bury their dead* (Mt 8:22), but called those living who do not hear the gospel in vain and believe in him. They do not hear in vain, *Arise, you sleeper; rise up from the dead, and Christ will enlighten you* (Eph 5:14). Of this sort of people the Lord himself said, *The hour will come, and it is already here, when the dead will hear the voice of the Son of God, and those who hear it will live* (Jn 5:25). Hence the following words of Peter, *For on this account the gospel was preached to the dead in order that they might be judged in the flesh like human beings, but might live in the spirit like God* (1 Pt 4:6), do not force us to understand that this took place in hell. *For on this account the gospel was preached* in this life *to the dead,* that is, to unbelievers and sinners in order that, when they have believed, *they might be judged in the flesh like human beings,* that is, in the different tribulations and in the death of the flesh itself. Hence the same apostle says in another passage that *it is time for the judgment to begin from the house of the Lord* (1 Pt 4:17), *but that they might live in the spirit like God,* because they were also put to death in the spirit when they were held in the death of unbelief and sinfulness.

22. Let anyone who is displeased with this explanation of the words of Peter or who, even if not displeased, still finds them insufficient, seek to understand them in relation to hell. If anyone can solve those problems by which, as I mentioned, I am disturbed, so that he removes all doubt about them, he should

share the solution with me. If he does that, those words will be able to be understood in both ways. This explanation of mine is not proven false. With regard to those questions that you sent earlier, apart from the vision of God by the body on which I need to write a larger work, I replied as well as I could, and through the deacon Asellus I sent the replies which I think you have already received. But in your recent memorandum to which I am now replying you had asked two questions, one longer, the other shorter, concerning the words of the apostle Peter and concerning the soul of the Lord. I again advise you not to hesitate to send me a copy of your letter containing the question about whether the substance of God can be seen in a bodily manner as if in a place, for in our house it has somehow or other gotten lost and cannot be found, although I looked for it for a long time.[8]

---

8. Augustine mentioned this misplaced letter in Letter 159, 1.

Letter 165

In 411 Jerome wrote from Bethlehem to Marcellinus, the imperial commissioner, and Anapsychia, his spouse. In reply to Marcellinus' question about the origin of souls, Jerome mentions the various theories and tells him that he can find what he himself holds in his *Defense against Rufinus* (paragraph 1). Jerome explains why he has not finished his commentary on Ezekiel (paragraph 2) and finally commends Oceanus to the imperial commissioner (paragraph 3).

To Marcellinus and Anapsychia, my truly holy lord and lady and son and daughter worthy of reverence by every duty of love, Jerome sends greetings in Christ.

1, 1. At last I have received from Africa the letter of Your Unanimity, and I do not regret the impudence by which, despite your silence, I have thrust my letters upon you in order that I might merit a reply and know that you are safe and sound—not by other messengers but most of all by your own words. I recall your little question about the state of the soul, in fact a question of greatest importance for the Church, namely, whether the soul has fallen from heaven, as the philosopher Pythagoras and all the Platonists and Origen think;[1] or is an emanation (ἀπορροία) from God's substance, as the Stoics, the Manichees, and the Hispanic heresy of Priscillian suppose;[2] or whether they were created long ago by God and are held in a storehouse, as certain men of the Church believe in their foolish conviction;[3] or are made by God every day and sent into bodies in accord with the words we read in the gospel,[4] *My Father is at work even now, and I am at work* (Jn 5:17); or whether they come by generation, as Tertullian, Apollinaris,

---

1. Pythagoras of Samos (c. 580 to c. 500 B.C.) was credited with teaching a theory of reincarnation. The Platonists, especially those whom we today call Neoplatonists, such as Plotinus and Porphyry, taught that the soul fell into bodies through a sin of pride. Origen of Alexandria (c. 185 to c. 254), a great Christian theologian, was accused of teaching that souls fell into bodies as places of punishment for prenatal sins.
2. The Stoics began after the death of Aristotle with Zeno of Citium; he seems to have identified the whole world with the substance of God. The Manichees, that is, the followers of Mani, taught that human souls were quite literally particles of God that had been captured in the great battle in the first times between good and evil. For the Manichees, see *Heresies* 46. For the Priscillianists, see *Heresies* 70; they were accused of teaching a doctrine on the nature of souls similar to that of the Manichees.
3. Jerome is probably alluding to Origen and Rufinus. Augustine too seems to have entertained such a view in *Genesis: A Refutation of the Manichees* II, 8, 10, where he says: "Perhaps the soul had been already made but was still as if in the mouth of God, that is, in his truth and wisdom." So too, in *Free Will* 3, 20, 57, he mentions the hypothesis that souls already exist in some secret place of God and are sent into bodies.
4. This view is creationism in accordance with which God creates individual souls for individual human beings.

and the majority of the Easterners suppose,[5] so that, just as a body is born from a body, so a soul is born from a soul and subsists in a condition like that of brute animals. I know that I once wrote what I thought on this point in my works in opposition to Rufinus,[6] against the book that he gave to Anastasius of holy memory, the bishop of the Roman Church. In that book he made a mockery of his faith, or rather of his perfidy, by his slippery, deceitful, and in fact stupid confession, when he tries to mock the simplicity of his audience. I think that your holy father, Oceanus, has those books. For the books of Rufinus were published long ago, spewing forth many slanders against us. You certainly have there a holy and learned man, the bishop Augustine, who could teach you *viva voce*, as they say, and explain his own view and, in fact, our view by himself.

2, 2. I earlier wanted to produce a commentary on the book of Ezekiel and to fulfill a promise often made to my eager readers but, when I began to dictate it, my mind was so troubled by the devastation of the Western provinces and especially the city of Rome that, in accord with the common saying, I was even ignorant of my own name and was silent for a long while, knowing that it was a time for tears.[7] But this year, after I commented on three books, there was a sudden attack of the barbarians. Of them your Virgil says, "The wide-ranging Barcaei,"[8] and holy scripture says of Ishmael, *He dwelled in opposition to all his brothers* (Gn 16:12). The barbarians have broken through the frontiers of Egypt, Palestine, Phoenicia and Syria, carrying everything with them like a torrent, so that it was by the mercy of Christ we were just able to escape their hands. But if, according to the renowned orator, "The laws fall silent amid battles,"[9] how much more do the studies of the scriptures, which need a multitude of books, silence, diligence on the part of copyists, and—what is true at least for me—security and leisure for dictating! I therefore sent two books to my holy daughter Fabiola, copies of which you can borrow from her if you wish. In view of the difficulties of the time I could not of course write others. When you read them and see the entryways, it will be easy to conjecture what the future house might be like. But I trust in the mercy of God, who has helped us in the very difficult beginning of the

5. Tertullian, the second-century African theologian, held for traducianism, the view that souls are propagated in the same way that bodies are. For Apollinaris of Laodocea, a fourth-century heretic who denied a human soul in Christ, see *Heresies* 55.

6. See Jerome's *Defense against Rufinus* (*Apologia contra Rufinum*) 2, 8, where he professes ignorance about which of the theories of the origin of the soul is true. He says, "I do not deny that I have read each of them, and I confess that I still do not know apart from that which the Church clearly hands down, namely, that God is the creator of souls and of bodies." Rufinus of Aquilea (c. 345 to c. 410), a priest who translated much of Origen into Latin, was once a close friend of Jerome, but the two had a falling out over Origen. When Rufinus was accused of heresy and was called to Rome, he wrote his *Defense for Pope Anastasius* (*Apologia ad Papam Anastasium*).

7. See Eccl 3:4.

8. Virgil, *Aeneid* 4, 42-43.

9. Cicero, *In Defense of Milo* (*Pro Milone*) 4, 10.

work I mentioned, that he will also help us in the all but last chapters of the prophet, which tell of the wars of Gog and Magog,[10] and in the last chapters, which describe the construction, variety, and dimension of the most sacred and mysterious temple.[11]

3, 3. Our holy brother, Oceanus, to whom you wish to be recommended, is so solid and fine a man and so learned in the law of the Lord that he could instruct you without your having to ask us and could explain our view on all the questions of the scriptures in accord with the measure of the talents we share in common. May Christ, our almighty God, keep you, my truly holy lord and lady, safe and prosperous for many years.

---

10. See Ez 38-39.
11. See Ez 40-43.

Letter 166

In 415 Augustine sent two letters to Jerome by means of the Spanish priest, Orosius. In *Revisions* 2, 45 Augustine calls them books and says the following of them:

> I also wrote two books for the priest Jerome, who was residing in Bethlehem—one, *The Origin of the Soul of Man*, the other, *The Opinion of the Apostle James*, where he said, *Whoever observes the whole law, but offends on one point, is guilty of all* (Jas 2:10), in order to consult him on both questions. In the first book I did not solve the question that I posed, but in the second one I was not silent about what I thought concerning its solution. But I also consulted him about whether he approved this. He wrote back, praising this consultation on my part, but his reply was that he did not have the leisure to reply. I did not want to publish these books as long as he was still alive in the hope that he would at some point reply and they might instead be published along with his response. After he died, however, I published the first book in order that the reader might be admonished either not to ask at all how a soul is given to those who are born or at least to admit on this most obscure issue a solution to this question that would not be opposed to the most evident truths held by the Catholic faith concerning original sin in infants, who are undoubtedly going to be condemned if they are not reborn in Christ. I published the second book in order to make known the solution that seemed correct to us on the matter that was dealt with in it. This work begins: "I have asked and am asking our God, who has called."

In Letter 166 Augustine asks Jerome's help with the complex question of the origin of the soul. He complains about the distance that separates them and that makes the exchange of letters difficult (paragraph 1). Augustine commends to Jerome Orosius, a young Spanish priest, who will carry the letter to Jerome (paragraph 2). Augustine assures Jerome that he knows that the soul is immortal, that it is not a particle of God, that it is incorporeal, and that it is set free from sin only by the mercy of God (paragraphs 3 to 5).

Augustine asks Jerome to resolve the question about where the soul contracted the guilt by which even the soul of an infant is carried off to condemnation if it dies without baptism (paragraph 6). He recounts the four hypotheses about the origin of souls that he had mentioned in *Free Will* (paragraph 7) and acknowledges that Jerome himself holds the position that individual souls are created for individual infants who are born (paragraph 8). Augustine complains that Jerome sent students to him and insists that he himself needs instruction (paragraph 9). Specifically Augustine wants Jerome to explain to him how original sin can be inherited according to the creationist theory (paragraph 10).

Augustine indicates that he can himself resolve some objections against the creationist position, such as the statement in Genesis that on the seventh day God rested from all his works (paragraphs 11 and 12). He addresses the question as to why God gives souls to infants he knows will soon die (paragraph 13). He also answers an objection that claims that the subsequent immortality of the soul indicates that the soul always existed and never came to be (paragraph 14) and a question about why God gives souls to infants conceived in adulterous unions (paragraph 15).

Other objections, Augustine admits, he cannot resolve, such as why infants endure all the physical sufferings that they undergo, since they have no personal sins for which they are justly punished (paragraph 16). Neither can he explain how it is just that some are born with mental defects (paragraph 17). He repeats what he had said about the suffering of infants in *Free Will* but insists that his sole purpose in that work was to show that God was not to be blamed, regardless of which of the four hypotheses was true (paragraphs 18 and 19). His answer in *Free Will* did not address the question of the souls of infants who died without baptism (paragraph 20). Hence Augustine asks Jerome why the souls of the newborn contract original sin if they are individually created for individual infants (paragraph 21).

He explores and rejects the opinion that the flesh of the newborn is the sole cause of its sin (paragraph 22) as well as the opinion that it is not the soul but the body that is saved by baptism (paragraph 23). After all, the latter opinion would mean that even the bodies of the dead should be presented for baptism (paragraph 24). The basic question is why it is that infants who die without baptism are condemned if each soul is created by God (paragraph 25). Augustine warns Jerome that certain scriptural passages, which are invoked to solve the problem, do not in fact solve it (paragraph 26). He points out that this same difficulty holds for those who maintain that souls exist elsewhere and are sent into bodies by God. He also gives his reasons for rejecting the view that souls sinned in some previous life and were sent into bodies as punishment. And he declines to discuss the view that all souls come to be from the one soul of Adam (paragraph 27). He again pleads for Jerome's help in answering this question and insists that whatever opinion on the origin of the soul turns out to be true will not be opposed to the faith of the Church that newborn infants cannot be set free from sin except by the grace of Christ (paragraph 28).

The Origin of the Soul

1, 1. I have asked and am asking our God, who has called us into his kingdom and glory,[1] that he may choose to render fruitful for us what I am writing to you, my holy brother Jerome, as I consult you on these matters about which I am ignorant. For, though I know you are much older than I, yet I am consulting you as an old man myself. But I think no age is too late for learning what is necessary, since, even if it is more fitting for old men to teach than to learn, it is more fitting for them to learn than not to know what they should teach. For I find nothing

---

1. See 1 Thes 2:12.

more troublesome in all the torments that I suffer over very difficult questions than the absence of Your Charity at so great a distance that I can scarcely send my letters and scarcely receive yours over a space neither of days nor of months but of several years. For, if it were possible, I would want to have you present every day to discuss with you whatever I wanted. And yet I ought not to have left undone what I could do if I could not do all that I wanted.

2. Now there came to me a pious young man, a brother in Catholic peace, a son in terms of age, our fellow priest in terms of dignity, Orosius, alert in mind, ready in speech, afire with zeal, a man who desires to be a useful vessel in the house of the Lord[2] for refuting the false and destructive teachings that have slain the souls of Spaniards much more tragically than the barbarian sword has slain their bodies.[3] He has hastened to us from there, almost from the very shore of the ocean, stirred by the idea that he could learn from me whatever he wanted concerning those matters he wanted to know. Nor was his coming without any benefit. For, first, he ceased to believe much of what was said about me; second, I taught him what I could and advised him where he could learn what I could not and encouraged him to go to you. Since in this matter he willingly and obediently took my advice and directive, I asked him to return from you to his own country by passing through ours. Having his promise, I believed that the Lord had granted me an opportunity to write to you about these matters that I want to know from you. For I was looking for someone to send to you, but I did not easily find someone suitable who would act with reliability, obey quickly and was experienced in traveling. And so, when I learned that this young man was the very sort of person for whom I was asking the Lord, I could not hesitate.

2, 3. Listen, then, to what I ask you to disclose to me, and do not be slow to discuss it. The question of the soul troubles many people, and I confess that I am among them. For I shall not pass over in silence what I hold most firmly regarding the soul; then I shall add what I would like you still to resolve for me. The human soul is immortal according to a certain manner of its own. For it is not immortal in every way like God, of whom scripture says that *he alone has immortality* (1 Tm 6:16). After all, holy scripture mentions a great deal about the soul's deaths, including the words, *Let the dead bury their dead* (Mt 8:22). But because it dies when separated from the life of God in such a way that it still does not entirely cease to live in its own nature, it is found to be mortal in some respect, while it is also not without reason said to be immortal. The soul is not a part of God.[4] For if it were, it would be absolutely immutable and incorruptible. And if it were such, it would not deteriorate or improve, nor would it begin to have in itself something that it did not have, and it would not cease to have what it

---

2. See 2 Tm 2:21.

3. Augustine refers to the massacres in Spain during 409 after the invasion by the Vandals, Alani, and Suevi.

4. The Manichees held that the soul was literally a part of God in us.

had, in terms of its dispositions. But there is no need of testimony from else-where about how it changes; anyone who pays attention to himself knows this. In vain, however, do those who want the soul to be a part of God say that the defilement and shame of it that we see in very wicked human beings and the weakness and illness that we perceive in all human beings comes to it not from itself but from the body. What difference does it make what causes it to be ill, since if it were immutable it could not become ill for any reason? For what is truly immutable and incorruptible cannot be changed and corrupted by contact with anything. Otherwise not only the flesh of Achilles, as the myths say, but all flesh would be invulnerable if no accident happened to it.[5] No nature is immu-table, therefore, that is mutable in some way, for some reason or in some part. It is wicked, however, to believe that God is anything but truly and supremely immutable. The soul, then, is not a part of God.

4. Though it is difficult for those who are a bit slow to be convinced that the soul is incorporeal, I still admit that I am convinced of it. But to avoid needlessly causing or deservedly suffering a controversy over a word (after all, where there is an agreement about the facts, there is no need to fight about words), if every substance or essence or that which in some way exists in itself, whatever it might more suitably be called, is a body, then the soul is a body. Likewise, if one wants to call only that nature incorporeal that is supremely immutable and is whole everywhere, then the soul is a body because it is not something of that sort. But if a body is only that which stands still or is moved through an area of space with some length, breadth and depth so that it occupies a larger place with a larger part of itself and a smaller place with a smaller part and is smaller in a part than in the whole, then the soul is not a body. It is, of course, stretched out through the whole body that it animates, not by a local diffusion but by a certain vital intention. For it is at the same time present as a whole through all the body's parts, not smaller in smaller parts and larger in larger parts, but more intensely in one place and less intensely in another, both whole in all parts and whole in the individual parts. For it does not otherwise perceive what it as a whole perceives in the body, though not in the whole body. After all, when something touches a small point in the living flesh, though that place is not the place of the whole body but scarcely seems to be in the body, it still does not escape the notice of the whole soul, nor does that which is perceived spread through all the parts of the body, but it is perceived only in the place where the sensation takes place. How, then, does that which does not take place in the whole body immediately reach the whole soul unless the soul is whole in the place where the sensation occurs and does not, in order to be whole there, abandon the other parts of the body? For those other parts live because it is present where nothing of the sort occurred. But if some-

---

5. Achilles was supposedly invulnerable except in his heel.

thing of the sort did occur there and both sensations occurred at the same time, both would at the same time likewise not escape the notice of the whole soul. Hence it could not as a whole be present at the same time in each and every part of its body if it were spread out through them, as we see that bodies spread out in areas of space occupy smaller areas with their smaller parts and bigger areas with their bigger parts. Hence, if the soul is to be called a body, it is certainly not like an earthly body or like a humid one or an airy one or an ethereal one. All such bodies are, of course, larger in larger places and smaller in smaller places, and none of them is present whole in some part of itself, but just as there are parts of the places, so they are occupied by parts of bodies. From this it is clear that, whether it should be called a body or not, the soul has a certain nature of its own created with a substance more excellent than all these elements of the world's mass. It cannot truthfully be thought of in some power of imagining bodily images, which we perceive through the senses of the flesh, but it is understood by the mind and perceived by life. I do not say these things to teach you what you know but to disclose what I hold most firmly regarding the soul, in order that, when I come to those things that I ask about, no one may think that I hold nothing regarding the soul either by knowledge or by faith.

5. I am certain that the soul has fallen into sin by no fault of God, by no necessity of God or of its own, but by its own will, and that it cannot be set free *from the body of this death* (Rom 7:24) either by the power of its own will, as if it were sufficient unto itself for this, or by the death of this body, but only *by the grace of God through Jesus Christ our Lord* (Rom 7:25). I am certain that there is absolutely no soul in the human race that does not need for its deliverance *the mediator between God and human beings, the man Jesus Christ* (1 Tm 2:5). But any soul that leaves the body at any age of the body without the grace of the mediator and his sacrament will both be punished and receive back at the last judgment its body for punishment. But if after its human birth, which came about from Adam, it is reborn in Christ and belongs to his society, it will have rest after the death of the body and will receive back its body for glory. These points are what I hold most firmly regarding the soul.

3, 6. Now listen, please, to what I am asking, and do not spurn me. In the same way may he who deigned to be spurned for us not spurn you. I ask where the soul contracted the guilt by which it is dragged into condemnation, even the soul of an infant overtaken by death, if the grace of Christ does not come to its rescue through the sacrament in which even infants are baptized. For you are not one of those who have now begun to mouth certain new ideas, saying that no guilt is contracted from Adam that needs to be removed from an infant by baptism. If I knew that you held such a view, in fact, I would by no means ask this of you or think that I should ask you; I only ask because I know that you do not hold such a view. But we possess your opinion on this matter, which is in accord with the most solidly grounded Catholic faith: when you refuted the folly of Jovinian,[6] also, you used the testimony from the Book of Job, *No one is clean in your sight, not even an infant who has lived a single day on the earth* (Jb 14:4-5 LXX). Then you added, "We are held guilty *in the likeness of Adam's transgression*"[7] (Rom 5:14). Your book on the prophet Jonah explains this strikingly and clearly enough where you said that infants were rightly forced to fast on account of original sin.[8] Hence it is not inappropriate that I ask you where the soul contracted this guilt from which it must be set free even at that age by the sacrament of Christian grace.

7. Some years ago, when I wrote certain books on free choice that passed into the hands of many and are possessed by very many, I thought that I should comment on the four opinions concerning the embodiment of the soul, namely, whether the other souls are propagated from that one soul that was given to the first man or whether new souls are even now created for each individual or whether, already existing somewhere, souls are either sent by God or fall of their own accord into bodies, in such a way that, whichever of these might be true, it would not interfere with my aim. For at that time I was opposing, to the extent I could, those—that is, the Manichees[9]—who try to introduce in opposition to God an evil nature endowed with its own principle. For I had as yet heard nothing of the Priscillianists,[10] who have blasphemous myths not much different from the Manichees. Hence I did not add the fifth opinion that you mentioned in your letter among the others to avoid omitting one, when you wrote back to Marcellinus, a man of pious memory and most dear to us in the grace of Christ,[11] when he questioned you on this point, namely, that the soul is a part of God.[12] I did not mention this opinion, first, because one asks about the soul's nature and not about its embodiment when one asks this question and, second, because those whom I was opposing held this view, and I was working most of all in order to keep the inculpable and inviolable nature of the creator separate from the defects and defilement of the creature. The Manichees, after all, maintain that the very substance of the good God was corrupted and oppressed and

---

6. For Jovinian, see *Heresies* 82; Jovinian was a monk who argued that marriage was as good as virginity and urged consecrated virgins to marry.

7. Jerome, *Answer to Jovinian* (*Adversus Jovinianum*) 2, 2.

8. See Rom 5:14 and Jerome, *Commentary on Jonah* (*Commentarium in Jonam*) 3, 5.

9. See *Heresies* 46 for the Manichees.

10. See *Heresies* 70 for Priscillian. Orosius, it seems, brought Augustine his first information on the Priscillianists. See Orosius' *Memorandum to Augustine on the Errors of the Priscillianists and Origenists* as well as Augustine's *To Orosius in Refutation of the Priscillianists and Origenists*.

11. Marcellinus, the imperial commissioner and friend of Augustine, who had presided over the Conference of Carthage in 411 at which the Donatists were defeated, was executed along with his brother on 13 September 413 for his alleged involvement in a plot against the emperor, Honorius.

12. See Letter 165, 1, 1.

brought to the necessity of sinning by the substance of evil, to which they attribute its own proper principle and rulers. Now that the error of this heretical opinion has been set aside, I desire to know which of the four remaining opinions one should choose. For heaven forbid that whichever one we ought to choose should attack this belief about which we are certain, namely, that every soul, even that of a tiny infant, needs deliverance from the bondage of sin and that there is no deliverance except through Jesus Christ and him crucified.

4, 8. Hence (to avoid dragging this out) you certainly hold that God even now creates individual souls for individuals who are being born. To avoid the objection to this view that God finished making all the creatures on the sixth day and rested on the seventh,[13] you use the testimony from the gospel, *My Father is at work even now* (Jn 5:17).[14] For you wrote to Marcellinus in that way in the letter in which you were so kind as to say of me, with great good will, that he had me in Africa and that I could easily explain this view. If I could have done this, he would not ask this of you, who are situated so far away, if he in fact wrote this to you from Africa. For I do not know when he wrote; I only know that he knew well my hesitation on this point because of which he wanted to ask you without consulting me. Although, even if he had consulted me, I would rather have exhorted him and been thankful for what you could have bestowed on us all if you had not preferred to reply briefly rather than to give an answer, I believe that you would not have labored superfluously in my case even though you thought that I knew very well what he had asked. See, I want that opinion of yours to be mine as well, but I state that it is not as yet.

9. You sent me disciples that I might teach them something that I have not yet learned. Teach me, then, what I should teach. For many demand of me that I teach them, and I confess to them that I am as ignorant of this as I am of many other things. And though they are respectful to my face, they perhaps still say among themselves, *Are you a teacher in Israel and do not know these things?* (Jn 3:10) The Lord, of course, said this to one of those who took delight in being called rabbi. For this reason he also came to the true teacher at night[15] because he who was accustomed to teach was perhaps embarrassed to learn. But it delights me more to listen to a teacher than to be listened to as a teacher. For I recall what he said to those whom he chose in preference to the rest; he said, *But do not be called, rabbi, by human beings; after all, one is your teacher, Christ* (Mt 23:8). No one else taught Moses, even when he taught him through Jothor,[16] and no one else taught Cornelius, even when he taught him earlier through Peter,[17] and no

---

13. See Gn 2:2.
14. See Letter 165, 1, 1.
15. See Jn 3:1-2.
16. See Ex 18:14-23.
17. See Acts 10:25-48.

one else taught Peter, even when he taught him later through Paul.[18] Whoever speaks the truth speaks the truth by the gift of him who is the truth. Why is it, then, that we still do not know these things and have been unable to discover them by praying, by reading, by thinking, or by reasoning? Is it not in order that we may be shown, not only with what great love we should teach the ignorant but also with what great humility we should take instruction from the learned?

10. Teach me, then, I ask you, what I should teach; teach me what I should hold, and tell me: If souls are created individually for the individuals who are born today, where do souls sin in infants so that they need the forgiveness of sin in the sacrament of Christ, given that they sin in Adam from whom sinful flesh is propagated?[19] Or if they do not sin, with what justice on the part of the creator are they made subject to the sin of another when they are inserted in mortal members propagated from him so that condemnation overtakes them unless they are helped by the Church, since it is not in their power to be able to be helped by the grace of baptism? With what justice are so many thousands of souls condemned which, in the deaths of infants, leave their bodies without the pardon of the Christian sacrament, if individual new souls created without any preceding sin of their own, but by the will of the creator, are united to newborn babies? After all, he created them and gave them to animate those babies, though he, of course, knew that each of them was going to leave its body with no sin of its own but without the baptism of Christ. Since, therefore, we cannot say of God that he forces souls to become sinful or punishes the innocent, and since we may not deny that the souls that leave their bodies without the sacrament of Christ, even those of infants, are carried off only to condemnation, I ask you: How is this opinion defended by which one believes not that souls are all created from the one soul of the first man but that individual souls are created for each individual, as that one soul was created for that one man?

5, 11. I think that I can easily refute the other objections that are raised against this opinion, such as the one by which some people think that they undermine it: How did God finish all the works of creation on the sixth day and rest on the seventh[20] if he still creates new souls? If we say to them what you cited from the gospel in the letter mentioned before, *My Father is at work even now* (Jn 5:17),[21] they reply, "He said, *He is at work*, because he governs natures already created, not because he creates new natures," so that it does not contradict the words of Genesis where we read with perfect clarity that God finished all his works. For, when scripture says that he rested, we must obviously understand this in the sense that he rested from creating new creatures, not from governing them. For at that point he was making those that were not in existence, and he rested from

18. See Gal 2:11-21.
19. See Rom 8:3.
20. See Gn 2:2.
21. See Letter 165, 1, 1.

making them because he had finished all the ones that he saw that he would make before they existed. And thereafter he did not create and make those that did not exist but created and made whatever he made from the ones that already existed. In that way both of these are shown to be true—the statement, *He rested from his works* (Gn 2:2), and the statement, *He is at work even now* (Jn 5:17), for the gospel cannot be opposed to Genesis.

12. But to those people who say these things lest it be believed that God makes new souls that did not exist, just as he made that one, but creates them from that one soul that already existed or sends them from some source or a storehouse that he made then, it is easy to reply that on those six days God created many things from the natures that he had already created, such as the birds and the fishes from the water and the trees, grass, and animals from the earth.[22] But it is clear that at that point he made those things that did not exist. For there was no bird, no fish, no tree, no animal, and he is correctly understood to have rested from having created things that were not in existence and that he created. That is, he is understood to have stopped so that thereafter he did not create things that did not exist. But now, when he is said not to send into bodies souls that already exist in some source, and not to pour them forth from himself like particles of himself, and not to derive them originally from that one soul, and not to bind them in the chains of the flesh in return for sins committed before they were in the flesh, but to create individual new souls for each individual newborn, he is not said to make something that he had not already made. For already on the sixth day he had made man to his image,[23] and he is of course understood to have done this in terms of his rational soul. And he now does this not by creating what did not use to exist but by multiplying what already existed. Hence the statement is true that he rested from creating things that did not exist, and the statement is true that he is at work even now because he not only governs the things that he has made but also creates in greater numbers not something that he had not yet created but something that he had already created. Either in that way or in some other we meet the objection against us regarding God's rest from his works, so that we do not on its account refuse to believe that new souls are even now made—not from that one, but just as that one was made.

13. For when someone says, "Why does he make souls for those whom he knows will soon die?" we can reply that the sins of their parents are revealed or punished by this. We can also rightly leave this to the governance of him who we know makes most beautiful and well-ordered the arrangement of all transitory things, which include the births and deaths of living beings, but we do not perceive this, although if we did perceive it we would be comforted with an ineffable delight. For it was not said in vain of God by the prophet who learned about

---

22. See Gn 1:11-12,20-25.
23. See Gn 1:26-27.

these things that were divinely inspired, *He produces the world in harmony* (Is 40:26 LXX). Hence the generosity of God has granted music, that is, a knowledge or perception of harmony, even to mortals who have rational souls in order to call their attention to something important. A human artist composing a song knows what length to give to what sounds in order that a melody may emerge and dissipate as subsequent sounds take the place of earlier ones. Hence, how much more does God—whose wisdom, by which he made all things, is preferable to all the arts—not allow any stretches of time in natures that are born and die, which are like syllables and words in relation to the parts of this age, to pass faster or slower in this marvelous song, as it were, of passing things, than the measure that he foreknew and predetermined demands! Since I would also say this of the leaf of a tree and of the number of our hairs, how much more do I say this of the birth and death of a human being, whose temporal life does not extend shorter or longer than God, who gives order to the times, knows harmonizes with the melody of the universe!

14. Their claim that nothing that begins in time can be immortal because "all things that come to be die, and those that grow become old,"[24] as a result of which they force people to believe that the human soul is immortal because it was created before all times, does not shake our faith. For, to pass over other things in silence, the immortality of the flesh of Christ began to be in time, and yet *he no longer dies, and death will no longer have dominion over him* (Rom 6:9).

15. But you said in the book against Rufinus that certain people attack this view because it seems unworthy of God to give souls to babies conceived in adultery.[25] From this they try to argue that on account of the merits of a life lived before embodiment souls can justly be brought, as it were, to prison cells of this sort. This objection does not bother me since I can think of many things by which this attack can be refuted. And your reply, that there is no sin on the part of the seed sown in the wheat that is said to be taken by theft but only in the one who stole the wheat, and that the earth ought not to have refused to make the seed sprout in its bosom because the sower spread it with an unclean hand, is a most elegant comparison. Even before I read your reply, this objection concerning babies conceived in adultery was causing me no difficulties on this issue, because I saw in general that God produces many good things even from our sufferings and our sins. But if the creation of any living being evokes inexpressible praise for the creator, if someone prudent and pious contemplates it, how much more does the creation, not of just any living being but of a human being, evoke such praise! But if one asks about God's reason for creating, no quicker or better reason is given in reply than that every creature of God is good. And what

---

24. Sallust, *The War with Jurgurtha* (*Bellum Jugurthinum*) 2, 3.
25. See Jerome, *Defense against the Books of Rufinus* (*Apologia aduersus libros Rufini*) 3, 28.

is more worthy of the good God than that he should make good things that no one can make but God?

6, 16. I say these things and other things that I can, as I can, against those who try to undermine the opinion by which souls are believed to be created for individuals, as that one soul was. But when it comes to the punishments of infants, I am, believe me, trapped in great difficulties, and I do not at all know how to reply. I mean not only the punishments that are involved in condemnation after this life, to which they must be brought if they left the body without the sacrament of Christian grace, but also those punishments that unfold before our eyes as we grieve in this life. If I wanted to count them, time would run out sooner than examples. They grow weak with illnesses; they are tormented by pains; they suffer from hunger and thirst; they become crippled in their members; they are deprived of their senses; they are troubled by unclean spirits. We must, therefore, show how they suffer these things justly without any evil cause on their part. For it is not permissible to say that these come about without God's knowledge and that he cannot resist those who cause them or that he either causes or permits them unjustly. We are correct to say that irrational animals are given to more excellent natures for their use, even if the latter are full of vices, just as we see most clearly in the gospel that pigs were given to the demons for the use that they desired.[26] But we are not correct, are we, to say this also of a human being? For a human being is an animal, but a rational animal, even if a mortal one. There is in those members a rational soul that is punished with great afflictions. God is good; God is just; God is omnipotent. To doubt this is the mark of a madman. Let the just cause be stated, then, of the great evils that come to be in infants. When, of course, adults suffer these evils, we are accustomed to say either, as in the case of Job, that their worth is being tested or, as in the case of Herod, that their sins are being punished, and it is left to human beings to conjecture[27] about other examples that are obscure from certain ones that God wanted to be clear. But this holds in the case of adults. Explain, however, what we should reply concerning the infants if there are no sins in them to be punished by such great penalties. For at that age there is no righteousness to be tested in them.

17. What shall I say about the diversity of talents? This, of course, lies hidden in infants, but it is drawn from these natural beginnings and appears in older children, some of whom are so slow and forgetful that they cannot learn even the first elements of language. Some are so stupid that they do not differ much from farm animals; people commonly call them morons. Perhaps someone will reply that their bodies are responsible for this. But according to the opinion that we want to be defended, did the soul choose a body for itself and make a mistake in choosing because it was deceived? Or, when it was being compelled to enter a

---

26. See Mt 8:31-32; Mk 5:12-13; and Lk 8:32-33.
27. I have followed the more common manuscript reading of *conjectare* in place of *conjecturae*.

body by the necessity of being born, because crowds of souls were already occupying other bodies, did it find no other body and thus occupied, like a place in a theater, not the flesh that it wanted but that which it could? Can we express these ideas and others of the same sort, or ought we to think them? Teach me, therefore, what we ought to think and what we ought to express in order that the reason may be clear to us why new souls are individually created for individual bodies.

7, 18. I myself said something in those books on free will not about talents, to be sure, but at least about the punishments that infants suffer in this life. I shall indicate the tenor of what I said and why it is not sufficient for me in respect to the question that we now have on our hands, and I shall insert in this letter the passage taken from the third book. For it runs as follows, "But regarding the torments of the body that afflict infants who because of their age have no sins, if the souls by which they are animated did not begin to exist before these human beings, a greater complaint and one full of mercy, as it were, is often set down when it is said: What evil have they done that they should suffer these things? As if innocence could have any merit before anyone could do any harm! But as God produces some good in the correction of adults when they are tortured by the pains and deaths of their little ones, who are dear to them, why should these things not happen since, after they have passed, they will be as if they did not happen in those to whom they happened? But those on whose account they happened will either be better if they were corrected by temporal losses and chose to live better lives, or they will be without excuse in the punishment of the judgment to come, if, despite the pains of this life, they refused to turn their desire to eternal life. But who knows what God reserves for the infants by whose torments the hardheartedness of adults is crushed or their faith or mercy is tested—who knows, then, what good recompense God reserves for these infants in the secrecy of his judgments? For, although they have done no good deeds, yet it is not as sinners that they have suffered. For the Church does not teach in vain that those infants who were slain when Herod sought to kill the Lord Jesus Christ[28] were received into the dignity of martyrs."[29]

19. I said these things at the time when I wanted to defend the very opinion we are dealing with now. For, as I mentioned a little before,[30] whichever of those four opinions on the embodiment of souls is true, I was striving to show that the substance of the creator is blameless and utterly remote from complicity in our sins. And therefore, whichever of them could be refuted and repudiated by the truth was not my concern at that time, since whichever of them rightly won out over the rest after they had all been examined by more careful discussion it

28. See Mt 2:1-18.
29. Augustine, *Free Will* 3, 23, 68.
30. See above 3, 7.

would leave me in full security for I was demonstrating that what I was doing also remains unrefuted in accord with all of them. But now, if I can, I want to choose the one correct account from all of them, and from this perspective I do not see that the defense of the view with which we are now dealing is firm and solid when I look more attentively at the points that I recalled from that book.

20. For what I said there is a kind of foundation of it: "But who knows what God reserves for the infants by whose torments the hardheartedness of adults is crushed or their faith or mercy is tested—who knows, then, what good recompense God reserves for these infants in the secrecy of his judgments?" But I see that this can be said with reason of those who either suffer something for the name of Christ or for the true religion, even without knowing it, or who have already been baptized by the sacrament of Christ. For they cannot be set free from condemnation without being united to the one mediator. And only in that way can they receive that recompense in return for those sufferings that they have endured here in various afflictions. Now, however, since this question cannot be resolved unless an answer is also given regarding these infants who expire after the severest torments without the sacrament of the Christian community, what recompense are we to think of in regard to those for whom condemnation has also been prepared besides? For with regard to the baptism of infants I replied somehow or other in that same book, not sufficiently, to be sure, but to the extent that it seemed necessary for that work. I said that baptism is beneficial even for those who are not aware of it and do not yet have faith of their own. But I did not think that I should say anything then with regard to the condemnation of the infants who leave this life without it, because I was not dealing with the question that I am dealing with now.

21. But though we leave out and belittle the sufferings that last for a short time and do not return once they are over, can we likewise belittle these words: *Through one man there came death, and through one man the resurrection of the dead. For, as in Adam all die, so all will also be brought to life in Christ* (1 Cor 15:21-22)? For, thanks to this clear, apostolic and divine statement it is made quite evident that no one enters into death except through Adam and no one enters into life except through Christ. That means *all* in both cases, because, just as all human beings belong to Adam by their first, that is, by their carnal birth, so all human beings who come to Christ come to their second, that is, to their spiritual birth. *All* was, therefore, said in the first place and *all* was likewise said in the second place because, just as all who die die only in Adam, so all who are brought to life are brought to life only in Christ. And for this reason whoever says to us that anyone is brought to life at the resurrection of the dead except in Christ is to be detested as a plague upon the faith that we share. Likewise, whoever says that the infants who leave this life without partaking of his sacrament are also brought to life in Christ certainly goes against the preaching of the apostle and condemns the whole Church, where the faithful hasten and run with

infants to be baptized precisely because they believe without a doubt that they absolutely cannot be brought to life except in Christ. The result, however, is that those who are not brought to life in Christ continue in that condemnation of which the apostle says, *Through the sin of the one all come to condemnation* (Rom 5:18). The whole Church believes that infants are born subject to this sin, and you yourself in arguing against Jovinian and explaining the prophet Jonah, as I mentioned a little before, declared this with the most true faith. And I believe that you did this also in other passages of your writings which I have either not read or do not recall at present. I am asking about the cause of this condemnation of infants because, if new individual souls are created for individuals, I do not see any sin of souls at that age, nor do I believe that any soul is condemned by God that he sees has no sin.

8, 22. Or should one perhaps say that in an infant there is only sinful flesh, but that a new soul is made for it, and that, if it lives according to the commandments of God with the help of the grace of Christ, its soul can attain the merit of incorruption for the flesh itself that it has tamed and subdued? But because in an infant the soul cannot yet do this, if it has not received the sacrament of Christ, it acquires for its flesh by this grace what it could not yet acquire by its actions. If, however, the soul of an infant passes away without that sacrament, it will certainly be in eternal life, from which no sin could separate it, but its flesh will not rise in Christ since it did not receive his sacrament before death.

23. I have never heard and never read this opinion, but I have clearly heard and *have believed, and on this account I have spoken* (Ps 116:1), for *the hour will come when all who are in the tombs will hear his voice, and those who have done good deeds will go forth for the resurrection of life* (Jn 5:28-29). This is the resurrection of which it is said, *And through one man there is the resurrection of the dead*, that is, by which *all will be brought to life in Christ* (1 Cor 15:21-22). *But those who have done evil deeds will go forth for the resurrection of judgment* (Jn 5:29). What, then, are we to understand here regarding those infants who, before they were capable of good or bad actions, are stripped of the body without baptism? Nothing is said here about such as them. But if their flesh will not rise because they did nothing either good or bad, neither will the flesh of those rise who, after receiving the grace of baptism, have died at the age when they were capable of neither good nor bad actions. If, however, these latter will rise among the saints, that is, among those who have done good actions, among whom are those others also going to rise except among those who have done evil actions? Otherwise, we would have to believe that some human souls will not receive back their bodies either for the resurrection of life or for the resurrection of judgment. This view is already objectionable by reason of its very novelty, even before it is refuted. Secondly, who would tolerate it if those who run to baptism with their infants believe that they run on account of their flesh, not on account of their souls? Blessed Cyprian was not creating some new decree but preserving

the most solid faith of the Church. In order to correct those who thought that an infant should not be baptized before the eighth day, he said not that the flesh but that the soul would be lost, and along with certain of his fellow bishops he declared that an infant can rightly be baptized as soon as it is born.[31]

24. But anyone may hold what he pleases contrary to an opinion of Cyprian in which he perhaps did not see what he should have seen. Only let no one hold another opinion contrary to the most clear faith of the apostle, who preaches that by the sin of the one all are led into condemnation,[32] from which condemnation only *the grace of God through Jesus Christ our Lord* (Rom 7:25) sets one free. In him alone all who are brought to life are brought to life. Let no one hold another opinion contrary to the most well-founded practice of the Church where, if the faithful ran to the Church for baptism for the sake of infant bodies, even the dead would be presented for baptism.

25. Since this is so, we must seek and give the reason why souls that are created new for any individuals who are born are condemned if infants die apart from the sacrament of Christ. For both holy scripture and the holy Church bear witness that they are condemned if they leave the body in that way. Hence let that view concerning the creation of new souls be mine if it does not attack this most well-founded faith; and if it does attack it, let it not be yours.

26. I do not want anyone to tell me that the words of scripture, *He fashioned the spirit of man in him* (Zec 12:1), and, *He fashioned their hearts individually* (Ps 33:15), should be interpreted in favor of this view. We must look for some absolutely solid and irrefutable evidence that does not force us to believe that God condemns some souls that are without any sin. For to create means either the same thing or more than to fashion, and yet scripture says, *Create a clean heart in me, O God* (Ps 51:12). Nor can the soul for this reason be thought in this passage to desire to be made before it was anything at all. Just as, when it already exists, it is created by being renewed by righteousness, so, when it already exists, it is fashioned by being shaped by doctrine. Nor do the words written in Ecclesiastes, *Then dust will turn to the earth, as it was, and the spirit will return to the Lord who gave it* (Eccl 12:7), support this view, which we want to be ours. For this supports those people more who think that all souls come from one soul. For, they say, dust turns to earth, as it was. And yet the flesh, of which this was said, does not return to the human being from which it was propagated but to the earth from which the first man was made. In the same way, the spirit propagated from the spirit of that one man does not return to him but to the Lord by whom it was given to him. But because this testimony sounds as if it is in favor of them so that it does not seem to be absolutely opposed to this opinion that I want to see defended, I only thought that I should warn Your Prudence not to try to rescue

---

31. See Cyprian, Letter 64, 2-6.
32. See Rom 5:18.

me from these difficulties by such testimonies. For, though by desiring it no one makes something to be true that is not true, I would nonetheless desire, if it were possible, that this view be true, just as I desire that, if it is true, you will defend it most clearly and irrefutably.

9, 27. But this difficulty also follows upon those who think that souls that already exist elsewhere and have been prepared from the beginning of God's works are sent by God into bodies. For this same question arises for them: If blameless souls go obediently where they are sent, why are they punished in infants if they end this life without having been baptized? There is, of course, the same difficulty in each view. Those people think that they get out of this question more easily who state that individual souls are inserted into individual bodies in accord with the merits of a previous life. For they think that to die in Adam means to suffer punishments in the flesh that was propagated from Adam, and they say that the grace of Christ sets free both infants and adults from this guilt. Indeed they say correctly, truly, and excellently that the grace of Christ sets free both infants and adults, but I do not believe, I do not accept, I do not agree that in another previous life souls sin and are hurled down from there into prisons of flesh. My first reason is that these people say that this is done through certain cycles, so that after some great number of years souls must return again to this burden of corruptible flesh and to suffering punishments. I do not know what can be thought that is more horrible than that idea. Secondly, if these people are right, has any righteous man died about whom we need not worry that he may sin in the bosom of Abraham and be cast down into the flames of that rich man?[33] After all, why couldn't one sin after leaving this body if one could also sin before? Finally, it is one thing to have sinned in Adam, because of which the apostle says, *In whom all have sinned* (Rom 5:12), and it is something far different to have sinned somewhere or other outside of Adam and on this account to be shoved into Adam, that is, into the flesh that was propagated from Adam, as into a prison. But I do not want even to discuss this opinion that all souls are made from one soul unless it is necessary, and I wish you to defend the opinion that we are now discissing, if it is true, so that this is no longer necessary.

28. But although, I desire, ask, hope for, and expect with ardent prayers that through you the Lord may remove my ignorance in this matter, if, nonetheless, I do not merit this (heaven forbid!), I pray that the Lord our God, in whom we believed to such an extent that we ought in no way to murmur against him if some things are not opened up for us when we knock, may give me patience.[34] We shall remember that he said to the apostles, *I have many things to say to you, but you cannot bear them now* (Jn 16:12). As far as I am concerned, I would count this among these things, nor do I, who know this, resent the fact that I am

---

33. See Lk 16:22-28.
34. See Mt 7:7-8.

unworthy for fear that I may be proved even more unworthy by this very fact. For I do not know many other things, likewise, that I cannot recall or count. And I would tolerate not knowing this if I did not fear that one of these opinions would invade careless minds contrary to that, truth that we hold with the most solid faith. But before I know which of them I should choose by preference, I declare that I am not being rash in holding this view, namely, that the one that is true is not contrary to the most solid and most well-founded faith by which the Church of Christ believes that not even infant human beings most recently born can be set free from condemnation except by the grace of the name of Christ, which he entrusted to us in his sacraments.

Letter 167

In 415 Augustine wrote to Jerome in Bethlehem concerning the opinion of the apostle James: *Whoever observes the whole law, but offends on one point, has become guilty of all* (Jas 2:10). See the introduction to the previous letter for the text of *The Revisions* in which Augustine refers to this letter as a book.

Augustine explains to Jerome that he did not want to add his question about the Letter of James to the previous letter (paragraph 1). Unlike the question about the origin of the soul, the present question deals with our living this present life and attaining eternal life (paragraph 2). Augustine quotes the verses leading up to the troublesome line in order to put it in context (paragraph 3).

Augustine explains without endorsing the doctrine of the philosophers that, if a person has one virtue, he has them all and that, if a person lacks one virtue, he lacks them all (paragraph 4). He shows how true prudence entails justice, courage, and temperance (paragraph 5). But, as far as the vices are concerned, there are those that are directly opposed to particular individual virtues, and there are those that bear a certain resemblance to particular virtues (paragraph 6). For example, Catiline had a quality that resembled courage but that was really a vice (paragraph 7). Hence, there are more vices than there are virtues (paragraph 8). At times one vice replaces another, but a single true virtue brings all the other virtues with it (paragraph 9).

Augustine leaves the previous question aside for further study and points out that the scriptures teach that no one is without sin (paragraph 10). But that does not mean that none of the faithful have any virtue, since piety and love are certainly virtues (paragraph 11). Augustine argues against the Stoics' view that someone who is making progress in wisdom does not have wisdom and rejects their comparison with a person instantly coming up out of the water in favor of the comparison with a person who gradually receives more and more light as he emerges from a cave (paragraphs 12 and 13).

Augustine apologizes for seeming to teach Jerome but insists that some sins are worse than others and that one person has more love than another (paragraph 14). The virtue necessary for living well is the love by which one loves what he ought to love, and one person can have more or less love or even no love at all (paragraph 15). Hence, because love of God and neighbor is the fulfillment of the law, one who sins against love becomes guilty of all the commandments since they all depend upon love (paragraph 16). So too, we all sin in many ways, but we sin more gravely or less gravely insofar as we love less or love more (paragraph 17). Furthermore, showing favoritism in ecclesiastical honors is no slight sin (paragraph 18).

Augustine explains that the law of freedom, of which James speaks, is the law of love and points out that the apostle teaches us to practice acts of mercy in order to receive forgiveness for our daily sins (paragraphs 19 and 20). Finally, Augustine praises Jerome's scholarly work and asks him to send him any better explanation of the words of James that Jerome himself may have discovered (paragraph 21).

The Book on the Opinion of James

1, 1. I wrote to you, Jerome, my honorable brother in Christ, asking a question about the human soul, namely: If individual new souls are created right up to the present for individuals who are born, where do they contract the bond of sin that we are certain must be removed, even in infants recently born, by the sacrament of Christ's grace? Since that turned into a large volume, I did not want to make it even larger with another question. But a question that is more urgently pressing ought much less to be neglected. Hence I ask and beg you by the Lord to explain to me something that I think will be of profit to many or, if you have or someone else has already explained this question, send it on to us, namely, how one should interpret what is found in the Letter of the apostle James, *For whoever has observed the whole law, but offends on one point, has become guilty of all* (Jas 2:10). This matter is of such great importance that I regret much that I did not write to you on it long ago.

2. For this question has to do with living the present life in such a way that we may come to eternal life, not with investigating the past that forgetfulness has completely wiped away, like that question that I thought needed to be asked about the soul. There is an eloquent story told that fits this matter quite aptly. A certain man fell into a well where there was so much water that it held him up so that he did not die instead of drowning him so he could not speak. Another man came along and, when he saw him, took pity and said, "How did you fall down there?" But the first man said, "Please, see how you might set me free from here, not how I fell down here." In that way, since we profess and state with the Catholic faith that the soul of an infant must be set free from the guilt of sin as if from a well, it is enough for him that we know the way his soul may be saved, even if we shall never know the way it came into this evil. But I thought that I should ask the question for fear that, of those opinions on the embodiment of the soul, we might hold one of them somewhat carelessly which denies that the soul of an infant must be set free, because it maintains that it is not present in this evil. With this truth, then, most firmly upheld, namely, that the soul of an infant must be set free from the guilt of sin and must be set free in no other way than by *the grace of God through Jesus Christ our Lord* (Rom 7:24-25), if we can also know the cause and origin of this evil, we are better prepared and instructed to stand up to the foolish talk not of people who want to discuss the matter but of those who want to quarrel over it. But, if we cannot, the work of mercy ought not to grow slack because the source of misery lies hidden. But, contrary to those who think they know what they do not know, we are safer to the extent that we are not unaware of our ignorance. For there are things that it is evil not to know, and there are

things that either cannot be known or need not be known or are of no consequence for the life we are seeking. But the question that I now am asking about the letter of the apostle James has to do with the actions by which we live this life and strive to please God in order that we may live forever.

3. How, then, I ask you, are we to understand, *Whoever has observed the whole law, but offends on one point, has become guilty of all*? Is a person who commits theft, or even someone who says to a rich man, *Sit here*, but to a poor man, *You, stand over there* (Jas 2:3), also guilty of murder, adultery, and sacrilege? But if he is not, how has someone who offends on one point become guilty of all? Or does what I mentioned about the rich man and the poor man not belong among those points on which, if one offends on any of them, he will become guilty of all? But we must remember the source of this statement and the ones that preceded and led up to it, on which it is dependant. It says, *My brothers, do not possess the faith of our Lord Jesus Christ, the Lord of glory, along with a favoritism toward persons. For, if a man enters your assembly in fine clothing and wearing a gold ring and a poor man enters in shabby clothing and you pay attention to the one clothed in fine clothing and say, Sit here, please, but say to the poor man, You, stand over there, or, Sit at my feet, have you not made distinctions among yourselves? And have you not become judges with wicked thoughts? Listen, my dearest brothers, has not God chosen the poor in this world to be rich in faith and heirs of the kingdom that he promised to those who love him? But you have dishonored the poor man* (Jas 2:1-6), that is, on account of the one to whom it was said, *You, stand over there*, when it was said to the one with the gold ring, *Sit here, please*. And then it continues expanding upon and explaining this statement more at length. It says, *Do not the rich oppress you with their power, and do they not drag you into court? Do they not blaspheme the good name that has been invoked over you? If you really fulfill the royal law according to the scriptures, You shall love your neighbor as yourself, you do well. But if you show favoritism toward persons, you commit sin and are convicted by the law as transgressors.* (Jas 2:6-9) See how it calls transgressors of the law those who say to the rich man, *Sit here*, and to the poor man, *Stand there*. And so that they would not think that it is a sin of no significance to transgress the law on this one point, it goes on and adds, *But whoever observes the whole law, but offends on one point, has become guilty of all. For he who said, You shall not commit adultery, also said, You shall not kill. If you do not kill, but commit adultery, you have become a transgressor of the law* on account of what it had said, *You are convicted by the law as transgressors.* Since this is so, it seems to follow (unless one shows that it should be interpreted otherwise) that the person who said to the rich man, *Sit here*, and to the poor man, *Stand there*, offering more respect to the former than to the latter, should be judged an idolater, a blasphemer, an adulterer, a murderer and—not to mention all of these,

which would take a long time—guilty of all serious sins, for by offending on one point he has become guilty of all.

2, 4. But does a person who has one virtue really have them all, and does a person who lacks one really have none? If this is true, the statement of James is confirmed. But I want this statement, which by itself is more certain for us than all the authorities of the philosophers, to be explained, not to be confirmed. And if that claim about the virtues and vices is true, it does not follow that on this account all sins are equal. For that claim about the inseparability of the virtues—though I may be mistaken, but if I have remembered the truth that I just barely remember—met with the approval of all the philosophers who said that the same virtues were necessary for living our life. But only the Stoics dared to argue this point concerning the equality of sins contrary to the common sense of the whole human race. You have refuted most clearly from the holy scriptures their foolishness in the case of that Jovinian[1] who was on this opinion a Stoic, but in hunting for and defending pleasures an Epicurean. In that most delightful and splendid discussion it was quite obvious that it did not meet with the approval of our authors or rather of the truth, which spoke through them, that all sins are equal. But I shall try to explain to the extent that I can with the Lord's help how it is possible that, even if this is true concerning the virtues, we are still not obliged on that account to admit the equality of all sins. And if I am successful, you will give your approval, but where I fall short of my endeavor you will make up the difference.

5. They argue that a person who has one virtue has them all and that someone who lacks one lacks them all, because prudence cannot be cowardly or unjust or intemperate. For, if it were one of these, it would not be prudence. But if it is prudence when it is courageous and just and temperate, then, when prudence exists, it has with it the other virtues. Thus also courage cannot be imprudent or intemperate or unjust. Thus temperance must be prudent, courageous, and just. Thus justice only exists if it is prudent, courageous, and temperate. And so where one of them is genuine, the others are too. But where the other virtues are lacking, the one that is there is not genuine, even if it seems like a genuine virtue in some respect.

6. For there are, as you know, certain vices that are clearly and distinctly contrary to certain virtues, as imprudence is to prudence. But there are certain vices contrary to certain virtues only because they are vices, but similar to the virtues by reason of their deceptive appearance, not like imprudence, but like cunning, which is opposed to that same prudence. What I now mean is that cunning that we more usually understand and speak of in the case of vicious persons, not as our scripture is accustomed to use when it often employs "cunning" in a good sense. For instance, it says, *Cunning as a serpent* (Mt

---

1. See Jerome, *Answer to Jovinian* (*Adversus Jovinianum*) 2, 30-33.

10:16), or, *That he may give cunning to the innocent* (Prv 1:4). And though the most eloquent among the writers of the Roman language said, "Nor did he lack deceit or the cunning to avoid it,"[2] when he uses "cunning" in a good sense, it is most rare among them but very frequent among our writers. Likewise, among the parts of temperance lavishness is most clearly contrary to frugality, but what is also commonly called stinginess is also a vice, similar to frugality not by its nature but by its very deceptive appearance. Likewise, justice is contrary to injustice by an obvious dissimilarity. A longing for revenge, however, often, as it were, imitates justice, but it is a vice. Cowardice is clearly contrary to courage; hardness, however, differs in nature from courage but misleads by its similarity to it. Constancy is a particular part of virtue; inconstancy is far removed from it and obviously stands in full opposition to it. But stubbornness likes to be called constancy, though it is not, because constancy is a virtue and stubbornness a vice.

7. In order, then, that it may not be necessary to mention the same points again, let us set forth an example from which the rest can be understood. As those who were able to know wrote of him, Catiline was able to endure cold, thirst, and hunger, and he "suffered hunger, cold, and a lack of sleep beyond what anyone could believe,"[3] and for this reason he seemed to his followers and to himself to be endowed with great courage. But this courage was not prudent, for it chose evil instead of good; it was not temperate, for it was defiled by the most shameful corruption; it was not just, for it conspired against the fatherland; and hence it was not courage either, but hardness gave itself the name "courage" to mislead the foolish. For, if it were courage, it would not be a vice but a virtue. But if it were a virtue, it would never be abandoned by the other virtues, which are like its inseparable companions.

8. For this reason, when the question is also raised about the vices as to whether they also all exist where there is one or whether none exists where one is lacking, it involves much effort because two vices are usually opposed to one virtue, both the one that is clearly its contrary and the other that resembles it by an apparent similarity. From this we see more easily that what Catiline had, which did not have the other virtues along with it, was not courage, but it is hard to persuade anyone that it was cowardice inasmuch as it included the practice of suffering and enduring certain very serious difficulties "beyond what anyone could believe." But for those whose sight is sharper, that hardness is perhaps seen to be cowardice because it neglected the labor of good activities by which true courage is acquired. But those who are not timid are daring, and those who are timid lack daring, and each is a vice, since a person who is courageous with

---

2. Sallust, *The War against Catiline* (*Bellum Catilinae*) 26.
3. Sallust, *The War against Catiline* (*Bellum Catilinae*) 5.

true virtue is neither rashly daring nor unwisely timid. Hence we are forced to admit that there are more vices than virtues.

9. As a result one vice is at times removed by another, as a craving for money is removed by a craving for praise; at times one vice withdraws in order that several may take its place, as when someone who was given to drink learns to drink moderately out of stinginess and ambition. Vices, therefore, can withdraw when other vices, not virtues, take their place, and for this reason there are more vices. But where one virtue has entered, all the vices that were present completely withdraw, because that virtue brings with it all the others. For the vices were not all present, but at times the same number and at times more were replaced by fewer, or fewer by more.

3, 10. We must inquire more carefully as to whether these things are this way. For it is not the word of God that says, "A person who has one virtue has them all, and someone who lacks one has none." Rather, this was the idea of human beings, of very intelligent, studious and leisured human beings, but of human beings nonetheless. But I do not know how I could say not of a man (from whom virtue gets its name[4]) but even of a woman who observes the fidelity of the marriage bed, that she does not have chastity, or that it is no virtue or an insignificant virtue, if she does this on account of the commandment and promise of God and is faithful to him from the beginning. I would also say the same thing of a husband who observes the same fidelity to his wife. Yet there are very many such persons, of whom I would say that none is without sin, and that sin, of whatever sort it is of course, comes from some vice. For this reason marital chastity in devout men and women is undoubtedly a virtue—for it is neither nothing nor a vice—but it does not bring with it all the virtues. For, if all the virtues were present, there would be no vice; if there were no vice, there would be absolutely no sin. But who is without some sin, that is, a certain tinderbox or root, so to speak, of sin, since the apostle who laid his head on the Lord's breast[5] cries out, *If we say that we have no sin, we deceive ourselves, and the truth is not in us* (1 Jn 1:8)? We need not emphasize this any longer with you; rather, I say this on account of others who may read this. For in fact in that same splendid work against Jovinian you have also proved this point from the holy scriptures.[6] There as well you quoted from this very letter, whose words we are now trying to understand, the statement, *For we all offend on many points* (Jas 3:2). For it did not say, "You offend," but, *We offend*, though the apostle of Christ was speaking. And though in this passage he says, *But whoever observes the whole law, but offends on one point, has become guilty of all* (Jas 2:10), he did not say

---

4. *Virtus* ("virtue") was said to be derived from *vir* ("man").

5. See Jn 13:25; 21:20.

6. See *Answer to Jovinian (Adversus Jovianianum)* 2, 2.

there that certain persons offend, but that all offend, not on one point but on many.

11. Heaven forbid, however, that any believer should think that so many thousands of Christ's servants, who truthfully say that they have some sin, for fear that they might deceive themselves and that the truth might not be in them, have no virtue, since wisdom is a great virtue. *He, however, said to the man, See, piety is wisdom* (Job 28:28). But heaven forbid that we should say that so many and such faithful and pious men of God do not have piety, which the Greeks call εὐσέβειαν or more clearly and fully θεοσέβειαν! But what is piety but the worship of God? And by what is he worshiped but by love? For *love from a pure heart and a good conscience and faith unfeigned* is a great and true virtue, for it is *the goal of the commandment* (1 Tm 1:5). It is rightly said to be *as strong as death* (Sg 8:6) either because no one conquers it, just as no one conquers death, or because in this life the measure of love goes as far as death, as the Lord says, *Greater love than this no one has than that he lay down his life for his friends* (Jn 15:13), or rather because, as death tears the soul away from the senses of the flesh, so love tears it away from the concupiscences of the flesh. When knowledge is useful, it serves love. For without love knowledge puffs us up with pride. But because love fills us up by building us up, knowledge will find no emptiness to puff up. Job showed that knowledge is useful when he defined it; after he had said, *See, piety is wisdom*, he immediately added, *But to hold back from evils is knowledge* (Job 28:28 LXX). Why, therefore, do we not say that one who has this virtue has them all, since *the fullness of knowledge is love* (Rom 13:10)? Or is a person endowed with more virtue to the extent that he has more love, while he has less virtue to the extent that he has less love, because love itself is virtue, and to the extent that virtue is less present, vice is more present? Where, then, virtue is full and perfect, no vice will remain.

12. Furthermore, the Stoics seem to me to be mistaken because they deny that a person making progress in wisdom has any wisdom at all. Instead they claim that a person has it when he is completely perfect in it, not because they deny that progress but because they say that a person is not wise at all unless by rising up from a certain depth he suddenly stands forth in the free atmosphere of wisdom. For just as it makes no difference for drowning a man whether he has over him many feet or one foot or one inch of water, so they say that those who are moving toward wisdom are certainly making progress, like men rising to the surface from the depths of the whirlpool, but unless by making progress they escape from all folly, as if by emerging out of it they do not have virtue and are not wise. But when they have escaped, they suddenly have the whole of wisdom, and no folly remains, and as a result there can be no sin at all.

13. This comparison in which folly is likened to water and wisdom to air, so that a mind rising up into wisdom, as if from drowning in folly, suddenly draws in air, does not seem to me to conform adequately to the authority of our scrip-

tures. But that comparison fits better in which vice or folly is likened to darkness while virtue or wisdom is likened to light, to the extent that these likenesses can be transferred from bodily things to intelligible ones. It does not, then, occur in the way in which someone rising from the water into the air can suddenly regain his breath when he passes through the surface of the waters. It occurs, rather, in the way in which someone going from darkness into light gradually receives light as he moves ahead. And until he has fully completed this move, we say that, like someone gradually emerging from a very deep cave, he is more influenced by the nearness of the light the more he approaches the entrance. In that way what is bright in him comes, of course, from the light toward which he is making progress, while what is still obscure in him comes from the darkness that he is leaving. And so *no one living will be righteous in the sight of God* (Ps 143:2), and yet *the righteous live by faith* (Hab 2:4; Rom 1:17). The saints are clothed with righteousness—one more, another less—and no one lives in this world without sin—here too one more, another less. But he is best who has the least sin.

5, 14. But what am I doing? As if I forgot to whom I am speaking, I have become like a teacher, though I was presenting to you what I would like to learn from you. But because I had decided to set forth my view for you to examine on the equality of sins, from which the question turned to the topic that I was discussing, I will at long last bring it to an end. For even if it is true that a person who has one virtue has them all and that a person who lacks one lacks them all, even so sins are not equal, because where there is no virtue there is of course no rectitude, but it does not follow that one evil is not worse than another and that one wrong is not worse than another. But I think that it is more true and more compatible with the sacred writings that the intentions of the soul are like the members of the body, not because they are seen in places but because they are perceived by our feelings. And one member receives more light, another less, while still another is completely without light and is in the dark because of a covering that excludes the light. In the same way each person is touched by the rays of pious love—more in one act, less in another, and not at all in a third—so that he can certainly be said to have one virtue, not to have another, and to have more or less of a third. For we can correctly say, "Greater love is found in this person than in that one," and, "Some love is found in this person and none in that," with regard to that love which is piety, and we can say of a single person that he has greater chastity than patience and greater chastity today than yesterday if he is making progress, and that as yet he has no continence but does have no small amount of mercy.

15. And to summarize in a general and brief statement the notion that I have of virtue, insofar as it pertains to living well, virtue is the love by which one loves what should be loved. This is greater in some, less in others, and not at all in still others, but it is not so perfect in anyone that it cannot be increased in him as long as he lives. But as long as it can be increased, then of course that which is less

than it ought to be comes from a vice. Because of that vice *there is not a righteous person on earth who will do good and not sin* (Eccl 7:21). Because of that vice *no living being will be righteous in the sight of God* (Ps 143:2). On account of that vice, *if we say that we have no sin, we deceive ourselves, and the truth is not in us* (1 Jn 1:8). On its account, however much progress we make, we must also say, *Forgive us our debts* (Mt 6:12; 11:4), though all our sins in words, deeds, and thoughts have been forgiven in baptism. A person who sees correctly, then, sees where and when and from whom we should hope for that perfection to which nothing can be added. If, however, there were not the commandments, there would surely be nowhere a person might look at himself with more certainty and see from what he should turn away, for what he should strive, for what he should give thanks, and for what he should pray. There is, then, a great benefit in the commandments if free choice is only given the help to pay greater honor to the grace of God.

5, 16. Since this is so, how does a person become guilty of all the commandments if he who has observed the whole law offends on one of them? Is it perhaps because *the fullness of the law is love* (Rom 13:10), by which God and neighbor are loved, on which commandments of love *the whole law and the prophets depend* (Mt 22:40), that one who acts against that love on which all the commandments depend rightly becomes guilty of all? But no one sins except by acting against that love, because *You shall not commit adultery, You shall not commit murder, You shall not steal, You shall not desire, and any other commandment there is is summed up in these words, You shall love your neighbor as yourself* (Rom 13:9-10). *Love of neighbor does no evil; the fullness of the law, however, is love* (Rom 13:9-10). Yet no one loves his neighbor without loving God, so that he pours out this love as much as he can upon his neighbor whom he loves as himself in order that his neighbor might love God. If he himself does not love God, he loves neither himself nor God. And for this reason a person who has observed the whole law becomes guilty of all the commandments if he offends on one of them, because he acts against the love on which the whole law depends. He therefore becomes guilty of all by acting against the love on which they all depend.

17. Why, then, are sins not said to be equal? Is it perhaps because a person acts against love more when he sins more gravely and that he acts against love less when he sins less gravely? And does he sin more and less and by that very fact become guilty of all the commandments, but more guilty by sinning more gravely or by sinning against more commandments, less guilty by sinning more lightly or against fewer commandments, with greater guilt to the extent he sins more and with less guilt to the extent he sins less? And yet even if he sins against only one commandment, is he guilty of all because he acts against that love on which all depend? If this is true, we have also in the same way resolved the problem about the statement of the man who had the grace of an apostle, *For we*

all offend on many points (Jas 3:2). For we do all offend, but one more gravely, another less gravely. To the extent that a person sins more or less, he is greater in committing sin to the extent that he is less in loving God and neighbor, and, on the other hand, he is less in committing sin to the extent that he is greater in the love of God and neighbor. He is therefore more full of sinfulness to the extent that he is more empty of love, and he will be most perfect in love when no weakness remains.

18. Nor should anyone, in my judgment, suppose that it is a slight sin to possess faith in the Lord Jesus Christ along with favoritism toward persons, if we take the difference between sitting and standing to refer to positions of honor in the Church. For who would tolerate it that a rich man is chosen for a position of honor in the Church when a better instructed and holier poor man is rejected? But if he is speaking about daily assemblies, who does not sin in this case, if he does in fact sin, when he so discriminates in his mind that he thinks that one person is better than another because he is richer? For he seems to have signified this when he said, *Have you not pronounced judgment within yourselves and become judges with unjust thoughts?* (Jas 2:4)

6, 19. The law of freedom, then, is the law of love, of which James says, *If you really fulfill the royal law according to the scriptures, You shall love your neighbor as yourself, you do well. But if you show favoritism toward persons, you commit sin and are convicted by the law as transgressors.* (Jas 2:8-9) And after that statement, which is most difficult to understand and about which I have already stated well enough what I thought should be said, he mentions the same law of freedom. He says, *Speak and act like persons who are beginning to be judged by the law of freedom* (Jas 2:12). And since he knew what he had said a little before, namely, that *we all offend on many points* (Jas 3:2), he suggests the Lord's remedy as a daily one for daily wounds, even though for lesser ones. For he says, *He who does not show mercy will receive judgment without mercy* (Jas 2:13). For on this topic the Lord also says, *Forgive and it will be forgiven you; give and it will be given you* (Lk 6:37-38). *But mercy exults in its superiority over judgment* (Jas 2:13). It does not say, "Mercy conquers judgment," for it is not opposed to judgment, but *exults in its superiority over judgment*, because many are rescued, but they are those who have shown mercy. For *blessed are the merciful because God will show them mercy* (Mt 5:7).

20. And it is indeed just that they be forgiven because they forgave and that it be given to them because they gave. To be sure, there is mercy in God when he judges and judgment in God when he shows mercy. For this reason we say to him, *I shall sing to you, Lord, of mercy and judgment* (Ps 101:1). For whoever, like someone overly righteous, looks forward to judgment without mercy, as if he were secure, calls forth the most just anger, which that man fears who says, *Do not enter into judgment with your servant* (Ps 143:2). Hence it is said to proud

people, *Why do you want to contend with me in judgment? For, when the just king shall sit upon his throne, who will boast that he has a chaste heart? Or who will boast that he is clean from sin?* (Prv 20:8-9 LXX) What hope is there, then, unless *mercy exults in its superiority over judgment—but toward those who have shown mercy by saying truthfully, Forgive us as we also forgive* (Mt 6:12; Lk 11:4), and by giving without complaint, *for God loves a cheerful giver* (2 Cor 9:7)? Finally, after this passage Saint James now speaks of the works of mercy in order to console those whom that statement had deeply terrified. He shows how even daily sins, without which no one lives in this life, are wiped out by daily remedies. Otherwise, since, when someone offends against one commandment, he becomes guilty of them all, he might by offending on many points—for *we all offend on many point*s (Jas 3:2)—bring a huge mass of guilt that he has accumulated little by little to the tribunal of the great judge, and he would not find the mercy that he did not show. Instead of this, by forgiving and pardoning others he should merit to have his debts forgiven and to receive the reward he has been promised.

21. I have said many things that have perhaps bored you. For you who do not expect to learn the very things that you approve, since you are accustomed to teach them. But if there is something in them that, insofar as it pertains to the truth—for I do not care much about the sort of language in which it is expressed—if there is, then, something in them that offends your learning, please write back and warn me and do not hesitate to correct me. For he is an unfortunate man who does not worthily honor the very important and very holy labors of your studies and does not, on their account, thank the Lord our God by whose gift you are such a man. And so, since I ought to be more willing to learn from anyone what I do not know to my disadvantage than eager to teach anyone what I do know, how much more justly do I demand of you this debt of love! For in the name of the Lord and with his help your teaching has contributed to the growth of the literature of the Church in the Latin language more than had ever before been the case. I especially ask by the Lord that, if Your Charity knows another way in which this statement, *Whoever observes the whole law, but offends on one point, has become guilty of all*, can be better explained, you be so good as to share it with us.

Letter 168

In 415 Timasius and James, two former disciples of Pelagius, who had given Augustine a copy of Pelagius' book, *Nature*, wrote to Augustine to thank him for his work, *Nature and Grace*. Their letter is important because it provides evidence that Pelagius wrote *Nature* earlier than had traditionally been thought. Hence, Pelagius most probably formulated his position on grace well before he came to Africa in the aftermath of Rome's fall to Alaric in 410, not subsequent to Augustine's attacks upon his position.[1]

To our truly blessed lord and rightly venerable father, bishop Augustine, Timasius and James send greetings in the Lord.

The grace of God brought to us by your word has so restored and refreshed us, blessed lord and rightly venerable father, that we say in all truth, *He sent his word and it healed them* (Ps 107:20). We find that Your Holiness has opened up the text of that small book with such care that we are stunned by the answers given to the individual points, whether in the matters that a Christian should refute and detest and flee from, or in those in which he[2] is not clearly shown to have been in error, although by some form of craftiness he believed that he should eliminate the grace of God in them as well. There is, however, one thing that strikes us in this great benefit, namely, that this splendid gift of the grace of God has shone forth somewhat late.[3] For, as it is, there are no longer present certain people whose blindness needed to be illumined by the brilliance of this pure truth. Still, we do not give up hope that this same grace will, by God's goodness, reach them, even if it is somewhat later, for *he wills all human beings to be saved and come to the knowledge of the truth* (1 Tm 2:4). As for ourselves, we earlier cast off our subjection to this error, after having been instructed by the spirit of love, which is present in you. We now also give thanks that we have learned to teach others what we earlier came to believe, since the rich explanation of Your Holiness makes the path more easy. [And in another hand there is written:] May the mercy of our God preserve Your Beatitude, keep you mindful of us, and bring you to eternal glory.

---

1. See Yves-Marie Deval, "La date du 'De natura' de Pélage. Les premières étapes de la controverse sur la nature de la grâce," *Revue des études augustiniennes* 36 (1990): 257-283, for an argument for an earlier dating of Pelagius's work.
2. Though they avoid mentioning his name, Timasius and James refer to Pelagius, whose book they had given to Augustine.
3. Augustine's *Nature and Grace* is too late for Pelagius and others of his followers who, by the time it was written, had moved on to Palestine.

Letter 169

In 415 Augustine wrote to his friend, Evodius, the bishop of Uzalis. He tells Evodius about the works he has just written and is presently writing (paragraph 1). Augustine explains that Paul's words, *He who does not know will not be known* (1 Cor 14:38), were not written about those who cannot distinguish by means of their intelligence the three persons in the Trinity but about certain persons who were causing trouble in the church of Corinth (paragraph 2). After all, God chose to save those who believe through the foolishness of preaching (paragraph 3), and Christ did not die only for those who have attained a certain degree of philosophical acumen (paragraph 4).

Hence, Augustine tells Evodius what they should believe regarding the Trinity, which always acts as a unity in creating, though the scriptures speak of the three separately (paragraph 5). Though our memory, understanding, and will provide an image of the Trinity, they also fall short of the Trinity in certain obvious ways (paragraph 6). The sound of the Father's voice and the form of the dove in which the Spirit appeared were not, however, assumed permanently into the unity of their persons, as the man was assumed into the unity of the person of the Word (paragraph 7). Hence, we can speak of Christ insofar as he is the Word and insofar as he has become man (paragraph 8). But the voice of the Father and the form of the dove were signs that performed their function and have ceased to exist (paragraph 9).

Augustine turns to an interpretation of the appearance of the Holy Spirit in the form of a dove at Christ's baptism (paragraph 10) and argues that the Trinity remained invisible and immutable, regardless of how any visions of it may have been produced (paragraph 11). Augustine congratulates himself for having taken the time to answer Evodius on these two questions (paragraph 12). He finally mentions the other works he has written, tells Evodius to send someone to copy them if he wants to have them all, and asks to be allowed to finish his works, which are needed by many people (paragraph 13).

Bishop Augustine sends greetings to Bishop Evodius.[1]

1, 1. If Your Holiness values so highly the knowledge of those writings with which I am much occupied and from which I do not want to turn aside to other things, send someone to copy them for you. For many projects have already been completed that we began this year before Easter at the approach of Lent. For we have added another two books to those three books on *The City of God* against the worshipers of demons, who are enemies of it. By these five books I think that I have argued sufficiently against those who think that we should worship the gods for the sake of the happiness of the present life and that we are an obstacle to

---

1. The CSEL edition omits the salutation.

that happiness, since they believe that such gods are hostile to the name of Christ. Next we must speak, as we promised in the first book, against those who suppose that the worship of their gods is necessary for the sake of the life after death, the life on account of which we are Christians. I have also dictated the explanation of three psalms in volumes of no small size, Psalms Sixty-Seven, Seventy-One, and Seventy-Seven. The others, which I have not yet dictated or commented on, are urgently awaited and demanded of us. I do not want to be distracted and kept from these by any questions arising unexpectedly. At present I do not want to give my attention even to the books of *The Trinity*, which I have had in hand for a long time and have not yet completed, for they involve much work and I think that they can be understood only by a few. Hence, the projects press upon us more insistently that we hope will be beneficial for more people.

2. For the apostle did not say on this topic, *One who does not know will be known* (1 Cor 14:38), as if someone were going to suffer that penalty if he could not distinguish with intelligence the ineffable unity of the Trinity in the same way as we distinguish in our mind memory, understanding, and will. The apostle said this with reference to something else. Read and you will see that he was speaking of those things that build up the faith and morals of many people, not of those things that gain an understanding among hardly a few, and only a slight understanding, such as one can have of so great a reality in this life. That is, he was placing a higher value on prophecy than on tongues in order that the latter might be employed without disorder, as if the spirit of prophecy[2] were forcing even the unwilling to speak. He wanted women to be silent in church in order that everything might be done properly and in order.[3] Since he was doing this, he said, *If anyone thinks himself to be a prophet or a spiritual person, let him know what I write to you, for it is a commandment of the Lord. If, however, someone does not know, he will not be known* (1 Cor 14:37-38). By these words he held in check and recalled to a peaceful order the restless who were the more ready for rebellion inasmuch as they seemed to themselves to excel in the spirit though they were disturbing everything by acting with pride. *If, now, anyone thinks himself to be a prophet or a spiritual person, let him know*, he says, *what I write to you, for it is a commandment of the Lord*—if anyone thinks himself to be such a person and is not at all, for one who is such a person undoubtedly knows it and needs neither admonition nor exhortation because he *judges all things and is judged by no one* (1 Cor 2:15). Those people, then, were fomenting rebellions and disturbances in the church. He teaches them to know the commandment of the Lord, for *he is not the God of rebellion, but of peace. If, however, anyone does not know, he will not be known*, that is, he will be rejected. For if you take it to refer to knowledge, God certainly knows those to whom he is going to say, *I*

---

2. See Rv 19:10.
3. See 1 Cor 14:34.40.

do not know you (Mt 7:23; Lk 13:25.27). Instead he signifies their rejection by this expression.

3. But the Lord says, *Blessed are the clean of heart because they shall see God* (Mt 5:8), and that vision is promised us in the end as the highest reward. Hence, if we are not now able to see clearly what we believe concerning the nature of God, there is no reason to fear that it was on this account that scripture said, *One who does not know will not be known* (1 Cor 14:38). *For, because in the wisdom of God the world has not known God through wisdom, it has pleased God to save those who believe through the foolishness of preaching* (1 Cor 1:21). This foolishness of preaching and the foolishness of God, *which is wiser than human beings* (1 Cor 1:25), draws many to salvation. For the salvation which that foolishness of preaching brings to the faithful embraces not only those who are not yet able to see by certain understanding the nature of God, which they hold by faith, but also those who do not yet distinguish in their own soul its incorporeal nature from everything bodily in the same way as they are certain that they live, know, and will.

4. For if Christ died only on account of those who can distinguish these things with certain intelligence, we labor in the Church to almost no purpose. But if, as the truth has it, the weak people among the faithful run to the physician to be healed by Christ, and by him crucified, so that where sin has abounded[4] grace might abound even more, it comes about in marvelous ways *through the depth of the riches of the wisdom and knowledge of God* and through *his inscrutable judgments* (Rom 11:33) that some who can distinguish incorporeal things from bodies think that for this reason they are important people and mock the foolishness of preaching by which believers are saved, while they themselves wander far from the one path that alone leads to eternal life. But many who boast in the cross of Christ and do not depart from the same path, even those who do not know those things that are discussed with great subtlety, because not a single infant perishes for whom he has died,[5] come to the same eternity, truth, and love, that is, to solid, certain, and complete happiness, where everything is clear for those who remain, see, and love.

2, 5. Hence let us with solid piety believe in one God, the Father, the Son, and the Holy Spirit, so that we do not believe the Son to be who the Father is, nor the Father to be who the Son is, nor the Father and the Son to be who the Spirit of them both is. Let us not think that in this Trinity there is any distance in time or place; rather, let us hold that these three are equal, coeternal, and absolutely one nature. The Father did not create one creature, the Son another, and the Holy Spirit still another; rather, each and every thing that was created or is created

---

4. See Rom 5:20.
5. Though the manuscripts and the contexts favor this reading, the passage seems open to the interpretation given by Jansenius that Christ did not die for all infants.

exists because the Trinity creates it. Nor is anyone set free by the Father without the Son and the Holy Spirit or by the Son without the Father and the Holy Spirit or by the Holy Spirit without the Father and the Son, but by the Father and the Son and the Holy Spirit, the one, true, and truly immortal, that is, absolutely immutable, God alone. Many things are said separately in the scriptures of the individual persons in order to present the Trinity, which, though inseparable, is a trinity. For example, just as they cannot be spoken of at the same time when they are mentioned by bodily sounds, though they exist inseparably at the same time, so in certain passages of the scriptures and through certain creatures they are also revealed individually and in sequence. For instance, the Father is revealed in the voice that boomed forth, *You are my Son* (Mk 1:11; Lk 3:22), and the Son is revealed in the man he assumed from the Virgin, and the Holy Spirit is revealed in the bodily form of the dove. These reveal separately those three that are not in any way separate.

6. To understand this somehow or other we use memory, understanding, and will. For, although we speak of these individually, each at its own time, we nonetheless do not use or speak of any of them without the other two. But these three should not for this reason be thought to be comparable to the Trinity so as to match it in every respect. For, in a discussion, to what likeness do we grant so great an aptness that it matches the thing to which it is to be applied in every respect, at least when one takes from a creature a likeness to the creator? This likeness, then, is first found to be unlike the Trinity insofar as these three, memory, understanding, and will, are in the soul but are not the soul. That Trinity, however, is not in God but is God. In that Trinity a marvelous simplicity is revealed because, in it, to exist is not something other than to understand, or anything else that is said of the nature of God. But since the soul exists even when it does not understand, its existence is one thing and its understanding is something else. Secondly, who would dare to say that the Father does not understand through himself but through the Son, just as memory does not understand through itself but through the intellect, or rather just as the soul itself, in which these are present, understands only through the intellect, just as it remembers only through the memory and wills only through the will? This likeness, then, is used in order that we might somehow understand that, just as when the individual names of these three, by which each of them is revealed, are spoken in the soul, yet each name is spoken by the three acting together when each name is said by remembering, understanding, willing, similarly there is no creature by which the Father alone or the Son alone or the Holy Spirit alone is revealed, which the Trinity, which acts inseparably, does not produce together. And for this reason neither the voice of the Father nor the soul and flesh of the Son nor the dove of the Holy Spirit was created except by the Trinity working together.

7. That sounding voice, which immediately ceased to exist, was of course not joined to the unity of the person of the Father, nor was that bodily form of the

dove joined to the unity of the person of the Holy Spirit. For, like that bright cloud that covered the savior along with the three disciples on the mountain,[6] or rather like that fire that revealed the same Holy Spirit,[7] it immediately ceased to exist once its function of being a sign was over. But because all these things were done in order to set free this nature, only a man was joined to the unity of the person of the Word of God, that is, of the only Son of God, by a marvelous and singular assumption, while the Word remained immutable in its nature, in which no imagining of the human mind should suppose any composition by which it might subsist. It is true that scripture says that the *the spirit of wisdom is multiple* (Wis 7:22), but it is also correctly said to be simple. For it is multiple because there are many things that it has, but it is simple because what it has is not something other than itself, just as the Son is said *to have life in himself* (Jn 5:26, 14:6) and is himself that same life. But the man was united to the Word; the Word was not united to the man by changing into the man, and in that way he is said to be the Son of God along with the man he assumed. Hence the same Son of God is immutable and coeternal with the Father, but only with regard to the Word, and the Son of God was buried, but only with regard to the flesh.

8. Hence, we must see in what sense the expressions that are used of the Son of God are meant. For the number of persons was not increased by the assumption of the man; rather, the same Trinity remained. For, just as in any man—apart from the one who was assumed in a singular manner—soul and body are one person, so in Christ the Word and the man are one person. And just as a human being is, for example, never said to be a philosopher except in terms of his soul, and yet we say without any absurdity, but speaking in a way that is utterly appropriate and commonplace, that a philosopher was killed, a philosopher died, a philosopher was buried, though all these happen in terms of the flesh and not insofar as he is a philosopher, so Christ is said to be God, the Son of God, the Lord of glory, and anything else of the sort insofar as he is the Word, and yet God is correctly said to have been crucified, though it is certain that he suffered this in terms of the flesh and not insofar as he is the Lord of glory.

9. But that sounding voice and the bodily form of the dove[8] and the fire like divided tongues which came to rest over each of them,[9] like those sounds and sights on Mount Sinai which were produced with a terrifying appearance,[10] and like that column of cloud by day and of flame by night,[11] were brought about to serve as signs and were then done with. In regard to these we must especially avoid believing that the nature of God, either of the Father or of the Son or of the

---

6. See Mt 17:5; Mk 9:6; Lk 9:34.
7. See Acts 2:3.
8. See Mt 17:5; Mk 9:6; Lk 9:34.
9. See Acts 2:3.
10. See Ex 19:18.
11. See Ex 13:21.

Holy Spirit, is mutable and subject to change, nor should it trouble us that at times the thing that serves as a sign receives the name of the thing that it signifies. The Holy Spirit was said to have descended in bodily form like a dove and to have remained over him. It was in this way that the rock was said to be Christ, because it signified him.[12]

3, 10. But I am surprised that you think that the sound of the voice that said, *You are my son* (Mk 1:11; Lk 3:22), could have been made at God's command by a bodily nature alone without the mediation of a soul, and that you do not think that the bodily form of any living being and the motion like something living could have been produced in the same way at God's command without any animal spirit intervening. For, if a bodily creature had obeyed God without the ministry of any life-giving soul in order to produce the sort of sounds that are usually produced by the animated body so that the form of articulate speech might be carried to the ears, why would it not obey in such a way that, without the use of the life-giving soul, the shape and motion of a bird might be presented to sight by the same power of the creator? Or perhaps the sense of hearing can manage this, while the sense of seeing cannot, though each of them is formed from the nearby matter of the body, as well as what sounds in the ears and appears to sight, and also the pronunciation of a word, the outlines of members and audible and visible motion. That is, a true body is what is perceived by the senses of the body and is nothing more than what is perceived by the senses of the body. For the soul, even in some living being, is perceived by no sense of the body. There is, then, no need to ask how the bodily form of the dove appeared, just as we do not ask how the words formed by an articulate body sounded. For, if it was possible that there was no need of a soul when scripture says that a voice—not something like a voice—was produced, for how much better reason was it possible that there was no need when it said *like a dove* (Mt 3:16; Mk 1: 10; Lk 3:22; Jn 1:32). For this expression signified only the bodily form presented to the eyes but did not indicate the nature of a living animal. In this way it was also said, *Suddenly a sound was produced from heaven as if a strong wind were blowing, and there appeared to them divided tongues like fire* (Acts 2:2-3). Here it mentions a certain sensible form like wind or like fire similar to these usual and familiar natures, but it does not seem to signify that these usual and familiar natures were themselves produced for a given period of time.

11. But if more subtle reasoning or a more refined investigation of the matter proves that the nature that is moved neither in time nor in place moves[13] only by means of that nature that is moved in time but not in place, the result will be that all those things were brought about by the help of a living creature, as they are brought about by the angels. To discuss this more carefully would take a long

---

12. See 1 Cor 10:4.
13. I have followed the reading *movere* in place of *moveri*.

time and is not necessary. In addition, there are visions that are seen by the spirit, as if by the senses of the body, not only by people who are asleep or insane but at times by people who are awake and of sound mind, not by means of the deceitfulness of mocking demons but by means of some spiritual revelation that is produced by incorporeal forms resembling bodies. These visions cannot be deciphered at all unless they are more fully revealed by the help of God and evaluated by the intelligence of the mind, hardly ever when they are occurring but generally only afterward, once they have passed. Since this is so, whether they seem to appear to our spirit as if to the senses of the body, either in bodily natures or only in a bodily appearance, but with a spiritual nature, when sacred scripture mentions these visions we ought not to pronounce judgment rashly about which of these two kinds they belong to and about whether they are produced by means of a living creature, if they are produced by a body. But we should believe without any doubt and also grasp by some sort of understanding that the invisible and immutable nature of the creator, that is, of the supreme and ineffable Trinity, is far removed and separate from the senses of mortal and carnal beings and from all change, whether it be for better or for worse or from one thing into another.

4, 12. You see how, though I am very busy, I was able to write these things to you at leisure on these two questions, that is, on the Trinity and on the dove in which the Holy Spirit was revealed not in his own nature but by a form acting as a sign. In the same way the Son of God was crucified by the Jews not in terms of his birth, of which the Father says, *Before the morning star I have begotten you* (Ps 110:3), but in terms of the man he assumed from the womb of the Virgin. I did not think that I ought to comment on everything that you put in your letter, but I believe that I have replied to the two topics on which you wanted to hear from me, if not in a way that is sufficient for your eagerness, then at least in a way that is obedient to your love.

13. But besides those two books I mentioned above, which I have added to the three, and the explanation of the three psalms, I have also written a book for the holy priest Jerome on the origin of the soul.[14] I asked him how he could defend the view of his that he explained to Marcellinus of pious memory,[15] namely, that individual new souls are created for those who are born, so that the most well-founded faith of the Church is not undermined, by which we believe unshakeably that all die in Adam[16] and are carried off into condemnation unless they are set free by the grace of Christ, which he brings about even in infants through his sacrament. I also wrote another book for him on how he thinks one should interpret the verse in the Letter to James, *But whoever observes the whole*

14. That is, Letter 166, which was also called *The Origin of the Soul.*
15. Marcellinus, the imperial commissioner, was executed for his alleged involvement in a plot against the emperor, Honorius, on 13 September 413.
16. See 1 Cor 15:22.

law, but offends on one point, has become guilty of all (Jas 2:10).[17] But in this book I also said what I thought, while in the former book on the origin of the soul I only asked, in a kind of consultative discussion, what he thought. I did not want to lose the opportunity provided by a certain very holy and enthusiastic young man, the priest Orosius, who came to us from the furthest reaches of Spain, that is, from the shore of the ocean, ablaze only with the love of the holy scriptures. I persuaded him to continue on to Jerome. In one small book I answered with as much brevity and clarity as I could, for this same Orosius, certain questions that were troubling him about the heresy of the Priscillianists and about certain opinions of Origen that the Church does not accept.[18] I also wrote a large book against the heresy of Pelagius at the urging of some brothers whom he had convinced of a destructive opinion opposed to the grace of Christ.[19] If you want to have all these, send someone to copy all of them for you. But allow me the free time to investigate and dictate the works that, since they are needed by many people, I think I should place before your questions, which concern very few.

---

17. That is, Letter 167, which was also called *The Opinion of James*.
18. That is, *To Orosius: An Answer to the Priscillianists and Origenists*.
19. That is, *Nature and Grace*.

Letter 170

Sometime after 415 Alypius and Augustine wrote to Maximus, a physician from Thaenae in Byzacena, to congratulate him on his recent conversion from the Arian heresy to the Catholic faith, though they are unhappy about those in Maximus' household who still remain Arians (paragraph 1). Augustine uses the text, *You shall adore the Lord your God and serve him alone* (Dt 6:13), to show how the Arians must either admit that the Father and the Son and the Holy Spirit are one God or not worship the Son and the Holy Spirit (paragraph 2). If, however, worship is owed to all three, then the Trinity is one God (paragraph 3). The Father did not create the Son out of nothing but generates him from his own substance; so too, the Holy Spirit proceeds from the Father and the Son and is not created by them (paragraph 4). The Trinity is not less in the individual persons than in all together and is not greater in all of them than in each person (paragraph 5). As a human being generates another human being of the same nature, so the Father generates the Son of the same nature. The two bishops distinguish names of natures from names of relations and reciprocal from non-reciprocal relations (paragraph 6). Terms that speak of the Son's generation from the Father indicate his origin, not his substance (paragraph 7). An Arian objection concerning the generation of the Son is shown to work against their position since, if God gives corruptible beings the ability to generate what they are, he himself certainly ought to be able to generate a Son of the same nature as he is (paragraph 8). Christ is said to be less than the Father on account of the form of the servant that he assumed, though he remains God along with the Father on account of the form of God that he did not lose (paragraph 9). Finally, Augustine urges Maximus to use his influence to bring his household into communion with the Catholic Church (paragraph 10).

To Maximus, our excellent and rightly honorable and pious brother, Augustine and Alypius send greetings in the Lord.

1. Since we asked from our holy brother and fellow bishop Peregrinus[1] not only about the bodily but especially about the spiritual well-being of you and your household, his replies, of course, made us happy about yours but sad about that of your household, because they have not yet been united to the Catholic Church by a conversion leading to salvation. And since we had hoped that this would soon take place, we are saddened that it has not yet occurred, my excellent and rightly honorable and pious brother.

2. Hence, greeting Your Charity in the peace of the Lord, we command and ask that you not put off teaching them what you have learned, namely, that there is only one God, to whom is owed the service that is called by the Greek term

---

1. Peregrinus was a deacon in the church of Hippo until the end of 415; he became bishop of Thaenae between then and 418. In 420 he and Alypius received Letter 22* from Augustine while they were on a mission to Italy. See Letter 171 to Peregrinus.

λατρεία. This very word is found in the law, where it says, *You shall adore the Lord your God, and you shall serve him alone* (Dt 6:13). If we say that he is God the Father alone, we shall receive the answer, "Therefore, we do not owe λατρεία to God the Son"—and that is wicked to say. But if we owe him λατρεία, how do we owe it to only one God, if we owe it to the Father and to the Son, unless the one God whom alone we are commanded to serve with λατρεία is said to be the only God in such a way that the Father and the Son and in fact the Holy Spirit as well are understood? Of him the apostle says, *Do you not know that your bodies are the temple of the Holy Spirit in you, whom you have from God, and you are not your own? For you have been purchased at a great price. Therefore, glorify*[2] *God in your body.* (1 Cor 6:19-20) Which God is this but the Holy Spirit, of whom he had said that our bodies are the temple? We owe λατρεία, then, to the Holy Spirit. For, if we were commanded to build a temple for him out of wood and stone, as Solomon did, we would certainly be shown to offer him λατρεία by building him a temple. How much more do we owe λατρεία to him for whom we do not build a temple but are a temple!

3. And for this reason, if we owe and offer λατρεία to the Father and to the Son and to the Holy Spirit—the λατρεία of which it is said, *You shall adore the Lord your God, and you shall serve him alone*— then the Lord our God whom alone we ought to serve with λατρεία is undoubtedly not the Father alone nor the Son alone nor the Holy Spirit alone but the Trinity, one God alone, the Father and the Son and the Holy Spirit. The Father is not the Son, nor is the Holy Spirit either the Father or the Son, since in that Trinity the Father is the Father only of the Son and the Son is the Son only of the Father, but the Holy Spirit is the Spirit of the Father and of the Son. But on account of their nature and inseparable life, which is one and the same, the Trinity is understood, as far as humanly possible, through faith which must come before understanding, to be the one Lord our God of whom scripture says, *You shall adore the Lord your God, and you shall serve him alone*, and of whom the apostle says in his preaching, *From him and through him and in him are all things; to him be glory forever and ever* (Rom 11:36).

4. For the only-begotten Son does not come from God the Father in the same way in which all creation, which he created from nothing, comes from him. For he begot the Son from his own substance; he did not make him out of nothing. Nor did he beget in time him through whom he created all times. For, just as a flame does not precede in time the brightness that it generates, so the Father never existed without the Son. For the Son is the wisdom of God the Father, of which scripture says, *For it is the brilliance of eternal light* (Wis 7:26). It is undoubtedly coeternal with the light whose brilliance it is, that is, with God the Father, and for this reason God did not make the Word in the beginning, as he made heaven and earth in the

---

2. From 401 on Augustine omits as an interpolation "and carry" *(et portate)* which is found in most Latin Fathers and the Vulgate.

beginning. Rather, *in the beginning was the Word* (Jn 1:1). The Holy Spirit also was not made out of nothing, like a creature, but proceeds from the Father and the Son[3] without being created either by the Father or by the Son.

5. This Trinity of one and the same nature and substance is not less in each person than in all, nor greater in all than in each person, but is as great in the Father alone or in the Son alone as in the Father and the Son together and as great in the Holy Spirit alone as in the Father and the Son and the Holy Spirit together. For, in order to have the Son begotten from himself, the Father did not make himself less, but he begot from himself an other than himself in such a way that he remained whole in himself and was as great in the Son as he was alone. Likewise, the whole Holy Spirit proceeding from another whole does not precede the principle from which he proceeds but is as great together with that other as he is when he comes from it, nor does the Holy Spirit diminish whence he comes when he proceeds from it or increase it when he is united to it. And these are all one without confusion; they are not three by division. Rather, though they are one, they are three, and though they are three, they are one. Hence, how much more does he who has granted to so many hearts of the faithful that they may be one heart[4] preserve in himself that these three are individually God and all together are not three gods but the one God whom we serve with all piety and to whom alone we owe that λατρεία.

6. Since in his goodness he arranges for beings born in time to give birth to offspring of their own substance, see how impious it is to say that he himself did not beget what he himself is, since by his gift a human being begets what he is, that is, a human being, not of another nature but of the same nature as he is, although he does not beget the father of his son, which is what he himself is. For these are names of a relationship, not of a nature, and for this reason names that are at times the same and at times different are used with respect to something else or to something related. The relations are, for example, the same when a brother is related to a brother, a friend to a friend, a neighbor to a neighbor, a relative to a relative, and so forth. It would be endless if we were to run through all of them. For in these this person is to that person the same thing that that person is to this person. But other relations are different, such as father to son, son to father, father-in-law to son-in-law, son-in-law to father-in-law, master to servant, and servant to master. The first person is not the same thing to the second as the second person is to the first, and yet they are both human beings. The relation is different, not the nature. For, if you pay attention to what the one is to the other, the first is not to the second what the second is to the first, because the first is the father, the second the son; or the first is the father-in-law, the second the

---

3. The expression *filioque* ("and the Son") is omitted in many manuscripts and in the CSEL edition.
4. See Acts 4:32.

son-in-law; or the first is the master, the second the servant. But if you pay attention to what each is in relation to himself or in himself, the first is the same as the second, because the second is a human being just like the first. Hence Your Wisdom understands from this that those from whose error the Lord has set you free do not have a good reason to say that the nature of God the Father and that of God the Son are different, because the first is the Father and the second the Son and that the Father did not beget what he himself is, because he did not beget the father of his son, which is what he is in relation to himself. For who would not see that these terms do not point to natures in themselves but signify one person in relation to another?

7. Such is also what they utter with a similar error, namely, that the Son is of another nature and of a different substance precisely because the Father is not God from another God, whereas the Son is God, to be sure, but from God the Father. Here too the expression indicates not the substance but the origin, that is, not what anyone is but from where he is or is not. For it is not true that Abel and Adam were not of one nature and substance because the first was a man from the other man while the second was from no man. If, then, there is a question about the nature of each of them, Abel is a man, and Adam is a man. But if there is a question about their origin, Abel came from the first man, but Adam came from no man. And so, if there is a question about the nature of each in the case of God the Father and God the Son, each is God, and the one is not more God than the other. But if there is a question about their origin, the Father is God from whom God the Son comes, but there is no God from whom God the Father comes.

8. And so, when they try to reply to this, they say in vain, "But a man generates with passion, while God has begotten his Son without passion." For this not only does not help them but in fact helps us very much. For, if God granted to temporal and corruptible things that they generate what they are, how much more has the one, eternal, and incorruptible Father generated what he himself is, namely, his only Son. And we are filled with great amazement because he has begotten him without any passion on his part and with such equality to him that he preceded him neither by power nor by age! But for this reason the Son attributes everything he has and can do not to himself but to the Father, because he does not come from himself but from the Father. For he is equal to the Father, but he received this too from the Father. Nor did he receive equality as if he were originally unequal; rather, he has been born equal. Just as he has always been born, so he has always been equal. The Father, therefore, did not beget someone unequal and give him equality once he was born, but by begetting him he gave him equality, because he begot an equal, not someone unequal. For this reason it was not robbery but natural to him to be equal to God in the form of God,[5] for he received equality by being born and he did not falsely claim it out of pride.

---

5. See Phil 2:6.

9. Hence he says that the Father is greater[6] because he *emptied himself, taking the form of a servant* (Phil 2:7) without losing the form of God. On account of this servant's form he became less not only than the Father but also than himself and the Holy Spirit, nor did he only become less than this most excellent Trinity but he also *became a little less than the angels* (Heb 2:9). He was less than human beings when he was subject to his parents.[7] On account of this servant's form, which he received when the fullness of time came, after emptying himself, he said, *The Father is greater than I* (Jn 14:28). But on account of the form of God that he did not lose, even when he emptied himself, he said, *The Father and I are one* (Jn 10:30). That is, he both became man and remained God. For the man was assumed by God, but God was not consumed in the man. Hence it is quite reasonable that as man Christ is less than the Father and that the same Christ, himself God, is equal to the Father.

10. Since, then, we rejoice with the great exultation of the people of God that you were united to this correct and Catholic faith in our presence, why are we still saddened over the sluggishness of your household? We beg you by the mercy of Christ that with his help you remove this sorrow from our hearts. For we ought not to believe that your authority could have had such power for leading your people astray and has no power for their correction. Or do they perhaps hold you in contempt because you came into union with the Catholic Church at this ripe age, though they ought to admire and respect you more because you have conquered your very old error by a certain youthfulness? Heaven forbid that they should oppose you when you speak the truth though they agreed with you when you wandered from the truth! Heaven forbid that they should refuse to hold the correct view with you with whom they were delighted to be in error! Only pray for them and insist with them; in fact, bring them with you into the house of God since they are with you in your house. Or feel shame or embarrassment at coming into the house of God without those who were accustomed to gather in your house, especially since our Catholic mother seeks some of them from you and seeks back others of them from you. It seeks those whom it finds in your company; it seeks back those whom it lost through you. Let her not be tormented by losses but, rather, happy with gains. Let her acquire children whom she did not have; let her not mourn those whom she did have. We pray to God that you do what we exhort you to do, and we hope in his mercy that, by the letter of our holy brother and fellow bishop, Peregrinus, and by the reply of Your Charity, our heart may be soon filled with joy and our tongue with exultation over this matter.[8]

---

6. See Jn 14:28.
7. See Lk 2:51.
8. See Ps 126:2.

Letter 171

Shortly after the previous letter, Alypius and Augustine wrote to Peregrinus, the bishop of Thaenae in Byzacena, where Maximus, the recipient of the previous letter, resided. They ask Peregrinus to find out whether their letter met with any success and ask him to tell Maximus that they are accustomed to write lengthy letters and to use paper even in writing to bishops and meant no offense to Maximus.

To Peregrinus, our most blessed lord and most dear and venerable brother and fellow bishop, Alypius and Augustine send greetings in the Lord.

We sent a letter to our honorable brother, Maximus, believing that he would gratefully receive it. At the next opportunity you can find, please write back to us whether we have met with any success. Let him know by all means that we are accustomed to write lengthy letters to our close friends, not only to lay persons, but also to bishops, just as this one was written, so that they may be written quickly and that the paper may be held more easily when they are read. I do not want him to think that we have done him an injury, since he perhaps does not know this custom of ours.

Letter 171 A

Most probably after the previous letter Augustine wrote to Maximus this letter, of which we have a fragment. Augustine describes the levels of the soul by which someone who desires purity of heart may ascend to the point of seeing with the mind the unity of the Trinity (paragraph 1) and he shows how the beatitudes and the cardinal and theological virtues form the steps by which one ascends to the vision of God (paragraph 2).

1. Begin with a fear of God, and try to conform your life and conduct to God's commandments, which we have received in order that we might act well, for *the fear of the Lord is the beginning of wisdom* (Ps 111:10 and Prv 1:7), where human pride is broken and crushed. Next with the mildness and meekness of piety, aim at not struggling in a spirit of stubbornness against the things that you do not understand and that seem to the uneducated absurd and contradictory in the holy scriptures, and at not superimposing your meaning upon the meanings of the divine books, but yield to them and meekly set aside your understanding rather than brazenly accusing their secrets. Third, when your human weakness begins to be disclosed to you for the sake of your self-knowledge and you know where you have fallen, how you drag along with yourself the penal bonds of mortality, since you were born of Adam, and how far you are wandering away from the Lord, and when you clearly see *another law in your members that resists the law of your mind and holds you captive under the law of sin that is in your members* (Rom 7:23), cry out, *Wretched man that I am! Who will set me free from the body of this death?* (Rom 7:24-25) in order that *the grace of God through Jesus Christ our Lord* (Rom 7:25) may console you in your mourning with the promise to set you free. Fourth, desire to bring about justice more intensely and more fervently than the wicked are accustomed to desire pleasures of the flesh, except that with the hope of God's help the ardor of this desire is peaceful and its flame more secure. But in this fourth stage of life prayers are constantly necessary so that those who hunger and thirst for justice may be satisfied in order that it may be not only not burdensome but even delightful to abstain from all of the pleasure that leads to the corruption either of oneself or of another, whether by struggling against it or by opposing it. In order that God may readily grant this, there is added the fifth beatitude, which gives the counsel to show mercy by helping the needy insofar as you can and by desiring that they may be helped by the Almighty insofar as you cannot. Now the task of mercy is twofold: when vengeance is foregone and when kindness is shown. The Lord briefly combined these two as follows, *Forgive and it will be forgiven you; give and it will be given to you* (Lk 6:37-38). But this work also contributes to the

purification of the heart in order that, as far as it is permitted in this life, we may be able to gaze upon the immutable substance of God with a pure intelligence. For something is held against us that must be loosened so that our sight may burst forth into the light; for this reason the Lord said, *But give alms, and see, all things are pure for you* (Lk 11:41). Hence there follows sixthly this purification of the heart.

2. But in order that a correct and pure gaze may be directed to the true light, neither those things that we do in a good and praiseworthy manner nor those that we cleverly and wisely contemplate are to be referred to the end of pleasing human beings or helping the needs of their bodies. For God wants to be worshiped gratuitously because there is nothing apart from him on account of which he is to be desired. When by the steps of a good life we have come, whether more slowly or more quickly, to this purity of understanding, then we may dare to say that by our minds we can touch to some extent the unity of the highest and ineffable Trinity, where there will be the highest peace, because there is nothing beyond to hope for. After all, when they have been reformed to the image of their origin and have been changed from human beings into children of God, they enjoy the immutability of the Father. For first, *Blessed are the poor in spirit* (Mt 5:3), where there is fear of God; then, *Blessed are the meek* (Mt 5:4), where there is docile piety; third, *Blessed are those who mourn* (Mt 5:5), where there is the knowledge of one's own weakness; fourth, *Blessed are those who hunger and thirst for righteousness* (Mt 5:6), where there is the courage to try to control one's desires; fifth, *Blessed are the merciful because God will be merciful to them* (Mt 5:7), where there is the counsel to help others so that you may merit to receive help. Then one comes to the sixth level at which it is said, *Blessed are the pure of heart because they will see God* (Mt 5:8), where we cannot preserve the pure intellect capable of understanding the Trinity in some small part if we seek human praise, though we do praiseworthy actions. Then at the seventh level we attain to the tranquility of that peace which the world cannot give. For if to those four virtues, which the philosophers were also able to investigate with remarkable industry, that is, to prudence, fortitude, temperance, and justice, we should also add and join for the perfect practice of religion these three, namely, faith, hope, and love, we of course find the number seven. For it is right that these three not be omitted, without which we know that no one can worship or please God.

Letter 172

In the beginning of 416 Jerome wrote to Augustine after having received Letters 166 and 167. He excuses himself for not having replied to Augustine's letters and tells him that he has spoken favorably about him in his recent work against the Pelagians (paragraph 1). He sends his greetings and the greetings of those with him to Augustine and the brothers with him (paragraph 2).

To Augustine, my truly holy lord and bishop, worthy of my veneration with deep affection, Jerome sends greetings in the Lord.

1. I welcomed the priest Orosius, an honorable man, my brother, and the son of Your Excellency, on his own merit and at your orders.[1] A most difficult time[2] has come upon us when it is better for me to be silent than to speak. As a result our studies have ceased for fear—to use the words of Appius—that our eloquence may be that of a dog.[3] And so I could not reply to the two books of yours that you dedicated to me,[4] books full of learning and resplendent with every sparkle of eloquence, not because I found anything blameworthy in them but because in the words of the blessed apostle, *Each person abounds in his own ideas* (Rom 14:5), *one in this way, another in that* (1 Cor 7:7). Certainly whatever could be said and drawn from the sources of the holy scriptures by your lofty mind you have stated and discussed. But I ask Your Reverence to allow me to praise your talent a little. For we converse among ourselves for the sake of gaining knowledge. But if enemies, and especially heretics, see differences of opinion between us, they will slander us by saying that they stem from rancor of the heart. Yet I have decided to love you, to cherish you, to honor you, to admire you, and to defend your statements like my own. To be sure, even in the dialogue that I recently published,[5] I was mindful, as was proper, of Your Beatitude. Let us make a greater effort to remove from the churches the very destructive heresy that constantly feigns repentance in order to have the possibility of teaching in the churches and of avoiding being expelled and dying outside, if it is seen in full daylight.

2. Your holy and venerable daughters, Eustochium and Paula,[6] are living lives worthy of their family and of your exhortation, and they specially greet

---

1. For Orosius, see Letter 166.
2. Not only was Pelagius acquitted by the Council of Diospolis in 415, but there was rioting around Jerome's monastery in Bethlehem, where several of the brethren were killed. See *The Deeds of Pelagius* 35, 66.
3. See Sallust, *History*, fragment 2, 37.
4. That is, Letters 166 and 167, also called *The Origin of the Soul* and *The Opinion of James*.
5. That is, *The Dialogue against the Pelagians* (*Dialogi adversus Pelagianos*).
6. Paula was a Roman widow who followed Jerome to Palestine, where she founded a monastery; Eustochium was her daughter, who succeeded her mother as superior of the monastery.

Your Beatitude, as does the whole brotherhood, which along with us tries to serve our Lord and savior. Last year we sent the holy priest Firmus to Ravenna and then to Africa and Sicily for the business of Eustochium and Paula, and we think that he is now staying in part of Africa. I ask that you greet with my respect the saints who remain at your side. I have also sent a letter to the priest Firmus. If it should come to you, do not delay to send it to him. May Christ the Lord keep you safe and mindful of me, my truly holy lord and most blessed bishop.

We suffer in this province a great poverty of copyists who use the Latin language, and for this reason we cannot obey your directives, particularly in the edition of the Septuagint that is marked with asterisks and slashes.[7] For we lost much of our earlier labor because of the deceit of a certain person.

---

7. See Letter 71, 2, 3, where Augustine describes Jerome's use of asterisks to indicate texts found in the Hebrew but missing in the Greek and of obelisks to indicate what is found in the Greek but not in the Hebrew.

Letter 173

Between 411 and 414 Augustine wrote to Donatus, a priest of the Donatist sect, who attempted to kill himself when it was ordered that he be arrested and brought to the Catholic Church. Augustine expresses concern for Donatus' well-being but points out that he injured himself (paragraph 1). He addresses Donatus' objection that no one should be forced to what is good (paragraph 2). Scripture provides many examples of people being forced to what is good (paragraph 3). Augustine argues that, if it was right to prevent Donatus from killing himself, it is right to prevent him from perishing eternally (paragraph 4). He deals with Donatus' interpretation of Paul's words about handing over his body to be burned and shows that Paul was not advocating suicide but stressing the importance of not separating oneself from the unity and love of the Church (paragraphs 5 and 6).

Donatus balked at the words accepted by the Donatist bishops at the Conference of Carthage, namely, that "one case is not prejudicial to another, nor one person to another." Augustine turns these words against Donatus himself (paragraph 7). He furthermore indicates how that statement shows that the Catholic Church is not made guilty, even if Caecilian had sinned (paragraph 8). He urges Donatus to read and study the acts of the conference (paragraph 9) and appeals to scripture to justify the use of force against the Donatists (paragraph 10).

To Donatus, a priest of the sect of Donatus, Augustine, a bishop of the Catholic Church, sends greetings.

1. If you could see the sorrow of my heart and my concern for your salvation, you would perhaps take pity on your soul, pleasing God[1] by hearing not our word but his, and you would not fix his scriptures in your memory so that you close your heart against them. You are unhappy because you are being dragged to salvation, though you have dragged so many of our people to destruction. For what do we want but that you be seized, brought here, and kept from perishing? But as for the injury you have suffered in the body, you did it to yourself, for you refused to use the mount that was immediately offered to you and you fell roughly to the ground. For the other man, your companion, who was brought along with you, arrived uninjured because he did not do such harm to himself.

2. But you do not think that even this ought to have been done to you, because you think that no one should be forced to what is good. Listen to what the apostle says, *He who desires the episcopacy desires a good work* (1 Tm 3:1), and yet so many are forced to accept the episcopacy against their will. They are led off,

---

1. See Sir 30:24.

imprisoned, kept under guard, and suffer so much that they do not want until they have the will to accept that good work. For how much better reason ought you to be dragged from the harmful error in which you are enemies to yourselves and brought to know or to choose the truth, not only in order that you may keep your ecclesiastical dignity in a manner conducive to your salvation but in order that you may not perish in the worst manner! You say that God gave us free choice and that, for this reason, a human being ought not to be forced even to what is good. Why, then, are those whom I mentioned above forced to something good? Listen, therefore, to what you do not consider. God mercifully brings to bear his good will precisely in order to direct the bad will of a human being. For who does not know that a human being is only condemned by the merit of a bad will and is only set free if he has a good will? Yet those whom we love are not for that reason to be left cruelly and with impunity to their bad will but, where we have the power, should be kept from evil and forced to what is good.

3. For, if a bad will should always be left to its freedom, why were the Israelites kept from evil by such severe scourges, when they murmured in rebellion, and were forced toward the land of the promise?[2] If a bad will should always be left to its freedom, why was Paul not permitted to use the wicked will by which he was persecuting the Church but was struck down so that he was blinded, blinded so that he was changed, changed so that he was sent, and sent so that he suffered on behalf of the truth the sort of evils he was committing in his error?[3] If a bad will should always be left to its freedom, why is a father warned in the scriptures not only to rebuke a stubborn child but to beat his back, so that, once he has been forced and subdued into good discipline, he might take direction?[4] For this reason the same author says, *You indeed strike him with a rod, but you set his soul free from death* (Prv 23:14). If a bad will should always be left to its freedom, why are the negligent shepherds rebuked, and why is it said to them, *You have not called back the wandering sheep; you have not searched for the one that was lost* (Ez 34:4)? And you are Christ's sheep; you bear the Lord's mark in the sacrament you have received, but you were wandering off and were lost. Do not be displeased with us because we call you back when you wander off and search for you when you are lost. For it is better that we do the will of the Lord who warns us to call you back to the fold than that we yield to the will of the wandering sheep and allow you to be lost. Do not, then, say what I constantly hear you say, "So I want to wander off; so I want to be lost." For it is better that, as far as we are able, we do not permit this at all.

---

2. See Ex 15:22-24.
3. See Acts 9:1-9.
4. See Sir 30:12.

4. Now the fact that you threw yourself into a well in order to die—this you certainly did with free will. But how cruel the servants of God would be if they abandoned you to this bad will of yours and did not set you free from that death! Who would not rightly blame them? Who would not rightly judge them to be wicked? And yet you willingly threw yourself into the water in order to die; they raised you up out of the water against your will in order that you might not die. You acted according to your will but to your own destruction; they acted against your will but for your well-being. If, then, this bodily well-being should be protected so that those who love them preserve it even in those who do not want this, for how much better reason is that spiritual well-being protected since, once it has been lost, eternal death is to be feared! And yet in the death that you wanted to inflict upon yourself, you would die not only in time but also for eternity. For, even if you were being forced not to salvation, not to the peace of the Church, not to the unity of Christ's body, not to a holy and undivided love but to some evils, you ought not thus to have inflicted death upon yourself.

5. Consider the divine scriptures and examine them to the extent you can, and see whether any of the righteous and faithful have ever done this when they suffered great evils from those who were driving them to eternal death, not to the eternal life to which you are being forced. I have heard that you said that the apostle Paul indicated that one ought to do this when he said, *Even if I hand over my body to be burned* (1 Cor 13:3). That is, because he said that without love he would have no profit from all such good things as the languages of men and angels, all the sacraments, all knowledge and all prophecy, all the faith to move mountains, and the distribution of one's possessions to the poor,[5] you thought that he also counted it among such goods that anyone might inflict death upon himself. But pay close attention and recognize in what way scripture says that a person should hand over his body to be burned. It is certainly not that anyone should cast his body into the fire when he is suffering persecution from an enemy, but when he is presented with the choice of either doing something evil or suffering something evil he should choose not to do evil rather than not to suffer evil. And thus he should hand his body over to the power of an executioner, just as those three men did who were being forced to adore the golden statue and, if they did not do so, the one who was forcing them threatened them with the furnace blazing with fire. They refused to adore the idol; they did not cast themselves into the fire.[6] And yet scripture also said of them that *they handed over their bodies so that they would not serve or adore any god but their God* (Dn 3:95). See in what sense the apostle said, *If I hand over my body to burn.*

6. But see what follows: *If I do not have love, it profits me nothing* (1 Cor 13:3). You are being called to this love; you are not being allowed to perish apart

---

5. See 1 Cor 13:1-3.
6. See Dn 3:13-21.

from this love, and you suppose that it profits you in some way to hurl yourself down to destruction, though it would have profited you nothing even if another person killed you, you who are enemy of love! But, placed outside the Church and separated from the structure of unity and the bond of love, you will suffer eternal punishment even if you are burned alive for the name of Christ. For this is what the apostle says, *Even if I hand over my body to burn, but do not have love, it profits me nothing* (1 Cor 13:3). Call your mind back to this sound consideration and sober thought; pay careful attention as to whether you are called to error and impiety and are suffering certain difficulties on account of the truth. If, however, you are living in error or impiety instead, while truth and piety are found in the place to which you are being called, because Christian unity and the love of the Holy Spirit are present there, why are you still trying to be your own enemy?

7. The mercy of God allowed both us and your bishops to come to Carthage in a very well-attended and large assembly and to discuss among ourselves in a most orderly fashion the disagreement between us.[7] The acts were written down; our signatures were also obtained. Read them, or allow them to be read to you, and then choose what you will. I have heard that you said that you could to some extent discuss with us the acts if we would omit the words of your bishops where they said, "One case is not prejudicial to another, nor one person to another." You want us to omit the words where the truth itself spoke through your bishops, though they did not know it. But you are going to say that they were mistaken on this point and carelessly fell into an erroneous view. We, however, say that they spoke the truth here, and we quite easily prove this by means of you yourself. For, if your bishops were chosen by the whole sect of Donatus to represent the case of all of them, and if the rest found agreeable and acceptable what they had done, and if you still do not want those bishops to be prejudicial to you on the point on which you think that they spoke rashly and incorrectly, then they spoke the truth, because "one case is not prejudicial to another, nor one person to another." And you ought to acknowledge there that, if you do not want the person of so many of your bishops represented by those seven to be prejudicial to the person of Donatus, a priest of Mutugenna,[8] how much less ought the person of Caecilian[9] to be prejudicial to the whole unity of Christ, which is not contained in the one village of Mutugenna but is spread out over the whole world, even if some evil were found in him.

8. See, we are doing what you wanted; we are dealing with you just as if your bishops had not said, "One case is not prejudicial to another, nor one person to

---

7. The Conference of Carthage was held in the beginning of June 411.
8. That is, the Donatus to whom this letter is addressed; Mutugenna was a town just west of Hippo in Numidia.
9. Caecilian was the bishop of Carthage who the Donatists claimed was ordained by a bishop who had surrendered the sacred books during the persecution under the emperor Decius.

another." Find what they ought to have said when the case and person of Primian[10] was raised as an objection for them. He condemned along with the rest those who condemned him, and those whom he condemned and detested he accepted back into their positions of honor. He preferred to acknowledge and accept the baptism that the dead had conferred — for it was said of them in that famous statement that the shores are full of the corpses of the dead[11]— than to subject that baptism to the rite of exsufflation and rescind it, and he annulled the whole statement that you are accustomed to make, although you misunderstand it: *One who is baptized by someone dead, what does his bath profit him?* (Sir 34:30)[12] If, therefore, they did not say, "One case is not prejudicial to another, nor one person to another," they would be held guilty in the case of Primian. But when they said this, they declared the Catholic Church innocent in the case of Caecilian.

9. But read the rest; examine the rest. See whether they were able to prove anything sinful against Caecilian, by whose person they were trying to condemn the Church. See whether they did not rather do many things in his defense and whether, by the many documents that they brought forth and read out against him, they did not simply strengthen the good case he had. Read these documents, or have them read to you. Consider all of them, examine them carefully, and choose which path you should follow: whether to rejoice with us in the peace of Christ, in the unity of the Catholic Church and in fraternal love, or to endure for a longer time the relentlessness of our love for you for the sake of your criminal dissent, the sect of Donatus, this sacrilegious division.

10. For you notice and often repeat, as I hear, what is written in the gospel, namely, that the seventy disciples abandoned the Lord and were left to the choice of their evil and impious dissent, but that it was said to the other twelve who remained, *Do you also want to go away?* (Jn 6:68) And you do not notice that the Church was then first beginning to grow with new seedlings and that there had not yet been fulfilled in it the prophecy, *And all the kings of the earth will adore him; all nations will serve him* (Ps 72:11). And to the extent that it is fulfilled the more, the Church uses greater power not only to invite but even to compel people to what is good. At that time the Lord wanted to indicate this, for, though he had great power, yet he first chose to teach humility. He also showed this quite clearly in that parable of the banquet where he sent word to those who

---

10. Primian was the Donatist bishop of Carthage at the time when the Maximianists split away from the Donatists. Despite having condemned the Maximianists, the Donatists accepted them back without rebaptizing those whom the Maximianists had baptized in their schism.

11. See Augustine, *Answer to Gaudentius, a Donatist Bishop* 1, 54. The line is from the Donatist Council of Bagai in April 394 in which the Maximianists were excommunicated.

12. The Vulgate adds, "and again touches a dead body," which is not found in the manuscripts and is omitted by the Donatists. Hence, the first part means: "One who washes after touching a dead body."

were invited and they refused to come. He said to his servant, *Go out into the squares and streets of the city, and bring here the poor, the weak, the blind, and the lame. And the servant said to his master, It has been done as you commanded, and there is still room. And the master said to his servant, Go out into the roads and pathways, and compel them to enter in order that my house may be full.* (Lk 14:21-23) See now how it was said of those who came earlier, *Bring them here*; it was not said, *Compel them.* In that way he indicated the beginnings of the Church that was growing to the point that it might also have the strength to compel. Then, after its strength and greatness were already built up, since it was necessary that human beings be compelled to enter the banquet of eternal salvation, after it was said, *What you commanded has been done, and there is still room,* he said, *Go out into the roads and pathways and compel them to enter.* Hence, if you were living quietly outside this banquet of holy unity, we would find you on the roads, as it were. But now, because on account of the many evil and savage acts that you commit against our people, you are, so to speak, full of thorns and thistles, we find you as if in the pathways and compel you to enter. One who is compelled is forced to go where he does not want to go, but after he has entered he eats willingly. Hold in check your wicked and wild heart, then, in order that you may find in the true Church of Christ the banquet of salvation.

Letter 173 A

In 416 or later Augustine wrote to Deogratias and Theodore, priests, and Titian and Comes, deacons, all of the church of Carthage, to reply to their request for a proof that the Holy Spirit is God. In his hurried reply he uses two scriptural texts to show that, if we are temples of the Holy Spirit, the Holy Spirit must be along with the Father and the Son the one God to whom we owe the service of latria. Augustine adds that, if this short answer is not enough, his correspondence ought to wait for his books on the Trinity, which he is arranging to publish.

To Deogratias and Theodore, his most beloved lords, holy brothers, and fellow priests, and to Titian and Brother Comes, fellow deacons, Augustine sends greetings.

Though it was not by your letter yet it was by a most reliable and faithful messenger that I learned of your desire that I write to you about where the Holy Spirit is proved to be God without any doubt and without any of the obscurity that slower minds cannot penetrate. Let Your Fraternity, then, know, to the extent that I can recall the holy scriptures on this point, that, if the words of the apostle, *Do you not know that your bodies are the temple in your midst of the Holy Spirit whom you have from God and that you are not your own? For you have been purchased at a great price. Glorify and carry God in your body* (1 Cor 6:19-20), are not enough for someone, I certainly do not know how he can be persuaded that the Holy Spirit is God by the authority of the divine scriptures. But by the reasoning that a human being, or such human beings as we are, can enter upon, this issue is debated with great labor. But let whoever yields to the most excellent authority of the divine scriptures first look at the words of scripture, *You shall adore the Lord your God, and you shall serve him alone* (Dt 6:13). This is expressed in Greek in such a way that we should not understand the service that we owe to human lords but the service that we should offer to God alone. This service is called latria, and for this reason idolatry is rightly condemned when the latria that should be offered only to the true God is offered to idols. But scripture does not say, "You shall adore the Lord your God alone." It says, *And you shall serve him alone.* It says, "alone," where it says, "You shall serve," that is, with that service that is called latria. To this service there belongs the temple, sacrifice, priest, and everything else of this sort. And for this reason the apostle would by no means say that our body is the temple of the Holy Spirit if we did not owe him that service that is called latria. But we would not owe him such service if he were not God, to whom it is owed, especially because he says that our bodies are members of Christ. For even those who deny that the Holy Spirit is God and maintain that Christ is greater than the Holy Spirit do not deny that Christ is God.[1] How, then, can the members of the greater be the temple of the lesser? Hence, the Holy Spirit is undoubtedly understood to be God not only because a temple can piously and correctly be built only for God but also because he is found to be one God along with the Father and the Son, for the Trinity is one God. Since the assignment of a temple pertains to that service that is called latria, and since scripture says, *You shall adore the Lord your God, and you shall serve him alone,* that is, you shall offer latria to him alone, precisely because, when latria is offered correctly, it is offered to God, and because latria is offered to one for whom a temple is built, and because there is only one God to whom latria is offered, the Father, Son, and Holy Spirit is undoubtedly one God. And this is why it said, *Glorify and carry God in your body,* of him of whom it had said, *Your bodies are the temple in your midst of the Holy Spirit whom you have from God.*

I preferred to dictate this as quickly as I could rather than put off the desire of Your Charity with some excuse. If you think this is too little, wait to read the books concerning the Trinity, which I now plan to publish in the name of the Lord. Perhaps they will persuade you of what this short letter cannot.

---

1. Augustine refers to the Macedonians, who denied the divinity of the Holy Spirit. See *Heresies* 52.

Letter 174

Augustine wrote Letter 174 to Aurelius, the bishop of Carthage and primate of Africa, when he sent him the books of *The Trinity,* which Augustine had finally completed in accord with the desire of Aurelius and others. Since the date of the completion of *The Trinity* is not known, the letter cannot be dated with any certitude, though it was most probably written after 420.

Augustine tells Aurelius that the theft of a number of the books by some of the brothers, who could not wait until Augustine had revised them and was ready to publish them, has prevented him from carrying out his original plan. But at the insistence of Aurelius and others he has agreed to finish off the work with the final books, making them fit as best he could with the earlier ones that had been stolen. He gives Aurelius permission to read and copy the books but asks that this letter be added at the beginning.

To Bishop Aurelius, our most blessed lord, holy brother and fellow priest, who deserves to be venerated with most sincere love, Augustine sends greetings in the Lord.

I began the books on the Trinity, which is the sovereign and true God, as a young man but published them as an old man.[1] I had, of course, put aside this work after I discovered that books were taken or stolen from me before I had completed them and before I had polished them after having checked them, as my intention had been. For that reason I had decided to publish them not individually but all at once, since the following ones are connected to the earlier ones in accordance with the progress of my investigation. Since, therefore, my plan could not be carried out on account of those men—because they were able to have in hand some of those books before I wanted—I left the dictation interrupted, thinking that I would complain about this fact in some of my writings so that those who could would know that those books were not published by me but taken from me before I thought they were fit for publication. But, compelled by the strongest requests of many brothers and especially by your command, I took care to complete, with the help of the Lord, this very laborious work, and I sent to Your Reverence by our son, the deacon Cresimus,[2] the same books that I had corrected, not as I wished but as I was able to do, so that they did not disagree very much with those copies that were taken from me and had already come into the hands of some people. And I gave permission that they be heard, copied, and

---

1. Augustine may have begun *The Trinity* as early as 399 or 400; he most likely finished it after 420.
2. The CSEL edition has *carissimum* ("most dear"), but following the conjecture of Dom De Bruyne I have read the proper name Cresimus.

read by anyone. If I had been able to carry out my plan in them, the books would have been less complicated and clearer as much as the difficulty in explaining such important topics and our ability would have permitted, though they would have contained the same ideas. There are, however, some who have the first four, or rather five, books without their introductions and the twelfth book without the last part, which is not a small one.[3] But if they can become familiar with this edition, they will correct everything if they want to and are able. I ask, however, that this letter be placed at the beginning of the same books, though set apart. Good-bye. Pray for me.

---

3. Hence it would seem that the monks had stolen books one through eleven as well as part of twelve.

Letter 175

In 416 the participants in the Council of Carthage wrote to Innocent, the bishop of Rome from 401 to 417, concerning the errors of Pelagius and Caelestius. The bishops explain their decision to condemn the teachings of Pelagius and Caelestius on account of the danger to the salvation of many that their teaching threatens (paragraph 1). The bishops ask that the Apostolic See add its authority to their condemnation, and they begin to point out the basic errors of the new heresy (paragraph 2). Even if the pope believes that Pelagius was acquitted in Diospolis, he should condemn the errors Pelagius taught (paragraph 3). Pelagius' teaching stands in opposition even to the prayers of priests for their people (paragraph 4) and contradicts the need for baptism on the part of infants. Hence, even if Pelagius and Caelestius have themselves been corrected, their teaching must be condemned (paragraph 5).

To Innocent, our most blessed and honorable lord and holy brother, Aurelius, Numidius, Rustician, Fidentius, Evagrius, Antonius, Palatinus, Adeodatus, Vincent, Publian, Theasius, Tutus, Pannonius, Victor, Restitutus, a second Restitutus, Rusticus, Fortunatian, Ampelius, Felix, Donatian, Adeodatus, Octavius, Serotinus, Maiorin, Posthumian, Crispulus, Victor, a second Victor, Leucius, Marianus, Fructuosus, Faustinian, Quodvultdeus, Candonius, Maximus, Megarius, Rusticus, Rufinian, Proculus, Thomas, Januarius, Octavian, Praetextatus, Sixtus, Quodvultdeus, Pentadius, Quodvultdeus, Cyprian, Servilius, Pelagius, Marcellus, Venantius, Didymus, Saturninus, Bazacenus, Germanus, Germanian, Juvantius, Majorinus, Juventius, Candidus, Cyprian, Aemilian, Romanus, Africanus and Marcellinus, who were present in the council of the church of Carthage.

1. After we had gathered as usual in solemn assembly at the church of Carthage and were holding the synod that had been convoked for various reasons, our fellow priest Orosius[1] gave us letters from our holy brothers and fellow priests, Hero and Lazarus,[2] a copy of which we decided should be added to this. Having read them, we denounced Pelagius and Caelestius[3] as the authors

---

1. For Orosius, see Letter 166, 1, 2, as well as Letter 172, 1.
2. Hero was bishop of Arles and Lazarus bishop of Aix-en-Provence. Both had been deposed from their sees; neither was able to be present at the Council of Diospolis in December of 415 because of the illness of one of them, though they were at the Council of Jerusalem in the summer of 415. See *The Deeds of Pelagius* 1, 2; 16, 39; 35, 62.
3. Pelagius was a monk of British origin who gathered about him a circle of Christian ascetics in Rome. After the fall of Rome he and his disciple Caelestius came to Africa. Caelestius was condemned by a Council of Carthage in 411 and then moved to the East. Pelagius moved to the East even earlier; he was tried at episcopal councils in Jerusalem and in Diospolis. See *The Deeds of Pelagius* for Augustine's account of the Council of Diospolis. See *The Perfection of Human Righteousness* for Augustine's refutation of Caelestius' teaching.

of a truly wicked error and one to be condemned by all of us. For this reason it came about that we asked that the action we took with regard to Caelestius almost five years ago here at Carthage be reread.[4] After it had been read out, as Your Holiness can see from what has been appended, it was agreed that the judgment was unequivocal by which the assembled bishops thought that the pronouncement of the bishops at that time had excised this great wound from the Church. Nevertheless, we judged in our common deliberation that, even if the same Caelestius is said to have afterward attained the priesthood, we ought to anathematize the authors of an opinion of this sort, unless they themselves most clearly anathematized these things.Thus, in order that, once the sentence pronounced against them is made known, we may procure the salvation if not of those men themselves, then at least of those who have been deceived or could be deceived by them.

2. Hence we believed, our lord and brother, that we should inform Your Charity of this action so that the authority of the Apostolic See might be added to the decrees of our humble selves in order to defend the salvation of many and to correct the perversity of some. For by their damnable arguments these heretics strive, not by defending free choice but rather by extolling it in sacrilegious pride, to leave no room for the grace of God by which we are Christians—the grace by which the very choice of our will becomes truly free when it is set free from the dominion of carnal desires. For the Lord says, *If the Son sets you free, then you will be truly free* (Jn 8:36). Faith in Jesus Christ our Lord obtains this help. But these heretics claim, as we have learned from some brothers who have also read their books, that the grace of God should be regarded as the way in which God established and created the nature of man such that it can by its own will fulfill the law of God, whether it be the law written by nature in the heart or the law given in writing. They hold that this same law also pertains to the grace of God because God gave it to human beings as a help.[5]

3. They do not want to acknowledge that grace by which, as was said, we are Christians. The apostle preached that grace when he said, *For I take delight in the law of God in terms of my inner self, but I see another law in my members that resists the law of my mind and that holds me captive under the law of sin that is in my members. Wretched man that I am! Who will set me free from the body of this death? The grace of God through Jesus Christ our Lord.* (Rom 7:22-25) But they do not dare to attack it openly. But what else are they doing when they do not cease from persuading natural human beings, who do not perceive what pertains to the Spirit of God,[6] that human nature alone can suffice of itself to

---

4. See *The Deeds of Pelagius* 11, 23, for the propositions of Caelestius that were condemned at the Council of Carthage in 411.
5. See Is 8:20 LXX.
6. See 1 Cor 2:14.

carry out righteousness and to bring it to perfection and to fulfill the command-ments of God? They do not heed what scripture says: *The Spirit helps our weak-ness* (Rom 8:26), and, *It does not depend on the one who wills or on the one who runs, but on God who shows mercy* (Rom 9:16), and, *We are one body in Christ, each members of one another, having different gifts in accord with the grace that has been given to us* (Rom 12:5.6), and, *By the grace of God I am what I am, and his grace has not been without effect in me, but I have labored more abundantly than all the others—not I, however, but the grace of God with me* (1 Cor 15:10), and, *Thanks be to God who has given us victory through our Lord Jesus Christ* (1 Cor 15:57), and, *Not that we are sufficient to have a single thought by ourselves, but our sufficiency comes from God* (2 Cor 3:5), and, *We have this treasure in earthen vessels in order that the excellence of virtue may be God's and not come from us* (2 Cor 4:7), and countless other such passages. If we wanted to gather all of them from the scriptures, a volume would not be enough. And we fear lest, by mentioning to you these passages that you proclaim from the Apostolic See with greater grace, we seem to act inappropriately, but we do so because, insofar as we are weaker, each of us suffers these heretics attacking us on every side and ever more audaciously.

4. If, therefore, Your Reverence thinks that Pelagius was justly acquitted by the episcopal proceedings that are said to have been carried out in the East, the error itself and the impiety that has so many defenders scattered in various places must also be anathematized by the Apostolic See. For Your Holiness should consider and feel along with us with your pastor's heart how pestilential and deadly for the sheep of Christ is what necessarily follows from the sacrilegious arguments of these men, namely, that we should not pray in order that we may not enter into temptation, about which the Lord warned even his disciples[7] and put into the prayer that he taught,[8] or that we ought not to pray that our faith may not fail, something for which he himself testifies that he prayed on behalf of the apostle Peter.[9] For, if these are placed in our power by the possibility of nature and the choice of the will, who does not see that we ask for them from the Lord to no purpose and that our prayer is a lie when in prayer we ask for those things that we obtain by the sufficient powers of our nature as it was created? Who does not see that the Lord Jesus should not have said, *Watch and pray*, but only, *Watch in order that you may not enter into temptation* (Mt 26:41)? Who does not see that he should not have said to the most blessed Peter, the first of the apostles, *I have prayed for you*, but I warn you or I command or order you, *that your faith may not fail* (Lk 22:32)?

---

7. See Mt 26:41.
8. See Mt 6:13.
9. See Lk 22:32.

5. Their claims are also opposed to our blessings, so that we seem to say in vain over the people whatever we ask for them from the Lord in order that, by living rightly and piously, they may be pleasing to him. And those prayers that the apostle prayed on behalf of the faithful are vain, when he said, *I bend my knees before the Father of our Lord Jesus Christ, from whom all fatherhood in the heavens and on earth takes its name, that he may grant you to be strengthened in virtue through his Spirit in accord with the riches of his glory* (Eph 3:14-16). If, then, we want to say in blessing over the people, "Grant them, Lord, to be strengthened in virtue through your Spirit," the argument of Pelagius and Caelestius speaks against us, when it claims that we deny free choice if we ask God for what lies in our own power. They say, "For, if we want to be strengthened in virtue, we can be such by the ability of nature that we do not receive now, but that we did receive when we were created."

6. They also deny that infants must be baptized for the sake of the salvation that is given through Christ the savior, and thus they slay them for eternity by this deadly doctrine when they promise that, even if they are not baptized, they will have eternal life and that the words of the Lord, *For the Son of Man came to seek and to save what was lost* (Lk 19:10), do not pertain to them. For they say, "These were not lost, nor is there anything in them that is saved or redeemed at so great a price, because nothing in them is damaged, nothing is held captive under the power of the devil, nor was the blood that we read was shed for the forgiveness of sins[10] shed for them." Although in his little book Caelestius confessed in the church of Carthage that the redemption of infants is also effected by Christ's baptism, many who are reported to be or to have been his disciples do not cease to defend these evil ideas, by which they try to overthrow, however they can, the foundations of the Christian faith. Hence, even if Pelagius and Caelestius have been corrected or say that they never held these views and deny that any writings brought forth against them are theirs, and even if there is no way of proving them guilty of lying, nonetheless, whoever teaches and maintains that human nature can suffice by itself for avoiding sins and observing the commandments of God and is, in that way, shown to be opposed to the grace of God that is expressed quite clearly in the prayers of the saints must without exception be anathematized, and anyone who denies that by the baptism of Christ infants are set free from perdition and receive eternal salvation must be anathematized. But, with regard to whatever further objections are raised against him, we have no doubt that, once Your Reverence has seen the episcopal proceedings that are reported to have been held in the East, Your Reverence will pronounce that judgment over which all of us may rejoice in the mercy of God. Pray for us, most blessed lord and pope.

---

10. See Mt 26:28.

Letter 176

In 416 the participants in the Council of Milevis also wrote to Pope Innocent to warn him of the grave dangers posed by the heresy of Pelagius. The bishops tell Innocent that it would be negligent on their part not to inform him of the dangers posed for the Church by the Pelagian heresy (paragraph 1). These heretics, they claim, deprive Christians of the Lord's Prayer by their emphasis on the sufficiency of unaided free choice (paragraph 2). The bishops point out two principal errors by which these heretics undermine the faith of the Church. First, they deny that we should ask God's help to fight sin and to act righteously, and secondly they deny that baptism offers any help to infants for attaining eternal life (paragraph 3). They inform Innocent that the instigators of this new heresy are Pelagius and Caelestius, whose salvation they desire (paragraph 4). Finally, they ask Innocent to correct these errors by the authority of the Apostolic See (paragraph 5).

To Pope Innocent, our most blessed and rightly venerable lord worthy of honor in Christ, Silvanus the Primate, Valentine, Aurelius, Donatus, Restitutus, Lucian, Alypius, Augustine, Placentius, Severus, Fortunatus, Possidius, Novatus, Secundus, Maurentius, Leo, Faustinian, Cresconius, Malcus, Litorius, Fortunatus, Donatus, Pontician, Saturninus, Cresconius, Honorius, Cresconius, Lucius, Adeodatus, Processus, Secundus, Felix, Asiaticus, Rufinus, Faustinus, Servus, Terence, Cresconius, Sperantius, Quadratus, Lucillus, Sabinus, Faustinus, Cresconius, Victor, Gignantius, Possidonius, Antoninus, Innocent, Felix, Antoninus, Victor, Honoratus, Donatus, Peter, Praesidius, Cresconius, Lampadius, Delphinus, from the Council of Milevis, send greetings in the Lord.

1. Because by a special gift of his grace the Lord has placed you in the Apostolic See and has offered to our times such a man that, if we passed over in silence before Your Reverence what recommendations we thought should be made on behalf of the Church, we would count it as a sin of negligence on our part rather than suppose that you could receive them with annoyance or indifference. We ask that you be so good as to apply your pastoral care to the great dangers of the weaker members of Christ.

2. A new and very dangerous heresy on the part of the enemies of the grace of Christ is attempting to rise up. By their impious arguments these people try to deprive us even of the Lord's Prayer. For, though the Lord taught us to say, *Forgive us our debts as we also forgive our debtors* (Mt 6:12), they say that in this life a human being can, once the commandments are known, come to so great a perfection of righteousness by free choice of the will alone, without the help of the grace of the savior, that it is not necessary for them to say, *Forgive us*

our debts. They claim that we should not interpret the words that follow, *Bring us not into temptation* (Mt 6:13), in the sense that we ought to ask God's help so that we may not fall into sin when we are tempted, but that this has been placed in our power and that the human will alone suffices to carry this out. They say this as if the apostle said in vain, *It does not depend on the one who wills or the one who runs, but on God who shows mercy* (Rom 9:16), and, *God is faithful who will not permit you to be tempted beyond your ability, but will give you along with the temptation a way out so that you can endure it* (1 Cor 10:13). In vain would the Lord have said to Peter, *I have prayed for you that your faith might not fail* (Lk 22:32), and to all his disciples, *Watch and pray that you may not enter into temptation* (Mt 26:41), if all this lay within human power. They contend with wicked presumption that little children, even if they are not renewed by any sacraments of Christian grace, will have eternal life. Thus they empty of meaning the words of the apostle, *Through one man sin entered the world, and through sin death, and in that way it was passed on to all human beings, in whom all have sinned* (Rom 5:12), and his words in another place, *Just as all die in Adam, so all are also brought to life in Christ* (1 Cor 15:22).

3. To omit, therefore, the many other things that they utter against the holy scriptures, we for the present single out the two points by which they strive completely to overthrow the whole Christian faith and which are the support of faithful hearts. They say that we should not ask God to be our helper to resist the evil of sin and to act with righteousness, and they say that the sacrament of Christian grace does not help infants to attain eternal life. In reporting these errors to your apostolic heart, we have no need to say much and to exaggerate so great an impiety by words, since they undoubtedly disturb you so that you cannot at all turn a blind eye to them and hold back from correcting them for fear that they may spread more widely and infect many or, rather, slay many in completely separating them from the grace of Christ in the name of Christ.

4. The authors of this most destructive heresy are said to be Pelagius and Caelestius, whom we of course prefer to be healed in the Church rather than to be cut off from the Church with no hope of salvation, if no necessity demands this. One of these, that is, Caelestius, is also said to have entered the priesthood in Asia; Your Holiness is better instructed by the church of Carthage about the proceedings against him a few years ago. But, as letters sent by certain of our brothers report, Pelagius is said to have taken up residence in Jerusalem and to be leading some people astray. Yet many more, who were able to investigate more carefully what he meant, fight against him on behalf of the grace of Christ and the truth of the Catholic faith, but especially your holy son and our brother and fellow priest, Jerome.

5. But we think that with the help of the mercy of the Lord our God, who deigns to guide you when you consult him and to hear you when you pray to him, those who hold such perverse and destructive ideas will more easily yield to the

authority of Your Holiness, which is derived from the authority of the holy scriptures, so that we may rejoice over their correction rather than be saddened by their destruction. But, whichever they choose, Your Reverence sees that you must firmly and quickly look after at least the many others whom they can trap in their snares if you turn a blind eye to them. We have sent this letter to Your Holiness from the council of Numidia, imitating the church of Carthage and our fellow bishops of the Province of Carthage, for we have discovered that they wrote concerning this matter to the Apostolic See, which you blessedly enlighten. [*And in another hand:*] Be mindful of us, and grow in the grace of God, our most blessedly and deservedly venerable lord and holy father worthy of honor in Christ.

Letter 177

In 416, Aurelius, the bishop of Carthage and the primate of Africa, Alypius of Thagaste, Augustine of Hippo, Evodius of Uzalis, and Possidius of Calama, wrote to Pope Innocent. The bishops tell Innocent that the people of God need his help in opposing the Pelagian heresy (paragraph 1). When Pelagius speaks of grace, he means the grace by which we were created with our own will, not the grace by which we are justified and saved (paragraph 2). Innocent should summon Pelagius to Rome for questioning, or at least handle this matter by letter, in order to determine what he means by grace (paragraph 3). If by grace Pelagius means free choice, the forgiveness of sins, or the commandment of the law, he still needs to admit the grace by which we are helped to overcome temptation and not to commit sin (paragraph 4). The bishops contrast the roles of the law and of grace (paragraph 5), and they mention that they have sent to Innocent Pelagius' *Nature* and Augustine's *Nature and Grace*, which was written as a reply to it (paragraph 6). If Pelagius denies that the book is his, he should condemn its content, since it makes grace to be what we received in being created (paragraph 7). The bishops quote from the apostle to show the genuine meaning of grace (paragraph 8). In his book Pelagius made grace to consist in the capability of the will that is received in creation (paragraph 9). The bishops argue that, if grace is the commandment of God, the promise of righteousness, or the capability of nature, Christ has died in vain (paragraph 10). Hence righteousness does not come from the law or through the capability of nature but from faith and the gift of God through Jesus Christ (paragraph 11). Though faith in Christ was hidden during the time of the patriarchs and was revealed in the New Testament, the patriarchs were saved by the same faith in Christ as we are (paragraph 12). The law made sin known, and sin was increased by transgression of the law so that we would have recourse to grace (paragraph 13). Like the Jews of old, the Pelagians think that they can attain righteousness through observing the law by their own free choice (paragraph 14). Pelagius must condemn his writings or, if he denies that they are his, he must condemn their contents for the sake of those who follow him (paragraph 15). The claim that some people can live without sin once they have been baptized is somewhat tolerable, but the question needs further examination (paragraph 16). The bishops explain the passage that says, *One who is born of God does not sin* (1 Jn 3:9) (paragraph 17). In any case no one should assert that he does not need to say for himself, *Forgive us our debts* (Mt 6:12) (paragraph 18). Finally, the bishops ask that the pope confirm by his reply the faith that they have stated (paragraph 19).

To Pope Innocent, our most blessed lord and brother rightly most worthy of honor, Aurelius, Alypius, Augustine, Evodius, and Possidius, send greetings in the Lord.

1. Concerning the two councils of the province of Carthage and of Numidia, we sent to Your Holiness letters signed by no small number of bishops in opposition to the enemies of the grace of Christ who place their trust in their own virtue

and as much as say to our creator, "You have made us human beings; but we have made ourselves righteous." They say that human nature is free so that they do not seek a deliverer to set it free; they say that human nature is saved so that they judge a savior unnecessary. For they say that it has such a great capability that, once it received its own powers in the beginning when it was created, it could by free choice, with no further help from the grace of him who created it, subdue and extinguish all desires and overcome all temptations. Many of these people rise up against us and say to our soul, *There is no salvation for it in its God* (Ps 3:3). The family of Christ, therefore, which says, *When I am weak, then I am strong* (2 Cor 12:10), and to whom its Lord says, *I am your salvation* (Ps 35:3), hopes, with a heart anxious in fear and trembling, for the help of the Lord also through the love of Your Reverence.

2. For we have heard that in the city of Rome, where Pelagius lived for a long time,[1] there are some people who side with him for various reasons. He is said to have convinced some of them of such ideas, but a larger number do not believe that he holds these ideas, especially since in the East, where he is living, it is said that ecclesiastical records have been produced by which he is believed to be exonerated. But if the bishops pronounced him Catholic, we should believe that it was for no other reason than that he said that he confessed the grace of God and said that a human being can by his own effort and will live righteously in such a way that he did not deny that one is helped in this regard by the grace of God. For, when they heard these words, the Catholic bishops could not have understood any other grace than that which they have frequently been accustomed to read in the books of God and to preach to the people of God—that grace of which the apostle says, *I do not cancel the grace of God. For, if righteousness comes through the law, then Christ has died in vain.* (Gal 2:21) This is undoubtedly the grace by which we are made righteous from being sinful and by which we are saved from infirmity, not the grace by which we were created with our own will. For if those bishops had understood that he meant the grace that we also share with unbelievers, along with whom we are human beings, but that he denied the grace by which we are Christians and children of God, who among the Catholic priests would—we do not say—hear him but would even tolerate him in their presence? Hence the judges should not be blamed because they understood the term "grace" with its customary meaning in the Church, not knowing what such persons commonly spread about either in the books of their teaching or in the ears of their followers.

3. We are not dealing with Pelagius alone, who has perhaps already been corrected—how we wish that he were!—but with many others scattered everywhere, who are verbosely contentious and drag off, as if overcome, weak and

---

1. Pelagius may have arrived in Rome as early as 380 and remained there until 410, when he came to Africa and then moved on to Palestine.

uneducated souls and wear out those who are solid in the faith by their very contentiousness. He should either be summoned to Rome by Your Reverence and carefully questioned about what he means by the grace by which he admits, if he really does admit it now, that human beings are helped to avoid sin and to live righteously, or you should handle this with him by letter. And when he has been found to say what the apostolic truth of the Church teaches, then he should be acquitted without any worry on the part of the Church and without any shadow of ambiguity. Then we should truly rejoice over his acquittal.

4. For, whether he says that grace is free choice or that grace is the forgiveness of sins or that grace is the commandment of the law, he mentions none of those things that pertain to the conquest of concupiscence and of temptations by the aid of the Holy Spirit. He who ascended into heaven and, taking captivity captive, gave gifts to human beings,[2] has most richly poured out upon us that Spirit.[3] For on this account we pray, in order to be able to overcome the temptation to sins, that the Spirit of God, whose pledge we have received,[4] may assist our weakness.[5] But one who prays and says, *Bring us not into temptation* (Mt 6:13), certainly does not pray that he may be a human being, that is, a nature. Nor does he pray that he may have free choice, which he already received when his nature was created. Nor does he pray for the forgiveness of sins, because he already said before, *Forgive us our debts* (Mt 6:12). Nor does he pray that he may receive the commandment, but he clearly prays that he may observe the commandment. For, if he is led into temptation, that is, falls in temptation, he certainly commits a sin that is against the commandment. He prays, then, that he may not sin, that is, that he may do no evil, as the apostle Paul prays for the Corinthians when he says, *But we pray to the Lord that you may do no evil* (2 Cor 13:7). Hence it is clear enough that, though the choice of the will undoubtedly exists, still its power does not suffice for not sinning, that is, for not doing evil, unless its weakness is helped. Prayer itself, then, is the clearest testimony to grace. Let Pelagius confess this grace and we shall rejoice that he is either correct or has been corrected.

5. We must distinguish the law and grace. The law is able to command; grace is able to help. The law would not command if there were no will. Nor would grace help if the will were enough. We are commanded to have understanding when scripture says, *Do not be like the horse and the mule, which do not have understanding* (Ps 32:9), and yet we pray that we may have understanding when it says, *Give me understanding that I may learn your commandments* (Ps 119:125). We are commanded to have wisdom when it says, *Be wise at last, you foolish people* (Ps 94:8), and yet we pray to have wisdom when it says, *But if any*

2. See Eph 4:8.
3. See Ti 3:6.
4. See 2 Cor 2:22.
5. See Rom 8:26.

*of you lacks wisdom, let him ask it of God who gives to all abundantly without
reproach, and it will be given to him* (Jas 1:5). We are commanded to have chastity when it says, *Let your loins be girt* (Lk 12:35), and yet we pray that we may
have chastity where it says,[6] *Since I knew that no one can be continent unless
God grants this and that this very point was a mark of wisdom, namely, to know
whose gift this was, I approached the Lord and beseeched him* (Wis 8:21).
Finally, lest it take too long to run through the complete list, we are commanded
not to do evil when it says, *Turn away from evil* (Ps 37:27), and yet we pray that
we may not do evil when it says, *But we pray to the Lord that you may do no evil*
(2 Cor 13:7). We are commanded to do good when it says, *Turn away from evil
and do good* (Ps 37:27), and yet we pray that we may do good when it says, *We
do not cease praying and making petitions on your behalf* (Col 1:9), and among
other things that he prays for on their behalf he includes, *That you may walk
worthy of God in all things pleasing, in every good work and word* (Col 1:10).
As, then, we acknowledge the will when we are commanded to do these things,
so let Pelagius acknowledge grace when we ask God for these things.

6. We have sent to Your Reverence a book that certain pious and honest
young servants of God gave us.[7] We even mention their names: they are called
Timasius and James. As we have heard and as you may be pleased to know, they
abandoned all the hope they had in this world thanks to the exhortation of
Pelagius himself, and they now serve God with lives of continence. After they
were eventually freed from the same error through some effort on our part and
under the inspiration of the Lord, they produced the same book, saying that it
was Pelagius' work, and they asked insistently that a reply be made to it. That
was done. The reply was sent to those young men, and they wrote back, thanking
God. We have sent you both of these: the book to which the reply was made and
the reply itself. And so that we would not be too burdensome, we marked the text
in those places where we ask that you do not hesitate to look. For example, when
the objection was raised for him that he denied the grace of God, he answered by
saying that grace was only the nature with which God created us.

7. If, however, he denies that this book or those passages in the book are his, we
do not claim that they are; let him anathematize them and let him confess most
clearly the grace that Christian doctrine expounds and preaches belongs only to
Christians. This grace is not nature but the grace by which nature is saved and
helped. This grace does not assist nature by some teaching that sounds in the ears or
by some visible help, like one who plants or one who waters from outside, but by

---

6. There is a lacuna here from before the quotation from Luke up to this point. I have translated the
Maurists' conjecture at filling the lacuna. The Jansenist Paschasius Quesnel suggested: "*Turn
aside from your desires* (Sir 20:17), and yet we pray that we may have continence where it
says."

7. The book was Pelagius' *Nature*, to which Augustine replied with his *Nature and Grace*. See
Letter 168 from Timasius and James, who thank Augustine for his work.

the ministry and hidden mercy of the Spirit, like the one who gives the increase, namely, God.[8] On the assumption that there is a good reason for doing so, let us call the grace of God that by which we have been created so that we are not nothing, nor are something like a corpse, which is not living, or like a tree, which does not have sensation, or like a cow, which does not have understanding, but that we are human beings, who exist, live, have sensation and understand. Let us also assume that we can offer thanks to our creator for so great a benefit. This, then can rightly be called grace since it was not given because of the merits of some preceding good works but because of the gratuitous goodness of God. But that grace is something else by which, having been predestined, we are called, made righteous and glorified, so that we can say, *If God is for us, who can be against us? He has not spared his own Son, but handed him over for all of us.* (Rom 8:31.32)

8. It was on this grace that the question focused when those whom Pelagius gravely offended and upset said to him that in his discussions he attacked it. He claimed to them that human nature was sufficient of itself through free choice not only to observe but also to fulfill completely the commandments of God. The teaching of the apostles not unreasonably calls by this name the grace by which we are saved and made righteous because of faith in Christ. Of this grace it is written, *I do not cancel the grace of God. For, if righteousness comes through the law, then Christ has died in vain.* (Gal 2:21) Of this grace it is written, *You have been separated from Christ, you who make yourselves righteous by the law; you have fallen away from grace* (Gal 3:4). Of this grace it is written, *But if it is by grace, it is no longer because of works; otherwise, grace is no longer grace* (Rom 11:6). Of this grace it is written, *A reward is given to one who works, not as a grace, but as something owed; to one, however, who does not work but believes in him who justifies the sinner, his faith is counted for righteousness* (Rom 4:4.5). And there are many other passages that you yourself can recall better, understand more wisely, and preach more brilliantly. But even if we are not incorrect to understand that the grace by which we were made human beings should be called grace, it would still be surprising if we read that it was spoken of in that way in any authentic writings of the prophets, the evangelists, or the apostles.

9. The objection, therefore, was posed for him concerning this grace, which is very familiar to believing Catholic Christians, in order that he would stop attacking it. Why is it that, when he himself posed this objection to himself in his own book, as if another person were attacking him in order that he might clear himself by replying, he made no other reply than that the nature of man as he was created includes the grace of the creator, and he said that one could without sin fulfill righteousness through free choice with the help of divine grace that God has given to a human being in the very ability of nature? One rightly replies to this, *The scandal of the cross, therefore, has been done away with* (Gal 5:11).

---

8. See 1 Cor 3:7.

Then Christ has died in vain (Gal 2:21). For, if he did not die for our sins and rise for our justification,[9] and if he had not ascended on high and, having taken captivity captive, had not given gifts to human beings,[10] would this ability of nature that he defends not be present in human beings?

10. Or did we perhaps not have the commandment of God, and did Christ die for that reason? On the contrary, this commandment already existed as something holy, just, and good.[11] It had already been said, *You shall not covet* (Ex 20:17). It had already been said, *You shall love your neighbor as yourself* (Lv 19:18), and in those words the apostle says that the whole law is summed up.[12] And since no one loves God unless he loves himself, the Lord says that the whole law and the prophets depends upon those two commandments.[13] Those two commandments were already given to human beings by God. Or had the eternal reward of righteousness not yet been promised? Pelagius himself does not say this, for in his writings he also stated that the kingdom of heaven was promised in the Old Testament. If, then, for acting righteously and bringing righteousness to fulfillment there already existed, through free choice, the ability of nature, if there already existed the holy, just, and good commandment of the law of God, if the everlasting reward had already been promised, then Christ died in vain.

11. Righteousness, therefore, comes neither through the law nor through the ability of nature but from faith and the gift of God through Jesus Christ our Lord, the one mediator between God and human beings.[14] If he had not died for our sins in the fullness of time and had not risen for the sake of our justification,[15] faith would certainly be emptied of meaning, both the faith of the people of the Old Testament and our faith. But if faith were emptied of meaning, what righteousness would remain for a human being, since a righteous person lives from faith?[16] For from the time sin entered the world through one man, and through sin death, and in that way passed on to all human beings, in whom all sinned,[17] one's own ability undoubtedly has set or does set no one free from the body of this death,[18] where another law resists the law of the mind.[19] For that ability was lost and needs a redeemer; it was wounded and needs a savior. But the grace of God sets it free through faith in the one mediator of God and human beings, the man

---

9. See Rom 4:25.
10. See Eph 4:8.
11. See Rom 7:12.
12. See Rom 13:9.
13. See Mt 22:37-40.
14. See 1 Tim 2:5.
15. See Rom 4:25.
16. See Hb 2:4.
17. See Rom 5:12.
18. See Rom 7:24.
19. See Rom 7:21.

Jesus Christ,[20] who, since he was God, made man and, while remaining God and having become man, himself remade what he made.

12. But I believe that he does not know that faith in Christ, which later was revealed, was hidden during the times of our ancestors. Yet by that faith they were set free by the grace of Christ—whoever were able to be set free in all the ages of the human race by the hidden but not blameworthy judgment of God. Hence the apostle says, *Having the same spirit of faith—the same, of course, that they had—in accord with the words of scripture, I believed; therefore, I have spoken, we also believe; therefore, we speak* (2 Cor 4:13). For this reason the mediator himself says, *Your father, Abraham, desired to see my day, and he saw it and rejoiced* (Jn 8:50). For this reason Melchizedek was able to prefigure the eternal priesthood when he offered the sacrament of the Lord's table.

13. The law was already given in writing, the law which the apostle says came along in order that sin might abound[21] and about which he says, *If the inheritance comes from the law, then it is no longer from the promise, but God gave it to Abraham through the promise. What, then, is the law? It was established for the sake of transgression until there should come the offspring to whom the promise was made. It was promulgated by angels through a mediator. But a mediator is not a mediator only for one. Yet God is one. Is the law, then, opposed to the promises of God? Heaven forbid! For, if a law were given that could bring to life, righteousness would certainly come from the law. But scripture enclosed all things under sin in order that the promise might be given to those who believe because of faith in Jesus Christ.* (Gal 3:18-22) Does this not show quite well that the law brought it about that sin was recognized and was increased by transgression? *For where there is no law, there is no transgression either* (Rom 4:15). And thus against the victory of sin we must take refuge in divine grace, which is found in the promises, and the law is not opposed to the promises of God. For through the law there comes knowledge of sin, and from the transgression of the law there comes an abundance of sin so that for deliverance we seek the promises of God, that is, the grace of God, and so that there begins to be in a human being not his own but God's righteousness, that is, the righteousness given by a gift of God.

14. Even now some people, *not knowing the righteousness of God*, as was then said of the Jews, *and trying to establish their own righteousness, are not subject to the righteousness of God* (Rom 10:3). For they think that they are made righteous through the law and that free choice is sufficient for them to observe it, that is, by their own righteousness drawn from human nature, not given by the grace of God, which is why it is called the righteousness of God. Hence it is likewise written, *For knowledge of sin came from the law. But now*

---

20. See 1 Tm 2:3.
21. See Rom 5:20.

apart from the law the righteousness of God has been made known, but the law and the prophets have borne witness to it. (Rom 3:20.21) When he says, *has been revealed,* he shows that it existed even then but, like that rain for which Gideon prayed, it was then hidden as if in the fleece but now has been revealed as if on the threshing floor.[22] Without grace the law could not have been the death of sin but would have been its power, as the apostle said, *The sting of death is sin, but the power of sin is the law* (1 Cor 15:50). And so, just as many flee from before the face of sin's reign to grace as it now lies revealed on the threshing floor, so a few fled to it as it then lay hidden in the fleece. But this distinction of the two eras pertains to the depth of the riches of the wisdom and knowledge of God, of which it was said, *How inscrutable are his judgments and unsearchable his ways!* (Rom 11:33)

15. Before the time of the law and at the very time of the law it was not the ability of a weak and needy nature that was damaged and sold under the power of sin but the grace of God through faith that justified our righteous forefathers who lived by faith, and it is the same grace now revealed and coming into the open that justifies us. Hence, let Pelagius anathematize the writings in which he argues against that grace—if not with contempt, then through ignorance—by defending the ability of nature to conquer sins and fulfill the commandments. Or if he denies that they are his writings or says that the passages which he denies are his own were inserted in his writings by his enemies, let him still anathematize and condemn them thanks to the fatherly exhortation and authority of Your Holiness. If he is willing, then let him learn how to remove the scandal, which is a burden for himself and harmful for the Church. The people who listen to him and who are wrongly fond of him do not cease up to the present moment to spread this scandal. For, if they know that the same book that they either believe or know is his has been anathematized and condemned by the authority of Catholic bishops and especially of Your Holiness, which we do not doubt carries greater weight with him, and by Pelagius himself, we do not think that they will dare to disturb faithful and simple Christian hearts by speaking against the grace of God that has been revealed through the suffering and resurrection of Christ. Rather, with the help of the merciful Lord and with your prayers united to ours and burning with love and piety, they will place their trust not in their own virtue but in the same grace, not only in order that they may be happy for eternity but also in order that they may be righteous and holy. Hence we thought that we should send on to Your Beatitude the letter written to him by one of ours, a man who, though he is a deacon of the Eastern church, is a citizen of Hippo, to whom Pelagius sent certain documents as if to establish his innocence since we judge it better and ask that you yourself forward it to him. For in that way he will more likely not disdain to read it, paying more attention to its sender than to its author.

---

22. See Jud 6:36-40.

16. But they claim that a human being can be without sin and easily observe the commandments of God if he wills to. When they say that this is done by the help of the grace that was revealed and given through the incarnation of his only-begotten Son, they seem to say this in a more tolerable fashion. But the question can reasonably be raised about where and when grace brings it about that we are completely without sin—whether it is in this life, in which the flesh has desires opposed to the spirit,[23] or in that life when *there will be fulfilled the word that is written, Where, death, is your victory? Where, death, is your sting? For the sting of death is sin.* (1 Cor 15:54-56) Hence this must be more carefully examined on account of others who have held and committed to memory in their writings the claim that even in this life a human being can be without sin—not from the first moment of his birth but from his conversion from sin to righteousness and from an evil to a good life. For they understood in this sense what scripture says of Zechariah and Elizabeth, namely, that they *walked in all the ordinances of the Lord without reproach* (Lk 1:6).[24] They interpreted the words, *without reproach*, as indicating sinfulness—not, of course, denying the help of grace but in fact piously confessing it, as is found in their other writings, not claiming that Zechariah and Elizabeth did this by the natural spirit of a human being but by the ruling Spirit of God. These people seem to have considered too little that Zechariah himself was, of course, a priest and that by the law of God all priests at that time had first of all to offer sacrifice for their own sins and then for the sins of the people.[25] Just as it is now proven by the sacrifice of prayer that we are not without sin, since we are commanded to say, *Forgive us our debts* (Mt 6:12), so it was then shown by the sacrifices of animals that the priests were not without sin, since they were commanded to offer those sacrifices for their sins.

17. But if it is the case that in this life we make progress by the grace of the savior to the extent that our evil desire lessens and our love increases and that we are made perfect in that next life when our evil desire is eliminated and love is made perfect, those words of scripture, *One who is born of God does not sin* (1 Jn 3:9), are said with reference to the love that alone does not sin. For to birth from God there pertains the love that must be increased and made perfect, not that desire that must be lessened and destroyed. And yet, as long as that evil desire exists in our members, it resists by its own law the law of the mind,[26] but one who has been born of God and does not obey its desires and does not offer his members to sin as weapons of iniquity[27] can say, *It is no longer I who do that, but the sin which dwells in me* (Rom 7:20).

---

23. See Gal 5:17.
24. Augustine is probably referring to Ambrose of Milan, who in his *Exposition of the Gospel according to Luke* (*Expositio evangelii secundum Lucam*) 1, 17-18, interpreted the statement that Zechariah and Elizabeth were "beyond reproach" in this sense.
25. See Lv 9:7; Heb 7:27.
26. See Rom 7:24.
27. See Rom 6:12-13.

18. But however this question may stand, since, even if no human being is found to be without sin in this life, it is still said to be possible by the help of grace and of the Spirit of God, and one must strive and pray that it may come about, it is more tolerable that a person is mistaken on this point. Nor is it diabolical impiety but human error to affirm that we must work for this and long for this, even if one cannot prove what one claims. For such a person believes that to be possible which it is certainly praiseworthy to want. For us, however, it is enough that there is no one among the faithful in the Church of God, in any state of progress toward or excellence of righteousness, who dares to say that the petition of the Lord's Prayer, *Forgive us our debts* (Mt 6:12), is unnecessary and says that he has no sin. Otherwise, he deceives himself, and the truth is not in him,[28] even though he now lives without reproach. For it is not just any human temptation but a serious sin that meets with reproach.

19. As for the other objections raised against Pelagius, Your Beatitude will undoubtedly judge concerning them as you see from the proceedings how he defended himself. The most gentle kindness of your heart will certainly pardon us for having sent to Your Holiness a letter perhaps longer than you had wanted. For we do not presume that our little stream increases your bountiful spring, but in this great trial of our time, from which we pray that he to whom we say, *Bring us not into temptation*, may set us free, we want you to test whether our stream, though small, flows from the same headwaters from which yours also flows in abundance, and by your replies we want you to console us concerning our common participation in the one grace.

---

28. See 1 Jn 1:8.

Letter 178

In 416 Augustine wrote to Hilary, most probably the bishop of Narbonne in Gaul. He informs him of the emergence of a new heresy and sums up the principal points of the Pelagian teaching (paragraph 1). He claims that such a doctrine undermines "the foundations of the whole Christian faith" and warns Hilary to be on guard against the followers of Pelagius, mentioning that two African councils have spoken against the new heresy and have sent letters to Rome (paragraph 2). Finally, Augustine asks that all Catholics condemn these errors (paragraph 3).

To Hilary, his blessed lord and venerable brother in the truth of Christ and fellow priest, Augustine sends greetings in the Lord.

1. Since our honorable son, Palladius, was setting sail from our shore when he asked for a favor, he bestowed on me an even greater one. For he asked that I not only commend him to Your Grace but also that I commend myself to your prayers, my blessed lord and venerable brother in the love of Christ. When I do this, Your Holiness will, of course, do what we both hope for from you. Your Holiness will hear from the courier whom I mentioned about our situation, since I know that in your love for us you are concerned about us, just as we are concerned about you in our love for you. Now I shall mention briefly what is most necessary. A certain new heresy inimical to the grace of Christ is trying to rise up in opposition to the Church of Christ but has not yet been clearly separated from the Church. This heresy arises from human beings who dare to attribute so much power to human weakness as to claim that the only things that pertain to the grace of God are our having been created with free choice and the ability not to sin and our having received from God commandments that we can fulfill. But they claim that we do not need any help from God to keep and fulfill the commandments. They admit that we need the forgiveness of sins because we are not able to undo the wrong actions that we did in the past. But they say that the human will is by its natural ability, without the help of the grace of God, sufficient from then on, thanks to virtue, for avoiding and conquering future sins and overcoming all temptations. They claim that even infants do not need the grace of the savior in order to be set free from perdition through baptism, since they contracted no infection of sin from Adam.

2. Your Reverence sees perfectly well, along with us, how inimical this idea is to the grace of God that has been granted to the human race through Jesus Christ our Lord and how they are trying to overthrow the foundations of the whole Christian faith. Nor ought we to be silent with you about how, with pastoral concern, you should watch out for such people whom we want and

desire to be healed in the Church rather than cut off from it. For, when I was writing this, I learned that in the church of Carthage a decree of the council of bishops was drawn up against them to be sent by letter to the holy and venerable Pope Innocent, and we ourselves have also likewise written to the same Apostolic See concerning the council of Numidia.[1]

3. For all of us who have hope in Christ ought to resist this pestilential impiety and with one heart condemn and anathematize it. It contradicts even our prayers when it allows us to say, *Forgive us our debts as we also forgive our debtors* (Mt 6:12), but allows it in such a way as to claim that a human being in this corruptible body, which weighs down the soul,[2] can by his own strength attain such great righteousness that it is not necessary to say, *Forgive us our debts*. But they do not accept the words that follow, *Bring us not into temptation* (Mt 6:13), in the sense that we should pray to God in order that he may help us to overcome temptations to sins but in order that no human misfortune may attack our body and afflict us, since it already lies in our power to conquer temptations to sins by the ability of our nature, so that we should think that it is useless to ask for this by prayers. We cannot in one short letter gather together all or even most of the arguments of so great an impiety, especially since, when I was writing these ideas, the couriers who were about to set sail did not allow me to delay longer. I think, however, that I have not been a burden to your eyes because I could not be silent about avoiding so great an evil with all vigilance and with the help of the Lord.

---

1. Augustine refers to the Councils of Carthage and of Milevis, both held in 416.
2. See Wis 9:15.

Letter 179

In 416 Augustine wrote to John, the bishop of Jerusalem, concerning the heresy of Pelagius. At the Council of Jerusalem, held in the summer of 415, John had sympathized with Pelagius, probably due at least in part to his feud with Jerome, who opposed Pelagius. Augustine explains that he is taking advantage of the opportunity provided by the courier, who plans to return immediately, and hopes that John will reply to him (paragraph 1). Augustine explains how he obtained a copy of Pelagius' book, *Nature*, and how in reply to it he wrote *Nature and Grace* (paragraph 2). He points out how in his book Pelagius calls grace merely the nature with which we are created and how he claims that free choice suffices itself for acting righteously (paragraph 3). Pelagius' teachings run counter to the prayers of Christians and are opposed to the blessings that priests ask God to bestow on their flocks (paragraph 4). Augustine explains to John why he is sending him a copy of Pelagius' book and a copy of his reply to it (paragraph 5). He tells John to question Pelagius about whether we need to pray to the Lord in order to avoid sin and about whether infants contract original sin from Adam (paragraph 6). In return Augustine asks for a copy of the proceedings of the Council of Diospolis at which Pelagius was allegedly acquitted, since Augustine has thus far only received a document that Pelagius had written in his own defense (paragraph 7). Augustine points out that Pelagius says in his book the opposite of what he said in the document written in his own defense (paragraph 8). Augustine tells John that, from what Pelagius said in his book, he will be able to see whether he ought to believe his other denials (paragraph 9). Augustine also insists that he has proof that the book was written by Pelagius (paragraph 10).

To John, his most blessed lord and rightly venerable brother and fellow bishop, Augustine sends greetings in the Lord.

1. I do not dare to be angry because I have not deserved to receive a letter from Your Holiness. For it is better to believe that a courier was unavailable than to suspect that Your Reverence has regarded me as unworthy of a reply, my most blessed lord and rightly venerable brother. But now, because I have learned that the servant of God, Luke, by whose hands I have sent this, will soon be returning, I shall offer abundant thanks to God and to Your Kindness if you are so gracious as to pay me a visit by letter. I hear that you are very fond of Pelagius, our brother and your son. I suggest that you show him such love that the people who know him and have carefully listened to him do not think that Your Holiness has been deceived by him.

2. For certain young men, sons of the finest families and well educated in the liberal arts, disciples of Pelagius, abandoned the hopes they had in this world

because of his exhortation and devoted themselves to the service of God.[1] But I found in them certain ideas opposed to the sound teaching that is contained in the gospel of the savior and explained in the letters of the apostles, that is, they were seen to argue against the grace of God because of which we are Christians and in which *through the Spirit we await in faith the righteousness for which we hope* (Gal 5:5). And when they began to correct their views through our instructions, they gave me a book that they said was by this same Pelagius, asking that I reply to it. After I saw that I ought to do this so that this wicked error might be more completely removed from their hearts, I read the book and replied.

3. In this book Pelagius calls grace only the nature in which we are created with free choice. But the grace which holy scripture commends by so many testimonies, teaching that we are justified by it, that is, made righteous, and are helped by God's mercy in doing or fulfilling every good work, something which the prayers of the saints most clearly reveal when they ask of the Lord what they are commanded by the Lord—this grace he not only does not mention, but he even says much against it. For he states and strongly maintains that by free choice alone human nature can suffice of itself for acting righteously and observing all the commandments of God. Hence, who would not see, when he reads the same book, how Pelagius attacks the grace of God of which the apostle says, *Wretched man that I am! Who will set me free from the body of this death? The grace of God through our Lord Jesus Christ* (Rom 7:24-25)? Who would not see that he leaves no place for the help of God on account of which we ought to say in prayer, *Bring us not into temptation* (Mt 6:13)? Who would not see that the Lord also seems to have said to Peter without any reason, *I have prayed for you that your faith might not fail* (Lk 22:32), if all this is accomplished in us without any help of God but by the power of our will?

4. These perverse and impious arguments not only contradict our prayers, by which we ask of the Lord whatever we read and hold that the saints asked, but are also opposed to our blessings, which we say over the people, desiring for them and asking from the Lord that *he may make them abound in love for one another and for all human beings* (1 Thes 3:12), that he may grant that they *may be strengthened in virtue according to the riches of his glory by his Spirit* (Eph 3:16), that *he may fill* them *with every joy and peace in believing*, and that they may abound *in hope and in the power of the Holy Spirit* (Rom 15:13). Why do we ask for them these things, which we know that the apostle asked from the Lord for the people, if our nature, created with free choice, can now offer all these things to itself of its own will? Why does the same apostle also say, *For whoever are driven by the Spirit of God are the children of God* (Rom 8:14), if we are driven by the spirit of

---

1. Augustine refers to Timasius and James, who had given him Pelagius' *Nature* and for whom he wrote *Nature and Grace*. See Letter 168, in which they thank Augustine, and Letter 177, in which the five bishops mention them to Pope Innocent.

our own nature to become children of God? Why does he likewise say, *The Spirit helps our weakness* (Rom 8:26), if our nature was created so that it does not need to be helped by the Spirit toward works of righteousness? Why did scripture say, *But God is faithful who will not permit you to be tempted beyond what you can bear, but will produce a way out along with the temptation in order that you can endure it* (1 Cor 10:13), if we were already created so that we could overcome all temptations by resisting them with the powers of free choice?

5. Why should I cite more texts for Your Holiness? For I feel that I am being a burden, especially since you are listening to my letter through an interpreter. If you love Pelagius, let him also love you, or rather let him not deceive himself and you. For, when you hear him confess the grace of God and the help of God, you think that he is saying what you hold in accord with the Catholic norm, since you do not know what he wrote in his book. For this reason I sent you his book and mine, in which I replied to it, so that Your Reverence may see from them what he calls the grace and help of God when people object to him that he speaks against the grace and help of God. Thereupon, show him by teaching him and exhorting him and by praying for his salvation, which must be found in Christ, so he may confess the grace of God that the saints of God are known to have confessed when they petitioned God for the things that God commanded them to do. For those things were not commanded except to display our will, and there would be no petitioning except so that a weak will would be helped by him who commanded.

6. Let him be asked openly whether he accepts that we must pray to God in order that we may not sin. But if he does not accept this, read in his hearing the words of the apostle, *But we pray to God that you may do no evil* (2 Cor 13:7). If, however, he accepts it, let him openly preach the grace by which we are helped in order that he himself may not do much evil. For those who are set free are all set free by this grace of God through Jesus Christ our Lord, because no one can be set free in any other way apart from it. On this account it was written, *Just as in Adam all die, so too all will be brought to life in Christ* (1 Cor 15:22), not because no one will be condemned but because no one will be set free in any other way. For, just as none are children of men except through Adam, so none are children of God except through Christ. None, therefore, can become children of men except through Adam, and none of them can become children of God except through Christ. Let him, therefore, openly state what he holds on this. Does he accept that even infants, who cannot yet desire or reject righteousness, are still set free by the grace of Christ? After all, on account of the one man *sin entered the world, and through sin death, and in that way it passed on to all human beings, in whom all have sinned* (Rom 5:12). Does he believe that the blood of Christ, which was certainly shed for the forgiveness of sins,[2] was also shed for them on account of original sin? It is especially on these points that we wish to know what he believes, what he holds,

---

2. See Mt 16:28.

and especially what he confesses and preaches. But on the other points on which objections are raised against him, even if he is proven to have been in error, one can more easily put up with him until he is corrected.

7. I also ask that you send us the proceedings of the ecclesiastical court by which he was allegedly acquitted. I ask this because of the desire of many bishops who are disturbed along with me by the uncertain rumor on this matter. But I alone wrote this letter because I did not want to lose the opportunity of a courier in a hurry to depart from us, who I heard could quickly return to us. Pelagius has already sent us in place of those proceedings not, in fact, any part of them but a sort of defense of himself that he himself wrote, in which he said that he was responding to the objections of the Gauls.[3] In that defense—to omit other things—when he was replying to the objection that he said a human being can be without sin and observe the commandments if he wills, he replied, "We said this, for God gave a human being this ability. We did not say that anyone is found who has never sinned from infancy to old age but that, having turned away from sin by his own effort and having been helped by the grace of God, a person can be without sin, but despite this he will be capable of sinning afterwards."

8. Your Reverence sees in this response of Pelagius that he confessed that the earlier life of a human being, which begins from infancy, is not without sin, but that he can be converted to a life without sin by his own effort and the help of the grace of God. Why, then, does he say in the book to which I replied that Abel lived this life so that he never sinned at all? For these are his words on this subject: "This can be correctly said with regard to those whom scripture recalls neither as good nor as bad. But with regard to those whose righteousness it recalls, it would also undoubtedly have recalled their sins if they were thought to have sinned in any way. Granted that in other times," he says, "because of the large numbers of people, scripture refrained from mentioning the sins of all. But right at the very beginning or the world, when there were only four human beings, what are we going to say?" he asks. "Why has scripture refused to mention the sins of everyone? Was it on account of the huge population, which did not yet exist? Or was it because it recalled only those who had committed sins but could not recall the one who had committed none? Certainly," he says, "in the first age scripture tells us of only four human beings: Adam and Eve and their sons, Cain and Abel. Eve sinned. Scripture tells us that. Adam also fell. The same scripture does not omit that fact. Moreover, scripture likewise testified that Cain sinned. It indicates not only their sins but also the nature of their sins. If Abel had also sinned," he says, "scripture would certainly have said so. If it did not, then he did not sin."[4]

---

3. That is, to Hero and Lazarus, the Gallic bishops who brought accusations against Pelagius at the Council of Jerusalem in the summer of 415.

4. Pelagius, *Nature*; Augustine quotes the same passage in *Nature and Grace* 37, 43-44.

9. I have quoted these words from his book, which Your Holiness will also be able to find in that volume, so that you may understand how you ought to believe him when he denies the other charges. Perhaps he will say that Abel himself committed no sin but that he was not for that reason without sin and, hence, cannot be compared to the Lord, who was the only one in mortal flesh without sin. For there was in Abel the original sin that he contracted from Adam but had not committed in his own person. I wish that Pelagius would say at least this so that for the present we could have his certain opinion on the baptism of infants! Or perhaps, because he said, "from infancy to old age," he might mean that Abel did not sin from infancy to old age, because he is shown not to have reached old age. His words do not indicate this; he said that a person's earlier life from the beginning was sinful, but that his later life could be without sin. For he declares that he did not say that "there is anyone who has never sinned from infancy to old age, but that, having turned away from sin by one's own effort and having been helped by the grace of God, a person can be without sin." For, when he says, "having turned away from sin," he shows that a person's earlier life was spent in sins. Let him, therefore, admit that Abel sinned, since he admits that the first part of his life was in the world and did not lack sins, and let him look at his book where it is clear that he said what in his defense he denied that he said.

10. But if he denies that this book or this passage in that book is his, I in fact have suitable witnesses, honest and faithful men, who are without a doubt admirers of his, by whose testimony I can defend myself. For they themselves gave the same book to me, and this passage can be read in it, and they said that it was Pelagius' book. This is at least enough to keep him from saying that it was written or falsified by me. Let each now choose among them whom to believe; it is not my intention to discuss this point any longer. We ask that you at least pass it on to him if he denies that he holds these ideas, which are objected to him as inimical to the grace of Christ. His own defense is so obscure that, if he has not misled by any ambiguous language Your Holy Wisdom, who has not known his other writings, we will congratulate you with great joy, for we do not care much whether he never held these perverse and impious teachings or has at some point turned away from them.

Letter 180

In 416 Augustine replied to a letter of Oceanus, a Roman nobleman and friend of Jerome. Augustine thanks Oceanus for the letters he sent him (paragraph 1). He explains what it is that troubles him about Jerome's theory that God creates individual souls for each infant that is born (paragraph 2). He argues that the use of figurative language does not constitute a lie (paragraph 3) but insists that Paul was not using figurative language in the Letter to the Galatians when he rebuked Peter (paragraph 4). Finally, Augustine asks Oceanus to send him the book that Jerome has written on the resurrection of the dead (paragraph 5).

To Oceanus, his rightly most dear lord and honorable brother among the members of Christ, Augustine sends greetings.

1. I received two letters from Your Charity, in one of which you mention a third and say that you sent it first. I do not recall having received it; on the contrary, I think I recall quite well that I did not receive it. Because of those that I received, however, I am very grateful for your kindness toward us. I was caught up in one storm after another of various occupations so that I could not immediately reply to them. Having now gained a drop of leisure time, I preferred to make some answer rather than maintain a long silence toward your most sincere love, and I preferred to bother you by my loquaciousness rather than by my silence.

2. I already knew what the saintly Jerome holds about the origin of souls, and I had read those very words that you quoted from his book in your letter. But the point that bothers certain people, namely, how God acts justly in giving souls to children conceived in adultery, is not what make the question difficult, since not even their own sins, much less those of their parents, can harm them if they are living good lives and have turned to God in faith and piety. But it is right to ask: If it is true that individual new souls are made out of nothing for individuals who are born, how does he, in whom there is no injustice,[1] justly condemn so many souls of countless infants, though God knows for certain that they will leave their bodies without baptism before the age of reason, before they can think or grasp anything right or wrong? There is no need to say more on this topic since you know what I want or rather what I do not want to say. I think that what I said is enough for someone wise. Nonetheless, if you have read something on this or heard something from his lips by which the question can be resolved, or if God granted you this knowledge when you were thinking about it, tell me, please, in order that I may be more grateful to you.

---

1. See Rom 9:14.

3. On the question of a dutiful or useful lie, which you thought should be resolved by the example of the Lord when he said that not even the Son knows the day or the hour of this world's end, I was delighted by the effort of your intelligence when I read it, but I do not by any means think that a figurative expression can rightly be called a lie. For it is not a lie when we call the day happy because it makes people happy or call lupine sad because by its bitter taste it makes sad the face of someone who is tasting it, just as God is said to know when he makes someone know.[2] You yourself mentioned that this was said to Abraham.[3] In no way are these lies, something that you yourself easily see. Hence, when blessed Hilary explained an obscure question by this kind of figurative speech and wanted us to understand that the Lord did indeed say that he did not know something insofar as he caused others not to know it by keeping it hidden, he did not excuse a lie but showed that it was not a lie.[4] And this holds not only in more familiar figures of speech but even in the one that is called metaphor, which is familiar to everyone because of our custom of speaking in that way. For does anyone claim it is a lie that vines bud,[5] that fields wave, that youths flower, because in these things he does not see the waters or stones or plants or trees from which these verbs have their proper sense?

4. But, given your mind and learning, you very clearly see how much what the apostle said differs from these examples. *When I saw that they were not living correctly in relation to the gospel, I said to Peter in the presence of everyone: If you, though a Jew, are living like a Gentile and not like a Jew, how do you force the Gentiles to live like Jews?* (Gal 2:14) There is no obscurity here as the result of a figure; the words are in plain language in their proper sense. The teacher of the nations, with God as his witness, had previously said to those whom he was bringing to birth in Christ, *But in what I am writing to you, look, I swear before God that I am not lying* (Gal 1:20). He spoke either the truth or a lie. If—God forbid!—it was a lie, you see what follows[6] . . . and horrified at both of these, he presents an argument for the truth, and in the apostle, Peter, an example of admirable humility.

5. But why delay on this any longer? For concerning the question between us, the previously mentioned venerable brother, Jerome, and I have dealt with this enough in writing. And in the recent work that he just published against Pelagius under the name Critobulus, he held the same view concerning what the apostles did and said as the most blessed Cyprian, which we have also followed.[7] The

---

2. See Gn 18:1-15.
3. See Gn 22:12.
4. Hilary, *The Trinity* (*De Trinitate*) 9, 62-57.
5. The Latin verb "*gemmare*: to bud" is derived from "*gemma*: gem."
6. There is a lacuna in the text at this point.
7. See Jerome, *Dialogues against the Pelagians* (*Dialogi adversus Pelagianos*) 1, 8 and Cyprian, Letter 71, 3. .

question about the origin of souls is not, in my opinion, a foolish one to ask, not on account of children born of adulterous parents but on account of the condemnation—heaven forbid!—of the innocent. If you have learned anything from so good and great a man that we can rightly give as an answer to those in doubt, please do not refuse to share it with us. In your letters you indeed appeared so learned and charming that it would be worth the effort for me to carry on a conversation with you in writing. I now ask that you do not delay to send to us the book of the same man of God that the priest Orosius[8] brought and gave to Your Charity to copy; in it Jerome is said to have argued splendidly concerning the resurrection of the flesh.[9] We did not immediately ask him for it because we thought that it should be copied and corrected, and we think that now abundant time has been allowed for both tasks. Live for God, mindful of us.

---

8. For the Spanish priest Orosius, see Letters 166, 2; 172, 1; and 175, 1
9. See Jerome, Letter 108, 22-25.

Letter 181

Probably in 416 Pope Innocent replied to Letter 175 from the participants in the Council of Carthage. Innocent tells the bishops that they have acted correctly and in accord with tradition in referring the issue to the judgment of the Apostolic See (paragraph 1). He congratulates the bishops for sending him the report on their council because their action will benefit the whole Church (paragraph 2). Heresy is like an infection that must be cured quickly or amputated in order that the whole body may not be infected (paragraph 3). Innocent points to some outrageous aspects of Pelagian teaching (paragraph 4). The Pelagians' denial of any need of God's daily help for living a good life is especially offensive to God (paragraph 5). The whole psalter is filled with evidence against them (paragraph 6). The first man sinned by his free will, and even now, after being redeemed by Christ, we need the daily help of grace (paragraph 7). Hence Innocent excommunicates those who hold and teach this heresy (paragraph 8), though he insists that, if the heretics come to their senses and condemn their errors, they are to be welcomed back into the Church (paragraph 9).

To Aurelius and all the holy bishops, his most beloved brothers, who were present at the council of the church of Carthage, Innocent sends greetings in the Lord.

1. In examining questions about God, with which it is proper that bishops and especially an authentic, legitimate, Catholic council deal with the greatest care, you have observed the patterns set by ancient tradition and have been mindful of Church discipline. In that way you have added strength to the vigor of our religion by true reason, no less now in consulting us than earlier when you issued the decree. For you wanted it to be referred to our judgment, knowing what is due to the Apostolic See, since all of us who have held this position desire to follow that apostle from whom the episcopacy itself and the whole authority of this name is derived. Following him, we know how to condemn what is evil and to approve what is praiseworthy, just as we approve the fact that in observing the teachings of our predecessors you did not think that they should be ignored. For they established it not by a human but by a divine decision that one should not regard as settled, whatever questions are dealt with, even in distant and remote provinces, before it comes to the knowledge of this see. In this way a correct declaration is upheld by the whole authority of this see, and—just as all waters go forth from their original source and the pure waters of their incorrupt spring flow through the different regions of the whole world—from this see the other churches learn what they should teach, whom they should absolve, and whom a stream fit for clean bodies should avoid like those persons filthy with a foulness that cannot be purified.

2. And so, dearest brothers, I am grateful that you have sent a letter to us by means of our brother and fellow bishop Julius, and while by it you are caring for the churches over which you preside, you are demonstrating your solicitude for the good of all, and you ask that we decree through all the churches of the world what at the same time benefits all. In that way the Church, once it has been confirmed by its norms and strengthened by this decree with its just declaration, may by this decree avoid those heretics and may be free from fear of those people who are instructed in perverse doctrine, who in fact are destroyed by the subtleties of words. For they argue under the semblance of the Catholic faith, breathing forth, as it were, a pestilential venom, and try to overthrow the whole discipline of the true doctrine, so that they might change for the worse the hearts of those who hold the correct teaching.

3. We must, therefore, heal this quickly so that the accursed disease does not attack souls over a longer time. Just as when a doctor sees that this earthly body has some ailment and thinks it a great proof of his art if by his intervention someone for whom hope has been abandoned quickly revives, so too, when he sees a wound with gangrene and applies plasters and other remedies in order to remove by them the wound that has developed, if he cannot heal what remains, in order that it may not corrupt the rest of the body with its infection, he cuts off the infected part with a knife so as to keep the rest whole and intact. We must, therefore, cut away the wound that has attacked an entirely pure and healthy body that lest, if it be removed later, the remains of this evil settle in the inner organs and be impossible to extract.

4. Should we still expect anything correct from these minds that think that they owe to themselves the fact that they are good and do not consider him whose grace they daily receive? But people of this sort receive no grace from God when they presume that they can attain without him as much as they hardly merit to receive who do ask him for it. For what can be so unjust, so barbarous, so ignorant of all religion, so hostile to Christian minds as to deny that you owe whatever you obtain as a daily grace to him to whom you admit you owe the fact that you were born? You will, then, be better in providing for yourself than he who caused you to exist can be for you! And since you think that you owe to him the fact that you live, how can you suppose that you do not owe to him the fact that you live a good life by receiving his daily grace? And when you deny that we need God's help, as if we were completely perfect as the result of our own ability, how do we invoke his help for us when we can be such people by ourselves?

5. For I would like to ask someone who denies the help of God what he would say. Is it that we do not merit it or that he cannot offer it? Or is there no reason on account of which each of us ought to ask for it? God's works testify that he can offer it, and we cannot deny that we need his daily help. For, if by his help we are living a good life, we call upon him in order that we may live a better and more

holy life, and if we have incorrect ideas and turn away from what is good, we need his help more in order to return to the right path. For what is so deadly, so headed for a fall, so exposed to all dangers as to think that by itself the free will that we received when we were born can be sufficient, so that we need now ask nothing further from the Lord? That is, having forgotten our maker, we refuse to acknowledge his power in order to prove that we are free, as if he who made you free at your birth had nothing more to give. They do not know that God's grace comes down upon us only when we beg for it with lengthy prayers and that, apart from it, we could never attempt to conquer the errors of earthly filth and a worldly body, since it is not free choice but only the grace of God that can make us capable of resisting.

6. For the psalmist, who would not correctly ask for it if free choice would have been more beneficial for him, cries out that he needs God's help. Though, in fact, that blessed man, who was already chosen by the Lord, needed nothing, yet he beseeches God and pleads, *Be my helper; do not abandon me, and do not forsake me, O God, my savior* (Ps 27:9). Do we, then, call upon free choice as our helper, while he calls upon God? Do we say that what we are by birth is sufficient, while he beseeches God not to abandon him? Are we not, I ask, clearly taught what we should pray for, when that man who was so blessed, as we said above, prays that God may not forsake him? For the heretics who hold these views must find fault with these words. Let them, therefore, accuse David for not knowing how to pray and for being ignorant of his nature. For, though he knew that he had such great resources in his nature, through the whole body of the Psalter he both proclaims and cries out that God is his helper, his constant helper; nor is it enough that God is his constant helper, but, prostrate in prayer, he begs that God not forsake him. As this great man recognized that it was necessary to ask God's help constantly, so he admitted that it was also necessary to teach this. How, then, are Pelagius and Caelestius, who have set aside any contrary arguments from the Psalms and rejected the teaching found in them, hopeful that they will persuade some people that we ought not to ask for God's help and do not need it? For all the saints testify that they can do nothing without it.

7. For the first man experienced long ago what free will can do when he unwisely made use of his good gifts, fell, and sank into the depths of transgression, and he found no way in which he could rise up from there. Misled by his freedom, he would have lain for eternity under the weight of his collapse if the coming of Christ had not later raised him up in accord with his grace. Through the purification of a new rebirth he washed away all past sin by the bath of baptism, and though he strengthened his condition so that he might live with more correctness and more stability, yet he did not deny his grace afterward. For, though he had redeemed man from his past sins, since he still knew that he could sin again, he reserved for his reparation many means by which he might correct him even after this. He offers daily remedies and, unless we strive, relying upon

and trusting in them, we will by no means be able to overcome human errors. For it is necessarily the case that, as we are victorious by his help, so we are again defeated without his help. But I could say more if it were not clear that you had said everything.

8. Whoever, then, seems to assent to the proposition which says that we do not need the help of God admits that he is an enemy of the Catholic faith and that he is ungrateful for God's gifts, nor are they worthy of communion with us since they defile it by preaching such doctrine. For, in following what they teach, they have of their own accord fled far from the true religion. Since all of this is included in what we profess and since we aim at nothing else by our daily prayers but how we may obtain mercy, how can we endure people making these boasts? What great error, I ask, so darkens their hearts that, if they themselves do not experience the grace of God because they are unworthy and do not deserve it, they do not consider what divine grace daily bestows upon others? For these people are all most deserving of blindness when they do not leave for themselves even the belief that they can be recalled from their errors by divine help. After all, in denying that help, they have completely removed it not from others but from themselves. They must be further separated and removed from the heart of the Church lest, if it occupies many minds for a longer time, this error later grow and become incurable. For, if they live for a long time with this impunity, they are bound to lead many into the wickedness of this way of thinking and to deceive the innocent, or rather the imprudent, who are now following the Catholic faith. For these Catholics will suppose that they hold the correct doctrine if they see that those people still remain in the Church.

9. Let the infected wound be removed from the healthy body, therefore, and after the effluvium of the raging disease is removed let the uninfected parts go on with a greater degree of caution, and let the purified flock be cleansed of this contagion of the sick animal. Let the integrity of the whole body be unimpaired, for we know you follow and maintain this integrity by this decree against them, and we preserve it along with you by our similar assent. Yet if they invoke some help of God upon themselves, which they have refused to do up to now, and acknowledge that they need his help in order to be set free from the defilement into which they have fallen by the perversity of their heart, let them, drawn as if into the light from ugly darkness, remove and renounce all those things by which their whole gaze was darkened and obscured so that they did not see the truth. Let them condemn the views that they have held up to now, and let them at some point turn their mind from this defilement to correct reasoning and, having been corrected, let them give and submit themselves to true counsels in order to be healed. If they do this, it will be in the power of the bishops to go to their help to some extent and to offer some care to such wounds, the care that the Church is accustomed to give to those who have come to their senses after a fall, so that having been called back from their sins, they may be brought back into the

sheepfold of the Lord. Otherwise, left outside and excluded from the great defenses of the fortress of the faith, they would be exposed to every danger and devoured and torn apart by the teeth of wolves. For they cannot resist those wolves by this perversity of doctrine, by which they have provoked them against themselves. But your warnings and the abundant testimonies of our law have sufficiently shown that an answer has been given to the heretics, and we do not think that anything remains for us to say since it is clear that you neither passed over nor excluded anything by which those heretics may be recognized as being rejected and completely refuted. For that reason we add no testimonies since your report is full of them, and it is quite clear that so many very learned priests have said everything necessary, nor is it right to believe that you have passed over anything that can help the case. [In another hand] Farewell, my brothers.

Letter 182

On 27 January 417 Pope Innocent wrote to Silvanus, the primate of Numidia, and to the participants in the Council of Milevis in response to Letter 176, which they had sent to him. Innocent congratulates the participants for their pastoral concern with regard to the leaders of the new heresy (paragraph 1). He expresses his pleasure over the fact that the bishops have consulted him and insists that it is right that they referred such a case to the chair of Peter (paragraph 2). He points out the errors of the Pelagians who by their teaching reject the help of God and destroy any reason for our daily prayers to God (paragraph 3). He insists that the help of God must be added to our free will and that the will can do nothing if it is deprived of God's protection (paragraph 4). Innocent also points out that the Pelagian claim that infants can attain eternal life without the grace of baptism is simply foolish (paragraph 5). Hence he declares Pelagius and Caelestius excommunicated until such time as they give up their error and return to the faith (paragraph 6). He says, however, that they are to be received back into the Church if they come to their senses and reject and condemn their errors (paragraph 7).

Innocent sends greetings in the Lord to Silvanus the primate, to Valentine, and to the other most beloved brothers who were present at the Synod of Milevis.

1. In the midst of the other cares of the Roman church and the tasks of the Apostolic See whereby, on the basis of the faith and with an aim to heal, we respond to questions coming from various sources, our brother and fellow bishop Julius unexpectedly brought me the letter of Your Charity, which you sent from the Council of Milevis out of a more ardent concern for the faith, to which you added the writings of the Synod of Carthage on a similar question. The Church rejoices greatly that shepherds manifest so much solicitude for the flocks entrusted to them. For they not only do not allow any of them to wander off but, if a meadow filled with an evil attractiveness has led any of them astray and if they have remained in error, they also want either to cut them off completely or to protect with the watchfulness of their original custody those who wrongly avoid what they have long sought. They are on guard against two outcomes. They fear that, by accepting back such people, others may be misled by a similar example or that, by rejecting them if they return, they may seem to be exposed to the teeth of wolves. Your present consultation is prudent and inspired by faith. For who could either tolerate a sheep's going astray or fail to welcome back one that makes amends? For, as I think it harsh to close one's eyes to sinners, so I judge it impious to refuse a hand to those who repent.

2. You act conscientiously and appropriately, therefore, in consulting the office of the Apostolic See, that mystical office, I say, to which, except for those

matters that lie outside, there pertains the solicitude for all the churches[1] over what judgment should be maintained in troubling affairs. You have followed the form of the ancient rule, which you know has been observed with me by the whole world. But I set aside this issue, because I do not believe that this has escaped the attention of Your Wisdom. Why did you endorse this practice by your action if it was not because you knew that responses always flow from the apostolic fountain through all the provinces for those who ask for them? I think that, especially when a question of faith is discussed, all our brothers and fellow bishops ought to refer it only to Peter, that is, to the source of their title and dignity, as Your Charity has now referred this question, which could benefit all the churches in common throughout the world. For these churches must necessarily become more cautious when they see that the inventors of these evils have been separated from communion with the Church by decrees of our judgment in response to the two synods.

3. Your Charity, then, will bring about a twofold good. For you will obtain a blessing for having observed the canons of the Church, and the whole world will enjoy your gift. For who among Catholics would want to hold further discussions with the enemies of Christ? Who would want to have in common with them even the light of life? Let the authors of the new heresy indeed be shunned! What could they have devised against the Lord that would be worse than when they destroy God's help and take away the reason for daily prayer? That is the same as to say, "What need do I have of God?" The psalmist rightly says against them, *There you have human beings who have not made the Lord their help!* (Ps 52:9) Because they deny the help of God, they say that a human being can be sufficient unto himself and does not need God's grace, though, when he is deprived of it, he is necessarily caught in the snares of the devil and falls when he tries to carry out by freedom alone all the commandments leading to life. Oh, the misguided teaching of most depraved minds! Notice, finally, that freedom itself deceived the first human being so that, when he applies its reins more loosely, he falls in the pride of transgression. Nor could he be rescued from this if the coming of Christ the Lord had not restored his state of pristine freedom by providing rebirth. Let him hear David as he says, *Our help is in the name of the Lord* (Ps 124:8), and, *Be my helper; do not abandon me or ignore me, O God, my salvation* (Ps 27:9). He said these things in vain if what he asked from the Lord with his tearful words lay in the power of his will alone.

4. Since this is so and since we read on every page of God's word that the help of God must be added to free will and that the will can do nothing if it is deprived of God's help, how do Pelagius and Caelestius, as you say, stubbornly claim for it alone this ability and—what should bring sorrow to all of us —even persuade many others of this? We could use many passages from the scriptures to defend

---

1. See 2 Cor 11:28.

this teaching if we were not aware that Your Holiness fully knows all the divine scriptures, especially since your report was filled with so many and such solid testimonies that they alone could cancel out this present teaching. And there is no need of obscure passages, since they do not dare and are unable to oppose the passages you quoted, which readily occurred to you. And so they try to take away the grace of God that we must ask for even after the freedom of our first state has been restored to us. Nor can we avoid the other devices of the devil except by the same grace.

5. The idea, however, which Your Fraternity states that they preach, namely, that infants can be given the rewards of eternal life even without the grace of baptism, is utterly foolish. For, unless they eat the flesh of the Son of Man and drink his blood, they will not have life in them.[2] But those who maintain that eternal life is given to them without rebirth seem to me to want to destroy baptism when they preach that these infants have what the faith holds is to be conferred on them only by baptism. If they hold that not being reborn does them no harm, they ought also to admit that the sacred waters of rebirth do them no good. But so that the wicked doctrine of useless human beings might be refuted by a quick argument on the part of the truth, the Lord cries out in the gospel, saying, *Allow the children to come to me, and do not keep them away from me* (Mt 19:14).

6. Hence we declare that Pelagius and Caelestius, that is, the inventors of these new ideas which, as the apostle said, have contributed to no edification but have rather generated utterly empty questions,[3] are excommunicated from the Church by the authority of our apostolic power until *they come to their senses and escape from the snares of the devil by whom they are held captive according to his will* (2 Tm 2:26). Until then they are unwelcome in the Lord's sheepfold, which they have chosen to leave in following the path of their misguided way. For those who cause us confusion and want to change the gospel of Christ must be cut off.[4] At the same time, however, we also command that an equal penalty be imposed upon whoever tries to defend that view by a similar obstinacy. For an equal punishment should bind not only those who do evil but also those who approve of those who do it, because I think there is not much difference between the mind of the one who does the evil and the approval of the one who consents to it. Furthermore, I add: A person generally learns to give up his error if no one agrees with him. And so, dearest brothers, let this judgment stand firm against the aforementioned persons. Let them be absent from the houses of the Lord; let them be without pastoral care lest the dreadful diseases of those two sheep perhaps infect the unwary crowd and the wolf with his rapacious heart rejoice

---

2. See Jn 6:54.
3. See 2 Tm 2:14.23.
4. See Gal 1:7; 5:12.

over the many slain carcasses of the sheep within the sheepfold of the Lord, while their guardians turn a blind eye to the wound from these two. We must be on the lookout lest by tolerating the wolves we seem to be hirelings rather than shepherds.

7. Since Christ the Lord indicated by his own voice that he did not want the death of the one who dies but only that he come back and live,[5] we command that, if they ever put aside the error of their teaching, come to their senses, and condemn those ideas by which they sinned and condemned themselves, they not be denied the usual medicine, that is, that they be taken back by the Church. Otherwise, if we reject them when they return, they might, while remaining outside the sheepfold, in fact be swallowed by the rabid jaws of the enemy who lies in waiting, jaws that they armed against themselves by the sharp points of their evil arguments. Farewell, my brothers. Given on 27 January during the consulate of the illustrious men, Honorius and Constantius.

---

5. Mt 9:13.

Letter 183

On 27 January 417 Pope Innocent wrote to the African bishops Aurelius of Carthage, the primate, Alypius of Thagaste, Augustine of Hippo, Evodius of Uzalis, and Possidius of Calama, in reply to Letter 177. Innocent thanks the bishops for their letter and confirms their condemnation of the Pelagian heresy (paragraph 1). He expresses his confidence that Pelagius' followers will more readily free themselves from his errors once they hear of his condemnation (paragraph 2). The evidence of Pelagius' acquittal at the Council of Diospolis is unclear (paragraph 3). Innocent hopes for the correction of Pelagius and outlines the steps he should take in order to be fully acquitted (paragraph 4). Finally, he reports that he read Pelagius' *Nature* and found in it many ideas opposed to the grace of God, and he calls upon Pelagius to condemn his errors in order that his followers may be recalled to the true faith (paragraph 5).

To his beloved brothers, Bishops Aurelius, Alypius, Augustine, Evodius, and Possidius, Innocent sends his greetings.

1. By our brother and fellow bishop Julius we have with great pleasure received your letter, my brothers, a letter filled with faith, supported by the whole vigor of the Catholic religion, and sent by two councils. For the whole tenor and composition of it, with its entire argument, consisted in the consideration of the daily grace of God and the correction of those who are opposed to it in order to be able to remove from them all error, offer them a suitable and worthy teacher to follow and, give them some passages from our law. But we have already said enough on these points previously, when we wrote back in reply to your reports what we thought both of their perfidy and of your view. But on this issue there is still something to say against them, nor are there ever lacking the means to conquer them since their heresy, which is fully defeated by the strength of our faith and the truth itself, is so wretched and wicked. For one who rejects and scorns all hope of life throws his heart into confusion by his hostile and damnable argument when he believes that there is nothing that he receives from God and that nothing remains that he should ask for in order to be healed. What does he have left who has taken this away from himself?

2. If, then, there are some people infected and induced to fall into error by their discourses and exhortations, persons whom such great perversity has taken hold of for its own defense and who commit and unite themselves to this teaching, hoping that there pertains to Catholic doctrine what is shown to be greatly abhorrent to it and completely opposed to it, they will hasten to return to the path of the correct way lest the error nourished, as it were, by these ideas lay siege to and take possession of their mind. For, wherever Pelagius is staying, he has deceived by that claim of his the minds of those who readily or unqualifiedly

believed his arguments, whether they dwell in this city or any place on this earth. Since we do not know them, we can neither reveal them nor deny their presence here. For, if they are here, they are hidden and do not dare to defend him when he teaches these ideas or to spread them about when one of us is present. In such a large number of people someone is not easily discovered, nor is there anywhere that he could be recognized. We believe that they can be easily corrected by the mercy and grace of God after they hear of the condemnation of him who has been discovered to be the stubborn and rebellious author of this teaching. Nor does it matter where they are since they must be healed wherever they can be found.

3. But we are not able to be persuaded that he was found innocent, though some lay persons have brought us copies of the proceedings by which Pelagius believed that he was tried and set free. We doubt whether the records are correct, because they arrived without any statement of that council, and we have not received a letter on the matter from those before whom Pelagius presented the reasons for his teaching. If Pelagius had been able to be convinced of his acquittal, we tend to think that he would have acted in such a way as to compel his judges to make it known by their letters, which could have been much more probable. But since there are recorded in those proceedings some objections, which he in part suppressed by dodging them and in part threw into total confusion by heaping many words upon them in return, he defended, as he could have thought good at the time, some ideas by false arguments rather than by true reason, denying some charges and giving others a false interpretation.

4. But I wish—and this is what is more to be desired—that he would turn away from the path of his error to the true road of the Catholic faith so that he might desire and want to be corrected, considering and recognizing the daily grace and help of God, so that he might truly be seen and found by all to have been corrected with clear reason, not by a proof from the proceedings but by a heart converted to the Catholic faith. For this reason we can neither approve nor find fault with the judgment of those bishops since we do not know whether the records are accurate; if they are accurate, it might be shown that he escaped by subterfuge rather than proved himself innocent with the full truth. If he is confident and knows that he does not deserve condemnation by us because he says that he has already condemned everything that he had said, he should not be summoned by us but should rather himself hasten to appear before us in order to be absolved. For, if he still has those ideas, when will he present himself for our judgment by reason of some letter, since he knows that he will be condemned? But if he must be summoned, it would be better if it were done by those who seem to be closer and are not separated by a huge distance of the earth. In any case he will not lack our care if he presents what stands in need of healing. After all, he can condemn his ideas and by means of a letter ask pardon for his error, as befits his return to us, my dearest brothers.

5. We have indeed examined the book that is said to be his and was sent to us by Your Charity. In it we read many things written against the grace of God, many blasphemies, nothing pleasing, and almost nothing that was not completely displeasing, deserving to be condemned and trodden underfoot by everyone. No one else but the person who had written these things would admit into his mind and hold ideas like that. For we did not consider it necessary here to discuss the law at length, as if Pelagius had been brought before us and were defending himself, since we have spoken about the whole issue with you who know all of it and rejoice with us in full agreement. For it is better to set forth these passages when we are dealing with those who are evidently imprudent in these matters. Who is there who holds the correct view and cannot discuss at length the ability of nature, free choice, every grace of God, and daily grace? Let Pelagius, therefore, anathematize those views of his so that those who have fallen because of his words and directives may know what the true faith holds. For they will be able to be called back more easily when they have seen that these views are condemned by their author. But if he chooses stubbornly to remain in this impiety, we must act in order to be of help at least to those who were led astray not by their own error but by the error of this man, so that they do not lose this medicine whose existence this man denies and from which he does not ask for healing.

[*In another hand:*] May God keep you safe, most dear brothers. Given on the sixth day before the Calends of February.

Letter 184

Before 416 Pope Innocent sent a brief letter of greetings to Aurelius of Carthage and Alypius of Thagaste.

Innocent greets Bishops Aurelius and Alypius.

The return to you of Germanus, my fellow priest, who is most dear to me, ought not to lack a proof of our esteem. For it seems to us somehow natural and reasonable to greet very dear friends through dear friends. We desire, therefore, that you, our most dear brothers, rejoice in the Lord, and we ask that you pour out similar prayers to God for us because, as you well know, we accomplish more by common and mutual prayers than by individual and private ones.

Letter 184A

In approximately 418 Augustine wrote to two monks, Peter and Abraham; he tells them that the answers to the questions that they posed can be found in many of his writings (paragraph 1). He explains the importance of baptism for infants who are still unable to commit any personal sin (paragraph 2) and the role of concupiscence of the flesh in the inheritance of original sin (paragraph 3). He points out that the monks should pray that God may grant faith to those who still do not believe (paragraph 4). Augustine tells them he has written the first ten books of *The City of God* against the pagans who worship idols (paragraph 5), and with the sort of pagans who have no religion at all he suggests that the monks should not discuss religion (paragraph 6). Having indicated where Peter and Abraham can expect to find the answers to their questions, he brings the letter to an end (paragraph 7).

To his most beloved lords and holy sons, Peter and Abraham, Augustine sends greetings in the Lord.

1, 1. Justice ought not and love cannot spurn your holy zeal; it leads you to think that you should ask me many questions in order that you may not be defenseless but able to oppose quarrelsome and impious teachings. But one letter, even though a long one, cannot contain a careful response to all of them. You know, however, that in many of our works I have already replied to all or almost all your questions as well as I could. If you read them, for I hear that you have taken up a life of service to God so that you have time for reading, either the whole teaching will become clear to you or, I think, not much will be lacking, especially since you have within you the interior teacher by whose grace you are the sort of men you are. For how does one human being help another to learn something if we are not taught by the Lord.[1] In accord with the help of the Lord, I shall nonetheless not deprive you of your expectation in this letter, at least by a short answer.

2. The Lord says, *One who believes and is baptized will be saved, but one who does not believe will be condemned* (Mk 16:16). When infants are baptized it is not said in vain but is truly the case that they are counted among the faithful, and for this reason they are also called new sons and daughters by the lips of all Christians. And it is certain that, if they do not believe, they will be condemned, but since they have added nothing to original sin by living bad lives, their punishment in that condemnation can correctly be said to be the slightest, but not to be none at all. If anyone, however, thinks that there will be no difference in punishments, he should read what scripture says, *It will be more tolerable for*

---

1. See Jn 6,45; Is 54,13.

174

Sodom on the day of judgment than for that city (Mt 10:15). Let the deceivers not seek a middle place for infants between the kingdom and punishment.[2] But let the infants cross over from the devil to Christ, from death to life, so that the anger of God does not remain over them.[3] Only the grace of God, indeed, sets them free from the anger of God. But what is the anger of God if not the punishment and penalty they deserve from the just God? For God is not agitated by some emotion in the way a mind subject to change becomes angry. Rather, what we call the anger of God is nothing but the just punishment of sin, and it is not surprising that this is passed on to our descendants.

3. Concupiscence of the flesh, of course, by which the seed is sown and children are conceived, did not exist before sin, nor would it have existed at all if the disobedience of the man was not followed by the disobedience of man's own flesh as a punishment in return. Although the good of marriage makes good use of that evil, marital intercourse, that is, licit and good intercourse for the sake of procreating children, cannot take place without it. It could, however, have taken place without it if human nature had by not sinning remained in the state in which it was created. For the genitals could, like the other body parts, be moved to perform their proper act by the command of the will instead of being aroused by the heat of passion. For who would claim that those words of God, *Increase and multiply* (Gn 1:22), are a curse upon sins rather than a blessing upon marriage? Apart from Christ, who was neither fathered nor conceived through this concupiscence (for his birth from the Virgin came about in a far different way), whatever is sown, conceived, and born through this concupiscence must be reborn in order to avoid punishment. For, even if a child is born of parents who have been reborn, carnal birth cannot offer the child what only spiritual rebirth offered the parents. In the same way only a wild olive tree is born not only of a wild olive tree but also of a domesticated olive tree. We have said much on these topics in our other writings, which I wish that you would read instead of obliging us to repeat the same things.

2, 4. But it is more difficult to reply to unbelievers, who are not bound by the authority of the Christian books. Nor can their error be corrected by the weight of divine scripture; on the contrary, against them scripture, which they openly attack, must be defended. But if the Lord also helps you in order to be able to do this, you still do too little with those people whom you desire to be Christians if you conquer their unbelief with truthful arguments if you do not also beg for

---

2. See Mt 19:23-24; 25:34-46; Dn 12:2; Lk 22:19; Mk 10:25; Jn 3:3-5. Against the Pelagian idea that the souls of unbaptized infants attained paradise, but not the kingdom of heaven, Augustine was adamant that there was no "third place" between heaven and hell. It was not until the time of Peter Lombard that the Church permitted a doctrine of limbo. The third canon of the Council of Carthage in 418 explicitly rejected the Pelagian view that infants dying without baptism attain paradise, but not the kingdom of heaven.

3. See Jn 5:24; 3: 36; Rom 3:5.

faith for them by prayers of supplication. And faith itself, as you know, is a gift of God, who imparts to each person the measure of faith,[4] and it is the sort of gift that necessarily precedes understanding. For the prophet was not mistaken when he said, *Unless you believe, you will not understand* (Is 7:9 LXX). And because [it was only by the gift of God that they could believe],[5] it was not for those who were already believers but for the still unbelieving Jews that the apostle prayed for faith when he said, *Brothers and sisters, the good desire of my heart and prayer to God is for their salvation* (Rom 10:1), for those, that is, who had killed Christ or who would surely kill him if they were given the power. For such men the Lord prayed himself when he was mocked as he hung on the cross,[6] and blessed Stephen prayed for them when he was being stoned.[7]

3, 5. There are two kinds of these unbelievers, whom we are accustomed to call either Gentiles or pagans by the commonly used term. One of them prefers the superstitions that they believe to the Christian religion; the other of them is tied to no sort of religion. I have given to certain books the title *City of God*. I think you have already heard of them, and I am trying in the midst of my work to complete those that still remain, if it is the Lord's will. Against the first kind of these people I have completed ten large volumes. The apostle described this kind when he said, *What the Gentiles sacrifice they sacrifice to demons, not to God* (1 Cor 10:20), and, to be sure, when he said, *They worshiped and served a creature rather than the creator* (Rom 1:25). The first five of these books refute those who maintain that the worship not of the one highest and true God but of many gods is necessary in order to attain or to retain earthly and temporal happiness. But the next five are against those who raise themselves up against this salutary teaching with a greater swelling and inflation of pride and think that they will come even to the beatitude that is hoped for after this life through the worship of many demons and gods. There their distinguished philosophers are also refuted by us in the three last books of those five. The remaining books, beginning with the eleventh, however many they will be, of which I have already completed three and have the fourth in my hands, will contain what we hold and believe concerning the city of God so that we may not seem to have wanted only to refute the views of others in this work and not also to state our own. The fourth book after the ten and the fourteenth of the whole work will, if the Lord wills, contain the answers to all the questions that you raised for me in your letter.

6. But I do not know whether one should have any discussion of a question of religion with the other kind of unbelievers, who do not believe that there is any divine power or believe that human affairs are of no concern to it, though in our

---

4. See Rom 12:3; 1 Cor 12:11.
5. There is a lacuna here in the manuscript. Within the brackets I have conjectured what might be missing.
6. See Lk 23:34.
7. See Acts 7:59.

times almost no one is found so stupid as to dare to say even in his heart, *There is no God* (Ps 13:1). There is, however, no lack of those other fools who say, *The Lord will not see* (Ps 93:7), that is, he does not extend his providence to these earthly concerns. Nonetheless, in these books, which I want Your Charity to read, while the city of God is defended, it will be shown to be believable, if God wills and for whom he wills, not only that God exists, which is something fixed in our nature that no impiety hardly ever extinguishes, but also that he has care for human affairs from the creation of human beings up to the bestowal of happiness upon the righteous along with the holy angels and up to the condemnation of the wicked along with the bad angels.

7. This letter, therefore, should not, dearest friends, be made any more burdensome. For we have sufficiently stated in it where you may hope to come to know what you want through our ministry, and in accord with our slight ability we have taken care that you can have those books, if you do not yet have them, through my holy brother and fellow priest, Firmus who loves you a geat deal and has quite carefully taught us that we should love you so that he may be grateful for your love in return.

Letter 185

In approximately 417 Augustine wrote to Boniface, the tribune of Africa, who later became the count of Africa, the same man for whom he also wrote Letters 185A, 189, and 17*. As the one in charge of implementing the punishments imposed upon the Donatists, Boniface had consulted Augustine about the character of Donatism. In *Revisions* 2, 48 Augustine treated the present letter as a book and gave it the title, *The Correction of the Donatists*. He says of it:

> At the same time I also wrote a book, *The Correction of the Donatists*, on account of those who refused to be corrected by the imperial laws. This book begins: "I express my praise and congratulations, and I am amazed."

Augustine begins by explaining the difference between the Donatists and the Arians, with whom Boniface was more familiar (paragraph 1). Scripture foretold that heresies and schisms would come to test our faith and love (paragraph 2). Along with the Catholics the Donatists recognize Christ in the scriptures, where they should also recognize the Catholic Church, which the scriptures foretold would spread throughout the whole world (paragraph 3). Even if Caecilian, the Catholic bishop of Carthage at the time the schism began, was guilty, as the Donatists claimed, they are still not justified in abandoning the unity of Christ (paragraph 4). It is not clear that Caecilian was guilty, but it is clear from the words of God that the Church would spread to all the nations (paragraph 5).

The Donatists were the first to appeal to the emperor when they took their case against Caecilian to Constantine (paragraph 6). The laws promulgated against the Donatists are actually for their benefit (paragraph 7). The Donatists must obey laws of the Christian emperors in defense of religious truth or submit to the penalties (paragraph 8). When the Donatists suffer under these laws, they are not martyrs because they do not suffer for the sake of justice (paragraph 9). It is not always wrong to persecute, just as it is not always right to be persecuted (paragraph 10). The wicked unjustly persecute the Church, while the Church justly persecutes the enemies of the Church (paragraph 11).

Augustine recounts the violent behavior of some of the Donatists, who have even resorted to killing themselves (paragraph 12). The laws of the emperors that force them into the unity of the Church are highly salutary (paragraph 13). The Church rightly tries to save them, even against their will and even at the risk that some will kill themselves rather than enter the Church (paragraph 14). Augustine continues his account of the Donatist violence and points out that their crimes kept many from entering into the Catholic Church (paragraphs 15 and 16). The Maximianist separation from the Donatists and their reconciliation with them provides a strong argument against the Donatists themselves (paragraph 17). Augustine explains that the terrible violence on the part of some Donatists brought the Catholics to appeal to the civil authorities (paragraph 18). The Christian emperors now use their power in the service of God (paragraph 19), as it was foretold that the kings of the earth would serve God (paragraph 20).

Though it is better to bring people to worship God by instruction than by fear of punishment and pain, the latter means are valuable too (paragraph 21). Christ himself used coercion in the conversion of Paul the apostle (paragraph 22). So, too, the Church has the right to use coercion to bring the Lord's lost sheep back to the fold (paragraph 23). Augustine explains the parable in which the Lord's servants are ordered to compel people to come in to the banquet from the roads and pathways (paragraph 24).

Augustine explains why he earlier did not want to use coercion against the Donatists and later changed his mind (paragraph 25). His earlier view failed to prevail because of the terrible way in which the Donatists treated the Catholic bishop of Bagai (paragraph 26). Augustine recounts the savage treatment that this bishop received from the Donatists (paragraph 27). Even Paul the apostle himself appealed to the protection of the emperor (paragraph 28). And great benefits have come to the church of Africa from the laws issued by the emperors (paragraph 29). For many Donatists have entered into union with the Catholic Church, though others have refused and turned to further violence (paragraph 30). The Catholic Church, nonetheless, meets their hatred and slander with love (paragraph 31).

As David in grief over the loss of Absalom was consoled by the preservation of his kingdom, so the Church is consoled by the salvation of many in her grief over the few who perish by their own hand (paragraph 32). Augustine develops a comparison between the Donatists and people who are in a building that we know is going to collapse and who threaten to kill themselves if we try to rescue them (paragraph 33). He argues that, if we could rescue even one person, we would have the obligation to do so, even if the rest kill themselves (paragraph 34).

Augustine replies to the Donatist objection that the Catholics are seeking their property (paragraph 35). If the Donatists enter the Church, they will have their own property as well as the property of the Church along with the Catholics (paragraph 36). He challenges the Donatist claim to righteousness and warns them against seeking to establish a righteousness of their own (paragraph 37). The Church in this world needs to pray daily for forgiveness of sins and will be without spot or wrinkle only in the next world (paragraph 38). All past sins are forgiven in baptism, but only if baptism is conferred within the Church (paragraph 39). For baptism makes righteous only those present in the body of Christ, which is the Church (paragraph 40). Scripture foretells the triumph of the righteous over the unrighteous, that is, of the Catholics over the Donatists (paragraph 41). For apart from the unity of Christ no one can be righteous (paragraph 42).

Augustine explains that the Donatists are not rebaptized when they enter the Catholic Church because they already have the mark of the king (paragraph 43). He also explains why the Donatists are allowed to retain positions of honor in the Church, though the previous practice of the Church had been more strict (paragraph 44). The rigorous discipline has been relaxed in order to heal the wound of schism (paragraph 45). The Donatists are received into the Church with their full honors, but they should also do penance for their error (paragraph 46). Just as the Donatists received back the Maximianists for the peace of their sect, so the Church welcomes back the Donatists for the peace of Christ (paragraph 47).

Augustine turns to the Donatist objection that they should not be forgiven if they have sinned against the Holy Spirit (paragraph 48). He explains that the sin against the Holy Spirit that will not be forgiven is not just any sin but the refusal, up to the end of one's life, to be in the unity of Christ's body (paragraph 49). Augustine warns the Donatists that they cannot have the Holy Spirit outside the body of Christ (paragraph 50). In closing, Augustine apologizes to Boniface for the length of his letter but promises him that he will find in it the answers to the questions that the Donatists raise (paragraph 51).

A Book on the Correction of the Donatists

1, 1. I express my praise and congratulations, and I am amazed, my most beloved son Boniface, that amid the concerns of armed warfare you intensely desire to know the things that pertain to God. From this it is truly evident that you serve the faith that you have in Christ even in a military setting. In order, therefore, to inform Your Charity briefly of the difference between the error of the Arians and that of the Donatists, the Arians say that the Father and the Son and the Holy Spirit have different substances. The Donatists, however, do not say this but confess that the Trinity has one substance. And if some of the Donatists say that the Son is less than the Father, they do not deny that he is of the same substance. But very many among them say that they believe about the Father and the Son and the Holy Spirit the same thing that the Catholic Church believes. Nor is this the question at issue with them, but to their misfortune they quarrel only about Church unity and, by the perversity of their error, carry on rebellious hostilities against the unity of Christ. But at times some of them, as we have heard, wanting to win the Goths to their side, when they see that they have some power, say that they believe the same thing as the Goths. But they are refuted by the authority of their predecessors, because not even Donatus himself is said to have held that belief, and it is his sect to which they boast of belonging.

2. But, my dearest son, do not let these things upset you. It was predicted, after all, that there would be heresies and scandals so that we might develop our minds in the midst of our enemies and that in that way our faith and love might be more tested—our faith, of course, in order that they may not deceive us, but our love in order that we may also work for their correction as much as we can, not merely striving so that they may not harm the weak and so that they may be set free from their wicked error, but also praying for them so that the Lord may

open their minds and they may understand the scriptures.[1] For in the holy books where Christ the Lord is revealed, his Church is also made known. But, though the Donatists come to know Christ only in the scriptures, with an amazing blindness they do not recognize his Church through the authority of the divine writings but design their own church through the vanity of human lies.

3. They recognize Christ along with us when we read, *They have pierced my hands and my feet; they have numbered all my bones. But they saw me and looked upon me. They have divided for themselves my clothes, and they cast lots for my tunic.* (Ps 22:17-19) But they refuse to recognize the Church in what follows a little later, *All the ends of the earth will remember and turn to the Lord, and all the families of the nations will adore in his sight, for kingship belongs to the Lord, and he will have dominion over the nations* (Ps 22:28-29). They recognize Christ along with us when we read, *The Lord said to me: You are my Son; today I have begotten you* (Ps 2:7). But they refuse to recognize the Church in what follows, *Ask me, and I shall give you the nations as your heritage and the ends of the earth as your possession* (Ps 2:8). They recognize Christ along with us in what the Lord says in the gospel, *It was necessary that Christ suffer and rise from the dead on the third day* (Lk 24:46). But they refuse to recognize the Church in what follows: *And that repentance be preached in his name through all the nations, beginning from Jerusalem* (Lk 24:47). And countless are the testimonies of the holy books, which I should not squeeze into this book. Just as Christ the Lord is seen in them either in his divinity equal to the Father, by which he was *the Word in the beginning, and the Word was with God, and the Word was God* (Jn 1:1), or in the lowliness of the flesh, which he assumed because *the Word became flesh and dwelled among us* (Jn 1:14), so his Church is seen to be not in Africa alone, as they rave in their most impudent vanity, but spread throughout the whole world.

4. For they prefer their contentions to the divine testimonies because, on account of the case of Caecilian, formerly bishop of the church of Carthage, against whom they brought charges that they could not and cannot prove, they split off from the Catholic Church, that is, from the unity of all the nations. And yet, even if the charges they brought against Caecilian were true and could at some point be proved to us, and we anathematized Caecilian, who is now dead, we should still not for the sake of any human being abandon the Church of Christ, which is not fashioned by quarrelsome opinions but is proved by divine testimonies, *because it is better to place one's trust in the Lord than in a human being* (Ps 118:8). For even if Caecilian sinned (and I say this without prejudice to the man's innocence) Christ did not for this reason lose his heritage. It is easy for one human being to believe true or false things about another, but it is crim-

---

1. See Lk 24:45; 1 Cor 11:19.

inal impudence to want to condemn the Church's communion, which stretches throughout the world, because of the crimes of a human being that you cannot prove to the whole world.

5. I do not know whether Caecilian was ordained by those who surrendered the books of God; I did not see it; I heard it from his enemies. It is not told me in the law of God, in the preaching of the prophets, in the holiness of the psalms, in the apostle of Christ, or in the words of Christ. But testimonies from the whole of the scriptures proclaim with one voice the Church spread through the whole world, with which the sect of Donatus is not in communion. The law of God said, *In your offspring all the nations will be blessed* (Gn 22:18, 26:4). God said through the prophet, *From the rising of the sun to its setting a pure sacrifice is offered to my name, because my name has been glorified among the nations* (Mal 1:11). God said through the psalm, *He will have dominion from sea to sea and from the river to the ends of the earth* (Ps 72:8). God said through the apostle, *Bearing fruit and growing in the whole world* (Col 1:6). The Son of God said with his own lips, *You will be my witnesses in Jerusalem, in all of Judea, and in Samaria, and to the ends of the earth* (Acts 1:8). Caecilian, the bishop of the church of Carthage, is accused by the quarrels of human beings; the Church of Christ, established in all nations, is praised by words of God. Piety, truth, and love do not permit us to accept against Caecilian the testimony of human beings whom we do not see in the Church to which God gave testimony. For those who do not follow the testimonies of God have lost the weight of human testimony.

2, 6. I add the fact that by their accusations they themselves referred the case of Caecilian to the judgment of Emperor Constantine. In fact, after the episcopal tribunals, in which they were not able to defeat Caecilian, they brought Caecilian himself, by their most persistent prosecution, to be examined by the aforementioned emperor. And now, in order to deceive the ignorant, they blame in us what they did first, when they say that Christians ought not to ask for anything from Christian emperors against the enemies of Christ. They did not dare to deny this in the conference that we held together at Carthage;[2] in fact, they dared to boast that their predecessors brought criminal charges against Caecilian before the emperor, adding, moreover, the lie that they won their case there and caused him to be condemned. How, then, are they not persecutors who, when they persecuted Caecilian by their accusations and lost to him, chose to claim for themselves false glory by a most impudent lie? For they not only thought it no sin if they were able to prove that Caecilian was condemned by means of their predecessors' accusations, but they even boasted of it in praise of themselves. Since the proceedings are very lengthy, especially for you who are occupied with other matters requisite for the Roman peace, it would take a great deal of time to read

---

2. Augustine refers to the Conference of Carthage held 1-8 June 411, at which the Donatist schism was in principle ended.

how the Donatists were defeated in every way at the conference itself, but you could perhaps read a synopsis of them, which I believe my brother and fellow bishop Optatus[3] has, or, if he does not have it, it could easily be obtained from the church of Sitifis,[4] since this book too is perhaps burdensome for a man with your concerns because of its length.

7. For the same thing happened to the Donatists as happened to the accusers of holy Daniel. For, just as the lions were turned against those men,[5] so the laws by which the Donatists wanted to destroy the innocent Caecilian have been turned against them. But by the mercy of Christ these laws, which seem to be against them, are rather in their favor since many Donatists have been corrected by them and are being corrected each day, and they give thanks that they have been corrected and set free from that mad destruction. And those who hated the laws now love them, and the more they hated the laws in their insanity, the more they are thankful, once they have recovered their health, that the laws so very conducive to their salvation were harsh toward them. And they are aroused by a similar love along with us for the others with whom they had been perishing. Hence, they strive equally with us in order that the others may not perish. For a doctor is troublesome to a raging madman and a father to an undisciplined son, the former by tying him down, the latter by beating him, but both because they act out of love. If, however, they neglect them and permit them to perish, this false gentleness is in fact cruel. After all, *the horse and the mule, which lack intellect* (Ps 32:9), resist with bites and kicks human beings who treat their wounds in order to heal them, and human beings are often put in danger from their teeth and hoofs and at times injured. But they still do not abandon them until they have brought them back to health by painful and tormenting medical interventions. How much more should one human being not abandon another, how much more should one brother not abandon another, lest he perish for eternity! For, once he has been corrected, he can understand what a great benefit he received when he was complaining of suffering persecution.

8. And so, as the apostle says, *While we have the time, let us do good for all without growing weary* (Gal 6:9-10). According to what is possible in each case, whether by the words of Catholic preachers or by the laws of the Catholic emperors, in part by those who obey the teachings of God, in part by those who obey the orders of the emperor, let all be called to salvation; let all be called back from destruction. For, when the emperors establish bad laws in favor of error and against the truth, those who hold the correct faith are put to the test and those who persevere win the crowns of martyrs. But when they establish good laws in favor of the truth and against error, those who act with violence are struck with terror

3. Optatus was the Catholic bishop of Milevis in Numidia.
4. Sitifis was the capital of Mauritania Sitifensis.
5. See Dn 6:21.

and those who act with intelligence are corrected. Whoever, then, refuses to obey the laws of the emperors that are issued against the truth of God earns a great reward, but whoever refuses to obey the laws of the emperors that are issued in favor of the truth of God earns a great punishment. After all, even in the times of the prophets all the kings are blamed who did not forbid or stop in the people of God practices that were instituted contrary to the commandments of God, and those who forbade and stopped them are praised beyond the merits of the others. And since King Nebuchadnezzar was a worshiper of idols, he established a sacrilegious law that the people were to worship a statue, but those who refused to obey his impious decree acted piously and faithfully. Yet the same king, once he was corrected by a miracle of God, established a pious and praiseworthy law in favor of the truth that whoever spoke blasphemously against the true God of Shadrach, Meshach and Abednego would be put to death along with his whole house.[6] If any individuals held this law in contempt and rightly suffered the penalty that had been established, they ought to have said what these Donatists say, namely, that they are righteous because they suffer persecution on account of the emperor's law. They would certainly say this if they were as insane as these Donatists are insane who divide the members of Christ, subject the sacraments of Christ to exsufflation,[7] and boast of being persecuted because they are forbidden to do these actions by the laws of the emperors, which they established for the sake of the unity of Christ, while the Donatists deceitfully boast of their own innocence and seek from human beings the glory of martyrs, a glory they cannot receive from the Lord.

9. But they are true martyrs of whom the Lord says, *Blessed are those who suffer persecution on account of justice* (Mt 5:10). Those, then, who suffer persecution on account of injustice and on account of the impious division of Christian unity are not true martyrs, but those *who suffer persecution on account of justice*. For Hagar suffered persecution from Sarah,[8] and Sarah who did this was holy, while Hagar who suffered persecution was sinful. Is holy David, whom wicked Saul persecuted, to be compared with this persecution that Hagar suffered?[9] There is a big difference, not because he suffered persecution, but because he suffered persecution on account of justice. And the Lord himself was crucified along with thieves,[10] but the reasons for their suffering separated those whom their suffering united. For this reason we should understand in the psalm the cry of true martyrs who desire to distinguish themselves from false martyrs,

---

6. See Dn 3:5.96.
7. Exsufflation was part of the rite of baptism in which the devil was "blown out" of the candidate for baptism. In repeating baptism the Donatists subjected the baptism of Christ to such disrespect.
8. See Gn 16:6.
9. See 1 Sm 18:8-11.
10. See Mt 23:38; Mk 15:27; Lk 22:33.

Judge me, O God, and distinguish my cause from that of an unholy people (Ps 43:1). The psalmist did not say, "Distinguish my punishment," but, *Distinguish my cause*. For the punishment of martyrs can be like that of the wicked, but their cause is different. And to martyrs there belongs that cry, *They have persecuted me unjustly; help me* (Ps 119:86). David thought that he was justly worthy of being helped because he was being persecuted unjustly. For, if he were being justly persecuted, he ought not to have been helped but corrected.

10. But if they think that no one can justly persecute anyone, as when they said in the conference that the true Church is the one that suffers persecution, not the one that inflicts it,[11] I omit saying what I mentioned above. For, if what they say is true, Caecilian pertained to the true Church when their predecessors persecuted him right up to the tribunal of the emperor with their accusations. For we say that he belonged to the true Church not because he suffered persecution but because he suffered on account of justice, but that the Donatists were separated from the Church not because they persecuted him but because they did so unjustly. This, then, is what we say. But if they do not look for the reasons why each person inflicts persecution or suffers it but think that it is a mark of a true Christian if one does not inflict but suffers persecution, they undoubtedly include in their definition Caecilian, who did not inflict but suffered persecution, but they exclude from that definition their own predecessors, who inflicted but did not suffer persecution.

11. But, as I said, I omit this. Here is what I say: If the true Church is the one that suffers and does not inflict persecution, let them ask the apostle which church Sarah symbolized when she persecuted her serving girl. He says that our free mother, the heavenly Jerusalem, that is, the true Church of God, was in fact symbolized by the woman who mistreated her serving girl.[12] But if we examine the question more carefully, that girl persecuted Sarah more by her pride than Sarah persecuted her by restraining her. For the serving girl was doing an injustice to her mistress, while Sarah was disciplining her pride. Next I ask: If good and holy people never persecute anyone but only suffer persecution, whose words do they think are found in the psalm where we read, *I shall persecute my enemies and seize them, and I shall not turn back until they collapse* (Ps 18:37). If, then, we want to speak or recognize the truth, that persecution is unjust which the wicked inflict upon the Church of Christ, and that persecution is just which the churches of Christ inflict upon the wicked. The Church, therefore, is blessed that suffers persecution on account of justice,[13] but those people are wretched who suffer persecution on account of injustice. The Church persecutes by

---

11. See *Acts of the Conference* (*Gesta collationis*) 3, 22, where the Donatist Petilian says, "For with us is found the true Catholic Church that suffers persecution, not the one that inflicts it."
12. See Gal 4:21-31.
13. See Mt 5:10.

loving; they persecute by raging. The Church persecutes in order to correct; they persecute in order to destroy. The Church persecutes in order to call back from error; they persecute in order to cast down into error. The Church, finally, persecutes and lays hold of enemies until they collapse in their vanity so that they may grow in the truth. They return evil for good[14] because we have at heart their eternal well-being, while they try to take from us even our temporal well-being. They love murder to the point that they commit murder upon themselves when they cannot murder others. For, just as the love of the Church labors to set them free from that perdition so that none of them dies, their madness labors either to kill us in order to feed their desire for cruelty or to kill themselves lest they seem to have lost the power to kill human beings.

3, 12. But those who do not know their habits think that they are now killing themselves when, at the occasion of the laws that were established on behalf of unity, so many peoples are being set free from their utterly insane dominion. But those who know what they were accustomed to do even before these laws are not surprised at their deaths but recall their conduct. Especially when the worship of idols still existed, long columns of their crowds came to the well-attended feasts of the pagans not to smash their idols but to be killed by the worshipers of idols. For, if they chose to smash their idols when they had lawful authority, they could have some vague claim to the title of martyrs if something happened to them. But they came only for the purpose of being killed, while the idols remained intact, for each of those very powerful young idolaters had the custom of offering to the idols as many Donatists as he killed. Certain Donatists also thrust themselves upon armed travelers in order to be killed, threatening in a terrifying manner that they would strike them if they were not killed by them. At times they obtained by force from transient judges that they be slain by executioners or the police. As a result it is reported that a certain man mocked them in ordering them to be bound as if to be killed and then left, and in that way he escaped their attack without shedding blood and without being harmed. It was a daily game for them to kill themselves by steep plunges or by water and flames. For the devil taught them these three kinds of death so that, when they wanted to die and did not find anyone to terrify into striking them with the sword, they might hurl themselves over cliffs or throw themselves into water or flames. Who are we to believe took possession of their heart[15] and taught them these things but him who suggested even to our savior, as if on the basis of the law, that he should throw himself down from the pinnacle of the temple?[16] They would drive the devil's suggestion from themselves if they carried Christ, the teacher, in their heart. But because they have given the devil a place in themselves, they either perish like the herd of pigs that a multitude of demons cast

---

14. See Ps 35:12.
15. See Sir 51:28.
16. See Mt 4:5-7; Lk 4:9-13.

down from the mountain into the sea[17] or, having been rescued from these deaths and gathered to the loving bosom of the Catholic mother, they are set free, just as that man was set free by the Lord when his father presented him to be healed of the demon and said that he was accustomed at times to fall into the water and at times into the fire.[18]

13. Hence they were shown a great mercy when they were first rescued against their will, even by those laws of the emperors, from that sect in which they learned these evil practices through the teaching of lying demons so that later they would be healed in the Catholic Church, once they had become accustomed to her good commandments and morals. For many of them, whose pious and fervent faith and love we now admire in the unity of Christ, give thanks to God with great joy that they are free from the error in which they thought those evil practices were good. And they would not now offer thanks willingly if they had not earlier also left that wicked community unwillingly. What shall we say about those who daily admit to us that they had long wanted to be Catholics but lived among those people with whom they could not be what they wanted because of the weakness of fear? For, if they said one word in favor of the Catholics among those people, they themselves and their homes would be completely destroyed. Who is so insane that he would say that these people should not be helped by the imperial orders so that they might be rescued from such a great evil, while those whom they feared are now forced to be afraid and are either themselves corrected by the same fear or at least, when they pretend that they have been corrected, spare those who have now been corrected and previously feared them.

14. Suppose that they want to kill themselves to prevent the deliverance of those who should be set free and that they want to inject fear into the piety of those setting them free in that way. And as a result, while we fear that certain wicked persons may perish, those who either had already wanted not to perish or could have been saved from perishing, if force were used, are not rescued from perdition. What does Christian love do in this case, especially since those who threaten us with their own self-inflicted and insane deaths are quite few in comparison with the people to be set free? What, then, does brotherly love do? While it fears the transitory fires of furnaces for a few, does it hand over all to the eternal fires of hell? Does it abandon to everlasting destruction all those who are now willing and were previously unable to come to perpetual life by means of the Catholic peace? Does it avoid the self-inflicted deaths of some who live as an impediment to the salvation of others whom they do not allow to live according to the teaching of Christ? For, in accord with the practice of their diabolical teaching they aim to teach them to rush at any occasion to the self-inflicted deaths that we now fear in those people. Or does it, instead, save those whom it can, even if those whom it cannot save perish by their

---

17. See Mt 8:32; Mk 5:13.
18. See Mt 17:14-18; Mk 9:16-26.

own choice? For it ardently desires that all may live, but it labors harder that all may not perish. Thanks be to the Lord that both among us—not, of course, everywhere, but in very many places—and in other parts of Africa the Catholic peace has thrived and is thriving without any deaths of these insane people. But these crimes occur where there is the kind of crazy and hurtful persons that used to do the same things even at other times.

4, 15. And before these laws were issued by the Catholic emperors, the teaching of Catholic unity and peace was gradually growing and individuals came over to it from that sect as each of them received instruction, chose to, and was able to do so, though among the Donatists frenzied crowds of wicked men disturbed the peace of the innocent in various cases. What master was not forced to fear his slave if his slave sought refuge under the protection of the Donatists? Who dared even to threaten a rioter or the instigator of a riot? Who was able to demand a reckoning from a slave who consumed his provisions or from a debtor who asked the Donatists for help and defense? Out of a fear of clubs and fires and imminent death the records of the worst slaves were destroyed so that they might go free. Lists of what they had extorted from creditors were handed over to debtors. Whoever ignored their harsh language was forced by harsher blows to do what they ordered. The homes of the innocent who had offended them were either razed to the ground or destroyed by fires. Some heads of families, men nobly born and well educated, were carried off barely alive after their attacks and chained to a mill stone; they were forced by beatings to make it turn, as if they were mere animals. For what help from the civil authorities was able to do anything against them by means of the laws? What official breathed easily in their presence? What banker was able to demand what they were unwilling to pay? Who tried to avenge those who were slain by their attacks? And yet their own madness exacted punishment from them. Some provoked the swords of men against themselves so those whom they threatened with death would kill them, while others killed themselves, some by jumping over cliffs, others by water, and still others by fires, and they threw away their bestial lives by punishments that they inflicted upon themselves.

16. Very many people found these actions horrifying when they were actually in that heretical superstition. And since they thought that it was sufficient for their innocence that they were displeased at such actions, the Catholics said to them, "If these sins do not defile your innocence, how can you say that the Christian world was defiled by either the false or at least the unknown sins of Caecilian? How do you separate yourselves by a wicked crime from Catholic unity as if from the threshing floor of the Lord, which must until the time of the winnowing have both the grain that will be stored in the barn and the chaff that will be consumed by fire?"[19] And in that way some of them were given a reason

---

19. See Mt 3:12; Lk 3:17.

to cross over to Catholic unity, ready to endure even the hatred of the wicked, but more of them, though they wanted to cross over, did not dare to make enemies of those men who had such license in expressing their rage. There were some, to be sure, who suffered from those most cruel men after they had crossed over to us.

17. It also happened that at Carthage some bishops of the sect of Donatus ordained a certain deacon by the name of Maximian, who arrogantly opposed his bishop, and made him a bishop in opposition to their bishop.[20] Thus they created a schism and divided the sect of Donatus among the people of Carthage. Since this displeased more of them, they condemned the same Maximian along with twelve bishops who were present and assisted at his ordination. But they gave the others who belonged to the same schismatic group the opportunity of returning by a set day. But afterward, for the sake of the peace of their sect, they received back with their full honors certain bishops from those twelve and from those given an extension who returned after the day that had been set. And they did not dare to rebaptize any whom the condemned bishops had baptized outside of their communion. This action of theirs began to serve as a strong argument against them in favor of the Catholic Church, so that their mouths were absolutely silenced. Word of this affair was spread about by every means—as it ought to have been—in order to heal the souls of human beings from schism, and it was shown, wherever it could be, by Catholic sermons and discussions that for the peace of Donatus they accepted back with their full honors even those bishops of theirs whom they condemned and that they did not dare to declare invalid the baptism that the condemned bishops or even those who were granted a delay conferred outside their church. And yet they raise as an objection against the peace of Christ the contamination of the whole world by some sins or other, and they declare invalid the baptism conferred even in those churches from which the gospel came to Africa. For these reasons many were ashamed, and in their embarrassment at the obvious truth they were corrected in greater numbers than usual and to a greater extent wherever they were able to breathe with a degree of freedom from the savagery of those people.

18. But then the Donatists became so inflamed with anger and were aroused by such goads of hatred that hardly any churches of our communion were able to be secure against their plots, acts of violence, and brazen robberies, and hardly any road was safe for those to travel who preached the Catholic peace against their madness and refuted their insanity with the plain truth. Things came to such a point that not only the laity or certain clerics but even Catholic bishops were faced with a dire situation. For either they had to be silent about the truth or they

---

20. In 393 Maximian was ordained bishop of Carthage in opposition to the Donatist bishop, Primian, whom Maximian and his followers deposed, thus creating the Maximianist schism in the sect of Donatus.

had to endure their cruelty. But, if they were silent about the truth, not only would this silence set no one free but many would also be lost through being led astray by them. If, however, the preaching of the truth provoked their fury to the point of rage, though some would be set free and our people would find strength, fear would again prevent the weak from following the truth. Since the Church was afflicted with these difficult conditions, whoever thinks that we should have endured everything rather than asking that the help of God be brought by means of the Christian emperors pays too little attention to the fact that no good reason could be given for this negligence.

5, 19. Those who do not want just laws to be established against their wickedness say that the apostles did not seek anything of the sort from the rulers of the earth. They do not take into account that it was a different time and that all things are done at their proper times. For what emperor then believed in Christ and would serve him by issuing laws in favor of piety and against impiety when those words of the prophet were still being fulfilled, *Why have the nations raged and the peoples planned folly? The kings of the earth rose up, and the princes came together against the Lord and against his anointed.* (Ps 2:1-2) There was as yet no realization of what it says a little later in the same psalm, *And now, O kings, understand; receive instruction, you who judge the world. Serve the Lord with fear, and exult before him with trembling.* (Ps 2:10-11) How, then, do kings serve the Lord with fear except by forbidding and punishing with religious severity actions done against the Lord's commandments? For he serves in one way because he is a man, and he serves in another way because he is king. For, because he is a man, he serves him by living a life of faith, but, because he is also a king, he serves him by upholding with appropriate force laws that command what is just and forbid what is unjust. In that way Hezekiah served God by destroying the groves, the temples of idols, and the high places erected contrary to the commandments of the Lord.[21] In that way Josiah served God by also doing the same sort of actions.[22] In that way the king of the Ninevites served God by compelling the whole city to placate the Lord.[23] In that way Darius served God by entrusting the smashing of the idol to the power of Daniel and by throwing Daniel's enemies to the lions.[24] In that way Nebuchadnezzar, about whom we have already spoken, served God by forbidding with a terrifying law all those living in his kingdom to blaspheme against God.[25] Kings, then, insofar as they are kings, serve the Lord when they do those things to serve him that only kings can do.

---

21. See 2 Kgs 18:4.
22. See 2 Kgs 23:4-20.
23. See Jon 3:6-9.
24. See Dn 14:21.41.
25. See Dn 3:96.

20. Since, then, the emperors did not yet serve the Lord at the time of the apostles and were still planning folly against the Lord and against his anointed so that all the predictions of the prophets might be fulfilled, they certainly could not at that time forbid acts of impiety by the laws; rather, they committed such acts. For the order of the ages changed so that even the Jews killed those who preached Christ, believing that they were offering a service to God, as Christ had foretold.[26] And the nations raged against the Christians, but the suffering of the martyrs conquered all. After the words of scripture began to be fulfilled, *And all the kings of the earth will adore him; all the nations will serve him* (Ps 72:11), who would say to the kings with a sober mind, "Do not be concerned about who in your kingdom defends or attacks the Lord's Church. It is no concern of yours who wants to be either religious or sacrilegious"? In the same way we cannot say to them, "It is no concern of yours who in your kingdom behaves morally or has no sense of shame." For, since God gave free will to human beings, why should adultery be punished by the laws and sacrilege be permitted? Or is it less serious for a soul to be unfaithful to God than for a woman to be unfaithful to her husband? Or, if sins that are committed not out of contempt for religion but out of ignorance should be punished more leniently, should they, then, be completely neglected?

6, 21. Would anyone doubt that it is better to bring human beings to worship God by instruction than by the fear or the pain of punishment? But because the former are better, it does not mean that the latter, who are not such, should be neglected. For it has benefited many, as we have found and continue to find by experience, to be first forced by fear or pain so that later they may be instructed or may put into practice what they have already learned verbally. Some of them quote for us the lines of a certain worldly author who said:

It is better, I believe, to hold children
In check by self-respect and kindliness than by fear.[27]

This is in fact true. But, just as they are better who are guided by love, so there are many whom fear corrects. For, to reply to them from the same author, they also read in him:

Unless you are forced by pain,
You do not know how to act correctly.[28]

But God's scripture also says on account of those better persons, *Fear does not exist along with love, but perfect love drives out fear* (1 Jn 4:18). And because of those who are less good but more in number, it says, *A stubborn servant will not*

---

26. See Jn 16:2.
27. Terence, *The Brothers* (*Adelphi*) 1, 57-58.
28. Terence, *The Brothers* (*Adelphi*) 1, 69-75; Augustine cites the words as they are abbreviated in Cicero's *Second Oration against Verres* (*Actionis in C. Verrem secundae*) 3, 62.

be corrected by words; for, even if he understands, he will not obey (Prv 29:19). When scripture said that he was not corrected by words, it did not command that he be abandoned; rather, it implicitly taught how he should be corrected. Otherwise, it would not say, *He will not be corrected by words*, but would simply say: *He will not be corrected.* In another passage, indeed, it says that not only a servant but even an undisciplined son should be restrained by beatings and with great benefit. For it says, *You beat him with a rod, but you free his soul from death* (Prv 23:14). And elsewhere it says, *He who spares the rod hates his own son* (Prv 13:24). Give me a man who says with right faith, true understanding, and all the strength of his soul, *My soul thirsts for the living God; when shall I come and stand before the face of God?* (Ps 42:3) and for such a person as this there is no need for fear not merely of temporal punishments or of imperial laws but even of hell. For he finds it so desirable a good to cling to God[29] that he not only holds in horror the loss of that happiness like a great punishment but also endures its postponement with difficulty. But before they say like good children, "We desire *to be dissolved and to be with Christ*" (Phil 1:23), many are first, like bad servants and in a sense like fleeing criminals, called back to their Lord by a beating with temporal scourges.

22. For who can love us more than Christ, who laid down his life for his sheep?[30] And yet, though he called Peter and the other apostles by words alone, in dealing with Paul, who was first Saul and later a great builder of his Church, but before that its fierce persecutor, he did not restrain him by words alone but laid him low by his power. And to press the man who was raging in the darkness of unbelief to desire the light of his heart, he first afflicted him with blindness of the body. If that were not a punishment, he would not have been healed of it later, and if his eyes were healthy when he saw nothing, though his eyes were open, scripture would not report that at the imposition of Ananias' hands some sort of scales that prevented his seeing fell from his eyes so that his sight might be restored.[31] What happens to their usual cry, "One is free to believe or not to believe. With whom did Christ use force? Whom does he compel?" See, they have Paul the apostle; let them acknowledge in him Christ first using force and afterward teaching, first striking and afterward consoling. It is amazing, however, how that man who came to the gospel, forced by bodily punishment, labored more for the gospel than all those who were called only by words.[32] And though greater fear drove him to love, his *perfect love cast out fear* (1 Jn 4:18).

23. Why, then, should the Church not force her lost children to return if those lost children were forcing others to perish. And yet their loving mother quite

---

29. See Ps 72:28.
30. See Jn 10:15.
31. See Acts 9:1-18; 13:9.
32. See 1 Cor 15:10.

warmly embraces even those whom they did not force but only misled, if they are called back to her bosom through fearsome but salutary laws.[33] And she is much over these than over those whom she had never lost. Does it not pertain to a shepherd's care to call back to the Lord's fold, once they have been found, even those sheep that were not snatched away with violence but were led astray by seduction and gentleness, that wandered off from the flock and began to belong to others? Does he not have to call them back, even by the fear and pain of beatings, if they want to resist? He ought especially to do so if the sheep have multiplied through fertility among runaway slaves and thieves, because it is more just that the Lord's brand should be recognized on them which is not violated in those whom we receive back but still do not rebaptize. For in that way the error of the sheep is to be corrected without destroying on it the mark of the redeemer. For suppose someone receives the mark of the king from a deserter who bears that mark, and suppose they both receive pardon and the deserter returns to the army, and the other begins to be in the army, where he had not been before. The mark on neither of them is canceled. Is it not rather recognized in both of them and treated with due honor, since it is the mark of the king? Because the Donatists cannot prove that it is something evil to which they are being forced, they contend that they ought not to be forced to what is good. But we show that Paul was forced by Christ; the Church, then, imitates its Lord in forcing the Donatists. The Church earlier waited without forcing anyone until the message of the prophets was fulfilled concerning the faith of kings and of the nations.[34]

24. From this we can without any absurdity understand the statement of the apostle where blessed Paul says, *We are prepared to punish every disobedience once your earlier obedience is carried out* (2 Cor 10:6). For this reason the Lord himself orders that guests first be invited to his great banquet and afterward forced. For, when his servants answered him, *Lord, we have done what you ordered, and there is still room*, he said, *Go out into the roads and pathways and force whomever you find to come in* (Lk 14:16, 21,23). In those who were first gently invited the earlier obedience is carried out, but in those who are afterward forced their disobedience meets with coercion. For what does *force them to come in* mean after he had first said, *Invite them*, and received the reply, *We have done what you ordered, and there is still room*? If he had wanted us to understand that they were to be forced by awesome miracles, many more divine miracles were produced for those who were first called, especially for the Jews, of whom scripture says, *The Jews seek signs* (1 Cor 1:22). At the time of the apostles such miracles also commended the gospel among the Gentiles so that, if the Lord ordered that guests be forced to come in by such miracles, we would rightly believe that it was rather the first guests who were forced. Hence, if the power

---

33. See Mt 18:12-13; Lk 15:4-7.
34. See Ps 72:11.

that the Church received as God's gift through the religion and faith of rulers is at the proper time forcing to come in those found on the roads and pathways, that is, those in heresies and schisms, they should not complain because they are being forced, but they should pay attention to where they are forced to go. The Lord's banquet is the unity of the body of Christ not only in the sacrament of the altar but also *in the bond of peace* (Eph 4:3). We can indeed say of these Donatists with complete truth that they force no one to what is good, for they force whomever they force only to what is evil.

7, 25. But before these laws by which they are being forced to come into the holy banquet were promulgated in Africa, some brothers, among whom I was included, thought that, though the madness of the Donatists was raging everywhere, we should not ask the emperors to give orders that this heresy be completely eliminated by establishing a punishment for those who chose to remain in it. Rather, we thought that we should ask that they establish laws so that those who preach the Catholic truth by speaking it or who read the scriptures to determine it should not suffer the Donatists' insane acts of violence. We thought that this could be achieved in some measure if they reaffirmed more explicitly against the Donatists, who denied that they were heretics, the law of Theodosius of most pious memory, which he promulgated against all the heretics in general, namely, "that any bishop or cleric of theirs, wherever he is found, should be fined ten pounds of gold."[35] We did not want all of them to be fined in that way but only those in whose territories the Catholic Church suffered some acts of violence from their clerics, from the Circumcellions, or from their people, so that, following a complaint from the Catholics who had suffered such violence, their bishops or other ministers would be held to the payment of the fine by the care of those in charge. For we thought that, if they were thoroughly frightened and did not dare to do anything of the sort, we could freely teach and hold the Catholic truth so that no one would be forced to it, but that those who wanted would follow it without the risk of having false and hypocritical Catholics. Other brother bishops of mine thought otherwise, who were older than I and who observed the examples of many cities and locales where we saw the solid and true Catholic Church, which was nonetheless established and strengthened there by such benefits from God, when human beings were forced into the Catholic communion by the laws of earlier emperors. But we obtained what I said that we should ask for instead from the emperors; it was decided by our council, and deputies were sent to the imperial court.

26. But God knew how necessary the fear engendered by these laws and a certain remedial suffering is for wicked or tepid souls and for that hardheartedness which cannot be corrected by words but which can yet be corrected by some

---

35. *The Theodosian Code* (*Codex Theodosianus*) 16, 5, 21.

moderately severe discipline. His great mercy brought it about that our delegates were not able to obtain what they had wanted to obtain. For there preceded us some very serious complaints of bishops from other places, who had suffered many evils from the Donatists and been removed from their sees. In particular the horrible and unbelievable attack upon Maximian, the Catholic bishop of Bagai, caused our legation not to get what it was after. For the law had already been promulgated that the heresy of the Donatists with all its great savagery—for it seemed more cruel to spare them than they themselves were cruel—not merely be prevented from using violence but not be permitted to go completely unpunished. And yet capital punishment was not to be imposed in order to maintain Christian gentleness even toward those unworthy of it, but fines were to be levied and exile established for their bishops and ministers.

27. The aforesaid bishop of Bagai had obtained before the ordinary judge, when the sentence was pronounced between the two parties, the basilica that the Donatists had taken over when it was Catholic. While he was standing at the altar, they attacked him with terrible violence and cruel madness and beat him horribly with clubs and weapons of that sort and, finally, with pieces of wood broken off from the same altar. They also struck him in the groin with a dagger, and the blood flowing from that wound would have left him dead if their greater savagery had not saved his life. For, when they dragged the seriously wounded man over the earth, soil blocked the hemorrhaging vein and stopped the flow of blood from which he was dying. Finally, after they abandoned him, our people tried to carry him off while chanting the psalms, but the Donatists became enraged with fiercer anger and snatched him from the hands of those who were carrying him, badly mistreating and putting to flight the Catholics, whom they surpassed by their great numbers and easily terrified by their savagery. Then, after having carried him to a tower, thinking that he had already died (although he was still alive), the Donatists pushed him off. But the bishop fell onto a pile of soft earth and was seen, recognized, and picked up by some people passing that way at night with a lamp. He was brought to a house of believers and, with much care, he recovered after many days from that desperate condition. But rumor had reported even overseas that he had been killed by the crime of the Donatists. After he arrived there, his being still alive was regarded as something completely unexpected, but by his many, large, and recent scars he proved that rumor had not without reason pronounced him dead.

28. He sought help from the Christian emperor, therefore, not for the sake of avenging himself but for protecting the church entrusted to him. If he had not done this, his suffering would not have been praiseworthy, but his negligence would have been blameworthy. For even the apostle Paul was not looking out for his own passing life but for the Church of God when he made known to the tribune the plan of those who had plotted to kill him; as a result armed soldiers

brought him to the place where he was to be brought in order to avoid their ambush.[36] He did not hesitate to appeal to Roman laws, declaring himself to be a Roman citizen, since it was not permitted to flog Roman citizens.[37] Likewise, in order that he might not be handed over to the Jews who desired to kill him, he demanded the help of Caesar, a Roman emperor but not a Christian one.[38] There he showed clearly enough what the ministers of Christ ought to do afterwards when they would find Christian emperors at a time of danger for the Church. As a result, then, when such cases were brought to his attention, the devout and pious emperor preferred to correct the error of that impiety completely by most pious laws and to bring back to the Catholic unity by terror and coercion those who bore the standards of Christ in opposition to Christ rather than merely to take away their freedom to act savagely while leaving them their freedom to be in error and to perish.

29. When the laws reached Africa, those especially who were looking for the opportunity or who feared the savagery of the Donatist fury or who were afraid of offending their own people immediately came over to the Church. Likewise many who were held in that heresy only by a habit that they inherited from their parents, people who never before knew the sort of cause this heresy had and never chose to investigate and evaluate it, became Catholics without any difficulty as soon as they began to pay attention and to find in it nothing that merited their suffering such great losses. Worry, in other words, taught those whom security had made negligent. But many who were less able by themselves to understand the difference between the error of the Donatists and Catholic truth followed the persuasive authority of all those whom we mentioned above.

30. Thus, though our true mother joyfully received great columns of people into her bosom, there remained obdurate multitudes which persisted in that plague with sorry stubbornness. From them many entered our communion as a pretense, while others remained hidden by reason of their small number. But a great many of those who entered only as a pretense were gradually corrected through becoming familiar with and hearing the preaching of the truth, especially after the conference and debate held between us and their bishops at Carthage. In certain places, however, where a more stubborn and less peaceful crowd prevailed and those fewer in number with a more positive attitude toward unity could not stand up to them, or where the crowds subject to the authority of a few persons of great power took the wrong side, the struggle lasted somewhat longer. Of these there are some with whom the struggle still goes on, and in that struggle Catholics, especially bishops and clerics, have endured many horrible and harsh sufferings, which it would take too long to discuss, when the eyes of

---

36. See Acts 23:12-32.
37. See Acts 22:24-29.
38. See Acts 25:11.

some were put out and the hands and tongue of a certain bishop were cut off. Some were even killed. I pass over the murders committed with great cruelty, the plundering of homes by attacks at night, and the burning not only of private dwellings but also of churches. And there were even some who threw the Lord's scriptures into those flames.

31. But the ensuing results consoled us who were afflicted with such evils. For, wherever these acts were committed by the wicked, there Christian unity made progress with more fervor and perfection, and the Lord is praised more abundantly who graciously granted that his servants gain their brothers by their sufferings and by their blood gather together into the peace of eternal salvation his sheep who had been scattered by their deadly error.[39] The Lord is powerful and merciful, and we daily ask that *he grant repentance* to the rest *and that they may come to their senses from the snares of the devil by whom they are held captive according to his will* (2 Tm 2:25-26). For these people only seek ways to slander us, and they repay good with evil[40] because they do not understand the attitude of love we maintain toward them and how, in accord with the Lord's command that he gave to shepherds through the prophet Ezekiel, we want to call back the straying sheep and find the lost ones.[41]

8, 32. But, as we once said elsewhere,[42] they do not blame themselves for what they do to us, and they blame us for what they do to themselves. For who among us would want not only that one of them should perish but even that he should lose anything? The house of David only merited to have peace when Absalom, David's son, was killed in the war that he waged against his father, though David ordered his men with great concern to keep him safe and alive so that he might survive to receive pardon from David's fatherly love. What, then, remained for him but to mourn his lost son and for his majesty to be consoled by the peace that had been gained for his kingdom?[43] In the same way, none other than her children are warring against their Catholic mother, for this small branch was broken off in Africa[44] from that great tree, which in fact is spread throughout the world by the development of its branches.[45] She is now in labor to give birth to them with love so that they may return to the root without which they cannot have true life.[46] If with the loss of some she gathers together the others, who are so many, especially since they are perishing, not like Absalom by the misfortune of war but rather by a death of their own choice, she soothes and heals the sorrow of her

39. See Mt 18:15; Ez 34:5-6.
40. See Ps 35:12.
41. See Ez 34:4-6.
42. See Letter 88, 8.
43. See 2 Sam 18:5-15.33; 22:1-51.
44. See Is 18:5; Rom 11:17.19.
45. See Lk 13:19, Mt 13:32; 24:14; Mk 4:32.
46. See Gal 4:19.

motherly heart by the deliverance of so many peoples. If you could only see their joy, eagerness, and enthusiasm in the peace of Christ and their frequent and joyous gatherings to hear and sing hymns and listen to the word of God, and on the part of many of them the very painful recollection of their past error and the joyful consideration of the truth that they have come to know! If you could only see their anger and hatred at the lies of their teachers, of which they are now aware, and at how they spread falsehoods concerning our sacraments! If you could also hear the admissions on the part of many of them that they earlier wanted to become Catholics but did not dare to among men of such great madness! If, then, you saw at a glance the congregations of these peoples throughout many regions of Africa who had been set free from that plague, you would then say that it would have been a mark of excessive cruelty if, out of fear that some desperate persons—by no one's reckoning comparable to the countless numbers of these people—would be consumed by their own fires and by their own choice, these people were to be abandoned to perish forever and be tormented in everlasting fires.

33. Suppose that two persons were living in one house that we most certainly knew was going to collapse and that they refused to believe us when we told them of this and insisted on remaining in it. If we were able to snatch them from there, even against their will, and afterwards showed them that the collapse was imminent in order that they would not venture to return again to that danger, I think that, if we did not do so, we would be rightly judged heartless. But if one of them said to us, "When you come in to snatch us, I will immediately kill myself," but the other wanted neither to leave nor to be snatched from there, though he would not dare to kill himself, what would we choose? To leave both of them to be crushed in the collapse or to rescue at least one by our merciful effort and to allow the other to perish not by our fault but rather by his own? No one is so impaired that he would not immediately judge what ought to be done in such cases. I have set before you this example of two persons, one who is rescued and the other lost. What, then, are we to think of a certain few who have been lost and a countless multitude of those who have been rescued? For those persons who perish by their own choice are not as many as the farms, fields, villages, towns, municipalities, and cities that are rescued by means of these laws from that deadly and eternal destruction.

34. But if we weigh more carefully the matter we are discussing, I think that, if there were many persons in the house that was going to collapse and if at least one person could be rescued from it and if, when we tried to do that, the others tried to kill themselves by hurling themselves down, we would console our sorrow over the others with the safety of at least the one. But we would still not permit them all to perish without rescuing anyone out of fear that others would destroy themselves. What, then, should we judge about the work of mercy that we ought to perform for human beings in order that they may gain eternal life and avoid eternal punishment, if an argument that is true and merciful compels us to

go to the aid of human beings in order to preserve their present state of well-being, which is not only temporal but also brief?

9, 35. They object to us that we desire their property and take it away. Would that they would become Catholics and possess not only their property but ours as well in peace and love along with us! But they are so blinded by their love of speaking slanderously that they do not notice how what they say is self-contradictory. They certainly say and seem to bewail that we are forcing them in a most hateful fashion into communion with us by the violent command of the laws. We would by no means do this if we wanted to own their property. Does any covetous person want a joint owner? Does anyone inflamed with the desire to have dominion or lifted up with the pride of ownership want to have a partner? Let them at least notice how those who were once their members, but who are now ours and are united with us in brotherly love, not only retain their property, which they had, but also have ours, which they did not have. Yet all those goods are now both ours and theirs if we are poor along with the poor. But if we personally possess things that are sufficient for us, those goods do not belong to us but to the poor. We somehow or other have charge of those goods, but we do not claim for ourselves ownership by an unjust appropriation of them.

36. Whatever, then, was owned in the name of the churches of the sect of Donatus the Christian emperors have by religious laws ordered to be transferred to the Catholic Church along with their churches. Since, therefore, the people of the same churches, who were being sustained by the same small properties, are now poor together with us, let the Donatists located outside the Church cease to desire the property of others but enter into the unity of our communion in order that we might together govern not just those goods that they say are theirs but also those that are said to be ours as well. For scripture says, *All things belong to you, but you belong to Christ. Christ, however, belongs to God.* (1 Cor 3:22-23) Under that head in his one body let us be one,[47] and let us do with all such goods what is written in the Acts of the Apostles, *They had one soul and one heart, and no one called anything his own, but they held all things in common* (Acts 4:32). Let us love what we sing, *See, how good and how pleasant it is for brothers to dwell in unity* (Ps 133:1), so that they may experience and know how truthfully their Catholic mother cries out to them what the blessed apostle writes to the Corinthians, *I do not seek your possessions, but you yourselves* (2 Cor 12:14).

37. But if we consider what is written in the Book of Wisdom, *And for this reason the righteous carried off the spoils of the wicked* (Wis 10:19), as well as what we read in Proverbs, *But the riches of the wicked are stored away for the righteous* (Prv 13:22 LXX), we will then see that we should not ask who has the possessions of the heretics but who are in the company of the righteous. We know, of

---

47. See Col 1:18.

course, that the Donatists claim for themselves such great righteousness that they not only boast that they have it but that they also bestow it on other human beings. They go so far as to say that someone whom they baptize is made righteous by them; here there only remains for them to say that someone who is baptized by them should believe in the one who baptizes him. For why should one not do so when the apostle says, *For one who believes in him who makes the sinner righteous his faith is counted as righteousness* (Rom 4:5)? Let him, therefore, believe in him if he makes him righteous so that his faith may be counted as righteousness. But I think that even they would be horrified at themselves if they venture even to think such thoughts. For only God is righteous and makes us righteous.[48] One can, however, say of these people what the apostle said of the Jews, namely, that *not knowing the righteousness of God and wanting to establish their own righteousness, they are not subject to the righteousness of God* (Rom 10:3).

38. God forbid that anyone of ours should say that he was righteous in such a way as to want to establish his own righteousness, that is, as if he gave it to himself, since God says to him, *What do you have that you have not received?* (1 Cor 4:7) God forbid that he should dare to say that he was without sin in this life in the same way as the Donatists said in our conference that they were now in that church that *has no spot nor wrinkle nor anything of the sort* (Eph 5:27). They do not know that this is only realized in those persons who leave this body either immediately after baptism or after the forgiveness of those debts that they ask in prayer to be forgiven. But in the whole Church it will be true that it has absolutely *no spot nor wrinkle nor anything of the sort*, when we will be able to say, *Where, O death, is your victory? Where, O death, is your sting? For the sting of death is sin.* (1 Cor 15:55-56)

39. But in this life, in which *the corruptible body weighs down the soul* (Wis 9:15), if their church is already so sinless, they should not say to God what the Lord taught us to pray, *Forgive us our debts* (Mt 6:12). For, after they have all been forgiven in baptism, why does the Church demand this? If even now in this life she has *no spot nor wrinkle nor anything of the sort*, they should disdain even the apostle John when he cries out in his letter, *If we say that we have no sin, we deceive ourselves, and the truth is not in us. But if we confess our sins, he is faithful and righteous who forgives us our sins and cleanses us from every iniquity.* (1 Jn 1:8-9) On account of this hope the whole Church says, *Forgive us our debts*, so that he may cleanse from every iniquity not those who are proud but those who confess their sins and so that Christ the Lord may present to himself on that day *a glorious Church that has no spot nor wrinkle nor anything of the sort* (Eph 5:27), the Church that he now cleanses *by the bath of water with the word* (Eph 5:26). For in baptism there is not a single past sin that is not

---

48. See 2 Mc 1:25; Rom 8:33.

forgiven—at least if the baptism is not conferred outside the Church in vain but is either conferred within the Church or, if it was conferred outside, the baptized person does not remain outside with it. And whatever sins those who live here after receiving baptism contract through human weakness are forgiven because of that bath. For it does not do someone who has not been baptized any good to say, *Forgive us our debts* (Mt 6:12).

40. Thus he now cleanses his Church *by the bath of water with the word* so that he may then present her to himself *having no spot nor wrinkle nor anything of the sort*, that is, entirely beautiful and perfect, when death will be swallowed up in victory.[49] Now, therefore, insofar as our having been born of God and our living from faith is having its effect upon us, we are righteous, but, insofar as we carry with us the remnants of the mortality derived from Adam, we are not without sin. For these words are true, *One who is born of God does not sin* (1 Jn 3:9), and these words are true, *If we say that we have no sin, we deceive ourselves, and the truth is not in us* (1 Jn 1:8). And so Christ the Lord is both righteous and makes us righteous, but we have been *made righteous gratuitously by his grace* (Rom 3:24). He, however, makes righteous only his own body, *which is the Church* (Col 1:24), and for this reason, if the body of Christ carries off *the spoils of the wicked* (Wis 10:19) and *the riches of the wicked are stored up* (Prv 13:22 LXX) for the body of Christ, the wicked ought not to remain outside so that they may speak slanderously but ought rather to enter so that they may be made righteous.

41. Hence those words that were written concerning the day of judgment, *Then the righteous will stand with great constancy over against those who oppressed them and carried off the fruits of their labors* (Wis 5:1), should not be understood in the sense that Canaan will stand against Israel because Israel carried off the fruits of the labors of Canaan.[50] Rather Naboth will stand against Ahab because Ahab carried off the fruits of the labors of Naboth.[51] Canaan was indeed wicked; Naboth was righteous. In the same way the pagan will not stand in opposition to the Christian who carried off the fruits of his labors when the temples of the idols were plundered or surrendered. But the Christian will stand in opposition to the pagan who carried off the fruits of his labors when the bodies of martyrs were struck down. In the same way the heretic will not stand in opposition to the Catholic who carried off the fruits of his labors when the laws of the Catholic emperors have prevailed. But the Catholic will stand in opposition to the heretic who carried off the fruits of his labors when the madness of the Circumcellions prevailed. Indeed, scripture itself resolves the question, for it does not say, "Then human beings will stand," but, *Then the righteous will stand* and *with great constancy*, because they will stand on a good conscience.

---

49. See 1 Cor 15:54.
50. See Jos 17:12-13.
51. See 1 Kgs 21:1-16.

42. But no one is righteous here with his own righteousness, that is, as if he himself produced it. Rather, as the apostle says, *As God has given to each one a measure of faith.* But he goes on and says, *For, just as we have many members in one body, though all the members do not have the same functions, so we, though many, are one body in Christ* (Rom 12:3-5). And for this reason no one can be righteous as long as he is separated from the unity of this body. For, just as if a member is cut off from the body of a living man it cannot retain the spirit of life, so a man who is cut off from the body of the righteous Christ can by no means retain the Spirit of righteousness, even if he retains the shape of the member that he received in the body. Let the Donatists, then, enter into the frame of this body, and let them possess the fruits of their labors not out of a desire to have dominion over them but out of the piety that makes good use of them. We, however, purify our will, as has already been said, of the filth of this desire, as even an enemy would judge, when we seek, as much as we can, that those very people to whom the fruits of those labors are said to belong may along with us in the Catholic communion make use of theirs and of ours.

10, 43. "But," they say, "this is what troubles us: If we are lacking righteousness, why are you seeking us?" We reply to them, "We are seeking you who are lacking righteousness so that you may not remain without righteousness. We are seeking those who are lost so that we may be able to rejoice over them when they have been found, saying, *A brother was dead and has come to life; he was lost and has been found* (Lk 15:32)." "Why, then," he asks, "do you not baptize me in order to wash away my sins?" I reply, "Because I do not do harm to the mark of the emperor when I correct the error of a deserter." "Why," he asks, "do I not at least do penance with you?" "If, in fact, you do not, you cannot be saved. For how will you rejoice over having been corrected unless you grieve over having gone astray?" "What, then," he asks, "do we receive with you when we cross over to you?" I reply, "You certainly do not receive baptism, which you were able to have outside the framework of the body of Christ but which could not do you any good. But you receive *the unity of the Spirit in the bond of peace* (Eph 4:3), *without which no one is able to see God* (Heb 12:14), and you receive the charity which, as scripture says, *covers a multitude of sins* (1 Pt 4:8)." Without that great good the apostle bears witness that nothing is of any value—neither the tongues of men and angels, nor the knowledge of all the mysteries, nor prophecy, nor faith so great that it can move mountains, nor the distribution of all one's possessions to the poor, nor one's body being tormented in fire. If, then, you place little or no value on so great a good, you deserve to be in error to your own misfortune; you deserve to perish if you do not cross over to Catholic unity.

44. "If, then," they ask, "it is necessary that we repent of having been outside the Church and in opposition to the Church in order that we may be saved, how may we remain among you as clerics or even as bishops after this penance?"

This would not be done—because it really ought not to be done, as we must admit—if the healing brought about by the restoration of peace did not compensate for it. But let them say this to themselves, and let those who have fallen into so great a death of schism grieve deeply and humbly so that they may come to life by this wound, as it were, of our Catholic mother. For, when the branch that was broken off is grafted on, another cut is made in the tree where it can be inserted in order that the branch that will perish without the life from the root may live. But when the branch grafted on begins to live off the tree that receives it, its strength and fruit follow. If, however, the branch does not begin to live off the tree, it dries up, but the life of the tree remains. For the method of grafting is such that the branch from elsewhere is grafted on without cutting off any branch that belongs to the tree, but not without a cut in the tree, though only a very small one. In that way, then, when the Donatists come to the Catholic root and are not deprived of the dignity of the clerical state or of the episcopacy, though this follows after their penance for their error, there is produced a wound of sorts in the bark that injures the integrity of the mother tree. But because *neither the one who plants nor the one who waters is important* (1 Cor 3:7), when our prayers have been poured out to God's mercy and the branches that were grafted on have peacefully taken hold, pour *love covers a multitude of sins* (1 Pt 4:8).

45. It was not a despair of receiving pardon but the rigor of discipline that brought it about that the Church established the rule that after penance for some crime no one should enter the clerical state or return to the clerical state or remain in the clerical state. Otherwise, one will be arguing against the keys given to the Church, of which it was said, *Whatever you loose on earth will be loosed in heaven* (Mt 18:18). But for fear that, even after his crimes have been discovered, a soul swollen with pride might proudly do penance in the hope of some ecclesiastical honor, it was decreed with the greatest severity that after having done penance for some crime worthy of condemnation no one should be a cleric so that, without any hope of a temporal dignity, the remedy of humility might be greater and more genuine. For even the saintly David did penance for his mortal sins and yet remained in his position of honor and, when blessed Peter shed most bitter tears, he certainly repented for having denied the Lord, and yet he remained an apostle. But the caution of those who came later should not for these reasons be considered useless, since, while they took away nothing belonging to salvation, they added something pertaining to humility by which salvation might be more securely protected. For they learned by experience, I believe, that some men merely pretended to repent for the sake of retaining or gaining positions of honor in the Church. For experience with many illnesses creates the need to find many medicines. But in cases of this kind where, because of the grave divisions of schism, it is not a matter of danger for this or that person but of the ruin of whole peoples, we need to reduce the severity in order that sincere love may help to heal greater ills.

46. Let these Donatists, therefore, have bitter sorrow for their detestable error, just as Peter had for his denials committed out of fear,[52] and let them come to the true Church of Christ, that is, to our Catholic mother. Let them be clerics in her; let them be bishops to her benefit, though they were opposed to her as enemies. We do not hate them; in fact, we embrace them, desire them, exhort them, and compel those whom we find on the roads and pathways to come in.[53] And in that way we still do not convince some of them that it is not their possessions but themselves that we seek. When the apostle Peter denied the savior, wept, and remained an apostle, he had not yet received the Holy Spirit, who had been promised.[54] But to a much greater degree did these Donatists not receive him when, in separation from the frame of the body, to which alone the Holy Spirit gives life,[55] they had the sacraments of the Church outside the Church and in opposition to the Church and fought in a kind of civil war with our own standards and weapons raised against us. Let them come; let there be peace in the strength of Jerusalem, the strength that is love. To that holy city it was said, *Let peace be established in your strength, and let there be an abundance in your towers* (Ps 122:6-7). Let them not raise themselves up in pride against the motherly concern that she had and still has to gather together them and the many peoples whom they have led and are leading astray. Let them not be proud because she receives them in that way; let them not ascribe to the evil of their pride what the Church does for the good of peace.

47. It is thus that she is accustomed to help the multitudes that are perishing through schisms and heresies. Lucifer was not pleased that this practice was implemented in receiving and healing those who had perished from the Arian poison.[56] And he who was not pleased by it fell into the darkness of schism after losing the light of love. The Catholic Church in Africa observed this practice with regard to the Donatists from the beginning in accord with the decision of the bishops who heard the case between Caecilian and the sect of Donatus in the church of Rome. After a certain Donatus, who was revealed to have been the author of the schism, was alone condemned, the bishops decided that the others, once they had been corrected, should be taken back with their positions of honor, even if they were ordained outside the Church. It was not because they were able to have the Holy Spirit, even outside the Church apart from the unity of the body of Christ, but it was especially on account of those whom they, while located outside the Church, could have led astray and prevented from receiving this benefit. It was, secondly, in order that their weakness might be able to be healed

---

52. See Mt 26:69-75; Mk 14:66-72; Lk 22:55-62.
53. See Lk 14:23.
54. See Jn 14:26; 16:13.
55. See Jn 6:64; 2 Cor 3:6.
56. Lucifer was the bishop of Cagliari in Sardinia from 354 to 270/371; see *Heresies* 81.

within the Church, after they had been received back with much kindness, when no stubbornness any longer closed the eyes of their heart against the evidence of the truth. But what else did they themselves have in mind when they received back with their full dignities the Maximianists when they saw that their people did not abandon them? For they were afraid that all those people might perish. The Donatists had condemned the Maximianists for their sacrilegious schism, as their council indicates, and they had ordained others in place of them. And they raised no opposition to or question about the baptism that the Maximianists had conferred when they were condemned and separated from them. Why, then, are the Donatists surprised or why do they complain or slander us because we received them back for the sake of the peace of Christ? And why do they not recall what they themselves did for the sake of the vain peace of Donatus, which is opposed to Christ? If this action of theirs is held against them and intelligently defended, they will not have anything at all to say in reply.

9, 48. But they say, "If we sinned against the Holy Spirit because we used the rite of exsufflation against your baptism, why do you seek us, since this sin absolutely cannot be forgiven us, for the Lord says, *If he sins against the Holy Spirit, it will not be forgiven him either in this world or in the world to come*" (Mt 12:32)? They do not notice that in accord with this interpretation no one should be set free. For who does not speak against the Holy Spirit and sin against him, whether he is not yet a Christian or is a heretical Arian, a Eunomian, a Macedonian, who says that the Holy Spirit is a creature, a Photinian, who says that he has no reality but that the Father alone is the one God, or one of the other heretics whom it would take long to mention? Should none of these be set free? Or were the Jews to whom the Lord says this not to be baptized if they believed in him? For the savior did not say, "It will be forgiven in baptism," but, *It will not be forgiven either in this world or in the world to come.*

49. Let them, therefore, understand that it is not every sin but a particular one that is meant by the sin against the Holy Spirit that absolutely will not be forgiven. For when he said, *If I had not come, they would have no sin* (Jn 15:22), he certainly did not want us to understand every sin, since they were filled with many great sins, but a particular sin which, if they did not have, all those that they had could be forgiven them, that is, the sin of not believing in him. For they would not have this sin if he had not come. In the same way, when he said, *He who sins against the Holy Spirit*, or, *He who says a word against the Holy Spirit*, he did not want us to understand every sin that is committed against the Holy Spirit by word or deed but a specific and particular sin. This sin is a hardness of heart up to the end of this life by which a person refuses to receive the forgiveness of sins in the unity of the body of Christ, to which the Holy Spirit gives life. For, after he said to his disciples, *Receive the Holy Spirit*, he immediately added, *If you forgive the sins of anyone, they will be forgiven him; if you retain the sins*

of anyone, they will be retained (Jn 20:22-23). Whoever, then, resists and refuses this gift of the grace of God or is somehow apart from it up to the end of this temporal life, *it will not be forgiven him either in this world or in the world to come*, that is, this sin that is so great that all sins are retained by it and that is not proved to have been committed by anyone until he leaves the body. Yet as long as he lives here, as the apostle says, *the patience of God leads to repentance* (Rom 2:4). But if with most obdurate iniquity, as the apostle goes on, he stores up for himself *in accord with his hard and unrepentant heart anger for the day of anger and of the revelation of the just judgment of God* (Rom 2:5), *it will not be forgiven him either in this world or in the world to come* (Mt 12:32).

50. But we should not abandon hope for these people with whom we are dealing or about whom we are dealing, for they are still living in the body. But let them seek the Holy Spirit only in the body of Christ; outside they have his sacrament, but internally they do not have the reality of him whose sacrament it is. And so they eat and drink it to their own condemnation.[57] For the one bread is the sacrament of unity, because, as the apostle says, *We, though many, are one bread, one body* (1 Cor 10:17). Hence the Catholic Church alone is the body of Christ, and its head is the savior of his body.[58] The Holy Spirit gives life to no one outside this body, because, as the apostle himself says, *The love of God has been poured out in our hearts by the Holy Spirit who has been given to us* (Rom 5:5). But one who is an enemy of unity has no share in the love of God. Those, therefore, who are outside the Church do not have the Holy Spirit. Of them scripture itself says, *Those who keep themselves separate are merely natural and do not have the Spirit* (Jude 19). But one who is in the Church only as a pretense does not receive the Spirit, because scripture says of such a person, For the *Holy Spirit of discipline will flee from a hypocrite* (Wis 1:5). One who wants to have the Holy Spirit, therefore, should avoid remaining outside the Church and should avoid entering her as a pretense, or, if he has entered her in that way, he should avoid remaining in that pretense so that he may truly grow in union with the tree of life.

51. I have sent you a long book and one that is perhaps a burden for you amid the tasks that keep you busy. If, therefore, you can read it at least in parts, the Lord will grant you understanding so that you may have answers for those who need to be corrected and healed, for our mother, the Church, commends them to you as to a faithful son in order that you may correct and heal them where you can and however you can, whether by speaking to them and replying to them or by bringing them to the teachers of the Church.

---

57. See 1 Cor 11:29.
58. See Eph 5:23.

Letter 185A

The following fragment of a letter of Augustine to Boniface, to whom he wrote Letter 185, was found in a tenth-century manuscript between two of Augustine's other writings.

It is highly pleasing to me that amid your civic duties you do not neglect also to show concern for religion and desire that people found in separation and division be called back to the path of salvation and peace.

Letter 186

Toward the middle of 416, Alypius, the bishop of Thagaste, and Augustine wrote to Paulinus, the bishop of Nola in Italy. Augustine and Alypius explain to Paulinus that, after having read a work of Pelagius, namely, *Nature*, they have come to realize that the Briton is an enemy of the grace of God (paragraph 1). They tell Paulinus that Pelagius' errors were reported to the Apostolic See by those who attended the Councils of Carthage and Milevis and that Pope Innocent had confirmed the condemnation of Pelagius (paragraph 2). The true grace of God not only wipes away sins but also helps us to avoid sin and to live rightly (paragraph 3). It is not our faith, good will, and good works that have saved us from the mass of perdition but the grace of God from which good works come (paragraph 4). Even our good thoughts do not come from ourselves but from God (paragraph 5). Before receiving grace no one has any good but only evil merits, even if his life has lasted only a single day on earth (paragraph 6).

The love that faith obtains is itself a gift of God (paragraph 7). The righteousness that makes us righteous comes from faith as a gift of God (paragraph 8). But the righteousness that comes from the law does not come from God (paragraph 9). Though faith merits righteousness, faith itself is a gift, so that no human merit precedes grace (paragraph 10).

The grace conferred on infants by baptism is obviously given gratuitously (paragraph 11). Yet some Pelagians have dared to deny the gratuitous character of this grace by supposing that infants are guilty of personal sins (paragraph 12). These people appealed to the struggle between Esau and Jacob in the womb as a sign of personal sin in Esau (paragraph 13). Augustine argues that the struggle between these twins was a miraculous sign but not evidence of free choice in them (paragraph 14). The apostle appealed to these twins as evidence of God's gratuitous choice of Jacob through grace (paragraph 15).

Some Pelagians object that God is unjust if he does not choose one person over another on the basis of merits, but Augustine and Alypius appeal to the teaching of the apostle that there is no injustice in God (paragraph 16). For the choice of Jacob over Esau did not depend on their works but on God, who showed mercy to Jacob and justice to Esau (paragraph 17). The apostle foresaw the Pelagian line of argument and answered them with the example of the potter who makes one vessel for an honorable purpose and another for a dishonorable purpose from the same lump of clay (paragraph 18). For through the sin of Adam the whole lump became subject to death, and from it no one is set free by his own merits (paragraph 19). Why one is set free and another is not falls under the inscrutable but just judgments of God (paragraph 20). Thus Esau is not unjustly condemned because he was subject to the sin he inherited from Adam (paragraph 21).

The Pelagians might object that it would have been better if both of the twins were set free, but that line of argument can go on endlessly (paragraph 22). The same question arises about why God creates those who he knows will be damned (paragraph 23). Augustine and Alypius appeal to the Letter to the Romans for an explanation of why God made vessels of anger for destruction (paragraph 24). In God's foreknowledge the number of the predestined is fixed (paragraph 25). Yet God created the others to reveal what free choice could do without grace and to emphasize the gratuity of grace toward the vessels of mercy (paragraph 26).

Augustine warns those who have other ideas and points to the propositions that Pelagius himself condemned when he was tried in Palestine (paragraph 27). In claiming that infants can have eternal life even if they die without baptism, Pelagius speaks against the words of the Lord, against the authority of the Apostolic See, and against what he himself condemned (paragraph 28). Augustine and Alypius warn Paulinus about those who persist in this condemned error of the Pelagians (paragraph 29). They insist that, if there is no original sin derived from Adam in newborn infants, the infants would be unjustly condemned if they died without baptism (paragraph 30). All those whom God calls and saves are called and saved by God's choice through grace (paragraph 31).

Augustine and Alypius cite the twelve propositions that Pelagius condemned at the Council of Diospolis and argues that the opposite of each of them must be held by a believer (paragraphs 32 and 33). In his recent books Pelagius continues to be unclear about what he understands by the help of God's grace (paragraph 34). Augustine and Alypius cite Pelagius' claim that grace allows us to carry out more easily what God commands (paragraph 35). They cite the passages of scripture that John, the bishop of Jerusalem, had used against Pelagius at his trial (paragraph 36). By his praise for human nature Pelagius empties of meaning the cross of Christ (paragraph 37). Though the Pelagians' refusal to believe is due to their will, we still ought to pray for them (paragraph 38).

Augustine and Alypius explain that they have written this letter not to support Paulinus' faith but to support his defense of the faith against these objectors (paragraph 39). They quote a passage from a letter of Paulinus that reveals the desperate need on the part of human beings for God's grace as we await the redemption of our body (paragraph 40). As long as we are in this life, we need to pray that we may not be brought into temptation (paragraph 41).

To Paulinus, their most blessed lord, brother, and fellow bishop, who deserves to be sincerely embraced in the heart of Christ, a brother who is more loveable than can be said, Alypius and Augustine send greetings.

1, 1. At long last God has provided us with a most reliable bearer for our letter, Brother Januarius, who is rightly very dear to us all. Even if we did not write, Your Sincerity could know everything about us by means of him as if he were a living and intelligent letter. We know that you loved as a servant of God Pelagius, who we believe had the surname "the Briton," in order that he might be distinguished from Pelagius, the son of Terence, but we do not know how you are at present disposed toward him. For we too not only have loved him but still love him. But our love for him now is different from what our love for him used to be. For we loved him then because we thought he held the correct faith, but we love him now in order that God's mercy might set him free from the views which he is said to hold that are hostile and contrary to the grace of God. For, though rumor spread this about concerning him for a long time, one ought not, of course, to have readily believed it, for rumor often carries lies. But in order that we might believe the rumor there was in addition the more recent event of our reading a certain book of his that certainly tries to convince us of views that wipe out from the hearts of the faithful a belief in the grace of God that has been given to the human race through the one mediator between God and human beings, the man Jesus Christ.[1] This book was handed over to us by servants of Christ who had heard him teaching such doctrines with great zeal and who had been his followers.[2] At their request we replied to the book with one treatise of ours because we saw that it was necessary to do so, though we did not mention the name of its author for fear that he would be offended and become more difficult to heal. That book of his contains and asserts many times and amply the same thing that he also states in a certain letter sent to Your Reverence in which he says that he should not be thought to defend free choice without the grace of God, since he says that the ability to will and to act, without which we can neither will nor do anything good, was implanted in us by the creator. In that way Pelagius' teaching would have us understand that the grace of God is something common to pagans and Christians, to the good and the bad, and to believers and unbelievers.

2. We were refuting, to the extent we could, these errors which empty of meaning the Lord's coming and of which we can say what the apostle says of the law, *If righteousness comes through nature, then Christ has died in vain* (Gal 2:21). We were refuting these errors in the hearts of those who held them in order that Pelagius too, once he came to know this, would, if possible, correct these views without being attacked. And in that way the harmfulness of his error would be destroyed, and the man would be spared embarrassment. But after we received a letter from the East that aired the same views in full openness, we ought by no means to have failed to help the Church with whatever episcopal authority we had.[3] Reports from two councils in Carthage and in Milevis were sent to the Apostolic See, therefore, before the ecclesiastical proceedings at which Pelagius was said to have been acquitted in the presence of some bishops

---

1. See 1 Tm 2:5.
2. The two disciples of Pelagius were Timasius and James, who gave Augustine Pelagius' work, *Nature*, against which Augustine wrote *Nature and Grace*. See Letter 168 to Timasius and James.
3. See *The Grace of Christ and Original Sin* 1, 35, 38, where Augustine cites Pelagius, who had included the letter to Paulinus in the dossier presented to Pope Innocent so as to establish his innocence.

of the Province of Palestine arrived either in our hands or in Africa.[4] We also wrote to Pope Innocent of blessed memory a personal letter in addition to the reports of the councils,[5] in which we dealt with this issue somewhat more at length. He replied to us on all these points in the way in which it was right and necessary for a bishop of the Apostolic See.[6]

3. You will now be able to read all these documents if perhaps some or all of them have not reached you. In them you will see that due moderation was preserved toward human beings so that they would not be condemned if they condemned these wicked teachings but that this new and deadly error was suppressed by the authority of the Church, with the result that we are very surprised that there are still certain people who try to oppose the grace of God through any error—at least if they have come to know that these actions have been taken. This grace of God through Jesus Christ our Lord, as the true and Catholic Church always holds, causes children along with adults to pass from the death of the first man[7] to the life of the second man[8] not only by wiping away sins but also by helping those who can already use the choice of the will not to sin and to live correctly. Hence without the help of this grace we can have no piety and righteousness either in our actions or even in our own will itself. *For it is God who produces in us both the willing and the action in accord with good will* (Phil 2:13).

2, 4. For who separates us from that solid mass of perdition except him who *came to seek and to save what was lost* (Lk 19:10)? For this reason the apostle asks, *For who sets you apart?* And if a man says, "My faith, my good will, my good work," he receives the answer, *For what do you have that you have not received? But if you have received, why do you boast as if you have not received?* (1 Cor 4:7) Of course he said all of this not so that a human being would not boast but so that *he who boasts would boast in the Lord* (1 Cor 1:31; 2 Cor 10:17), *not on the basis of works, lest anyone perhaps be filled with pride* (Eph 2:9). It is not that good works are rendered useless by that pious thought, for *God repays each one according to his works* and *everyone who does good has glory, honor, peace* (Rom 2:6.10). Rather it is that works come from grace, not grace from works. For *the faith that works through love* (Gal 5:6) would do nothing unless *the love of God* were poured out *in our hearts by the Holy Spirit who has been given to us*

---

4. Pelagius was acquitted by a council of bishops at Diospolis in Palestine in December of 415. Augustine was unable to obtain a copy of the acts of that council until 417. The letter he mentions was written by Bishops Hero and Lazarus, who had been present at Diospolis; see Letter 175, 1. The Councils of Milevis and of Carthage in 416 sent Letters 175 and 176 to Pope Innocent to notify him of their condemnation of Pelagius.

5. That is, Letter 177.

6. That is, in Letters 181, 182, and 183.

7. See Rv 11:18.

8. See 1 Cor 15:47.

(Rom 5:5). Nor would faith itself be present in us *unless God* imparted *to each the measure of faith* (Rom 12:3).

5. It is, therefore, good for a human being to say truthfully with all the strength of free choice, *I shall preserve my strength with you* (Ps 59:10). For the man who thought that he could preserve what God gave him without God's help left for a distant region and used up everything, living wastefully. And worn down by the misery of hard servitude, he came to his senses and said, *I shall rise up and go to my father* (Lk 15:18). When would he have had this good thought if the most merciful Father had not secretly inspired him with it? Understanding this, that minister of the New Testament said, *It is not that we are able to think something by ourselves, as if from ourselves; rather, our ability comes from God* (Eph 3:6-7). Hence, when the psalmist said, *I shall preserve my strength with you*, so that he would not arrogate to his own strength the fact that he preserves it, as if it had come to his mind that, *unless the Lord preserves the city, those who guard it keep watch in vain* (Ps 127:1) and that *he who guards Israel does not slumber nor sleep* (Ps 121:4), he adds the reason why he became able to guard it or rather is the guard who preserves it. He says, *For God is my helper* (Ps 59:10).

6. Let this fellow,[9] then, recall, if he can, his own merits because of which God deigned to become his helper as if it were God who was helped. Let him recall whether he sought or was sought, that is, by him who *came to seek and to save what was lost* (Lk 19:10). For, if he wants to seek what he merited before grace in order that he might receive grace, he will be able to find his own evil merits, not good ones, even if the grace of the savior finds him having life for one day on earth.[10] For, if a human being does some good action in order to merit grace, *his reward is assigned to him not as grace but as something owed. But if he believes in him who makes the sinner righteous* so that *his faith is counted as righteousness* (Rom 4:4-6)—for *the righteous live by faith* (Hb 2:4; Rom 1:17; Gal 3:5; Heb 10:38)—before he is justified by grace, that is, before he is made righteous, what is a sinner but a sinner? If he received what he deserved, what would he receive by his merit but punishment? *If*, then, *it is by grace, it does not come from works; otherwise, grace is no longer grace* (Rom 11:6). What is owed is payment for works, but grace is given gratuitously; that is where it gets its name.

3, 7. But if anyone says that faith merits the grace of doing good actions, we cannot deny it; in fact, we most gratefully admit it. For we want these brothers of ours, who boast much of their good works, to have this faith by which they might obtain the love that alone truly produces good works. But love is so much a gift of God that it is called God.[11] Those, then, who have the faith by which they

---

9. Augustine refers to Pelagius without naming him.
10. See Jb 14:5 LXX.
11. See 1 Jn 4:8.

obtain justification have come through the grace of God to the law of righteousness; for this reason scripture says, *I heard you at an acceptable time, and I helped you on the day of salvation* (Is 49:8; 2 Cor 6:2). Hence, in those who are being saved through the choice of his grace,[12] God as a helper *produces the willing and the action in accord with good will* (Phil 2:13), *because for those who love God all things work out for the good* (Rom 8:28)—and if all things, then certainly the love itself that we obtain by faith in order that we may love through his grace him who first loved us[13] so that we might believe in him and so that by loving him we might do good works, which we did not do in order that we might be loved.

8. But the people who look for rewards as if they were owed to their merits, and who do not attribute their merits to the grace of God but to the strength of their own will, do not attain the law of righteousness, as it was said of Israel according to the flesh, though they pursue the law of righteousness. Why? Because they pursue it not on the basis of faith but on the basis of works. For this is the righteousness coming from faith that the Gentiles attained, of whom scripture says: *What, then, shall we say? For the Gentiles, who did not know righteousness, have attained righteousness, but the righteousness that comes from faith. But Israel, while pursuing the law of righteousness, did not attain to the law of righteousness. Why? Because they pursued it not on the basis of faith but as if on the basis of works. For they stumbled on the stumbling block, as it is written, See, I set a stumbling block in Zion, a stone of scandal, and one who believes in him will not be put to shame.* (Rom 9:30-33; Is 28:16; 8:14) This is the righteousness from faith by which we believe that we are justified, that is, made righteous by the grace of God through Jesus Christ our Lord so that we may be found in him, not having our own *righteousness that comes from the law, but that which comes through faith in Christ. This righteousness from God is found in faith* (Phil 3:9), in the faith, of course, by which we believe that righteousness is given to us by God and is not produced in us by us by our own strength.

9. For why did the apostle say that the righteousness that comes from the law was his own and not from God, as if the law does not come from God? Who but an unbeliever would have such an idea? But because the law commands by the letter and does not help by the Spirit, whoever hears the letter of the law so that he thinks that it is sufficient for him to have known what it commands or forbids and is confident that he will fulfil it by the power of his choice and does not in faith take refuge in the life-giving Spirit for help in order that the letter may not kill him in his guilt—that man certainly has a zeal for God, but not with knowl-

---

12. See Rom 11:5; Phil 2:13.
13. See 1 Jn 4:19.

edge. For, not knowing the righteousness of God, that is, the righteousness that is given by God, and wanting to establish his own righteousness so that it comes only from the law, he is not subject to the righteousness of God.[14] *For the end of the law is Christ for the righteousness of everyone who believes* (Rom 10:2-4), as the same apostle says, *in order that we may be the righteousness of God in him* (2 Cor 5:21). *Made righteous, then, by faith, let us have peace with God through our Lord Jesus Christ* (Rom 5:1), but *made righteous gratuitously by his grace* (Rom 3:21), so that faith is not proud.

10. And let him not say to himself, "If it comes from faith, how is it gratuitous? For why is what faith merits not a repayment rather than a gift?" Let a believer not say this because, when he says, "I have faith in order to merit justification," he receives the answer, *For what do you have that you have not received?* (1 Cor 4:7) Though faith, then, obtains justification, as God has also granted to each the measure of faith itself,[15] no human merit precedes the grace of God, but grace itself merits an increase in order that, once increased, it may also merit to be made perfect with the will accompanying, not leading, following along, not preceding. Hence he who said, *I shall preserve my strength with you* (Ps 59:10), and went on to give the reason, *Because God is my helper*, as if he were looking for the merits by which he got this and found nothing in himself prior to the grace of God, says, *My God, his mercy will precede me* (Ps 59:11). As much as I shall ponder antecedent merits, he says, *his mercy will precede me*. Hence, in preserving with God the strength that God gave him, he does not lose it because God preserves what that man received as God's gift. And he does not merit more grace except by knowing in piety and in faith him from whom all good gifts come to him and by knowing that this realization does not come from himself so that he does not have even this without its also coming from God. For this reason the apostle says very well, *We have not received the spirit of this world, but the Spirit who is from God, in order that we may know what God has given us* (1 Cor 2:12). And for this reason even the merit of a human being is a gratuitous gift, and no one merits to receive anything good from the Father of lights, from whom every best gift comes down,[16] except by receiving what he does not merit.

4, 11. But it is much more merciful and undoubtedly more gratuitous that the grace of God through Jesus Christ our Lord is offered to infants so that their birth from Adam may not harm them and their rebirth in Christ may profit them, for in them the mercy of God comes long before even the awareness of their receiving it. And if at this early age they leave the body, they certainly receive eternal life and the kingdom of heaven knowingly by the merit of that gift that they did not

---

14. See Rom 10:2-4.
15. See Rom 12:3.
16. See Jas 1:17.

know here, when of course it was of benefit to them. In these infants the merits of the later gifts are nothing else than the earlier gifts, and in giving the earlier gifts the grace of God works in such a way that the will of the recipients does not precede it, accompany it, or follow it. For such a great benefit is given not only to those infants who do not desire it but even to those who struggle against it—something that would be counted as a great sacrilege on their part if the choice of the will were already capable of anything in them.

12. We said this for the sake of those who, being unable to search out the inscrutable judgments of God in the area of grace,[17] ask why from the mass coming from Adam, which because of only one person fell as a whole into condemnation, God makes one vessel for honor and another for dishonor.[18] And yet they dare to make infants guilty of personal sins, and thus those who cannot have either a good or a bad thought are supposed to be able to merit punishment or grace through free choice, though the truth from the lips of the apostle who says, *Because of the one* all entered *into condemnation* (Rom 5:16), in fact shows quite well that they are born subject to punishment so that they may be reborn in grace not by merit but by mercy. *Otherwise, grace is no longer grace* (Rom 11:6) if it is not given as grace from God's riches but is a recompense for human merits. It alone sets one apart from punishment in such a way that, though punishment is owed to all because of Adam, grace through the one Jesus Christ is owed to no one but is gratuitous. In that way grace can truly be grace. Thus the judgments of God, like God himself, can be inscrutable, when he separates infants whom no merits distinguish. But his judgments can never be unjust because *all the ways of the Lord are mercy and truth* (Ps 25:10). Therefore when one person is offered the gift of mercy, he has no reason to boast of human merit, because this does not come *from works, lest anyone be filled with pride* (Eph 2:9). But when another person receives punishment in accord with the truth, he has no reason for just complaint, for he receives in recompense what is rightly owed to sin. For the one *in whom all sinned* (Rom 5:12) is certainly not unjustly punished in each individual as well. In their punishment we are more clearly shown what is given to the vessels of mercy through a grace that is not owed but is true grace, that is, gratuitous.

5, 13. The apostle says most clearly, *Through one man sin entered the world, and through sin death, and in that way it was passed on to all human beings in whom all sinned* (Rom 5:12). It is annoying to notice and displeasing to state, but we are in fact compelled to say how they argue against him, saying that even infants have personal sins through free choice. For it would be either a sign of our helplessness to omit through silence or a sign of our arrogance to pass over in contempt what those great and clever minds were able to think up. They say,

17. See Rom 11:33.
18. See Rom 9:21.

"Look, Esau and Jacob fought in the womb of their mother and, when they are born, one takes the place of the other, and the hand of the second found holding onto the foot of the first proves that the struggle was in some sense still going on. How, then, is there no choice of their own will either for good or for evil in infants performing these acts, as a result of which rewards or punishments follow upon preceding merits?"[19]

14. To this we say that those movements and the supposed fight of the infants were signs of important things not because they involved choice but because they were a miracle. After all, we are not going to assign free choice of the will to donkeys because an animal of this kind, as scripture says, *a beast of burden without a voice, replying with the voice of a human being, restrained the madness of the prophet* (2 Pt 2:16). But what are these people, who claim that such movements were not prodigies but voluntary acts and were produced not with regard to the infants but by them, going to reply to the apostle? For, since he saw that he should mention these twins as a proof of the gratuitousness of grace, he said, *When they were not yet born and did nothing either good or bad, in order that God's plan might remain in accord with his choice, it was said not because of works but because of his call that the older would serve the younger* (Rom 9:11-13). And then adding the testimony of a prophet who said these things afterward, but who was explaining God's ancient plan regarding this matter, he says: *As scripture said, I loved Jacob, but I hated Esau* (Rom 9:13; Mal 1:2-3).

15. The teacher of the nations in faith and truth testifies that those as yet unborn twins did nothing good or bad in order that he might emphasize grace. And so when he said, *The older will serve the younger*, we understand that this *was said not because of works but because of his call in order that God's plan might remain in accord with his choice*, not in order that human merit might come first. He does not mean the choice of the human will or of nature since the condition of death and condemnation was equally present in both of them, but he undoubtedly means the choice of grace, which does not discover those to be chosen but makes them such. Speaking of this grace in the following parts of the letter, he says, *So, then, in this time as well a remnant has been saved by the choice of grace. But if it is grace, it is not because of works; otherwise, grace is no longer grace.* (Rom 11:5-6) This passage agrees well with the one where it is mentioned that it said, *The older will serve the younger, not because of works but because of* God's *call*. Why, then, do they so impudently oppose the most illustrious teacher of grace with regard to the free choice of infants and the actions of those not yet born? Why do they say that grace is preceded by merits? It would not be grace if it were assigned in accord with merits. Why do they argue against the salvation that was sent to those who were lost and that came to

---

19. See Gn 25:22.25 and Hos 12:3.

those who were unworthy with a line of argument that, however clever, however lengthy and eloquent, is hardly Christian?

6, 16. "But how," they ask, "is there not injustice in God if by his love he separates those whom no merits from their works separate?" They say this to us as if the apostle himself did not see this, did not pose this question, and did not answer it. He certainly saw what human weakness or ignorance could think up when it heard these ideas and, posing the same question for himself, he asked, *What, then, shall we say? Is there injustice in God?* and he immediately replied: *Heaven forbid!* And giving the reason why he said, *Heaven forbid!* that is, why there is no injustice in God, he did not say, "For he judges the merits or works even of the infants, even if they are still located in the womb of their mother." For how could he say this who had said of those who were not yet born and of those who had done nothing good or bad that *it was not said because of works but because of his call: The older will serve the younger* (Rom 9:11-12)? But when he wanted to show why there is no injustice in God in these matters, he said, *After all, God said to Moses: I will take pity on whom I will take pity and I will show mercy to whom I will show mercy* (Rom 9:15; Ex 33:19). What did he teach us here but that it pertains not to the merits of human beings but to the mercy of God that anyone is set free from that mass coming from the first man,[20] which rightly deserved death, and that thus there is no injustice in God? For he is not unjust either in canceling or in exacting what is owed. After all, forgiveness is gratuitous only in a case where punishment could be just. And from this it is seen more clearly how great a benefit is conferred upon one who is set free from the punishment he deserved and is made righteous gratuitously,[21] because the other who is equally guilty is punished without injustice on the part of God who punishes him.

17. Finally, he goes on to add, *And so, it does not depend on the one who wills or on the one who runs, but on God who shows mercy* (Rom 9:16-18; Ex 9:16). This was said on account of those who were set free by grace and made righteous. But on account of those on whom the anger of God remains,[22] because God also makes good use of them to teach the others whom he deigns to set free, he went on to add, *For scripture says of Pharaoh: I have raised you up in order to reveal my power in you and in order that my name might be proclaimed in the whole world* (Rom 9:17). Then, concluding with regard to both, he said, *Hence, he shows mercy to whom he wills, and he hardens whom he wills* (Rom 9:18); of course he does neither out of any injustice but both out of mercy and truth. And yet the brazen weakness of human beings is disturbed, that is, of those who try to

---

20. See Rom 9:21.
21. See Rom 3:24.
22. See Jn 3:36.

fathom the inscrutable depth of the judgments of God[23] in accordance with the conjectures of the human heart.

18. Posing this question for himself as an objection, the apostle says, *And so, you say to me: What complaint still remains? For who can resist his will?* (Rom 9:19) Let us suppose that this objection is made to us. What else, then, ought we to answer but what the apostle answered? Or if such questions trouble us too, because we too are human beings, we ought all together to listen to him as he says, *Who are you, O human being, to answer back to God? Does the pot say to him who fashioned it, Why did you make me that way? Or does the potter not have the power to make from the same lump of clay one vessel for honor and another for dishonor?* (Rom 9:20-21; Is 45:9; 29:16) If this lump were so positioned in the middle that, as it merited nothing good, so it merited nothing bad, it would seem with good reason to be an injustice that vessels were made from it for dishonor. But since the whole lump fell into condemnation because of the one sin through the free choice of the first human being, the fact that vessels are made from it for honor is not due to his righteousness, because no righteousness preceded grace, but to the mercy of God. The fact, however, that a vessel is made for dishonor is not to be attributed to the injustice of God—heaven forbid that there should be any injustice in God!—but to his judgment. Whoever holds this along with the Catholic Church does not argue against grace in favor of merits but sings to the Lord of his mercy and judgment,[24] so that he does not ungratefully reject his mercy or unjustly accuse his judgment.

19. For it is another mass of dough of which the same apostle says, *But if the dough offered is holy, then the whole lump is holy, and if the root is holy, then the branches are too* (Rom 11:16). That lump comes from Abraham, not from Adam, that is, from the sharing in the sacrament and the similarity in faith, not from our mortal lineage. But this latter lump or, as we read in many manuscripts, this mass, is wholly subject to death because *through one man sin entered the world, and through sin death, and thus it was passed on to all human beings in whom all sinned* (Rom 5:12). Because of mercy there is made out of it *one vessel for honor*, but by judgment there is made *another for dishonor* (Rom 9:21). In the first case no merits precede the grace of God who sets free, nor in the latter do sins escape the justice of God who punishes. In more adult ages, of course, this is not seen so clearly to be opposed to the quarrelsome when they fight on behalf of human merits, as if protected by some sort of obscurity. But against their argument the apostle discovered those of whom, *though they were not yet born and had not done anything good or bad, it was said, not because of works but because of his call: The older will serve the younger* (Rom 9:11-12).

---

23. See Rom 11:33.
24. See Ps 101:1.

20. Because in this area *the judgments of God are* too deep and *inscrutable and his ways unsearchable*, let a human being for the present hold that there is no injustice in God. But let him admit that, as a human being, he does not know the justice by which God shows mercy to whom he wills and hardens whom he wills.[25] And thus let him know by reason of the unshakeable truth that he holds, namely, that there is no injustice in God, that, though no one is made righteous by him because of any preceding merits, neither is anyone hardened except by merit. For it is piously and truthfully believed that, by making sinners and unbelievers righteous, God sets them free from the punishment they deserve, but if it is believed that God condemns anyone who does not deserve it and who is subject to no sin, it is not believed that God is free from injustice. In a case, then, in which someone unworthy is set free, God deserves more gratitude to the extent that the punishment the person deserved was more just. But in a case where someone who does not deserve it is condemned, neither mercy nor truth prevails.

21. "How," they ask, "was Esau not undeservedly condemned if *it was said, not because of works but because of God's call: The older will serve the younger* (Rom 9:11-12)? For, just as no good works of Jacob came first in order that he would receive grace, so no evil works of Esau came first in order that he should meet with punishment." There were no works either good or bad in either of the two, that is, no personal works, but both were subject to him *in whom all sinned* (Rom 5:12) so that all died in him. For those who from that one man were going to be many in themselves were then one in him. Hence, that sin would have been his alone if no one had come from him. But now no one is exempt from the sin of him in whom our common nature existed. If, then, the two, who had not done any good or bad actions of their own, were nonetheless born guilty because of their origin, let the one who is set free praise God's mercy and let the one who is punished not blame his judgment.

7, 22. If we say here, "How much better it would be if both were set free!" nothing more appropriate will be said to us than, *Who are you, O human being, to answer back to God?* (Rom 9:20). For he knows what he is doing and what number there ought to be, first, of all human beings and, secondly, of the saints, just as he knows what the number should be of the stars, of the angels, and—to speak of earthly things—of cattle, of fish, of birds, of trees, of plants, and of the hairs on our heads. Now we can still say in our human way of thinking, "Because all the things he made are good, how much better it would be if he doubled their number or multiplied them so that there were many more than there are." For if the world could not contain them, could he not make it larger to the extent he wanted? And yet, to whatever extent he made them more or made the world

---

25. See Rom 9:18.

more capacious and larger, the same things could still be said about making them more, and there would be no limit to limitless things.

23. For, whether it is the grace by which persons without righteousness are made righteous, about which we are not permitted to doubt, or free choice, as certain people want, that always comes first, and either punishment or reward follows upon its merit, it can still be objected: "Why were they created at all, since God undoubtedly foreknew that they would sin so that they would be condemned to eternal fire?" For, though he did not cause their sins, who but God, nonetheless, created their natures? The natures by themselves were no doubt good, but in them the defects of sins were going to come into existence from the choice of their will—and in many cases the sort of sins that would receive eternal punishment. Why did he do this except because he willed to? But why did he will to? *Who are you, O human being, to answer back to God? Does the pot say to him who fashioned it: Why did you make me so? Does the potter not have the power to make from the same lump of clay one vessel for honor and another for dishonor?* (Rom 9:20-21)

24. And now let us cite what follows: *But if God, wanting to reveal his anger and to demonstrate his power, endured with great patience the vessels of anger that were made for destruction in order to make known the riches of his glory toward the vessels of mercy* (Rom 9:22-23). See, there the reason is given to a human being to the extent it ought to be given to him, at least if one who defends the freedom of his choice in the slavery of such weakness grasps this. See, the reasons have been stated. Who are you, then, to answer back to God if, wanting to reveal his anger and to demonstrate his power, God endured in great patience the vessels of anger destined for destruction? After all, the all-good God can make good use even of evil persons, for the evil are not such because of their creation by God but because their nature, which was created good by God the creator, was damaged by the wickedness of their will. *He endured with great patience the vessels of anger that were made for destruction* (Rom 9:22) not because he needed the sins of either angels or human beings, for he does not need even the righteousness of any creature, but *in order to make known the riches of his glory toward the vessels of mercy* (Rom 9:23), so that in their good works they would not be filled with pride as if over their own abilities but would humbly understand that, unless God's grace, which is not owed to them but is gratuitous, came to their help, their merits would receive the recompense that they saw was given to the others in the same lump.

25. The predetermined number and multitude of the saints is, therefore, certain in God's foreknowledge. *For those who love God*, a gift which he gave them through the Holy Spirit poured out in their hearts,[26] *all things work together*

---

26. See Rom 5:5.

for the good for those who have been called according to his plan. For those whom he foreknew he also predestined to be conformed to the image of his Son, in order that he might be the firstborn among many brothers. But those whom he predestined he also called. (Rom 8:28-30) Here we ought to understand: *according to his plan.* For there are also others who are called but not chosen.[27] And for this reason they are not called according to his plan. *But those whom he called*—that is, *according to his plan*—*he also made righteous. But those whom he made righteous he also glorified* (Rom 8:30). These are *the children of the promise* (Rom 9:8); these are the chosen who are being saved by his choice through grace, when it says, *But if it is because of grace, it is not because of works; otherwise, grace is no longer grace* (Rom 11:5-6). These are the vessels of mercy,[28] in whom God makes known even through the vessels of anger the riches of his glory. The Holy Spirit makes these to have *one heart and one soul* (Acts 4:32), which blesses God and does not forget all the gifts of him who pardons all their sins, who heals all their illnesses, who redeems their life from their corruption, who crowns them in his mercy,[29] because it *does not depend on the one who wills or on the one who runs, but on God who shows mercy* (Rom 9:16).

26. But the other human beings, who do not belong to this company, though their soul and body were made by the goodness of God, and whatever their nature has apart from the defect, which the audacity of a proud will inflicted upon it, was created by God in his foreknowledge. He created them so that in these human beings he might show what the free choice of one who abandons him is capable of without grace and so that the vessels of mercy, which have been separated from that lump not by the merits of their works but by the gratuitous grace of God, might realize the gift that has been given to them *in order that every mouth might be shut* (Rom 3:19) and in order that *he who boasts might boast in the Lord* (1 Cor 1:31; 2 Cor 10:17).

8, 27. *Whoever teaches another doctrine and does not agree with the sound words of our Lord, Jesus Christ* (1 Tm 6:3), who said, *The Son of Man came to seek and to save what had been lost* (Lk 19:10 Mt 18:11)—for he did not say, "what was going to be lost," but, *what had been lost*, in order to show that the nature of the whole human race had perished by the sin of the first human being—*Whoever*, therefore, *teaches another doctrine and does not agree with the teaching that is in accord with piety* (1 Tm 6:3), defending human nature as if it were safe and free, in opposition to the grace of the savior and in opposition to the blood of the redeemer, and pretending to bear the name "Christian"—what is

---

27. See Mt 20:16; 22:14.
28. See Rom 9:22-23.
29. See Ps 103:2-4.

such a person going to say about the separation of infants? Why is one taken up into the life of the second man, while another is left in the death of the first man? If he says that the merits of free choice came first, the apostle has answered what we said above about those who were not yet born and did nothing good or bad.[30] But if he says what is still defended in the books that Pelagius is reported to have published quite recently, although he is now seen to have condemned in the episcopal court in Palestine those who say that the sin of Adam harmed Adam alone and not the human race, that is, if he says that both infants were born without sin and did not contract anything from the condemnation of the first human being, since he certainly does not dare to deny that one who has been reborn in Christ is adopted into the kingdom of heaven, let him reply what will happen with one who has been carried off by this temporal death before being baptized and without any sin of its own. We do not think that he will say that God will condemn to eternal death an innocent human being who does not have original sin prior to the years in which he could have had personal sin. And so he is forced to reply what Pelagius was forced to condemn in the ecclesiastical court in order that he might somehow be declared Catholic, namely, that infants have eternal life even if they are not baptized. For, if he does not say this, what else will remain but eternal death?

28. And in this way he will argue against the statement of the Lord, who says, *Your fathers ate manna in the desert and died. This is the bread coming down from heaven so that, if anyone eats it, he may not die.* (Jn 6:49-50) For he was not talking about the death that even those who eat this bread must suffer. And a little later he says, *Truly, truly, I say to you: Unless you eat the flesh of the Son of Man and drink his blood, you will not have life in you* (Jn 6:54)—that life, of course, which will exist after this death. And he will argue against the authority of the Apostolic See where, when it dealt with this issue, it used this testimony from the gospel lest unbaptized infants be thought capable of having life.[31] And he will argue against the words of Pelagius himself before the bishops who heard his case, the words he expressed when he condemned those who said that unbaptized infants have eternal life.[32]

29. We have mentioned this because some people with you or rather in your city, at least if what we have heard is true, fight with such stubbornness in defense of this error that they say that it is easier for them to abandon and despise even Pelagius, who condemned the people who hold these views, than to give up the truth, as they see it, of this opinion. But if they yield to the Apostolic See or rather to the very teacher and Lord of the apostles, who says that they will not have life in them unless they eat the flesh of the Son of Man and drink his

---

30. See Rom 9:11.
31. See Letter 182, 5.
32. See *The Deeds of Pelagius* 11, 23.

blood—something that only the baptized, of course, can do—they will finally admit that unbaptized infants cannot have life and, for this reason, are still punished by eternal death, though less harshly than all those who have also committed personal sins.

30. Since this is the case, let them be so bold as to argue and let them strive to persuade those whom they can that the just God, in whom there is no injustice,[33] will condemn to endless death infants who are innocent of personal sins if they are not bound by and subject to that sin from Adam. If this is absolutely absurd and completely alien to the justice of God, and if no one who bears in mind that he is a Christian of the Catholic faith denies or doubts that infants do not have life in themselves if they have not received the grace of rebirth in Christ and are without the food of his flesh and the drink of his blood[34] and that they are, for this reason, subject to everlasting punishment, there then remains the fact that, because they have not done anything good or bad,[35] the punishment of their death is just because they died in him *in whom all sinned* (Rom 5:12). Hence, they are brought to life only in him who could neither contract original sin nor commit personal sin.

31. He himself *called us, not only from the Jews, but also from the Gentiles* (Rom 9:24). For he gathered the children whom he willed even, despite her unwillingness, from the Jerusalem that killed the prophets and stoned those sent to her both before his incarnation as prophets and, after *the Word was made flesh* (Jn 1:14), as apostles and as the thousands who laid at the feet of the apostles the money from the sale of their possessions.[36] All these were, of course, children of the Jerusalem that was unwilling to be gathered, but they were still gathered against her will. Of them he says, *If I cast out demons by Beelzebub, by whom do your children cast them out? Hence, they will be your judges.* (Mt 12:27) Of these it was foretold, *If the children of Israel will be like the sand of the sea, a remnant will be saved* (Rom 9:27; Is 10:22; Hos 1:10). The word of God cannot fail to be true, nor *has he rejected his people whom he foreknew* (Rom 11:2), and *this remnant was saved by his choice through grace* (Rom 11:5). *But if it is by grace*—which must be said with frequency—*it is not because of works; other-wise, grace is no longer grace* (Rom 11:6). These are, of course, not our words but the words of the apostle. What, therefore, he cried out to the Jerusalem that was unwilling that her children be gathered, we shout out against those who do not want the children of the Church, who are willing, to be gathered and against those who have not been corrected, even after the judgment that was pronounced concerning Pelagius in Palestine. He would have emerged from there as a

---

33. See Rom 9:14.
34. See Jn 6:54.
35. See Rom 9:11.
36. See Acts 4:23-35; 2:41; 4:4.

condemned man if he himself had not condemned the statements against the grace of God that were raised as objections to him, statements that he could not disguise.

9, 32. Besides those statements that he dared to defend by some sort of argument, however he could, certain statements were raised as objections, and if he had not anathematized them without any ambiguity he himself would have left anathematized. For it was objected that he said: "Adam was created mortal so that he was going to die whether he sinned or did not sin," and, "His sin harmed him alone and not the human race," and, "Newborn infants are in the same state in which Adam was before his transgression," and, "The whole human race does not die through the death or transgression of Adam, nor does the whole human race rise through the resurrection of Christ," and, "Infants attain eternal life, even if they are not baptized," and, "If wealthy persons who have been baptized do not renounce all their possessions, they have no merit, even if they seem to do something good, and they cannot possess the kingdom of God,"[37] and, "God's grace and help is not given for individual actions, but consists in free choice or in the law and teaching," and, "The grace of God is given in accord with our merits,"[38] and, "Only those who have become completely without sin can be called children of God," and, "Free choice does not exist, if one needs the help of God, because each person has in his own will the power to do or not to do something," and, "Our victory comes not from the help of God but from free choice," and, "Pardon is not given to penitents in accord with God's grace and mercy but in accord with their merit and labor, since they were worthy of mercy because of their penance."[39]

33. Pelagius condemned all these statements, and the proceedings themselves sufficiently testify that he in no way produced any argument in their defense. For this reason it follows that whoever accepts the authority of that episcopal court and the confession of Pelagius himself ought to hold what the Catholic Church has always held: Adam would not have died if he had not sinned. His sin harmed not him alone but also the human race. Newborn infants are not in the same state in which Adam was before the transgression, and so the apostle's brief statement applies to them: *Death came through one man, and the resurrection of the dead came through one man. For, just as all die in Adam, so all will also be brought to life in Christ.* (1 Cor 15:21-22) For this reason it turns out that, if they are not baptized, infants are unable to attain not only the kingdom of heaven but also eternal life. It must be admitted as well that wealthy persons who have been baptized, even if they do not give up their riches, cannot be excluded from the kingdom of God. The apostle described people of this sort in

---

37. See *The Deeds of Pelagius* 11, 23-24; 33, 57; 35, 65.
38. See *The Deeds of Pelagius* 14, 30-31; 17, 40; 35, 65.
39. See *The Deeds of Pelagius* 18, 42; 35, 65.

writing to Timothy, *Command the rich people of this world not to have proud thoughts and not to place their hope in the uncertainty of riches, but in the living God who gives us all things in abundance for our enjoyment. Let them be rich in good works; let them give readily, share with others, and store up for themselves a good foundation for the future in order that they may attain true life.* (1 Tm 6:17-19) It must be confessed that the grace and help of God is given for individual actions and that it is not given in accord with our merits so that it may be true grace, that is, given gratuitously through the mercy of him who said, *I will take pity on whom I will take pity, and I will show mercy to whom I will show mercy* (Ex 33:19 LXX). It must be confessed that they can be called children of God who say daily, *Forgive us our debts* (Mt 6:12; Lk 11:4). Of course they would not truthfully say this if they were absolutely without sin. It must be confessed that free choice exists even if it needs God's help. It must be confessed that, when we fight against temptations and sinful desires, though we do in that case have a will of our own, our victory does not come from it but from the help of God. Otherwise, the words of the apostle would not be true, *It does not depend on the one who wills or on the one who runs, but on God who shows mercy* (Rom 9:16). It must be confessed that to those who repent pardon is granted in accord with the mercy of God, not in accord with their merits, since the apostle said that repentance itself is a gift of God, when he says of certain people, *In case God should perhaps give them repentance* (2 Tm 2:25). Whoever assents to the Catholic authority and to the words expressed in the ecclesiastical proceedings against Pelagius must confess all these things unconditionally and unambiguously. For we should not believe that the statements opposed to these are truly condemned if these statements to which they are opposed are not held in a believing heart and uttered in an open confession.

10, 34. Nor is what Pelagius holds on this issue seen clearly enough in the more recent books that the same Pelagius is said to have published after that trial, though he seems to acknowledge the help of divine grace. For at times he considers the power of the will like a balanced scale, so that he holds that it is as capable of not sinning as it is of sinning. But if that is so, no room remains for the help of the grace without which we say that the choice of the will is incapable of not sinning. At times, however, he admits that we are protected by the daily help of grace, though we have a strong and healthy free choice for not sinning, which he ought to admit is weak and sick until all the illnesses of our soul are healed.[40] For he did not pray for the weakness of his body who said, *Have mercy on me, Lord, because I am weak; heal me, Lord, because my bones are troubled* (Ps 7:3), since, in order to show that he was praying for his soul, he went on to say, *And my soul is greatly troubled* (Ps 7:4).

---

40. See Mt 4:23.

35. Pelagius, then, seems to believe that the help of grace is granted as something extra, that is, so that, even if it were not granted, we would still have a strong and healthy free choice for avoiding sin. But so that we may not be thought to be rash in suspecting him of this and so that no one might say that Pelagius holds that free choice is strong and healthy for avoiding sin, though it cannot accomplish and carry this out without the grace of God, just as we say that sound eyes are healthy for seeing, though they can in no way do this if they lack the help of light, in another passage he shows more clearly what he meant or thought where he says, "The grace of God is given to human beings in order that they may more easily accomplish by grace what they are commanded to do by free will."[41] Where he says, "more easily," what does he want us to understand but that, even if grace is lacking, one can through free choice carry out either easily or even with difficulty what is commanded by God?

36. Where, then, are the words, *What is a human being that you are mindful of him* (Ps 9:5)? Where, finally, are those testimonies that the bishop of the church of Jerusalem mentions that he cited for Pelagius himself, as you can read in the proceedings, when it was reported to him that Pelagius said that a human being could be free from sin without the grace of God?[42] For he set forth three very important testimonies against such an impious presumption, in the words of the apostle, *I have labored more than all those; not I, however, but the grace of God with me* (1 Cor 15:10), and, *It does not depend on the one who wills or on the one who runs, but on God who shows mercy* (Rom 9:16), and, *Unless the Lord builds the house, in vain have its builders labored* (Ps 127:1). How, then, is what God commands carried out, even with difficulty, without his help, since, if the Lord does not build, the builder is said to have labored in vain? And scripture does not say, "It does in fact depend on the one who wills and on the one who runs, but it is easier when God shows mercy." Rather scripture says, *It does not depend on the one who wills or on the one who runs, but on God who shows mercy*, not because a human being has no will and does not run, but because one can do nothing unless God shows mercy. Nor did the apostle say, "I too." Rather he said, *Not I, however, but the grace of God with me*, not because he himself did nothing good, but because he would do nothing if grace did not help. And yet, that perfect equilibrium of the capability of free choice for both good and evil did not leave room for even the ease that he at least seems to have confessed when he said, "They can more easily fulfil God's commands through grace." For, if the good is done more easily through grace, while evil is done most easily without grace, this capability is not in perfect equilibrium.

11, 37. But what else? We ought not only to be careful to avoid these people, but we ought also not to be hesitant to teach and admonish them, if they allow us.

---

41. See *The Grace of Christ and Original Sin* 1, 8, 9 and 27, 28.
42. See *The Deeds of Pelagius* 14, 37.

Yet we undoubtedly offer them more if we pray that they may be corrected so that they may neither perish with their fine minds nor cause others to perish because of their damnable presumption. For *they have zeal for God, but not in accord with knowledge* (Rom 10:2); but *not knowing the righteousness of God, that is,* the righteousness that comes from God, *and wanting to establish their own, they are not subject to the righteousness of God* (Rom 10:3). Since they are called Christians, they ought certainly to be on guard against this more than the Jews, about whom the apostle said this. Otherwise they will trip over *the stumbling block* (Rom 9:32), when they craftily defend nature and free choice, just like the philosophers of this world who worked hard in order to be thought or in order to think that they achieved for themselves the happy life by the power of their own will. Let these people beware that they do not empty of meaning the cross of Christ by their wordy wisdom.[43] For them this is to trip over the stumbling block. For, even if human nature remained in that state of wholeness in which it was created it would not in any way preserve itself without the help of its creator. Since, then, without the grace of God it could not guard the well-being it received, how could it without the grace of God repair the well-being it lost?

38. But we ought not to cease to pray for them on the grounds that, if they are not corrected, it must be attributed to the will of those who refuse to believe that they need the grace of the savior, even for what they think lies in the power of their will alone. On this issue the Pelagians resemble very closely the Jews, of whom the apostle said that, *not knowing the righteousness of God and wanting to establish their own, they are not subject to the righteousness of God* (Rom 10:3), and the Jews certainly failed to believe because of a sin of their own will. For they were not forced against their will to be unbelievers, but by refusing to believe they were guilty of the sin of unbelief. And yet the will is not sufficient by itself to come to believe the truth unless God helps it by grace, since the Lord himself said when he was speaking of those who did not believe, *No one comes to me unless it has been given him by my Father* (Jn 6:66). For the same reason, though the apostle zealously preached the gospel to them, he saw that it was still not enough unless he also prayed for them. For he said, *Brothers, the good desire of my heart and my prayer to God aims at their salvation,* and then he added the words that we mentioned, *For I bear witness to them that they have zeal for God, but not in accord with knowledge* (Rom 10:1-2), and so on. Therefore, holy brother, let us pray for them.

12, 39. You surely see along with us the wicked error that holds them captive. For your letters are fragrant with the most pure odor of Christ; in them you are seen to love and confess his grace most sincerely. But we thought that we should speak with you on this at length. We did so, first of all, because it is most

---

43. See 1 Cor 1:17.

pleasant. For what ought to be more pleasing to the sick than the grace by which they are healed or more pleasing to the sluggish than the grace by which they are roused or more pleasing to the willing than the grace by which they are helped? Secondly, we did this in order that, if we could do anything by our argumentation with God's help, we might lend support not to your faith but to your defense of the faith against persons such as these just as we have also been helped by the letter of Your Fraternity for this purpose.

40. For what could be richer or more filled with a most true profession than that passage in a letter of yours where you humbly deplored that our nature did not remain as it was created, but was damaged by the father of the human race. You said, "*I am poor and sorrowing* (Ps 69:30), since I am still fashioned from the squalor of the earthly image and still carry more of the first than of the second Adam in the senses of my flesh and in my earthly actions.[44] How shall I dare to make a portrait of myself for you when I am shown to reject the image of the heavenly man by my earthly corruption?[45] Shame encloses me from both sides. I am ashamed to portray what I am; I do not dare to portray what I am not. I hate what I am; I am not what I love. But what good will it do wretched me to hate iniquity and to love virtue,[46] since I do rather what I hate and I do not in my laziness strive to do what I love? In my discord I am torn apart by inner warfare, while *the spirit has desires opposed to the flesh and the flesh has desires opposed to the spirit* (Gal 5:17) and the law of the body attacks the law of the mind with the law of sin.[47] Unhappy man that I am, who have not eliminated the poisoned taste of the hostile tree even by the wood of the cross![48] For there remains in me that paternal poison by which through his transgression our father infected the whole of his race,"[49] and the many other things that you put together concerning this misery, while groaning in expectation of the redemption of your body, in the knowledge that you are not yet saved in fact but in hope.[50]

41. But perhaps, when you said these things, you portrayed someone else rather than yourself, and you do not endure any untimely and odious difficulties from the flesh with its desires opposed to the spirit, though you do not consent to it. Yet you and anyone else who experiences this and awaits the grace of God by which we might be set free *from the body of this death* (Rom 7:4) were clearly not present at the time openly and in your own person but were present in that man in a hidden way when he touched the forbidden food and contracted the

---

44. See 1 Cor 15:47-49.
45. Paulinus wrote this letter to Bishop Severus who had asked him to have a painting of him and his wife sent to him.
46. See Ps 45:8; Heb 1:9.
47. See Rom 7:23.
48. See Gn 3:6.
49. Paulinus of Nola, Letter 30, 2.
50. See Rom 8:23-24.

perdition that was going to spread far and wide through all human beings, unless he who was not lost came, thanks to a virgin, by another path *to seek and to save what was lost* (Lk 19:10; Mt 18:11). But what letter of yours is not filled with fervor about praying for and demanding with groans the help to make progress and to live correctly? What writing is there of yours, of whatever length, in which there is not scattered amid the groans of piety what we say in prayer, *Do not bring us into temptation* (Mt 6:13; Lk 11:4)? Let us, therefore, console, exhort, and help one another in all these ways to the extent that the Lord grants. But those things we have heard about some people, things over which we grieve and which we do not want readily to believe, Your Holiness will hear from our common friend by means of whom, when he returns in good health by God's mercy, we hope to be assured about everything.

Letter 187

Toward the middle of 417 Augustine wrote to Claudius Postumus Dardanus, the prefect of the praetorium of the Gauls, a Catholic layman in Italy, in reply to two questions. In *Revisions* 2, 49 Augustine treated the letter as a book and called it *The Presence of God*. He says of it:

> I wrote a book on the presence of God in which our intention was especially to refute the Pelagian heresy, though it was not explicitly mentioned. I also discussed in it with much effort and subtlety the presence of the nature that we say is the true and sovereign God and his temple. This book begins as follows: "I admit, my most beloved brother, Dardanus."

Augustine apologizes for this slowness in replying to Dardanus' questions (paragraph 1). Furthermore, the questions that Dardanus poses are difficult to answer, at least if one does so in a more than superficial way (paragraph 2). Dardanus had asked how Christ was in heaven when he hung upon the cross and promised the good thief that he would be with him that day in paradise (paragraph 3). Augustine commends Dardanus for his correct understanding of Christ as fully God and fully man (paragraph 4).

If as man Christ promised that the thief would be with him that day in paradise, paradise cannot be in heaven since Christ's body was in the tomb and his soul descended into the underworld (paragraph 5). In the scriptures "the underworld" seems to imply a place of punishment, and Christ could hardly have gone there, though he perhaps went to the bosom of Abraham (paragraph 6). Christ's words to the thief are much easier to understand if he spoke them as God, because as God he is everywhere (paragraph 7). As God Christ is one with the Father, while as man he is less than the Father (paragraph 8). While Christ as God was in heaven, he was also on earth as man (paragraph 9). But as man Christ is not present everywhere (paragraph 10).

Augustine warns against thinking of God's omnipresence in bodily terms (paragraph 11). He uses the examples of health and immortality to show how even bodily qualities are not greater in larger bodies and smaller in smaller ones (paragraph 12). He explains the difference between quality and quantity (paragraph 13). God, however, is spread out through the whole world, not as a quality of it but as a substance that creates the world (paragraph 14). Furthermore, the Father, Son, and Holy Spirit do not divide the world among themselves into three parts, but each is whole everywhere (paragraph 15).

Though God is present everywhere, he does not dwell in all persons (paragraph 16). Even in those in whom God does dwell, he does not dwell equally in all of them (paragraph 17). God, who is whole everywhere, is also whole in himself, because he is not contained by those in whom he is present and does not need them (paragraph 18). God is present as a whole to all things and is whole in those in whom he dwells, though they receive him, some more, others less, in accord with their capacity (paragraph 19). The members of Christ's body are individually temples of God and all together are the temple of God (paragraph 20). Not all who know God belong to his temple, and yet baptized infants, who do not know God, do belong to his temple (paragraph 21).

Dardanus' second question concerns John the Baptist's leaping in the womb of his mother at the visit of Mary (paragraph 22). John's leaping for joy in his mother's womb was a miracle that God performed in the infant, not something that the infant did by his own human power (paragraph 23). The miracle produced in John does not provide us with a rule for thinking about what infants are capable of (paragraph 24). That is, we should not credit infants with the use of reason and free choice (paragraph 25).

The Holy Spirit, nonetheless, dwells in baptized infants, though they do not know it (paragraph 26). He is making such infants into his temple and will bring that temple to perfection as they make progress and persevere in making progress (paragraph 27). In this life we must ask God to forgive our sins, but in the next life the Church will be without stain or wrinkle (paragraph 28). Augustine distinguishes between those in whom God does not dwell and those in whom he does dwell; he also points out that among those in whom he does dwell there are many infants who do not know that they are temples of the Holy Spirit (paragraph 29).

Hence there are two events in a given human being, birth in accord with the first Adam and rebirth in accord with the second Adam, namely, Christ (paragraph 30). Christ alone was conceived without concupiscence and born without original sin (paragraph 31). Baptism is the one means of sanctification by which we become temples of God (paragraph 32). Only by being reborn through the grace of baptism do we become members of the body of Christ (paragraph 33).

Christ is the one mediator between God and human beings for all human beings, whether of the Old or the New Testament (paragraph 34). Though God is present everywhere, he dwells only in those whom he makes his temple (paragraph 35). God at times works miracles in those in whom he does not yet dwell (paragraph 36). The sanctification of Jeremiah in the womb need not mean that he did not need to be reborn but only that he was predestined (paragraph 37).

The temple of all those in whom God dwells, as long as it is in this world, is symbolized by Noah's ark tossed about by the waves (paragraph 38). Augustine explains the senses in which the fullness of divinity can be said to dwell in Christ in a bodily manner (paragraph 39). Yet the difference between the way the divinity dwells in Christ and in any other holy person is very great because in no other saint is the Word united with a man to form one person (paragraph 40). Finally, Augustine tells Dardanus that he has with God's help explained as well as he could how God is present everywhere, how he dwells in the saints in heaven and on earth, and how Christ as God is present everywhere and dwells in his temple but, as man, is in a particular place in heaven (paragraph 41).

The Presence of God

Augustine sends greetings to Dardanus.

1, 1. I admit, my most beloved brother, Dardanus, who are more illustrious for me in the love of Christ than in your high office in this world, that I have replied to your letter later than I should have. Do not ask the reasons for this. For I fear that you may bear with me less patiently when I make long excuses than you have borne with me for replying so tardily. I would prefer that you readily pardon my offense rather than pronounce judgment on my defense. Whatever those reasons were, believe me that I could not have had any contempt for you. For I would, on the contrary, have replied most quickly if I held you in contempt. Nor, because I have at long last written back, have I now at long last produced something that is worthy of your reading and that I could rightly dedicate to you, but I preferred to reply somehow or other rather than to allow this summer also to pass with me still owing you this debt. Nor did your high office frighten me or make me hesitant since your kindness is more pleasing than your office is a cause of mistrust. But the more love I have for you, the more difficult I find the means to satisfy the great eagerness of your pious love.

2. In addition, besides the flame of mutual love that makes us love even those whom we have never seen, provided we believe that they possess what we love, in which respect you have, of course, anticipated me and made me fear that your opinion and expectation are mistaken about me—besides this, therefore, you asked me such questions in your letter that, if just anyone asked them, they would also become no small labor for my leisure, which is something that I lack. But when you who are by no means satisfied by their superficial solution ask them, since you search out their depths, and when you ask them of someone who is most busy, besieged and surrounded by mountains of other cares, I leave it to your wisdom and benevolence to imagine how forgiving I deserve to find you, either because I have not answered for a long time or if even now I do not answer in a way that corresponds to the greatness of your desire.

2, 3. And so you ask, "How are we to believe that *the mediator between God and human beings, the man Jesus Christ* (1 Tm 2:5), is now in heaven, since, when hanging on the tree and just about to die, he said to the believing thief, *Today you will be with me in paradise* (Lk 23:43)? And perhaps you are saying that from this we should understand that paradise is located in some part of heaven or that, since God is everywhere, the man, who is in God, is spread out everywhere as well, and you want it to be understood that he who is everywhere could also be in paradise.

4. Here I ask or rather recognize how you understand Christ the man. Certainly not like some heretics, as the Word of God and flesh, that is, without a human soul, so that the Word took the place of a soul for the flesh, or as the Word

of God, soul and flesh but without a human mind, so that the Word of God took the place of a human mind for the soul.[1] You certainly do not understand Christ the man in that way but rather as you said above, when you said that you understand Christ as almighty God by the norm of faith, so that you would not believe him to be God unless you also believed him to be a complete man. Of course, when you say "complete man," you want us to understand by that term a whole human nature. But it is not a complete man if either a soul is lacking to the flesh or a human mind to the soul.

5. If, then, we think that the phrase, *Today you will be with me in paradise* was said in terms of the man, paradise ought not to be thought to be in heaven on the basis of those words. For on that very day the man Jesus Christ was not going to be in paradise but in the underworld in terms of his soul and in the tomb in terms of his flesh. For the gospel is perfectly clear about the fact that his flesh was laid in the tomb on that day. But the teaching of the apostle declares that his soul descended to the underworld[2] when blessed Peter uses the testimony from the psalms in this regard and shows that it was predicted, *For you will not leave my soul in the underworld, nor will you allow your holy one to see corruption* (Ps 16:10; Acts 2:27). The first part was said of the soul because it was not left in the underworld, from where it moved so quickly, but the second part was said of the body because it could not be corrupted in the tomb on account of the short time before the resurrection. But no one understands paradise to be in the tomb. And if anyone should be so absurd as to try to maintain this because that tomb was in a garden, he would surely be held back from this opinion by the fact that the thief to whom it was said, *Today you will be with me in paradise*, was not with Christ in that tomb on that day, nor would the burial of the flesh, which in death experiences no joy or sorrow, be offered him as a great gift in return for his faith, since he would be thinking of a place of rest where he would be conscious.

6. What remains then, is that if *Today you will be with me in paradise*, was said in terms of the man, paradise would be understood to be in the underworld where Christ was on that day in terms of his human soul. But I could not easily say whether the bosom of Abraham, where the wicked rich man saw the poor man at rest while he himself was in the torments of the underworld,[3] should be denoted by the term "paradise" or should be thought to belong to the underworld. For we read that scripture said about that rich man, *But the rich man also died, and he was buried in the underworld* (Lk 16:22), and, *Since he was in torments in the underworld* (Lk 16:23). At the death or rest of the poor man, however, the underworld is not mentioned, but it says, *It happened that the poor man died and was carried to the bosom of Abraham* (Lk 16:22). Then Abraham

---

1. Augustine refers to the Arians and the Apollinarists; see *Heresies* 44 and 45.
2. See Mt 27:60; Mk 15:46; Lk 23:53,; Jn 19:41-42.
3. See Lk 16:23.

says to the rich man in the fire, *A great chasm has been placed between you and us* (Lk 16:26), as if between the underworld and the place of the blessed. For one does not readily find anywhere in the scriptures the term "underworld" used in a good sense. Hence it is often asked: "If the underworld is correctly understood as only a place of punishment, how are we piously to believe that the soul of Christ was in the underworld?" But it is a good answer that he descended there in order to help those who needed his help. For this reason blessed Peter says that he destroyed the pains of the underworld in which *he could not be held* (Acts 2:24). But if both the region of those who are suffering and that of those at rest, that is, both where that rich man was tormented and where that poor man was happy, should be believed to be in the underworld, who would dare to say that the Lord Jesus came only to the penal parts of the underworld and was not present with those who were at rest in the bosom of Abraham? If he was there, that should be understood to be the paradise which he graciously promised to the soul of the thief on that day. If that is so, "paradise" is a general term for where one lives happily. For scripture was not prevented from calling the Church as well a paradise full of fruit[4] because the place where Adam was before his sin was called paradise.

3, 7. There is a much easier interpretation and one free from all these ambiguities if Christ is understood to have said, *Today you will be with me in paradise*, not insofar as he was a man but insofar as he was God. On that day Christ the man was going to be in the tomb in terms of his flesh and in the underworld in terms of his soul. But the same Christ, as God, is always everywhere. For he is the light that shines in the darkness, though the darkness does not grasp it.[5] He is the power and wisdom of God, of which scripture says that it *stretches from end to end mightily* and arranges *all things pleasingly* (Wis 8:1) and reaches *everywhere on account of its purity, and nothing impure* is found *in it* (Wis 7:24-25). Wherever, then, paradise is, whoever of the blessed are there, they are there with him who is everywhere.

8. For Christ is God and man. It is as God, indeed, that he says, *The Father and I are one* (Jn 10:30), but it is as man that he says, *The Father is greater than me* (Jn 14:28). He is also the Son of God, the only-begotten of the Father,[6] and the Son of Man *from the offspring of David according to the flesh* (Rom 1:3). Hence, when he speaks or when scripture speaks of him, we should consider both of them and see what is said in terms of what. For, just as one human being is a rational soul and flesh, so too the one Christ is the Word and a man. Hence, as the Word, Christ is the creator, for *all things were made through him* (Jn 1:3), but, as a man, Christ was created. For *he came to be from the offspring of David*

4. See Gn 2:8.
5. See Jn 1:5.
6. See Jn 1:14.

according to the flesh (Rom 1:3) and *came to be in the likeness of human beings* (Phil 2:7). Likewise, since there are two elements in a human being, soul and flesh, in terms of his soul he was sad unto death,[7] and in terms of his flesh he suffered death.[8]

9. And yet when we call Christ the Son of God we do not exclude the man, nor when we call the same Christ the Son of Man do we exclude God. For as man he was on earth, not in heaven where he is now, when he said, *No one goes up into heaven except him who has come down from heaven, the Son of Man who is in heaven* (Jn 3:13); though as the Son of God he was in heaven, as the Son of Man he was still on earth and had not yet ascended into heaven. Similarly, as the Son of God, he is the Lord of glory, but as the Son of Man he was crucified. Yet, the apostle says, For, *if they had known, they would never have crucified the Lord of glory* (1 Cor 2:8). And for this reason the Son of Man as God was in heaven, and the Son of God as man was crucified on earth. Consequently, just as he could correctly be called the Lord of glory when he was crucified, though that suffering pertained to his flesh alone, so he could correctly say, *Today you will be with me in paradise*, though as regards his lowly human condition he was going to be in the tomb in terms of his flesh and in the underworld in terms of his soul on that day. But in accord with the immutability of God he had never left paradise because he is always everywhere.

10. Do not doubt, therefore, that the man Christ Jesus is now in heaven, from where he will come, and recall to mind and maintain with faith the Christian confession that he rose from the dead, ascended into heaven, is seated at the right hand of the Father, and will come from nowhere else when he will come to judge the living and the dead.[9] And, as the angel's voice testified, he will come just as he was seen going to heaven,[10] that is, in the same form and substance of the flesh, to which he certainly gave immortality, but did not take away its nature. In accord with this form he should not be thought to be spread out everywhere. For we must be careful not to defend the divinity of the man in such a way that we remove the reality of his body. It does not follow, however, that what is in God is everywhere, as God is. For scripture also says of us that *we live, move, and have our being in him* (Acts 17:28), and yet we are not everywhere, as he is. But that man [Jesus] is in God in a different way because, as God, he is in the man in a different way, in a manner that is proper to him and singular. For one person is God and man, and the two are the one Jesus Christ, everywhere as God, in heaven as man.

---

7. See Mt 26:38; Mk 14:34.
8. See Acts 3:18.
9. See Mk 16:19; Lk 22:69; Col 3:1; Heb 1:3; 10:12; 12:2.
10. See 2 Tm 4:1; Acts 1:10-11.

4, 11. And yet, when we say that God is everywhere, we must resist carnal thinking and withdraw the mind from the senses of the body so that we do not suppose that God is spread out through all things as if by spacial magnitude in the same way that the earth, or a liquid, or air, or this light is spread out. For every magnitude of this sort is smaller in a part than in its whole. But he is present, rather, in the way that wisdom, which is great, is present in a man whose body is small. And if there are two wise persons, one of whom is larger in body, but neither is wiser, there is not greater wisdom in the larger, or less in the smaller, or less in one than in the two, but as much in this one as in that one, and as much in each as in both. For, if they are absolutely equal in wisdom, both of them are not more wise than each individually, just as, if they are equally immortal, both of them do not live longer than each individual.

12. Finally, though the immortality of the body, which came first in the flesh of Christ and is promised to be ours in the end, is something great, it is certainly not great in terms of mass but in terms of a certain incorporeal excellence, though it will be possessed by the body. For, though an immortal body is smaller in a part than in the whole, its immortality is as complete in a part as in the whole, and though some members are larger than others, still they are not more immortal. Similarly, now, when we are healthy in every part in accord with the sort of health present in the body, we do not say that the health of the whole hand is greater than that of the finger because the whole hand is larger than the finger. But in those unequal parts the health is equal, since smaller members are compared to larger ones in such a way that one member which cannot be as large as another can still be as healthy. Yet there would be greater health in larger members if the larger members were healthier. But when that is not so and the larger and the smaller ones are just as healthy, there is certainly a different quantity in the size of the members but an equal health in the unequal members.

13. Since, then, a body is a substance, its quantity consists in the size of its mass, but its health is not its quantity but its quality. The quantity of a body, therefore, could not do what its quality could. For with parts so distant, which cannot all be together, since each of them occupies its own amount of space, smaller parts smaller spaces and larger parts larger spaces, the quantity could not be whole and as large in each individual part. Rather the quantity is larger in larger parts and smaller in smaller parts, and in no part is there as much as in the whole. But the quality of the body, which is called health, is as great in the larger parts as in the smaller, when the whole body is healthy. For those parts that are less large are not for that reason less healthy, nor are the larger parts more healthy. Heaven forbid that the substance of the creator is incapable of what a quality of a created body is capable of.

14. Hence God is spread out through all things. Indeed, he says through the prophet, *I fill heaven and earth* (Jer 23:24) and what I cited a little before concerning his wisdom, *It stretches from end to end mightily and arranges all*

things pleasingly (Wis 8:1). Scripture likewise says, *The Spirit of the Lord filled the world* (Wis 1:7), and a certain psalm says to him, *Where shall I hide from your spirit, and where shall I flee from your face? If I go up to the heavens, you are there; if I go down to the underworld, you are present.* (Ps 139:7-8) But God is spread out through all things not such that he is a quality of the world but such that he is the substance that creates the world, rules it without any toil, and contains it without any burden. Yet he is not spread out in space like a mass such that in half of the body of the world there is half of him and half of him in the other half, being in that way whole in the whole. Rather, he is whole in the heavens alone and whole on the earth alone and whole in the heavens and in the earth, contained in no place, but whole everywhere in himself.

15. So it is with the Father, with the Son, with the Holy Spirit, with the Trinity, one God. For they do not divide the world among themselves into three parts that they individually fill, as if the Son or the Holy Spirit would not have anywhere to be in the world if the Father occupied the whole of it. It is not that way with the true, incorporeal, and immutable divinity. For they are not bodies that would have a greater magnitude in the three than in each individually. Nor do they fill places with their masses such that they cannot be present at the same time in distant places. For, when the soul is present in the body, it experiences not only confinement but even a sort of expansion, not of bodily spaces but of spiritual joys, when there occurs what the apostle says, *Do you not know that your bodies are in you the temple of the Holy Spirit, whom you have from God?* (1 Cor 6:19) Nor can one say except most foolishly that the Holy Spirit has no room in our body because our soul fills the whole of it. How much more foolishly does one say that the Trinity is hindered anywhere by any confinement such that the Father and the Son and the Holy Spirit cannot be together everywhere!

5, 16. But it is much more marvelous that, though God is whole everywhere, yet he does not dwell in all persons. For it cannot be said to all persons what the apostle said, or what I just said, or this: *Do you not know that you are the temple of God and that the Holy Spirit dwells in you?* (1 Cor 3:16) For this reason the same apostle says of some people just the opposite: *But whoever does not have the Spirit of Christ does not belong to him* (Rom 8:9). Now who except someone utterly ignorant of the inseparability of the Trinity would dare to suppose that the Father or the Son could dwell in someone in whom the Holy Spirit does not dwell or that the Holy Spirit could dwell in someone in whom the Father and the Son do not? Hence we must say that God is everywhere by the presence of his divinity but not everywhere through the indwelling of grace. For, on account of this indwelling, in which we undoubtedly recognize the grace of his love, we do not say, "Our Father who art everywhere," though this is also true, but, *Our Father who art in heaven* (Mt 6:9), in order that we may rather call to mind in prayer his temple. For we ourselves ought both to be his temple and, to the extent that we are, to pertain to his society and adopted family.[11] For, if the people of God, when not yet made equal to his angels, are called his temple[12] while still on pilgrimage, how much more so is his temple in heaven where there are the people of the angels,[13] to whom we shall be gathered and made equal when, after the end of our pilgrimage, we receive what God has promised!

17. Since, therefore, he who is everywhere does not dwell in all persons, neither does he dwell equally in all the persons in whom he dwells. For why did Elisha ask that the Spirit of God, who was in Elijah, might be in him in a double amount?[14] And why in all the saints are some holier than others except by having God dwelling in them more abundantly? How, then, is what we said above true, namely, that God is whole everywhere when he is more in some persons and less in others? But we should not carelessly look at what we said, namely, that in himself he is whole everywhere but is not whole everywhere in those persons who receive him, some more and others less. He is said to be everywhere, there-fore, because he is absent to no part of reality; he is said to be whole because he does not offer a part of himself as present to a part of reality and another part of himself to another part of reality, equal parts to equal parts, but a smaller part to a smaller part and a larger part to a larger part. But he is equally present as a whole not only to the whole of creation but also to each part of it. Some persons are said to be far from him who became unlike him by sinning, and some persons are said to draw near to him who receive his likeness by living a pious life. In the same way eyes are said to be further from the light to the extent that they are more blind. For what is as far from the light as blindness, even if light is present and floods sightless eyes? But eyes are rightly said to draw near to the light when by an increase in health they improve by recovering their keenness.

6, 18. But I see that I must explain more carefully what we thought that we could not understand distinctly enough when we said that God is whole every-where unless we added "in himself." For how is he everywhere if he is in himself? He is everywhere, of course, because he is absent nowhere. But he is in himself because he is not contained by those things to which he is present, as if he could not exist without them. For take from bodies their places and they will be nowhere, and because they will be nowhere they will not exist. Take the bodies themselves from their qualities and there will be no place for the qualities to be, and so they necessarily do not exist. For, when a body is equally healthy or equally white through its whole mass, its health or whiteness is not greater in one part than in another and not greater in the whole than in a part of it, because it is agreed that the whole is not more healthy or more white than the part. But if it

---

11. See Rom 8:15.23; Gal 4:5.
12. See Lk 20:36.
13. See 2 Cor 5:6.
14. See 2 Kgs 2:9.

were unequally healthy or unequally white, it could be that there is greater health or whiteness in a smaller part, since smaller members can be more healthy or more white than larger ones. To that extent it is clear that large and small are not said of qualities by reason of mass. Yet, if the mass itself of a body, however big or small it may be, were completely removed, there would be nowhere for its qualities to be, even though they were not to be measured by mass. But if God is received less by one to whom he is present, he is not therefore himself less. For he is whole in himself, and he is not in those in whom he is in such a way that he needs them, as if he could not exist apart from them. But just as he is not absent from one in whom he does not dwell, and he is present as a whole although that person does not have him, so he is present as a whole to one in whom he dwells, though that person does not receive him wholly.

19. For God does not divide himself in order to dwell in human hearts or bodies, giving one part of himself to one person and another part to another, like the daylight through the doorways and through the windows of houses. But a better image would be this: a deaf person does not grasp a sound of any sort, though it is something bodily and passing; someone hard of hearing does not grasp it completely; and, in those with hearing, when they draw equally near to it, one grasps more than another to the extent that his hearing is sharper, but less to the extent that his hearing is less sharp, though the sound does not vary with more or less loudness but is equally present to all in the place where they are. How much more excellently is God, an incorporeal and immutably living nature, who cannot be extended and divided like a sound over stretches of time and who does not need an airy space in which to make himself present to others but, remaining in himself in his eternal stability, able to be present to all things in his totality and to individual things in his totality. And yet those in whom he dwells possess him in accordance with their different capacities, some more, others less, and he himself makes them a most beloved temple for himself by the grace of his goodness![15]

20. And scripture has spoken of a division of gifts as if over the parts and members of one body in which all of us together are one temple and individuals are individual temples.[16] For God is not greater in all than in each individual, and it often turns out that many persons possess him less and one person possesses him more. But when the apostle said, *But there are divisions of gifts*, he immediately added, *but the same Spirit*. Likewise, after he had mentioned these divisions of gifts, he said, *But one and the same Spirit produces all these, distributing particular gifts to each one as he wills* (1 Cor 12:11). And so, though he distributes, he himself is not distributed because he is one and the same. But the apostle described those divisions as the divisions of the members in a body, because the ears cannot do what the eyes can, and so the other

15. See 1 Cor 3:16; 6:19; 2 Cor 6:16.
16. See 1 Cor 12:4.

members are harmoniously assigned different functions. When we are healthy, these members enjoy a single and undivided health, and there is not a greater health in one member and a lesser in another but, though they are unequal, they enjoy a common and equal health. Christ is the head of this body; the unity of his body is expressed by our sacrifice. The apostle briefly signified this when he said, *We, though many, are one bread, one body* (1 Cor 10:17.14). Through our head we are reconciled with God, because in him the divinity of the Only-Begotten came to share in our mortality in order that we might share in his immortality.

21. This mystery is far from the hearts of the proud and wise, who for this reason are not Christians and hence not truly wise. I also mean the wisdom of those who knew God, because the apostle says, *Though knowing God, they did not glorify him as God or give him thanks* (Rom 1:21). You, however, know the sacrifice in which we say, "Let us give thanks to the Lord our God." From the lowliness of this sacrifice their pride and arrogance is far distant. And it is something quite amazing that God dwells in some who do not yet know God and does not dwell in some who do know him. For they do not pertain to the temple of God who, *though knowing God, did not glorify him as God or give him thanks,* whereas infants made holy by the sacrament of Christ and reborn by the Holy Spirit do pertain to the temple of God,[17] though at their age they surely cannot yet know God. Hence, before knowing him the latter could possess him whom the former could know but could not possess. But most blessed are they for whom to possess God is the same as to know him! Such knowledge is most complete, most true, and most happy.

7, 22. Here it behooves us to examine the question that you added after the signature on your letter: "If infants still do not know God, how could John exult even before he was born in the womb of his own mother at the arrival and presence of the mother of the Lord?"[18] For, after you mentioned that you read my book, *The Baptism of Infants,* you went on to say: "I want to know what you think about pregnant women, since the mother of John the Baptist answered with a pledge of faith on behalf of the child."

23. These are, of course, the words of Elizabeth, the mother of John: *Blessed are you among women, and blessed is the fruit of your womb. And how is it that the mother of my Lord should come to me? For, see, when the words of your greeting reached my ears, the infant in my womb leapt with joy.* (Lk 1:41-44) But as the evangelist already said, *She was filled with the Holy Spirit* (Lk 1:41), in order that she might say this. It was undoubtedly through his revelation that she knew the meaning of that exultation of the infant, that is, the coming of the mother of him whom he himself would precede and point out. This, then, could

---

17. See Ti 3:5.
18. See Lk 1:41-44.

be the meaning of the great event that was meant to be known by adults, though it was not known by that infant. For, when this was narrated earlier in the gospel, it did not say, "The infant believed in her womb," but, *The infant leapt.* Nor did she say, "The infant leapt in my womb with faith," but, *The infant leapt with joy.* Now we see the leaping not only of children, but also of animals, which certainly does not come from some faith or devotion or any rational thought. But it is clearly something unusual and novel that an infant leapt in the womb and did this at the arrival of the woman who was going to give birth to the savior of human beings. This is the reason why it is marvelous; this is the reason why it is to be numbered among the great signs; this is the reason for that leaping and greeting given in return, as it were, to the mother of the Lord. Just as miracles are usually produced, this leaping was produced by divine power in the infant, not by the infant with human power.

24. And yet, even if the use of reason and will was developed so early in that infant that within the womb of his mother he could recognize, believe, and assent—acts that other infants have to await a later age to perform—this too must be counted as a miracle of God's power and not taken as an example for human nature. For, when God willed it, even a dumb beast spoke reasonably, but human beings had not been admonished by that to await the counsel of donkeys in their deliberations.[19] Hence, I neither hold in contempt what happened in John's case nor do I frame a rule from it of what I should maintain regarding infants. On the contrary, I declare it a miracle in his case, because I do not find it in others. That struggle of the twins in Rebekah's womb has some likeness to this, but it too was a miracle insofar as, because of it, the woman sought an explanation from God and received the answer that the two infants symbolized two peoples.[20]

25. But if we wanted to prove by words that infants, who do not know even human matters, do not know the plans of God, I fear that we may seem to do an injustice to our very senses when we try by speaking to persuade people of a point on which the obviousness of the truth most easily surpasses all the powers and function of speech. Do we not see, even when they begin to produce some sort of signs in articulated sounds and to pass from infancy to the start of speaking, that they still think and say such things that, if they had remained and continued to be such as the years increased, no one, or only someone really stupid, would doubt that they were stupid? Or perhaps the possibility remains that we are to believe that children are wise amid the wails of infancy or even in the silence of the womb but that, after they have begun to speak with us, they have come to the ignorance that we laugh at by growing up. You see how absurd it is to entertain this thought since the mind of children that bursts forth in words

19. See Num 22:28.
20. See Gn 25:22-23.

of any sort—though compared to the thoughts of adults their mind is certainly almost none at all—can still be called intelligence when compared to that with which they are born. But why, when they are helped by the grace of Christ in that great bulwark of salvation, is the fact that they struggle, with whatever cries and gestures they can, not held against them? And why is all their resistance ignored until the sacraments are conferred on them, by which there is wiped away what they contracted by the condemnation at their origin? Is it not because they know so little what they are doing that they are not judged to do those actions? But if they were using the choice of reason and will, by which assent ought to be given to that rite of sanctification, what Christian could fail to know what a great sin it would be to resist so great a grace and how the conferral of baptism could not only do them no good but would even increase their guilt?

8, 26. We say, therefore, that the Holy Spirit dwells in baptized infants, although they do not know it. For they do not know the Holy Spirit, though he is in them, any more than they know their own mind, though its reason, which they cannot as yet use, is asleep like a little ember to be stirred up with the advance of age. Nor should this seem surprising in infants since the apostle also says to certain adults, *Do you not know that you are the temple of God and that the Spirit of God dwells in you?* (1 Cor 3:16) Of such persons he had said a little before, *But a natural human being does not perceive what pertains to the Spirit of God* (1 Cor 2:14). And so they did not perceive with knowledge the Holy Spirit who was dwelling in them and, though the Holy Spirit was dwelling in them, they were still natural and not yet spiritual because they could not yet perceive by knowledge the Spirit dwelling in them.

27. But he is said to dwell in such persons because he acts in them in a hidden manner so that they might be his temple, and he brings this to fulfilment in those who make progress and who persevere in making progress. *For we are saved in hope* (Rom 8:24), as the apostle says, though he says in another place, *He saved us through the bath of rebirth* (Ti 3:5). Though he says in this verse, *He saved us*, as if this salvation were already given, he explains in the other verse how this should be understood, when he says, *For we were saved in hope. Hope, however, that is seen is not hope. For who hopes for what he sees? But if we hope for what we do not see, we await it in patience.* (Rom 8:24-25) For many things are said in the divine scriptures as if they already happened, though they are understood to be still matters of hope. This is why the Lord said to his disciples, *Everything that I heard from my Father I have made known to you* (Jn 15:15). This was so clearly said in accordance with hope for what was to come that he afterwards said to them, *I have many things to say to you, but you cannot now bear them* (Jn 16:12). The Spirit, therefore, carries out in the mortals in whom he dwells the construction of his dwelling, which he brings to completion, not in this life but in another after it, when *death* will be swallowed up *in victory* and it will be said to

it, *Where, O death, is your victory? Where, O death, is your sting?* (1 Cor 15:54).
But what is death's sting except sin?[21]

28. On this account, even now that we have been reborn *of water and the
Spirit* (Jn 3:5) and the purification of that bath has removed all our sins, whether
sins from our origin in Adam, *in whom all sinned* (Rom 5:12), or sins of our own
thoughts, words, and deeds, because we still remain in this life, which is *a temptation on earth* (Jb 7:1), we rightly say, *Forgive us our debts* (Mt 6:12). And the
whole Church says this prayer, the Church that the savior cleanses *by the bath of
water with the word in order to present* her *to himself as glorious, with no stain
or wrinkle or anything of the sort* (Eph 5:26-27). He will certainly do this when
she has been made perfect in reality, whereas now she walks in hope as she
makes progress. For how is she now *with no stain or wrinkle or anything of the
sort* when, either in all human beings belonging to her who now make use of the
reason of their mind and the choice of their will and carry about the burden of
mortal flesh or at least in many of her members, which even those contentious
persons have to admit, she truthfully says, *Forgive us our debts* (Mt 6:12)?

29. Since, therefore, he makes more and more righteous those mortals who
are making progress, in whom he dwells, and hears them when they pray and
cleanses them when they confess in order to present to himself an immaculate
temple for eternity,[22] he is rightly said not to dwell in those who, though knowing
God, did not glorify him as God or give thanks (Rom 1:21). For, by worshiping
and serving *a creature rather than the creator* (Rom 1:25), they did not want to
be the temple of the one true God. And so, when they wanted to have him along
with many gods, they more easily brought it about that they did not have him
than that they made him one among the many false gods. And he is rightly said to
dwell in those whom he called according to his plan and took under his protection in order to make them righteous and glorify them, even before they can
know his incorporeal nature that is whole everywhere, to the extent that it can be
known by a human being in this life *in part through a glass and in an enigma* (1
Cor 13:12), when one has made great progress. For there are many in whom he
dwells of the sort to whom the apostle says, *I could not speak to you as to spiritual people, but only as to carnal people. As if to little ones in Christ I gave you
milk as a drink, not solid food, for you were not yet capable. But even now you
are not capable.* (1 Cor 3:1-2) To these people he indeed also says this: *Do you
not know that you are the temple of God and that the Spirit of God dwells in you?*
(1 Cor 3:16, 6:19) If the last day of this life overtakes people of this sort before
they reach spiritual maturity of mind when they are not fed milk but solid food,[23]
he who dwells in them will make perfect in them what they lack in intelligence

---

21. See 1 Cor 15:55-56.
22. See 2 Cor 4:16.
23. See Heb 5:12.

here, because they did not withdraw from the unity of the body of Christ, who became for us the way, and from the fellowhsip of the temple of God.[24] Hence, in order that they may not withdraw, they perseveringly hold in the Church the rule of faith common to the small and the great, and they walk in the way they have come until God reveals it to them, if they have different ideas, and they do not teach as the truth their carnal thoughts because they have not become hardened in clinging to their quarrelsome defenses, but they perspire in a sense as they walk, that is, as they make progress, begging for the clarity of understanding through the piety of faith.[25]

9, 30. Since this is so, the two events that take place in one human being, birth and rebirth, pertain to two men: one to the first Adam, the other to the second Adam, who is called Christ. The apostle said, *But first there came not what is spiritual, but what is natural; afterward there came what is spiritual. The first man from the earth is earthly; the second man from heaven is heavenly. The earthly are like the earthly man, and the heavenly are like the heavenly man. Just as we have borne the image of the earthly man, let us also bear the image of him who is from heaven.* (1 Cor 15:46-49) Again he says, *Death came through one man, and the resurrection of the dead came through one man. For, just as all die in Adam, so we will all also be brought to life in Christ.* (1 Cor 15:21-22) He said *all* both times because no one enters into death except through the first man and no one enters into life except through the second man. In the first we see what the choice of a man could do to bring about death, but in the second we see what the help of God could do to bring about salvation. Finally, the first man was only a man, but the second is God and man. Sin was committed through abandoning God; righteousness is not attained without God. And for this reason we would not die if we had not come from the members of the first man by carnal procreation, nor would we live if we were not members through a spiritual union with the second man. Hence we needed to be born and to be reborn, but Christ needed only to be born on our account. For we pass from sin to righteousness by being reborn; Christ did not pass from sin to righteousness, but in being baptized he commended more highly by his humility the sacrament of our rebirth, symbolizing our old human being by his suffering and our new human being by his resurrection.

31. For the disobedience of concupiscence, which dwells in our mortal flesh with the result that those same members are aroused even apart from the choice of our will, is brought back to its proper limits by marital righteousness so that from parents legitimately united children may be born who need to be reborn. Yet Christ did not want his flesh to come through such a coupling of man and woman. Rather, he who had no such concupiscence when he was conceived,

24. See Jn 14:6.
25. See Phil 3:15-16.

took *took the likness of sinful flesh* (Rom 8:3) from a virgin for our sake, in order to purify sinful flesh in us. The apostle says, *As through the sin of one all entered into condemnation, so through the righteousness of one all come to the righteousness of life* (Rom 5:18). For no one is born apart from the working of carnal concupiscence which is derived from the first man, who is Adam, and no one is reborn apart from the working of spiritual grace which is given through the second man, who is Christ. Hence, we belong to the first by being born, and we belong to the second by being reborn, and no one can be reborn before being born. He was certainly born in a singular way who had no need to be reborn, because he did not pass from sin, in which he never was, nor was he conceived in iniquity, nor did his mother nourish him in her womb amid sins.[26] For the Holy Spirit came over her, and the power of the Most High overshadowed her. Hence, the Holy One who was born of her is called the Son of God.[27] For the good of marriage does not extinguish but controls the disobedience of the members so that, once carnal concupiscence has been somehow limited, it may become marital chastity. But in conceiving her holy child the Virgin Mary, to whom it was said, *And the power of the Most High will overshadow you* (Lk 1:35), did not burn with the ardor of concupiscence under such a shadow. With the exception, then, of this cornerstone,[28] I see no way in which human beings are built into a house of God to order to have God dwelling in them unless they are reborn,[29] and they cannot be reborn before they are born.

10, 32. John had not yet seen the light of day but leapt, nonetheless, with joy, and who would believe that this could have happened except by the working of the Holy Spirit? And the Lord said to Jeremiah, *Before you emerged from the womb, I sanctified you* (Jer 1:5). Whatever opinion, therefore, we may have about pregnant women or, better, about human beings still in the wombs of their mothers, whether we think that they can or cannot be given some means of sanctification, that sanctification by which we are individually made temples of God and made into one temple of God belongs only to those who have been reborn, and only human beings who have been born can be reborn. No one, however, ends well the life in which he was born unless he is reborn before he comes to its end.

33. But suppose someone says that a human being is already born, even when he is still in the womb of his mother, and uses as testimony from the gospel that it was said to Joseph about the pregnant virgin, the mother of the Lord, *For what is born in her is the work of the Holy Spirit* (Mt 1:20). A second birth does not follow after this birth, does it? Otherwise, rebirth will not be the second but the

---

26. See Ps 51:7.
27. See Lk 1:35.
28. See Is 28:16; 1 Pt 2:6; Eph 2:20.
29. See 2 Cor 6:16.

third birth. But when the Lord was speaking about this, he said, *Unless one is born again* (Jn 3:3), counting as first the birth that takes place when a mother gives birth, not when she conceives and is pregnant—the birth from her, not the birth in her. For we do not refer to as reborn a human being to whom a mother gave birth, as if he were born again after he had already been born once in the womb. But without counting the birth that makes her pregnant, a human being is said to be born at birth in order that he can be reborn *of water and the Spirit* (Jn 3:5). In accord with this birth the Lord himself is also said to have been born in Bethlehem of Judah.[30] If, therefore, a human being can be reborn by the grace of the Spirit in the womb, he is then reborn before he is born, because it still remains for him to be born. He is reborn, therefore, before he is born, which is in no way possible. Hence, human beings who have been born are transferred into the frame of the body of Christ as if into the living structure of the temple of God, which is his Church, not because of works of righteousness that they were going to perform but by being reborn through grace, as if taken from the mass of ruins to serve as the foundation of the building. For, apart from this building, which is being constructed to order to be made happy as the eternal dwelling place of God, the life of every human being is unhappy and should be called death rather than life. Whoever, therefore, has God dwelling in him so that the anger of God does not remain on him[31] is no stranger to this body, to this temple, and to this birth. But everyone who is not reborn is a stranger to it.

11, 34. Further, he who was revealed as the mediator wanted to be the manifest sacrament of our rebirth. But for the righteous of old he was something hidden, though they too were being saved by the same faith that was going to be revealed. For we do not dare to prefer the saints of our time to the friends of God through whom these events were foretold to us. For God teaches that he is the God of Abraham, the God of Isaac, and the God of Jacob[32] and says that this is his name for eternity. But if for the saints of old circumcision is thought to have taken the place of baptism, what answer shall we make regarding those who were pleasing to God before this commandment was given, though not without faith? For, as was written to the Hebrews, *it is impossible to please God without faith* (Heb 11:6). *But, having the same Spirit of faith*, the apostle says, *on account of which scripture says, I believed, and for this reason I spoke, we too believe, and for this reason we speak* (2 Cor 4:13; Ps 116:10). He would not say *the same* unless they had the same Spirit of faith as he had. But, as they believed that the incarnation of Christ would come when the same sacrament was hidden, so we also believe that it has taken place. And both we and they are waiting his future coming for judgment. For there is no other *mystery of God* (Rv 10:7; Am 3:7)

---

30. See Mt 2:1.
31. See Jn 3:36.
32. See Ex 3:15.

but Christ, in whom those who have died in Adam must be brought to life. For, *just as all die in Adam, so all will also be brought to life in Christ* (1 Cor 15:22), as we have explained above.

12, 35. Hence God, who is present everywhere and whole everywhere, does not dwell in all but only in those whom he makes his most blessed temple or most blessed temples, rescuing them *from the power of darkness* and transferring them *into the kingdom of his beloved Son* (Col 1:13), which begins with their rebirth. But "his temple" is said in different senses. It is said in a symbolic sense when the temple is made by human hands from lifeless things, as a tabernacle is made from wood, veils, skins, and other such furnishings, just as the temple was constructed by Solomon from stones, wood, and metals. "Temple" is said in another sense of the true reality itself that is signified by these symbols. For this reason it says, *And you like living stones are being built as a spiritual house* (1 Pt 2:5), and for this reason scripture also says, *For we are temples of the living God, as God says, I will dwell in them and walk in their midst, and I will be their God, and they will be my people* (2 Cor 6:16; Lv 26:12).

36. Nor should it disturb us that God produces something miraculous through certain persons who do not or do not yet belong to this temple, that is, through those in whom God does not or does not yet dwell, such as the man who was expelling demons in the name of Christ though he was not a follower of Christ, and Christ commanded that he be permitted to continue in order to spread his name, which was beneficial to many.[33] He also said that there would be many who would say to him on the last day, *We have worked many miracles in your name*, to whom he would certainly not reply, *I do not know you* (Mt 7:22-23), if they belonged to the temple of God, which he makes blessed by his indwelling. Before he was incorporated into this temple by rebirth, Cornelius the centurion also saw an angel sent to him and heard him saying that his prayers had been heard and his almsgiving found acceptable.[34] For God does these things because he is present everywhere or through his angels.

37. For, though some interpret the sanctification of Jeremiah before he left the womb as a symbol of the savior who did not need rebirth, it can still, even if it is taken as applying to the prophet himself, not unsuitably be understood in terms of predestination. In the same way the gospel calls those who had not as yet been reborn the children of God where, when Caiaphas said of the Lord, *It is to your advantage that one man die for the people and that the whole nation not perish*, the gospel immediately goes on to add, *But he did not say this by himself. Rather, because he was the high priest that year, he prophesied that Jesus would die for the people and not only for the people, but in order to gather together into*

---

33. See Mk 9:37-39.
34. See Acts 10:1-4.

one the children of God who had been scattered. (Jn 11:50-52) He called children of God those people located in all the other nations apart, of course, from the Hebrew nation, who were not yet believers and not yet baptized. How, then, did he call them children of God except in terms of the predestination in accordance with which the apostle also says that God chose us in Christ before the creation of the world?[35] But that gathering of them together into one was going to make them children of God. For *into one* was not said in the sense of "into some bodily place," since the prophet foretold concerning such a calling of the nations, *And they will adore him, each from his own place, all the isles of the nations* (Zep 2:11). Rather, *gather together into one* was said in the sense of "into one Spirit" and "into one body," of which Christ is the one head.[36] Such a gathering is the building of the temple of God. It is not carnal birth but spiritual rebirth that produces such a gathering.

13, 38. God dwells, therefore, in individuals as in his temples and in all gathered together into one as in his temple. As long as this temple is tossed about on the waves of this world, like the ark of Noah, there is taking place what is written in the psalm, *The Lord dwells in the flood* (Ps 29:10), although we can also suitably understand *The Lord dwells in the flood* to refer to the many peoples of the believers in all nations, which the Apocalypse refers to by the term *waters.*[37] But there follows, *And the Lord will sit as king for eternity* (Ps 29:10), that is, in his temple now located in eternal life after the waves of this world. God is present everywhere, therefore, and is present whole everywhere, but he does not dwell everywhere but only in his temple, to which he is kind and merciful through grace. But when he dwells in them, he is received by some more and by others less.

39. But the apostle says of our head, *The fullness of divinity dwells in him corporeally* (Col 2:9), not corporeally because God is a body; rather, he used the word in a transferred sense, meaning that God did not dwell corporeally, in a temple made by human hands, but symbolically, that is, by symbols foreshadowing what was to come. For, by a word that is also used in a transferred sense, he calls all those practices shadows of what was to come.[38] For the sovereign God, as scripture says, *does not dwell in temples made by hand* (Act 17:24). Or, as another possibility, he said *corporeally* because God dwells, as if in a temple, in the body of Christ that he assumed from the virgin. This is why, when the Jews were seeking a sign, he said, *Destroy this temple, and in three days I shall raise it up.* In explaining what this means the evangelist went on to say, *He said this of the temple of his body* (Jn 2:19, 21).

---

35. See Eph 1:4.
36. See Col 1:18; Eph 1:22-23.
37. See Rv 17:15.
38. See Col 2:17; Heb 10:1.

40. What follows then? We believe that there is this difference between the head and the other members—that in any member, however eminent, such as some great prophet or apostle, although the divinity dwells in him, *all the fullness of divinity* does not dwell in him as it does in the head, which is Christ.[39] For in our body there is sensation in each member, but not as much as in the head, where there are the five senses. For in the head there is sight, hearing, smell, taste, and touch, but in the other members there is only touch. Or, apart from the fact that *the fullness of divinity* dwells in that body as in a temple, is there another difference between that head and the excellence of any member? There clearly is, because the singular assumption of that man formed one person with the Word. For of no saint could or can or will it be able to be said, *And the Word become flesh* (Jn 1:14). No saint by any excellence of grace has received the title "the Only-Begotten" in the same way that he who was the very Word of God before all ages bears this same title after assuming the man. That assumption, then, is singular, nor can it in any way be shared by some human saints, no matter how outstanding in wisdom and holiness. Here we have a clear and evident proof of God's grace. For who would be so sacrilegious as to dare to say that some soul could bring it about by the merit of his free choice that he be another Christ? How, then, would one soul alone have merited to belong to the person of the only-begotten Word through free choice, which is naturally given to all in common, unless a singular grace had bestowed this? One may preach this grace, but one may not choose to pronounce judgment on it.

41. If we have properly examined these ideas in accord with our strength and with God's help, when you stretch yourself to think of God as present everywhere and not spread out in separate places as if by some mass or extension, but whole everywhere, turn your mind away from all images of bodies that human thought usually considers. For we do not think of wisdom in that way, nor of justice, nor, finally, of love. Of it scripture says, *God is love* (1 Jn 4:16). But when you think of his dwelling place, think of the unity and the assembly of the saints, especially in heaven, where he is chiefly said to dwell because his will is done there by the perfect obedience of those who dwell there, and then on earth, where he dwells as he builds his house, which will be dedicated at the end of the age. But do not doubt that Christ, our Lord, the only-begotten Son of God, who is equal to the Father, and the same Christ, Son of Man, than whom the Father is greater, is as God present whole everywhere and is in the same temple of God as the God who dwells there, while he is present in a place in heaven on account of the limits of his true body. But since it is a delight for me to converse with you, I do not know if I have preserved the limits of a normal letter; it is as if I were compensating for my long silence by my long-windedness. But since by your piety and good will, with which you have anticipated me, you have become

---

39. See Col 1:18; Eph 1:22.

deeply rooted in my heart so that I truly converse with you as a friend, thank God for whatever you see has been usefully developed by the work of our pen. But if you see any defects of mine, pardon them as a very dear friend, desiring a remedy for me with the same sincere love with which you also grant me pardon.

Letter 188

At the end of 417 or the beginning of 418 Alypius and Augustine wrote to Juliana, the widow of Olybrius and daughter-in-law of Proba, concerning Demetrias, the daughter of Juliana and Olybrius, who had recently taken vows as a consecrated virgin. Augustine dedicated his work *The Excellence of Widowhood* to Juliana and wrote Letters 130 and 131 to Proba. Like many Roman aristocrats, the family had fled Rome and come to Africa after 410, and like many Christian aristocrats of Rome, the family was influenced by the ascetic teachings of Pelagius, who in 414 wrote a letter to Demetrias at the request of Juliana to exhort her to the life of virginity.

Augustine and Alypius thank Juliana for her letter, which is no longer extant, in which she informed them of Demetrias' having taken vows as a virgin (paragraph 1). Because of their close relationship Augustine and Alypius venture to warn Juliana and Demetrias about those who destroy the faith (paragraph 2). Though Juliana claimed that no one in her family has ever been tainted with heresy, the bishops warn her of the heresy of Pelagius, which claims that we can have from ourselves whatever virtue we might have (paragraph 3).

The bishops warn that Demetrias must not believe that she has the good of virginity from herself alone, as Pelagius said in his letter to her (paragraph 4). Pelagius' claim that spiritual goods can only come from Demetrias is poison and is opposed to the words of the apostle (paragraph 5). Virginity is a gift of God and a treasure that we carry in vessels of clay (paragraph 6). The human will needs to be helped by God, who not merely teaches us what to do but inspires us with love so that we do it (paragraph 7). Scripture clearly teaches that continence is a gift of God for which one ought to pray to God (paragraph 8).

Hence Demetrias should boast only in the Lord, since all her reasons for boasting are found only in the Lord (paragraph 9). Juliana and her family may have always had the correct faith about the Trinity, but there are other ways in which one can fall into most dangerous errors, as Pelagius has done (paragraph 10). Careful examination will show that Pelagius admits grace only in the sense of the nature with which we were created, in the sense of free choice, in the sense of teaching, or in the sense of the forgiveness of sins (paragraph 11). The bishops challenge Juliana to find in Pelagius' book the grace by which the will is helped to do the good (paragraph 12). His book lacks the grace that the apostle commends, by which we are helped by the gift of love to live pious and righteous lives (paragraph 13). The bishops especially want Demetrias to boast only in the Lord. They ask Juliana whether the book is really the work of Pelagius, as they are convinced it is (paragraph 14).

Alypius and Augustine send greetings in the Lord to Juliana, their lady who deserves to be honored in Christ with due regards and their rightly illustrious daughter.

1, 1. It was a cause of joy and pleasure for us that your letter, revered lady, found us both present together in Hippo. We are together sending this reply to it, rejoicing to know of your good health and with mutual love reporting to you ours in turn, which we are confident is dear to you, our lady, who deserves to be honored in Christ with due regards, and rightly illustrious daughter. We know very well, however, that you are aware of the great religious love we owe you and the great concern we have for you both before God and among human beings. Although our humble selves came to know first by letter and then also by your physical presence that you were pious and Catholic, that is, true members of Christ, *when,* nonetheless, *you received the word of God that we preached* through our ministry, *you received it,* as the apostle says, *not as the word of human beings, but as the word of God, which it truly is* (1 Thes 2:13). With the help of the savior's mercy and grace, such great fruit has emerged from our ministry in your house that, though her human marriage was already arranged, the saintly Demetrias preferred the spiritual embrace of that husband, more handsome than the sons of men,[1] whom virgins marry in order to have a greater fecundity of spirit and in order not to lose the integrity of their flesh. But we would not have known how that faithful and noble virgin received at that time that exhortation of ours if we had not learned from your most joyful message and truthful testimony that, shortly after our departure, she had taken vows as a holy virgin and that we workers had been given this great gift of God, which he plants and waters through his servants but gives through himself.[2]

2. Since this is the case, no one will blame us if we are concerned, because of our closeness to you, to warn you to avoid teachings opposed to the grace of God. For, though the apostle commands us to continue to preach the word not only when it is opportune but also when it is inopportune,[3] we do not in any event consider you to be among those to whom our words or writing would seem inopportune, when we say that you should carefully avoid what does not pertain to sound doctrine. For this reason, then, you were so grateful to receive our admonition that you said in the letter to which we are now replying, "I sincerely give abundant thanks for so pious an admonition, since Your Reverence urges me not to give a hearing to these people who often corrupt the venerable faith with their evil writings."

3. You then go on to say, "But Your Holiness knows that I and my home are far removed from such persons, and all our family follows the Catholic faith to

---

1. See Ps 45:3.
2. See 1 Cor 3:5-7.
3. See 2 Tm 4:2.

the point that it has never strayed into any heresy and has never fallen not only into those sects from which it is difficult to free oneself but even into those which are seen to have some small errors." It is this that compels us more and more not to remain silent with you about those who try to corrupt even those teachings that are sound. For we regard your home as no small church of Christ. Nor, of course, are those people in a small error who think that we possess it from ourselves if we have any righteousness, continence, piety, or chastity, because God created us so that, besides the fact that he discloses knowledge to us, he gives us no further help so that by loving we may do what by learning we know that we should do. That is, they claim that nature and doctrine are by themselves the grace and help of God for living righteously and correctly. But they deny that we are helped by God so as to have the good will in which is found our living righteously and the love of God itself, which among all the gifts of God is so outstanding that it is also said to be God.[4] By it alone we carry out whatever we carry out of the law and counsels of God. They say instead that we ourselves are by our own choice sufficient by ourselves for this. It should not seem to you that it is a slight error to want to claim to be Christians, but to refuse to listen to the apostle of Christ. For, after he said, *The love of God has been poured out in our hearts*, lest anyone should think that we have this only from our own choice, he immediately added, *through the Holy Spirit who has been given to us* (Rom 5:5). You understand what a great and what a deadly mistake one makes if one still does not confess that this is a great grace of the savior, who, ascending on high, took captivity captive and gave gifts to human beings.[5]

2, 4. How, then, could we hold back from warning you, to whom we owe so much love, that you should avoid such teachings, since we read the book for the holy Demetrias, and we want rather to learn from your reply who wrote it and whether it reached you. In that book a virgin of Christ might read, if this were not wrong, reasons to believe that she has her virginal holiness and all her spiritual riches from herself alone and in that way, before she has attained perfect happiness, she might learn to be ungrateful to God. God keep her from this! For the following are words written to her in the same book: "And so you have even here," he says, "reasons by which you are rightly placed ahead of others; in fact, even more on this account. For the nobility of your birth and the wealth of your family are understood not to be yours, but no one but you yourself will be able to bestow spiritual riches upon you. For these riches, then, which can only come from you and can only exist in you, you are rightly to be praised; for these riches you are rightly to be placed ahead of others."[6]

4. See 1 Jn 4:8.16.
5. See Eph 4:7-8; Ps 68:19.
6. Pelagius, *A Book for Demetrias (Liber ad Demetriadem)* 11.

5. You certainly see the great harm to be avoided in these words. For the statement, "These goods can exist only in you," is very well and most truly said. This is clearly solid food. But the statement, "They can come only from you," is entirely poisonous. God forbid that this virgin of Christ should willingly listen to this if she piously understands the proper poverty of the human heart and, for this reason, knows that she is in her heart adorned only by the gifts of her spouse. Let her rather hear the apostle when he says, *I have betrothed you to one man, to present a chaste virgin to Christ. But I am fearful that, as the serpent seduced Eve by his cunning, so your minds may also be drawn away from chastity, which is found in Christ.* (2 Cor 11:2-3) And for this reason, concerning these spiritual riches let her also not listen to the man who says, "No one apart from you yourself will be able to bestow these upon you," and, "They can come only from you and can exist only in you." Rather, let her listen to the man who says, *We have this treasure in vessels of clay in order that the excellence of virtue may be God's and not ours* (2 Cor 4:7).

6. Let her also listen to the same true and pious teacher concerning the sacred continence of a virgin, which she does not have from herself but which is a gift of God, though one bestowed upon someone who believes and is willing. When he was dealing with this topic, he said, *I would wish all to be like me, but each has his own gift from God, one this gift, another that* (1 Cor 7:7). Let her listen to him who is not only her spouse but the only spouse of the universal Church when he says of such chastity and integrity, *All do not accept this teaching, but only those to whom it has been given* (Mt 19:11), so that she may understand that she ought to thank God and our Lord that she has such a great and outstanding gift rather than listen to the words of anyone that she has it as from herself. We do not say that they are the words of someone who flatters and humors her for fear that we might seem to judge rashly the secrets of human hearts, but at least they are the words of someone who praises her erroneously. Indeed, *every best gift and every perfect gift,* as the apostle James also says, *is from above, coming down from the Father of lights* (Jas 1:17). From this source, then, holy virginity also comes, in which you are willing and glad to be surpassed by your daughter, after you by birth, before you by action, from you by generation, ahead of you in honor, coming after you in age, going before you in holiness. In her that begins to be yours which could not be in you. She has not married in terms of the flesh so that beyond you she might be made spiritually greater not only for herself but also for you. For by that reckoning you are also less than her because you married so that she might be born. These are God's gifts, and they are certainly yours, but they *do not come from you* (Eph 2:8). For you have *this treasure* in earthly and still fragile bodies, as if *in vessels of clay so that the excellence of virtue may be God's and not yours* (2 Cor 4:7). Do not be surprised when we say

that they are yours but do not come from you, for we also speak of our daily bread, and yet say, *Give us,*[7] so that it may not be thought to come from us.

7. Hence, as scripture says, *Pray without ceasing; in all things give thanks* (1 Thes 5:17-18). For you pray in order that you may persevere and make progress; you give thanks because this does not come from yourselves. For who has separated you from that mass of death and destruction stemming from Adam? Was it not he who *came to seek and to save what was lost* (Lk 19:10; Mt 18:11)? Or, when a person hears the apostle saying, *Who has set you apart?* will he reply, "My good will, my faith, my righteousness," without hearing what immediately follows, *For what do you have that you have not received? And if you have received, why do you boast as if you have not received?* (1 Cor 4:7, 9-11) We do not want, therefore, when a consecrated virgin hears or reads, "No one but you yourself will be able to bestow spiritual riches upon you. For these riches, which can only come from you and can only exist in you, you are rightly to be praised; for these riches you are rightly to be placed ahead of others"—we certainly do not want her to boast as if she had not received. Let her say, *In me, O God, are the vows of praise that I will pay to you* (Ps 56:12), but because they are in her and do not also come from her, let her also remember to say, *O Lord, by your will you have given virtue to my beauty* (Ps 30:8). For, even if they come from her on account of personal choice, without which we do no good work, still they do not come only from her, as this fellow said. Unless one's own choice is helped by the grace of God, a good will cannot exist in a human being. *For it is God*, the apostle says, *who produces in you both the willing and the action in accord with good will* (Phil 2:13), not, as they think, merely by revealing the knowledge in order that we might know what we ought to do, but also by instilling love in order that by loving we may do what we have come to know through learning.

8. For he knew what a great good continence was who said, *And since I knew that no one can be continent unless God grants this* (Wis 8:21-22). Hence he knew not only how great a gift it was and with what desire we should want it but also that it could not exist unless God grants it. For wisdom had taught him; for he says: *And this too was a mark of wisdom: to know whose gift this was.* And yet knowledge was not enough for him; but he says *I approached the Lord, and I begged him for this* (Wis 8:21-22). God, then, helps us not only so that we may know what we should do but also so that by loving we may do what we know from learning. No one, therefore, can have not only knowledge but also continence unless God grants it. For this reason, though he already had knowledge, he begged that he might also have continence in order that there might be in him what he knew did not come from him. Or if on account of his own free choice it came from him to some small degree, it still did not come only from him,

---

7. See Lk 11:3.

because no one can be continent unless God grants this. But concerning the spiritual riches among which is certainly also included this bright and beautiful continence, he does not say, "They can exist in you and come from you." Rather, he says, "They can only exist in you and come from you," so that she might believe that, just as they can exist nowhere but in her, so they can come from no one but her and so that she might for this reason boast as if she had not received.[8] May *the merciful Lord* (Ps 103:8) keep this from her heart!

3, 9. With regard to the Christian discipline and humility of the holy virgin in which she was raised and educated, we too certainly think that when she read these words, if she did in fact read them, she groaned, humbly beat her breast, perhaps even wept, and with trust prayed to the Lord, to whom she was consecrated and by whom she was made holy, in order that, just as those words were not hers but someone else's, so her faith might not be such that she would believe that she has something about which she might boast, but not in the Lord.[9] For her reasons for boasting are in fact in her and not in the words of others, as the apostle says, *But let each one test his own work, and then each will find reason to boast in himself and not in another* (Gal 6:4). But God forbid that her reason for boasting is she herself rather than he to whom she says, *O my reason for boasting, you who raise up my head* (Ps 4:4). In that way her reason for boasting is in her in a salutary manner when God, who is in her, is himself her reason for boasting. From him she has all the good gifts because of which she is good, and she will have all those by which she will be better to the extent that she can be better in this life and by which she will be perfect when God's grace, not human praise, will make her perfect. For her *soul will be praised in the Lord* (Ps 34:3), *who satisfied* her *desire with good gifts* (Ps 103:5). For he also inspired her with this desire so that his virgin would not so boast of some good as if she had not received it.[10]

10. Please assure us by replying, then, whether we are mistaken about this attitude of hers. For we know very well that you are and have been, along with all your family, worshipers of the undivided Trinity. But human error does not sneak up on one on this point alone, so that one holds something different concerning the undivided Trinity. For there are other doctrines on which one errs in a most destructive way, such as the one on which we have spoken in this letter, perhaps longer than was sufficient for your faith-filled and chaste wisdom. And yet we do not know to whom one does injury if not to God and, for this reason, to that Trinity, if one denies that some good, which comes from God, does come from God. May God keep that sin from you, as we believe he has. May God absolutely forbid that this book, from which we believed that we should cite

---

8. See 1 Cor 4:7.
9. See 1 Cor 1:31.
10. See 1 Cor 4:7.

some readily intelligible words, produce some such idea—I do not say in your soul or in that of your daughter, a consecrated virgin, but even in the souls of any male or female servant of yours of the lowest rank.

11. But if you pay more careful attention to the things in it that he seems to say in defense of grace and the help of God, you will find them so ambiguous that they can refer either to nature or to doctrine or to the forgiveness of sins. For they are forced to admit that we ought to pray in order that we may not enter into temptation,[11] and they can understand this in terms of their reply that we are helped toward this insofar as, when we pray and knock, the understanding of the truth is opened up for us. In that way we learn what we should do, but our will does not receive the strength to do what we learn. And when they say that, by the grace and help of God, Christ the Lord was set before us as a model for living a good life, they limit this to the same teaching, that is, insofar as we learn from his example how we ought to live, but they do not want us to be helped so that by loving we might also do what we know through learning.

12. Or at least find something in that same book, if you can, where, apart from nature, apart from the choice of the will which belongs to nature, apart from the forgiveness of sin and the revelation of doctrine, he admits the sort of help of God that he admits who said, *Since I knew that no one can be continent unless God grants this, and this too was a mark of wisdom: to know whose gift this was, I approached the Lord and begged him for this* (Wis 8:21). For, when he prayed, this man did not want to receive the nature in which he was created. Nor was he concerned about the natural choice of the will with which he was created. Nor did he desire the forgiveness of sins, for he desired instead the continence by which he might avoid sin. And he did not desire to know what he should do, since he admitted that he already knew whose gift this was. But he wanted to receive such a strength of will, such an ardor of love from the Spirit of wisdom as would suffice for carrying out the great task of continence. If, then, you can find anything of the sort in that book, we will give you most ample thanks if you would be so kind as to let us know by replying.

13. For words fail me to express how much I desire that a clear confession of the grace that the apostle strongly commends[12] be found in the writings of those people, which many read because of their cleverness and eloquence. The apostle says that God gives to each person a measure of the faith[13] without which it is impossible to please God,[14] the faith from which the righteous live,[15] the faith *that works through love* (Gal 5:6), the faith before which and without which no

---

11. See Mt 26:4; Mk 14:38; 22:46.
12. See Rom 12:3.
13. See Rom 12:3.
14. See Heb 11:6.
15. See Rom 1:17; Gal 3:11; Heb 10:38; Hab 2:4.

one's works are to be judged good, since *everything that does not come from faith is sin* (Rom 14:23). He says that, in order that we may live piously and righteously, God does not help us only by the revelation of knowledge, for knowledge without love puffs one up with pride,[16] but also helps us by inspiring us with the love *that is the fullness of the law* (Rom 13:10), which builds up our heart without puffing it up with pride as knowledge does. But up to now we have never found anything of the sort in their writings.

14. Yet we would very much wish that these things were in this book from which we have taken the words that we cited. There, in praising Christ's virgin as if no one besides herself could bestow on her spiritual riches and as if she could have these only from herself, he does not want her to boast in the Lord[17] but to boast as if she had not received.[18] Though he did not explicitly name her or you, revered lady, he nonetheless mentions that he was asked by the mother of a virgin to write to her. In a certain letter of his in which the same Pelagius very clearly puts his own name and does not pass over the name of the virgin, he says that he wrote to her and strives to prove by the testimony of the same book that he most openly confesses the grace of God, which he is said either not to mention or to deny. But we ask that you be so good as to inform us whether this is the book in which he set forth those words about spiritual riches or whether it reached Your Holiness.

---

16. See 1 Cor 8:1.
17. See 1 Cor 1:31; 2 Cor 1:17; Jer 9:23-24.
18. See 1 Cor 4:7.

Letter 189

In approximately 417 Augustine wrote to Boniface, a Christian general, the tribune of Africa, who later become the count of Africa. Augustine also wrote to him Letter 185, a book called *The Correction of the Donatists*, as well as Letter 185A, which survives only as a short fragment, and Letter 17*. In the present letter he first explains why he is writing to Boniface in so hurried a manner (paragraph 1). He tells him that the whole of Christian life is summed up in the commandment to love God and one's neighbor (paragraph 2). In that love all the saints have pleased God in this life and have come to the vision of God in the next (paragraph 3). He tells Boniface that he should not suppose that a soldier cannot please God and points to many biblical examples of good men in arms (paragraph 4). Augustine reminds Boniface that, while he fights against visible enemies, namely, the barbarians, other Christians fight against invisible enemies, namely, the devil and his angels (paragraph 5). Even in war, however, one ought to aim at peace (paragraph 6). Moreover, Augustine warns Boniface that his life should be adorned with the virtues of marital chastity, sobriety, and frugality (paragraph 7). Finally, Augustine tells Boniface to offer thanks to God for the goodness he already has and to pray to God for the virtue he still lacks and for the forgiveness of those sins that no one lacks (paragraph 8).

To his illustrious lord and rightly excellent and honorable son, Boniface, Augustine sends greetings in the Lord.

1. I had already written a reply to Your Charity, but when I was looking for an opportunity to send the letter, my most beloved son Faustus, who was on his way to Your Excellency, turned up. After he had received the letter that I had already produced to carry to Your Benevolence, he informed me that you greatly desire that I write for you something that would build you up for the eternal salvation that you hope for in our Lord Jesus Christ. And though I was busy, he insisted that I not delay to do this because he sincerely loves you, as you know. In order to accommodate him since he was in a hurry, I preferred to write something quickly rather than to disappoint your devout desire, my illustrious lord and rightly excellent and honorable son.

2. This, then, I can say briefly: *Love the Lord your God with your whole heart and with your whole soul and with your whole strength*, and, *Love your neighbor as yourself* (Mt 22:37.39; Mk 12:30-31; Lk 10:27; Dt 6:5; Lv 19:18). For this is the word that the Lord shortened upon the earth,[1] when he said in the gospel, *Upon these two commandments the whole law and the prophets depend* (Mt 22:40). Make progress daily in this love, then, both by praying and by doing good, in order that with the help of him who commanded and gave this love to

---

1. See Rom 9:28.

you it may be nourished and grow until, when it has become perfect, it makes you perfect. For this is the *love* that, as the apostle says, *has been poured out in our hearts through the Holy Spirit who has been given to us* (Rom 5:5); this is the love of which he likewise says, *The fullness of the law is love* (Rom 13:10); this is the love through which faith works so that he again says, *Neither circumcision nor the lack of circumcision does any good, but the faith that works through love* (Gal 5:6).

3. By this love, then, all our holy forefathers, the patriarchs, prophets, and apostles, pleased God. By this love all true martyrs fought against the devil to the point of shedding their blood, and because this love neither grew cold nor gave out in them,[2] they conquered. By this love all good believers daily make progress, desiring not to come to a kingdom of mortal beings but to the kingdom of heaven,[3] not to a temporal but to an everlasting inheritance,[4] not to gold and silver but to the incorruptible riches of the angels, not to some goods of this world about which one lives in fear, and which cannot be taken with one when he dies but to the vision of God, whose sweetness and delight surpass not only all the beauty of bodies but even all the splendor of souls, however just and holy. He surpasses all the magnificence of the angels and powers; he surpasses not only whatever can be said, but even whatever can be thought of him. Nor should we give up all hope for this great promise because it is so very great, but we should instead believe that we shall attain it because he who promised it is so very great. For, as blessed John the apostle says, *We are children of God, and it has not yet been revealed what we shall be; we know that when he appears, we shall be like him, because we shall see him as he is* (1 Jn 3:2).

4. Do not suppose that no one can please God who as a soldier carries the weapons of war. Holy David carried them, and the Lord bore a great a testimony to him. The centurion also carried them who said to the Lord, *I am not worthy that you should enter under my roof, but only say the word, and my servant will be healed. For I too am a man placed under authority, having soldiers under me. And I say to this one: Do this, and he does it.* Of him the Lord also said, *Truly, I tell you, I have not found such great faith in Israel* (Mt 8:8-10; Lk 7:6-9). Cornelius carried them, to whom the angel was sent and said, *Cornelius, your almsgiving was found acceptable, and your prayers have been heard* (Acts 10:31).[5] Then he told him to send someone to the apostle Peter and to hear from him what he should do. And Cornelius also sent a pious soldier to the apostle so that he would come.[6] The soldiers also bore arms who came to John, the holy

---

2. See Mt 24:12.
3. See Mt 7:21.
4. See Heb 9:15.
5. See also Acts 10:4, though the words Augustine cites come later in the chapter.
6. See Acts 10:5-7.

precursor of the Lord and friend of the bridegroom, in order to be baptized.[7] Of John the Lord himself said, *Among those born of women there has not arisen one greater than John the Baptist* (Mt 11:11). And when they asked him what they should do, he replied to them, *Strike no one; slander no one; be content with your wages* (Lk 3:3). He certainly did not forbid them to carry arms as soldiers, since he commanded them to be content with their wages.

5. Those who have abandoned all these worldly activities and also serve God with the perfect continence of chastity certainly have a greater place before God. *But each person*, as the apostle says, *has his own gift from God, one this gift, another that* (1 Cor 7:7). Hence others fight against invisible enemies by praying for you; you struggle against visible barbarians by fighting for them. Would that all would have the one faith because there would be less of a struggle and the devil along with his angels would be more easily defeated! But because in this world it is necessary that the citizens of the kingdom of heaven suffer temptations among those who are in error and are wicked so that they may be exercised and put to the test like gold in a furnace,[8] we ought not to want to live ahead of time with only the saints and the righteous in order that we may merit to receive this reward at its proper time.

6. Think of this first, then, when you take up your weapons for a fight, namely, that even your bodily strength is a gift of God. For in that way you will bear in mind not to act against God by means of the gift of God. For, when one has given his word, he should keep it, even with an enemy against whom he is waging war. How much more ought one to keep his word with a friend for whom he is fighting! Your will ought to aim at peace; only necessity requires war in order that God may set us free from necessity and preserve us in peace. For we do not seek peace in order to stir up war, but we wage war in order to acquire peace. Be, therefore, a peacemaker even in war in order that by conquering you might bring to the benefit of peace those whom you fight. For *blessed are the peacemakers*, says the Lord, *because they will be called the children of God* (Mt 5:9). But if human peace is so sweet because of the temporal salvation of mortals, how much sweeter is the peace of God because of the eternal salvation of the angels! And so, let necessity and not the will be the cause of slaying the enemy in battle. Just as violence is brought to bear upon one who rebels and resists, so mercy is now owed to one who is defeated or captured, especially to one about whom there is no fear for the disturbance of the peace.

7. Let marital chastity adorn your conduct; let sobriety and frugality adorn it as well. For it is very shameful that lust conquer a man who is not conquered by another man and that he who is not conquered by the sword is overcome by wine. If you lack worldly riches, do not seek them in the world by wrongdoing, but if

---

7. See Lk 3:12.
8. See Wis 3:5-6.

you have them, store them away in heaven by doing good works. Worldly riches ought not to fill a manly and Christian heart with pride if they are present or crush it if they withdraw. We should rather bear in mind the words of the Lord, *Where your treasure is, there also is your heart* (Mt 6:21; Lk 12:34). And, of course, when we hear that we should lift up our heart, we ought to respond truthfully what you know that we respond.[9]

8. And in these matters I know that you are quite zealous. I am both greatly delighted by your reputation and congratulate you greatly in the Lord. Hence this letter should be for you a mirror in which you see the sort of man you are rather than one in which you learn the sort of man you ought to be. Nonetheless, whatever you find in it or in the holy scriptures that you still lack for a good life, press on to acquire it by action and prayer, and offer thanks to God for what you have as to the source of the goodness that you have. And in all your good actions glorify him and humble yourself. For as scripture says, *Every best gift and every perfect gift is from above, coming down from the Father of lights* (Jas 1:17). But however much you progress in the love of God and neighbor and in true piety, do not believe as long as you are living in this life, that you are without sin. Do we not read in the scriptures concerning this life: *Is not the life of human beings on earth a temptation?* (Jb 7:1) Hence, since it is always necessary for you, as long are you are living in this body, to say in prayer, *Forgive us our debts, as we forgive our debtors* (Mt 6:12; Lk 11:4), remember to forgive quickly if anyone has sinned against you and has asked pardon from you so that you may be able to pray truthfully and obtain pardon for your sins. I have written this in a hurry for Your Charity because the haste of the courier was pressing me. But I thank God that in some way or other I did not fail to comply with your desire. May the mercy of God always protect you, my excellent lord and rightly illustrious and honorable son.

---

9. Augustine alludes to the prayers at the beginning of the Preface of the Mass where the celebrant says, "Lift up your hearts," and the congregation responds, "We have lifted them up to the Lord."

Letter 190

In the summer or fall of 418 Augustine wrote to Optatus, the bishop of Milevis, who had written a letter not to Augustine but to others at Caesarea in Mauretania, where Augustine was present on account of ecclesiastical business at the request of Pope Zosimus. Optatus was a prominent Catholic opponent of Donatism and had written against Parmenian a work called *The Donatist Schism* (*De schismate Donatistarum*). Letter 190 was found within a year of its composition by Vincent Victor, a convert from Rogatism, a Donatist sect, and Vincent wrote two books in which he complained about Augustine's professed ignorance about the origin of souls. Augustine wrote in reply his four books of *The Nature and Origin of the Soul*.

In the present letter Augustine explains to Optatus that he was consulted by the recipients of Optatus' letter regarding the origin of the soul and, therefore, decided to write to Optatus on this question (paragraph 1). Augustine explains that he has not come to a definite position on either the propagation of souls or their individual creation (paragraph 2). The heart of the Christian faith, however, is found in the doctrine of original sin, from which no one is set free apart from the grace of Christ (paragraph 3). Furthermore, Augustine is certain that the soul is not the creator but a creature, not born of God but made, that it is a spirit, not a body, and that souls do not sin before birth (paragraph 4). Regardless of its origin, no soul is released from the contagion of death and sin except through the one mediator, Christ Jesus (paragraph 5). The patriarchs of the Old Testament were saved through the same faith in Christ through which we are now saved (paragraph 6). The law was given to teach us how much we need grace (paragraph 7). All the righteous, whether before or after the incarnation of Christ, are saved only by faith in his incarnation (paragraph 8).

Augustine appeals to Paul to explain why God creates those who he foreknows will be condemned and not receive mercy (paragraph 9). God gives many gifts to sinners and uses them to teach the greatness of his grace toward the vessels of mercy (paragraph 10). If God created only those whom he would bring to rebirth, the benefit that he bestows on those who are saved would remain hidden (paragraph 11). God creates so many who are destined for condemnation in order to reveal the greatness of his mercy toward those who are gratuitously rescued from the condemnation all deserve (paragraph 12).

Hence, if the view that new souls are created for newborn individuals does not undermine the faith of the Church regarding the need for baptism, it can be held (paragraph 13). But if Optatus cannot find proof for creationism, he should not rashly jump to the conclusion that souls are propagated from the soul of Adam (paragraph 14). There are problems in maintaining that the soul is spiritual and that it is propagated in the same way as bodies are (paragraph 15). The question of the propagation of souls cannot be resolved by observation or by the testimony of scripture (paragraph 16). Scriptural texts that favor one position over the other are not decisive and can easily be interpreted in the other sense (paragraphs 17 to 19).

In his short letter Jerome favored creationism but did not reveal his reasons for doing so (paragraph 20). Until Jerome replies to Augustine's letter or Augustine finds a solution elsewhere, he cannot defend creationism (paragraph 21). Augustine warns Optatus to beware of the new heresy of Pelagius and Caelestius. They are not heretics because they hold creationism but because they deny the need for the baptism of infants (paragraph 22). Pope Zosimus has confirmed the teachings of the African councils on the need for infants to receive forgiveness of sin in baptism (paragraph 23). Creationism can be defended provided that it does not destroy the inheritance of original sin (paragraph 24). Christ's soul alone was born without sin (paragraph 25). Finally, Augustine expresses his hope that Optatus will receive his letter with gratitude and wishes him well (paragraph 26).

To Optatus, his most blessed lord, his brother worthy of being loved with sincere love, and his fellow bishop, Augustine sends greetings in the Lord.

1, 1. I received no letter of Your Holiness that was sent to me, but the letter that you sent to Caesarean Mauretania arrived while I was present in Caesarea, where a pressing work of the Church imposed upon us by the venerable Pope Zosimus of the Apostolic See had taken us. Hence it happened that I also read what you wrote, when the holy servant of God, Renatus, a brother most dear to us in Christ, handed your letter over to me. Since he asked and was very insistent with me, though I was occupied with other matters, I was forced to respond to it. In addition to this there arrived, while we were staying in the aforementioned town, another holy brother of ours, who deserves to be mentioned with respect and, as I learned from him, is a relative of yours by the name of Muressi. He reported to me that Your Reverence had also sent a letter to him about this matter, and he consulted me about this very question so that he might convey to you what I thought about it either by my response or by his, namely, whether souls come into existence by propagation like bodies and stem from that one soul that was created for the first man or whether the omnipotent creator, who, to be sure, *works up to now* (Jn 15:7), creates new individual souls for individual persons without any propagation.

2. Before I give Your Holiness any advice on this matter, I want you to know that I never dared to state a definitive opinion on this question in my many works and never impudently dared to put into writing to instruct others what was not clear in my own mind. It would take too long to set forth in this letter the facts and reasons whose consideration has influenced me so that my assent is inclined toward neither view but remains undecided between the two. Nor is this so necessary that, without it, it is impossible to discuss this question; even if it is not sufficient for removing our hesitation, it is at least sufficient for avoiding rashness.

3. For this is the truth upon which the Christian faith above all rests: *Through a man death came, and through a man the resurrection of the dead. For, as in Adam all die, so too in Christ all will be brought to life* (1 Cor 15:21-22), and, *Through one man sin entered this world, and through sin death, and in that way death was passed on to all men in whom all sinned* (Rom 5:12), and, *Judgment, indeed, came after the one for condemnation, but grace came after many sins for producing righteousness of life* (Rom 5:16), and, *Through the sin of one man all entered into condemnation, but through the righteousness of one man all entered into righteousness of life* (Rom 5:18), and any other testimonies that state that no one is born of Adam who is not bound by the chain of sin and condemnation and no one is set free from it except by being reborn in Christ.[1] We ought to hold this with unshaken faith so that we know that anyone who denies this certainly does not belong to Christ's faith and does not have any share in the grace of God that is given through Christ to children and adults. Hence there is no danger if the origin of souls remains hidden, provided that their redemption is clearly known. For we do not believe in Christ in order to be born but in order to be reborn, however we may have been born.

4. But it is only to a certain point that it is not dangerous to say that the origin of souls remains hidden. For we believe that it is not a part of God but a creature, not born of God but created by him and destined to be adopted by him into his family by a wonderful concession of grace, not by an equal dignity of nature. We believe that it is not a body but a spirit, certainly not the creator but a creature, and we believe that it did not come into this corruptible body, which weighs down the spirit,[2] because it was forced into it by the merits of a bad life it previously lived in the heavens or in other parts of the world. For, when he was speaking of Rebekah's twins, the apostle said that, before they were born, they had not as yet done anything good or bad. Hence scripture did not say that the older would serve the younger because of works, since the one was not distinguished from the other by any works, but because of God's calling.[3]

2, 5. Now that all of this has been most firmly established, then if it is so buried and concealed in the hidden works of God that not even the clear words of God's scripture reveal whether we must believe that, when they were not yet born, they had not done anything good or bad, because individuals receive souls that have not been propagated from others but are immediately created from nothing, or because, though they were originally in their parents, they themselves did not yet exist and live their own personal lives, that faith still remains unimpaired by which we believe that no human being, whether an adult or a child, however young, is set free from the contagion of the ancient death and the bondage of sin,

1. See Jn 3:3.
2. See Wis 9:15.
3. See Rom 9:11-12; Gn 25:23.

which was contracted by our first birth, except through the one mediator of God and human beings, the man Jesus Christ.[4]

6. By the most salutary faith in Christ, who is both God and man, those righteous people were also saved who, before he came in the flesh, believed that he would come in the flesh.[5] For our faith is the same as theirs, since what they believed would come about we believe has come about. For this reason the apostle Paul says, *But having the same Spirit of faith, in accord with which scripture says, I believed, and for this reason I spoke, we also believe, and for this reason we speak* (2 Cor 4:13; Ps 116:1). If, then, those who foretold that Christ would come in the flesh have the same Spirit of faith as those who proclaim that he has come, the sacraments could be different in accord with different times and yet refer in perfect harmony to the unity of the same faith. It is recorded in the Acts of the Apostles when the apostle Peter says, *Now, then, why do you tempt God by trying to impose a yoke upon the neck of the disciples that neither our fathers nor we were able to carry? But we believe that we are saved through the grace of Jesus Christ, just as they were.* (Acts 15:10-11) If, then, even those men, that is, the fathers, who were unable to carry the yoke of the old law, believed that they were saved through the grace of the Lord Jesus, it is evident that this grace also caused the righteous of old to live from faith, *For the righteous live from faith* (Rom 1:17; Gal 3:11; Heb 10:38; Hb 2:4).

7. *But the law entered in so that sin might abound* (Rom 5:20) and grace might abound even more and heal the abundance of sin. *For, if a law were given that could give life, righteousness would surely come from the law* (Gal 3:21). Still he added next the benefit for which the law was given, when he said: *But scripture enclosed all things under sin so that the promise might be given to believers on the basis of faith in Jesus Christ* (Gal 3:22). Hence the law had to be given in order to reveal human beings to themselves more clearly, lest a proud human mind should think that it can be righteous by itself, and lest, not knowing the righteousness of God, that is, the righteousness that a human being has from God, and wanting to establish its own righteousness, that is, a righteousness supposedly gotten by its own powers, it would not become subject to the righteousness of God.[6] And so it was necessary that by the addition of the commandment that says, *You shall not desire* (Ex 20:17; Dt 5:21; 7:25; Rom 7:7; 13.9), the proud sinner should commit the crime of transgression and that thus his weakness, which was not healed but exposed by the law, might seek the remedy of grace.

8. Hence, since all the righteous, that is, the true worshipers of God, whether before the incarnation or after the incarnation of Christ, lived or live only

---

4. See 1 Tm 2:5.
5. See 1 Jn 4:2; 2 Jn 7.
6. See Rom 10:3.

because of faith in the incarnation of Christ, in whom there is the fullness of grace, the statement of scripture, *There is no other name under heaven in which we must be saved* (Acts 4:12), holds true for the salvation of the human race from the time when the human race was damaged in Adam. For, *just as all die in Adam, so too all will be brought to life in Christ* (1 Cor 15:22), because, just as no one enters the kingdom of death without Adam, so no one enters the kingdom of life without Christ. Just as through Adam all lack righteousness, so through Christ all human beings become righteous. Just as through Adam all the children of this world became mortal as punishment, so too through Christ all the children of God become immortal by grace.

3, 9. But the apostle mentioned with greater brevity in proportion to his greater authority why those people were created who the creator foreknew were destined for condemnation, not for grace. For he says that God, wanting *to show his anger and to demonstrate his power*, endured *with much patience the vessels of anger, which were made for destruction, in order to make known the riches of his glory toward the vessels of mercy* (Rom 9:22-23), and before that he had said that God, like a potter of clay, *makes from the same lump of clay one vessel for honor and another for dishonor* (Rom 9:21). But it would rightly be thought to be unjust that the vessels of anger were made for destruction if the whole lump of clay were not condemned because of Adam. The fact, then, that they become vessels of anger by being born is due to the punishment that they deserve, but the fact that they become vessels of mercy by being reborn is due to the grace that they did not deserve.

10. God, therefore, reveals his anger, which is certainly not a disturbance of the mind like what we call anger in a human being but a just and determinate punishment, for the propagation and punishment of sin is derived from the root of disobedience. And *a human being born of a woman*, as is written in the Book of Job, *has a short life and one full of anger* (Jb 14:1 LXX). They are vessels of that with which they are full; hence, they are called vessels of anger. He also shows the power by which he makes good use of sinners, bestowing on them many natural and temporal goods and adapting their malice to test good people and to warn them by comparison with sinners so that through sinners the good may learn to thank God that they were separated from them not by their merits, which were the same in the same lump of clay, but by God's mercy. This is most clearly seen in infants. When they are reborn through the grace of Christ and, ending this life at their tender age, pass into an eternal, happy life, it cannot be said of them that they are separated by their free choice from other infants who die without this grace in the condemnation of the whole lump.

11. But if only they were created from Adam who would be recreated by grace and if, apart from those who are adopted as children of God, no other human beings were born, the gift that is given to those who do not deserve it

would remain hidden because the punishment that they deserve would be given to none of those coming from that same root that deserves condemnation. But since *he endured with much patience the vessels of anger, which were made for destruction*, he not only showed *his anger* and revealed *his power* by inflicting punishment but, by making good use of those who were not good, he also made *known the riches of his glory toward the vessels of mercy* (Rom 9:22-23). For in that way a person who has been gratuitously justified learns what he is given when he is separated, not by his own merit but by the glory of God's most bountiful mercy, from someone else who is condemned, with whom he himself deserved to be condemned with equal justice.

12. But God willed that so many be created and born who he foreknew would not pertain to his grace that they outnumber by an incomparable amount those whom he graciously predestined to be children of the promise for the glory of his kingdom.[7] As a result, even by the very multitude of those rejected he showed that it is of no importance in the sight of the just God how great is the number of those justly condemned. And those who are redeemed from that condemnation can also understand from this that what they see was given to so great a part of that mass was deserved by that whole mass, not only in the case of those who add many sins to original sin by the choice of their bad will but also in the case of the many infants who, while subject only to the bond of original sin, are taken from this life without the grace of the mediator. For this whole mass would receive the punishment of just condemnation that they deserved if the potter, who is not only just but also merciful, did not make from it other vessels for honor as a grace, not as something they deserved,[8] when he goes to the help of infants who cannot be said to have any merits, and gives grace for the first time to adults in order that they may have some merits.

4, 13. Since this is so, if your statement is not intended to say that, on account of the innocence of their recent birth, before they use their free choice for sinning, new souls cannot be subject to original condemnation, but if you confess with the Catholic faith that, even if they leave the body at that tender age, they will be condemned to perdition unless they are set free by the sacrament of the mediator, who *came to seek and to save what was lost* (Lk 19:10; Mt 18:11), investigate where or why or when they began to deserve condemnation if they are newly created. Do this, of course, so that you do not make God or some nature that God did not create the author either of their sin or of the condemnation of those who are innocents. And if you find what I admonished you to seek, which I admit that I have not found, defend it as well as you can and maintain that infant souls are new in such a way that they do not come from any propagation, and share with us out of brotherly love what you find.

---

7. See Rom 9:8; Gal 4:28.
8. See Rom 9:21.

14. But if you do not discover why or how the souls of infants come to be sinful, even though they have no bad will in themselves by which they are forced to contract from Adam the grounds for being condemned, since you believe that they were not propagated from that first sinful soul but that they are enclosed in sinful flesh as new and innocent, do not rashly give your assent to the other position so that you believe that they were derived from that one soul by propagation. For someone else might discover what you could not, or at some point you may discover what you cannot now discover. For, if they follow the opinion of Tertullian, those who claim that souls are propagated from the one soul that God gave to the first human being and say that in that way they are derived from their parents certainly maintain that they are not spirits but bodies and come into existence from bodily seeds.[9] What can be said that is more perverse than that? Nor should one be surprised that Tertullian had this wild idea, for he also thought that God, the creator himself, was only a body.

15. Once this madness has been driven from the heart and lips of a Christian, whoever admits that the soul, as is true, is not a body but a spirit, and still holds that it is transmitted from the parents to the children, does not face any difficulties from the fact that the true faith preaches that all souls, even those of infants, whom the Church certainly baptizes not for a false but for a true forgiveness of sins, contract original sin. That sin was committed by the first man's own will, was passed on to all his descendants by birth, and can be removed only by rebirth. But when one begins to consider and weigh what is being said, it is surprising if any human mind grasps how from the soul of the parent the soul comes into existence in the offspring or is transmitted to the offspring, as one lamp is lighted from another and the second flame comes into existence from it without any loss to the first. Does an incorporeal seed of the soul by some hidden and invisible path run all by itself from the father into the mother when the child is conceived in the mother or—what is more incredible—is this incorporeal seed hidden in the seed of the body? But when seed is sown to no avail without producing any conception, does the seed of the soul not go forth at the same time, or does it with the greatest speed and in an instant of time return to its source, or does it perish? And if it perishes, how is the soul immortal if its seed is mortal? Or does the soul receive immortality at the point when it is formed so that it lives, just as it receives righteousness when it is formed so that it is wise? And does God fashion the soul in a human being, even if the soul is derived from another soul through seed, in the same way as he fashions in a human being the members of the body, though the body is derived from a body through seed? For, if a spiritual creature were not fashioned by God, scripture would not have said, *He who fashions the spirit of a human being within him* (Zec 12:1). And if souls are signi-

---

9. See Tertullian, *Against Praxeas* (*Contra Praxean*) 7.

fied by hearts in the words, *He who individually fashioned the hearts of human beings* (Ps 33:15), who would doubt that they can be fashioned? But the question is whether they are fashioned from the one soul of the first man, just as God individually fashions the faces of human beings, but from the one body of the first man.

5, 16. Since on this issue these and many such questions are raised that cannot be explored by any sense of the body and that are far removed by our experience and are hidden in the most secret depths of nature, a human being should not be embarrassed to admit that he does not know what he does not know. Otherwise, if he lies about knowing, he may never merit to know. But who denies that God is the creator and maker not only of one soul but of every soul, except someone who is most clearly refuted by the words of God? For he says through the prophet without any ambiguity, *I have made every breath* (Is 57:16 LXX), wanting us, that is, to understand "souls," which the following words reveal. He himself, then, made not just the one breath that he breathed into the first man, who was made from the earth, but every breath, and he himself still makes every breath. The question is, nonetheless, whether he makes every breath from that one breath, just as he makes every body of a human being from that one body, or whether he makes new bodies out of that one body but makes new souls out of nothing. For who makes various kinds of things in accord with their principles even by means of seeds but him who made the seeds themselves without the use of seeds? Where an issue that is by its nature obscure surpasses the limitation of our mind and a clear testimony from God's scripture offers no help, it is rash to presume to make a definitive statement about it on the basis of human conjecture. But we say that human beings are born new, both in their soul and in their body, in terms of the personal lives that they begin to live. Still in terms of original sin they are born old, and for this reason they are made new by baptism.

17. I have not yet, therefore, found anything certain about the origin of the soul in the canonical scriptures. For those who claim that new souls come into existence without any propagation also include among the testimonies by which they strive to prove this those two that I mentioned a little before: *He who fashions the spirit of a human being within him* (Zec 12:1), and, *He who individually fashioned the hearts of human beings* (Ps 33:15). You see how their opponents can respond to them, for it is uncertain whether, when he fashions souls, he fashions them out of another or out of nothing. But among the others that testimony seems the most important which we read in the book of Solomon's preacher, *And the dust will return to earth, as it was, and the spirit will return to God, who gave it* (Eccl 12:7). But the response to this is very easy! "The body will return to the earth from which the first body of a human being was made, and the spirit will return to God by whom the first soul of a human being was made. For, they say, just as our body returns to that from which the first body was made, though

our body was propagated from that first body, so our soul returns not to nothing, because it is immortal, but to God, by whom the first soul was made, though our soul was propagated from that soul." And for this reason what scripture says about the spirit of any human being, namely, that *it will return to God, who gave it*, does not resolve this most obscure question, because God certainly gave it, whether from that one spirit or from no other spirit.

18. Similarly, those who defend the propagation of the soul with ill-considered rashness can suppose that, among the other testimonies that they think support their cause, no testimony supposedly clearer and more explicit will be brought forth in their favor than that found in the Book of Genesis: *But all the souls who entered Egypt along with Jacob, those who came from his loins* (Gn 46:26 LXX). For they can believe on the basis of this supposedly most evident testimony that parents propagate souls for their children, because it seems to have been stated quite clearly that the souls too and not merely the bodies of the children came from the loins of Jacob, and so they also want us to understand the whole from the part in the words that Adam spoke when his wife was presented to him, *Now this is bone from my bones and flesh from my flesh* (Gn 2:23). For he did not say, "And soul from my soul," but, just as it is possible that, when the flesh is mentioned, both are understood, so scripture here mentioned the souls and yet wanted us also to understand the bodies of the children.

19. But this testimony, which seems so clear and evident, would not suffice for resolving this question even if in the words, *those who came from his loins*, the relative pronoun were found in the feminine gender so that we would under-stand that souls came from there.[10] It would not suffice because we see that the body alone can be signified by the term "soul" by a certain figure of speech according to which the container is signified by its contents. In that way a certain poet said, "They crown the wines,"[11] when the cups of wine were crowned with garlands. For the wine is the content, the cup the container. Just as, then, we call the church the basilica that contains the people, who are properly called the church, so that by the term "church," that is, the people who are contained, we signify the place that contains them, so, because souls are contained in bodies, the bodies of the children can be understood when their souls are mentioned. In that way we also interpret more correctly the statement in the law that says that one is unclean who comes upon a dead soul,[12] that is, the body of a dead person, when we understand by the expression "dead soul" a dead body that contained the soul, because, when the people, that is, the church, are absent, that place is still called the church. This would be the answer if, as I said, the feminine gender

---

10. The relative pronoun in the Latin text is masculine so that it seems to refer to the children rather than to their souls.
11. Virgil, *Aeneid* 1, 724.
12. See Nm 9:6-10.

were used in the words, *those who came from the loins of Jacob*, that is, those souls. But now, since the masculine gender was used in the expression, *those who came from the loins of Jacob*, who would not prefer to understand it as "all the souls of those who came from the loins of Jacob," that is, the souls of human beings? And so even in this way the human beings to whom those souls belonged could be understood to have come from the loins of their father only in terms of the body, and the number of those souls refers to as many human beings.

6, 20. But I would like to read the little book of yours that you mention in your letter, in case you cited there some testimonies that are not ambiguous. But since a friend most dear to me and most devoted to theological writings[13] had asked me what I held on this question, and since without any embarrassment I had admitted to him my confusion and ignorance,[14] he wrote to a most learned man who resides across the sea,[15] and that man wrote back that Marcellinus should consult me instead.[16] For Jerome had not known that Marcellinus had already done so and was unable to learn anything certain and definitive from me. He indicated in that same short letter of his, however, that he believed that souls are created rather than propagated. At the same time he also pointed out, since he himself is in the east, that the western Church usually held for the propagation of souls. Having found this greater opportunity, I wrote to him a long book to consult him and to ask him first to teach me and only then to send me persons whom I should teach.[17]

21. You can read this book of mine here, a book not of a teacher but of an inquirer and of a person desiring rather to know, but it must not be sent anywhere or given to anyone elsewhere except when, with the Lord's help, I see from his answer what Jerome holds. For I am most ready and willing to defend it if he can explain to me how souls do not come from Adam and still meet with their just lot of condemnation from him, unless they attain forgiveness of sins by being reborn. For God forbid that we should believe either that the souls of infants receive a fictitious purification from sins in the bath of rebirth or that God or some nature which God did not create is the source of the defilement from which they are purified. Until, therefore, he either writes back or I somehow learn, if God wills, why, if the soul does not take its origin from that sinful soul, it is subject to original sin, which must be present in all infants and into which God does not force an innocent soul, because he is not the author of sin, nor does any nature of evil, because there is none, I do not dare to preach anything of the sort.

---

13. That is, Marcellinus, the military commander of Africa, who was executed by Count Marinus near Carthage.
14. See Letter 143, 6, 11 to Marcellinus.
15. That is, Jerome.
16. See Letter 165, 1, 1.
17. See Letter 166.

22. But if you willingly or patiently allow me, I admonish you, my dearest brother, not to rush because of a lack of caution into the new heresy that tries to overturn the established foundations of the most ancient faith by arguing against the grace of God, which Christ the Lord bestows with ineffable goodness upon infants and adults. Its authors, or at least its fiercest and best known advocates, are Pelagius and Caelestius, and by the vigilance of councils of bishops along with the help of the savior, who watches over his Church, as well as by two venerable bishops of the Apostolic See, Pope Innocent and Pope Zosimus, they have been condemned throughout the whole world, unless they are corrected and also do penance. On the chance that they have not yet come into the hands of Your Holiness, we have taken care to send copies of their recent letters concerning Pelagius and Caelestius, sent from the aforementioned see either to Africans in particular or to all the bishops of the world.[18] We have sent them by means of the brothers to whom we have given this letter so that they may deliver them to Your Reverence. But the Pelagians are not heretics because they say that souls do not derive their origin from that first sinful soul, which can perhaps be said for some good reason or can go unknown without loss of the faith. But from this they try to establish—and for this reason they are judged to be outright heretics—that the souls of infants contract no sin from Adam that must be wiped away by the bath of rebirth. For the argument of Pelagius on this matter, which is appended to the letter from the Apostolic See among his other teachings deserving of condemnation, runs as follows: "If the soul," he says, "is not transmitted by generation, but only the flesh has the transmitted sin, the flesh alone, then, deserves punishment. For it is unjust that a soul born today, not stemming from the mass of Adam, should bear so ancient a sin of another person, for reason does not allow that God, who forgives personal sins, would impute a single sin committed by someone else."

23. If, then, you can maintain that souls are created new apart from any propagation, so that they are shown by a just reason not foreign to the Catholic faith to be, even in that case, subject to the sin of the first man, defend what you hold as best you can. But if you cannot keep souls exempt from propagation except by at the same time setting them free from every bond of sin, refrain entirely from such a line of argumentation. For the forgiveness of sins in the baptism of infants is not a fiction, nor is it done merely verbally but in actual fact. For, to use the words that we read in the letter of the blessed Bishop Zosimus, *"The Lord is faithful in his words* (Ps 145:13), and his baptism has the same fullness of power in its reality and in its words, that is, in the action, confession, and forgiveness of sins, in every sex, age, and condition of the human race. Only one who is a slave

---

18. Augustine refers to Letters 182 and 183 from Pope Innocent to the participants in the Councils of Carthage and of Milevis as well as to the *Tractoria* of Pope Zosimus, which was sent to the universal Church but survives only in fragments.

of sin is set free, and only one who was before held captive by sin can be said to be redeemed, as scripture says, *If the Son sets you free, you will be truly free* (Jn 8:36). For through him we are reborn spiritually; through him we are crucified to the world. By his death there is destroyed that sentence of death which was introduced and passed on to every soul and contracted by all of us through generation from Adam. Because of that sentence absolutely everyone who has been born is held guilty before being set free by baptism."[19] These words of the Apostolic See contain the Catholic faith that is so ancient and well-founded, so certain and clear, that it is impious for a Christian to doubt it.

24. Since, then, the sentence of death contracted by generation, not by one or a few but by every soul, is destroyed by the death of Christ, if you can maintain that souls are free from propagation in such a way that they are shown by a completely orthodox argument to be bound by this decree of condemnation that can be destroyed only by the death of Christ, not because of their propagation but because of this debt of the flesh, not only defend it since no one is preventing you but also teach us how we can defend it with you. But if you cannot defend what you hold regarding the newness of souls in any other way than by saying that they are not bound by the sin of the first man or that perfectly innocent souls are made sinful not through their own propagation but by the author of their flesh, either God or some sort of evil nature, it is better that the origin of the soul lie hidden (provided that we, nonetheless, have no doubt that it is a creature of God) than that God be said to be the origin of sin or that some evil nature opposed to God be introduced or that the baptism of infants be considered to be inneffectual.

25. But that Your Charity may hear something definitive from me on this question, which should not be considered a matter of little moment but, on the contrary, highly necessary: However the soul may take its origin, whether souls are propagated from that one soul or from no other soul, it is not permissible to have any doubt that the soul of the mediator did not contract any sin from Adam. For, if no soul is propagated from any other when all souls are held bound by the sinful flesh that has been propagated, how much less ought we to believe that the soul whose flesh came from the Virgin could come by propagation from that sinful soul. For the soul of that flesh was not conceived through lust but through faith, in order that it might be *in the likeness of sinful flesh* (Rom 8:3), not in sinful flesh. But if the other souls are held guilty on account of the sin of the first sinful soul because they were propagated from it, certainly that soul that the Only-Begotten united to himself either did not contract sin from it or was not derived from it at all. For he who destroyed our sins could not but derive for himself a soul without sin, or he who created a new soul for that flesh that he

---

19. The citation is from the now lost *Tractoria* of Pope Zosimus, which he wrote in the summer of 418.

made from the earth without any parent could not but create a new soul for the flesh that he assumed from a woman without the work of a man.

26. I have made this reply, as best I could, to a letter that was not sent to me but to persons very dear to us and to Your Holiness. My reply is not as learned as you desired, but it is filled with concerned love. If you gratefully accept my fraternal and beneficial warning and abide by it, not falling into error but wisely remaining in the peace of the Church, thanks be to God. But if you are surprised that I still do not know these things, or even if you are not surprised, and if you do not refuse to teach me something certain about the origin of souls in harmony with the faith that is perfectly certain and clear, much greater thanks be to God. Mindful of us, may you always live for the Lord, my most blessed lord and brother who are loveable with a pure love.

Letter 191

It was perhaps in 418 that Augustine wrote to the Roman priest Sixtus, who later succeeded Celestine as the bishop of Rome in 432 and exercised his office until 440. Under Pope Zosimus (18 March 417 to 26 December 418), Sixtus had favored the Pelagians, but then he supported Celestine's anti-Pelagian stance. Augustine's Letter 194 to Sixtus is an important statement of Augustine's doctrine on grace. In the present letter Augustine thanks Sixtus for his letter to Alypius and himself and congratulates him on having seen the light and come to the defense of the grace of God (paragraph 1). He goes on to remind Sixtus that those who continue openly to teach the Pelagian doctrine must be punished with a salutary severity but that the Church must also be on guard against those who still cautiously spread in whispers Pelagian beliefs and those who hold such beliefs, though they are silent about them (paragraph 2).

To Sixtus, his venerable lord, holy brother, and fellow priest, who is to be embraced with the love of Christ, Augustine sends greetings in the Lord.

1. The letter of Your Grace sent to me by means of our brother, the priest Firmus, arrived in Hippo when I was away.[1] I was able to read it afterward when I returned, although its bearer had already left there. Since that time this is the first opportunity, and a most gratifying one, to present itself for sending a reply by means of our most beloved son Albinus, an acolyte. But because the two of us to whom you wrote at the same time were not then both together,[2] it turned out that you received a single letter from each of us, not one from both. The bearer of this letter has departed from me with the intention of going by way of my venerable brother and fellow bishop Alypius, so that he might write another letter to you. He also carried to him the letter of yours that I had already read. With what great joy it filled us! Why should one try to say what cannot be expressed? I do not think that you yourself realize this, but believe us about the great good you did in sending such answers to us. For as you are a witness to your own mind, so we are to ours about how ours is affected by the perfectly transparent sincerity of your letter. For we quickly and joyfully copied your short letter on this subject that you sent to the blessed primate Aurelius,[3] by means of the acolyte Leo,[4] and we read it with great eagerness to those to whom we could. In it you explained to us what you hold on that most pernicious teaching and what you hold against it on the grace of God, which is given to infants and adults and to which that

---

1. Augustine was in Mauretania at the time.
2. Sixtus had written to both Alypius and Augustine.
3. That is, the bishop of Carthage and primate of Africa.
4. The NBA edition identifies this Leo as the future pope who succeeded Sixtus in 440 and died in 461.

teaching is most opposed. With what great joy do you imagine we read this longer letter of yours and with what great care do you suppose that we have offered it and are still offering it to whatever others we can in order that it might be read to them! For what could one read or hear with more pleasure than so pure a defense of the grace of God against its enemies from the lips of one who earlier was claimed to be an important patron of those same enemies? And for what ought we to offer greater thanks to God than that his grace is so defended by those to whom it is given against those to whom it is not given or to whom his gift is not pleasing, because by the hidden but just judgment of God they are not given the gift that makes it pleasing?

2. For this reason, my venerable lord and holy brother who are to be embraced in the love of Christ, although you do very well when you write about this to the brothers among whom those heretics are accustomed to brag about your friendship, this greater concern remains for you. Not only must those who dare more freely to spread about this error so opposed to the Christian name be punished with a salutary severity, but on account of the weaker and simpler sheep of the Lord we must also be most carefully on guard with pastoral vigilance against those who in fact continue, though very cautiously and timidly, to whisper this error in the ears of believers, entering into their homes, as the apostle says, and doing with habitual impiety the other things that follow.[5] Nor should those be neglected who out of fear suppress in deep silence what they believe but do not cease to hold the same misguided views. Before this plague was condemned by the most clear judgment of the Apostolic See,[6] some of them, to be sure, were able to come to your attention, though you now see that they have suddenly fallen silent. Nor is it possible to know whether they have been healed except when they not only do not speak about those false teachings but even defend the truth opposed to them with the same zeal with which they are accustomed to defend those teachings. And yet these people must, of course, be treated with a certain gentleness. For what need is there to terrify those whose silence itself shows that they are terrified enough? Nor should they be passed over in terms of medical care because their wound is hidden. For, even if they should not be terrified, they should nonetheless be taught, and in my opinion they can be taught more easily while the fear of severity assists the teacher of the truth in them so that, once they have come to know and love his grace, they may with the Lord's help battle against what they now do not dare to say.[7]

---

5. See 2 Tm 3:6-9.
6. That is, by Pope Zosimus in 418 in his *Tractoria* which is no longer extant.
7. The end of the Letter is lost.

Letter 192

Toward the end of 418 Augustine wrote to Celestine, a deacon of the Church of Rome, who succeeded Pope Boniface in 422 and died in 432. Augustine tells Celestine that he gladly pays the debt of love that he owes him because love is increased, not lost, when it is given to another (paragraph 1). Unlike a debt of money, the debt of love is never fully paid, nor is love lost in payment of our debt of love (paragraph 2).

To his venerable and highly beloved lord, holy brother, and fellow deacon, Celestine, Augustine sends greetings in the Lord.

1. Although I was far away when the letter of Your Holiness, which was sent to me by means of the cleric Projectus, arrived in Hippo, after I returned and once I had read it I recognized that I owed you a reply and was looking for a chance to pay my debt.[1] And, see, suddenly there was provided the most pleasing opportunity by our dearest brother, the acolyte Albinus, who was about to leave us.[2] And so, rejoicing over your well-being, which is something I desire very much, I pay my debt by sending greetings to Your Holiness. But I always owe the debt of love, for it alone, even when paid, always holds one in debt. For that debt is paid when love is given, but the debt is still owed even after it has been paid. Nor does one cease to have the debt when it is paid; rather it is increased by being paid. For we pay the debt by having love, not by lacking it. And the debt cannot be paid unless one has love, and one cannot have love unless one pays the debt. In fact when we pay the debt, love increases in us, and we acquire it more to the extent that we pay the debt of love to more persons. Yet how may we deny to our friends what we owe even to our enemies? But if we are wary in giving love to our enemies, we are safe in bestowing it on our friends. Love, nonetheless, does everything it can to receive the love that it gives even from those to whom it gives good in turn for evil. We, of course, desire the enemy whom we truly love to become a friend, for we only love him if we want him to be good, and he will certainly not be good unless he loses the evil of his hostility.

2. Love, then, is not paid out like money. For, apart from the fact that money is diminished by being given to someone else, while love is increased, they also differ from each other by the fact that we will be more benevolent to someone to whom we give money if we do not look for its return, but one cannot truly give love without demanding repayment for his love. For, when money is received, it accrues to the recipient but leaves the giver, but love not merely increases in the

---

1. Augustine was in Mauretania on Church business.
2. See Letter 191, 1.

278

one who demands love from the person he loves, even if he does not receive it, but the person from whom he receives love begins to have it at the point when he gives it in return. Hence, my lord and brother, I gladly give love and joyfully receive love in return. I still ask for the love I receive, and I still owe the love I return. For we ought docilely to listen to the one teacher, of whom we are both disciples; he commands us through his apostle, saying, *Owe no one anything except that you have love for one another* (Rom 13:8).

Letter 193

In approximately 418 Augustine wrote to Marius Mercator, a Catholic layman, an Italian who later lived in Constantinople. He wrote two works against Pelagianism, which he sent to Augustine and which are no longer extant.[1] In the present letter Augustine apologizes for not having replied to Mercator's first letter and expresses his pleasure at receiving his second one (paragraph 1). He thanks Mercator for sending him his books against the Pelagian teaching (paragraph 2).

Augustine notes that, if the heretics hold that baptized infants believe through those who present them for baptism, they have taken a big step in the right direction, since they thereby admit that without baptism infants are non-believers who will, according to the Lord's words, be condemned (paragraph 3). In fact, if they admit that baptized infants believe, the whole controversy is practically speaking settled (paragraph 4).

As Mercator reported, the Pelagians pointed to Enoch and Elijah as having escaped death, but Augustine does not see how this helps their case (paragraph 5). God could bring about eternal life without the intervention of death for those he wanted to (paragraph 6). The question as to why the penalty for sin remains once the sin itself has been wiped out in baptism presents more of a problem, and on this issue Augustine refers Mercator to his books on the baptism of infants (paragraph 7). Or perhaps the Pelagians are troubled that no one now lives without sin as Enoch supposedly did so that he merited to escape death. Augustine points out that it is not certain that Enoch has escaped death (paragraph 8).

Paul's words about those found living at the coming of Christ present another problem (paragraph 9). Augustine would like to hear what more learned persons have said on the passage (paragraph 10). Whether those living at Christ's coming are taken to be the righteous or those still in their bodies, it remains true that Christ will judge the living and the dead (paragraph 11). Whichever interpretation one takes, it does not seem relevant to the Pelagian cause (paragraph 12). Augustine asks Mercator to let him know if he has found a definite resolution to the question about those found living at Christ's coming and says that he prefers to learn rather than to teach (paragraph 13).

---

1. Marius Mercator later wrote a *Memorandum on the Name of Coelestius (Commonitorium super nomine Coelestii)* and a *Memorandum against the Heresy of Pelagius and Coelestius on the Writings of Julian (Commonitorium adversum haeresim Pelagii et Coelestii, seu scripta Juliani)*. These works are no longer extant.

To Mercator, his most beloved lord and son worthy of praise and of most sincere love among the members of Christ, Augustine sends greetings in the Lord.

1, 1. The letter of Your Charity, which you sent earlier and which I received in Carthage, filled me with such great joy that I was most grateful to receive even your later letter, in which you were angry with me because I had not replied to you. For your anger was not the beginning of a state of animosity but a proof of love. The fact that I did not reply from Carthage was not due to a lack of couriers, but other more urgent matters kept us very occupied with and intent upon them until we left there. But after we left there, we went on to Caesarean Mauretania where the needs of the Church carried us. While the different things thrust upon our senses through all those lands pulled our attention this way and that, no one was insistently reminding me to reply to you and there was no opportunity to find a courier. Then, upon returning from there, I found the other letter of Your Sincerity already filled with sharp complaints and another book against the new heretics filled with testimonies from the holy scriptures. After I had read it somewhat in haste, I felt obliged to reply also to the first one you sent since a very good opportunity presented itself in your dearest brother, Albinus, an acolyte of the church of Rome.

2. Heaven forbid, therefore, my dearest son, that I should be negligent in welcoming you when you write to me or send me your writings to examine or that I should hold you in scorn because of proud vanity, especially since my joy over you is greater to the extent that it comes to me unexpected and unforeseen. For I admit that I did not know that you had made so much progress. And what should be more desirable for us than that they become more and more numerous who refute the errors that attack the Catholic faith and lay ambushes for weak and ignorant brethren and who fiercely and faithfully defend the Church of Christ against *profane innovations in language* (1 Tm 6:20)? For, as scripture says, *The multitude of the wise is the good health of the world* (Wis 6:26). I looked into your heart in your writings as much as I could, and I found a heart that I should embrace and exhort to stretch out with most persevering diligence toward the things that are ahead,[2] as the Lord helps your strength, for he has given you that strength in order that he may make it grow.

2, 3. But the people who wandered off, whom we are trying to call back to the way, have drawn close to the truth to no small degree concerning the baptism of infants, when they admit that an infant, no matter how recently born from its mother, nonetheless believes through those who present the child to be baptized. For they say, as you write, that infants do not believe in the forgiveness of sins in the sense that infants, who they think have no sin, receive the forgiveness of sins. But since infants also receive the same bath that produces the forgiveness of sins

---

2. See Phil 3:13.

in whoever receives it, they believe that this forgiveness, which is not produced in them, is produced in others. When, therefore, they say, "They do not believe in that sense, but they believe in this sense," they certainly are clear that infants believe. Let them, therefore, hear the Lord: *Whoever believes in the Son has eternal life, but whoever does not believe in the Son will not have life, but the anger of God remains over him* (Jn 3:36). Hence, because infants become believers through others who present them to be baptized, they are certainly unbelievers through those people (if they are among such) who do not believe that they should be presented for baptism, since they do not believe that it does them any good. And for this reason, if infants in that way believe through believers and have eternal life, they are certainly unbelievers through unbelievers and will not see life, but the anger of God remains over them. For scripture did not say "comes over them" but *remains over them*, because it was already in them from their origin, and it is by no means taken away from them except by *the grace of God through Jesus Christ our Lord* (Rom 7:25). Concerning this anger we read in the Book of Job, *A man born of a woman has a short life and one full of anger* (Job 14:1 LXX). Why, then, does the anger of God remain over the innocence of an infant if not because of the condition and defilement of original sin? Concerning this defilement it is likewise written in the same book that no one is immune from it, not even an infant *who has lived one day on the earth* (Job 14:5 LXX).

4. The fact that we argue against them most persistently has, therefore, not failed to accomplish something in these people, and Catholic voices echo in their ears from one side and another, since, though they wanted to argue against the sacraments of the Church, they admitted, nonetheless, that infants believe. They do not, therefore, promise them life even if they have not been baptized. Of what other life is it said, *Whoever does not believe the Son will not see life* (Jn 3:36)? And let them not say that they are excluded from the kingdom of heaven in such a way that they still defend them from condemnation. For what but condemnation is signified by the anger that the Lord testifies remains over one who does not believe? They have in fact come quite close to us, and apart from a dispute over minor points the case is ended. For, if they grant that infants believe, just as the statement, *One who is not reborn of water and the Spirit will not enter the kingdom of heaven* (Jn 3:5), is binding for them, so undoubtedly is this one, which is also from the same Lord, *One who believes and is baptized will be saved, but one who does not believe will be condemned* (Mk 16:16). Because, then, these people admit that infants are believers when they are baptized, they should not doubt that, if they do not believe, they are condemned, and they should be so bold as to say, if they can, that they are condemned by a just God, though they contract no sin from their origin and have no infection of sin.

5. But regarding the point that you mentioned in your letter, namely, that they raise as an objection to us that Enoch and Elijah did not die but were taken from this life from the midst of human beings along with their bodies, I do not understand how it helps them with respect to the issue that we are dealing with. For I omit the fact that it is said that they too are going to die afterward, as most people interpret the Revelation of John concerning those two prophets. He says about them without mentioning their names that these two holy men will at some time appear with the bodies in which they are now living in order that they too might die for the truth of Christ, like the other martyrs.[3] Having, then, omitted this interpretation, however it stands with the question that they have raised, how, I ask you, does it help them? For, if God, who pardons sins for so many of his faithful, also willed to spare some of them this punishment of sin, who are we to answer back to God[4] and ask why one person receives this gift and another that one?[5]

6. We state, therefore, what the apostle states with full openness: *The body is indeed dead on account of sin, but the spirit is life on account of righteousness. But if the Spirit of him who has raised up Christ from the dead dwells in you, he who has raised up Christ from the dead will also bring to life your mortal bodies through his Spirit dwelling in you.* (Rom 8:10-11) But we do not say this in the sense that we deny that God can now, in those whom he wants, produce without death what we believe he will doubtlessly produce in so many after their death, nor is that statement for this reason false, that *through one man sin entered this world and through sin death, and in that way it was passed on to all human beings* (Rom 5:12). For this was said because, if death had not entered through sin, there would be no death. For, when we also say, "All are sent to hell on account of sins," do we say something false because all human beings are not sent to hell? That statement is certainly true not because every human being is sent there but because no one is sent there except as punishment for sins. The statement, *Through the righteousness of one all human beings come to righteousness of life* (Rom 5:18), is also a statement of this sort to the opposite effect. For all human beings do not share in the righteousness of Christ, but this was said because no one is made righteous except by Christ.

7. That question, then, is not without reason more disturbing, namely, why the punishment of sin remains when the sin does not remain. That is, if the death of the body is punishment for sin, it is a greater problem that an infant dies after it has been baptized than that Elijah did not die after he had been justified. For, after the sin of the infant is canceled, it is a problem that the punishment of sin takes place; it ought not to be a problem if, after Elijah's sin is canceled, the

---

3. See Rev 11:3-7.
4. See Rom 9:20.
5. See 1 Cor 7:7.

punishment of sin does not take place. If, then, in the books on the baptism of infants,[6] with which I know that you are quite familiar, we resolved as best we could with the Lord's help the question about the death of the baptized, namely, why, once sin has been abolished, the punishment of sin still follows, how much less should we be disturbed by the question that we are asked: "Why did the righteous Elijah not die if death is the punishment for sin?" It is as if the question were: "Why did the sinful Elijah not die if death is the punishment of sin?"

8. But these people might raise another objection from another angle and ask: "If Enoch and Elijah were so sinless that they did not suffer even death, which is the punishment for sin, how is it that no one lives in this life without sin?" They might ask this as if we would not give them the more probable answer: "Those whom the Lord wanted to live after their sins had been removed were not allowed to live here because here no one can live without sin." But these and similar responses could be given to them if they proved from elsewhere that those men were never going to die. But since they cannot prove this, it is better to believe that Enoch and Elijah will die at the end of the world, and, since it is better to believe that they will meet death, there is no reason that they should want to raise those two men as an objection to us since they will in no way help their case.

4, 9. But those of whom the apostle said, when he was speaking of the resurrection of the dead, *And we, the living who remain, will be snatched up with them in the clouds to meet Christ in the air, and in that way we will be with the Lord forever.* (1 Thes 4:16) certainly raise a question, but on account of those people themselves, not on account of our opponents. For, even if they are themselves not going to die, I do not at all see how it helps our opponents, since the same sort of things can be said of these people as were said of those two prophets. But, with regard to the words of the blessed apostle, he really seems to state that at the end of the world, at the Lord's coming, when the resurrection of the dead will take place, certain persons will not die but will be found alive and will be changed suddenly into that immortality that is also given to the other saints and will be snatched up along with them, as he says, in the clouds. Nothing else has come to my mind whenever I have chosen to think about these words.

10. But I would prefer to hear from more learned persons on this. Otherwise we may find that the apostle also said to those who think that some living people will be transferred to perpetual life without death having preceded, *You fool, what you sow is not brought to life unless it first dies* (1 Cor 15:36). For how is what we read in most manuscripts, *All of us will rise* (1 Cor 15:51), possible unless all of us die? There is certainly no resurrection unless death has come first. And what some manuscripts have, namely, *All of us will fall asleep*, makes

---

6. See *The Merits and Forgiveness of Sins and Baptism of Infants* 2, 3, 49-34, 56.

us understand this same point much more easily and clearly, and anything else of the sort that is found in the holy writings seems to force us to the conclusion that no human being should be thought to attain immortality unless death has come first. Hence, when the apostle said, *And we, the living who remain at the coming of the Lord, will not arrive ahead of those who have already fallen asleep. For the Lord himself at the sound of a command, at the word of an archangel, at the blast of a trumpet, will come down from heaven, and those who have died in Christ will rise first; then we, the living who remain, will be snatched up with them in the clouds to meet Christ in the air, and in that way we will be with the Lord forever* (1 Thes 4:14-16). I would like, as I said, to hear from more learned persons on these words and, if they can explain them so that we can understand from them that all human beings who are living or who will live after us are going to die, I would like to correct what I once held on this. For we ought not to be teachers who cannot be taught, and it is certainly better that a little fellow be corrected than that a rigid one be broken, for what we have written exercises and trains our weakness or that of others, even though our writings are not established with anything like the authority of the canon of scripture.

11. For, if no other meaning can be found in these words of the apostle and if it is clear that he wanted us to understand what the words themselves seem to cry out, that is, that at the end of the world and at the coming of the Lord there will be some persons who will not be stripped of the body but will be clothed over with immortality, *in order that what is mortal may be swallowed up by life* (2 Cor 5:4), what we confess in the rule of faith will undoubtedly be in accord with this view, namely, that the Lord will come to judge the living and the dead.[7] Thus we would not understand here the living as the righteous and the dead as those lacking righteousness, though the righteous and those lacking righteousness are going to be judged. Rather we would understand the living as those whom his coming will find not yet to have left their bodies and the dead as those who have already left them. If it is established that this is the case, we must examine how we should then interpret the words, *What you sow is not brought to life unless it first dies* (1 Cor 15:36), and, *All of us will rise*, or, *All of us will fall asleep* (1 Cor 15:51), in order that they may not be opposed to this view by which it is believed that they will live with their bodies for eternity without having tasted death.

12. But whichever of these interpretations is found to be truer and clearer, how is it relevant to their case whether all are punished by the death they deserve or some are spared suffering death? For it is clear that death not only of the soul but also of the body would not take place if sin had not come first and that the power of grace is more wonderful in the coming to life of the righteous into eternal blessedness than in their not meeting with the experience of death.

---

7. See 2 Tm 4:1.

Enough has been said on account of the people about whom you wrote to me, though I do not think that they now say that, even if Adam had not sinned, he would have died at least in the body.

13. But, with regard to the question of the resurrection, we must bring to bear a more careful examination on account of those who, it is thought, are not going to die but to pass from this mortality to immortality without death intervening, and if you have either heard or read something or have been able to think of something on this question that has been resolved and settled by arguments that are reasonable and complete, I ask that you not hesitate to send it to me. For I prefer—something I must admit to Your Charity—to learn rather than to teach. We are also admonished about this by the apostle James, who says, *Let each be quick to listen and slow to speak* (Jas 1:19). The sweetness of the truth, therefore, ought to invite us to learn, but the necessity of charity ought to force us to teach. Here we should rather hope that this necessity passes away, because of which one human being teaches another, so that we may *all be taught by God* (Jn 6:45 ; Is 54:13). And yet we are taught by God when we learn those matters that pertain to true piety, even when a human being seems to teach them, because *neither the one who plants nor the one who waters is important, but only God who gives the increase* (1 Cor 3:7). Since, therefore, if God did not give the increase, the apostles who planted and watered would not be important, how much more are you or I or any human beings of this time unimportant, when we think that we are teachers!

Letter 194

In 418 Augustine wrote to the Roman priest Sixtus, to whom he had written Letter 191 and who was elected the bishop of Rome in 432. The letter subsequently played an interesting role in the controversy on grace when some monks from a monastery in Hadrumetum found a copy of it in the library of Evodius, the bishop of Uzalis. Shocked by Augustine's teaching on grace, the monks concluded that their superior ought not to rebuke them for misconduct but should simply pray that God would give them grace since, if they misbehaved, it was due to a lack of grace. As a result, Augustine had to write two works for the abbot of the monastery, Valentine, namely, *Correction and Grace* and *Grace and Free Will*. See Letters 214 and 215 for further background on the controversy.

Augustine begins by expressing his joy at hearing that Sixtus, whose letter to Augustine is no longer extant, has now condemned the Pelagians, though it has been rumored that he earlier favored their views (paragraph 1). He distinguishes various kinds of supporters of the Pelagian position and the different manners in which they should be dealt with (paragraph 2). The Pelagians are simply wrong in claiming that free choice is done away with if one holds that it is impossible to have a good will without God's help (paragraph 2). They wrongly charge God with favoritism on the grounds that grace is not given in accord with previous merits (paragraph 3). They claim that it is unjust if, when two people are in the same situation, God shows mercy to one and not to another (paragraph 4) and that it is unjust that one is set free and the other is condemned (paragraph 5).

Augustine insists that God justifies sinners without any preceding merits but that why he justifies one person and not another is hidden in the unsearchable ways of God (paragraph 6). Although at the Council of Diospolis Pelagius condemned those who say that grace is given in accord with merits, he continues to teach what he condemned (paragraph 7). Pelagius teaches that the grace given without any preceding merits is the human nature with which we are created (paragraph 8). Pelagians also say that this grace given previous to any merits is the forgiveness of sins, but they hold that faith obtains this forgiveness (paragraph 9). Augustine shows from Paul that even faith is a gift of God (paragraph 10). After all, Christian faith must include love, which is a gift of the Holy Spirit (paragraph 11). God's foreknowledge of believers differs from his foreknowledge of those who do not believe (paragraph 12). The Pelagian defenders of free choice ask what complaint God can have with them since no one can resist his will (paragraph 13). Some people do merit to have their hearts hardened, but there is no merit by which others obtain mercy (paragraph 14). We do not merit to receive faith (paragraph 15). Even prayer is a gift of God (paragraph 16). When the Holy Spirit is said to intercede for us with inexpressible groans, we must understand that he makes us groan (paragraph 17). Without the Spirit no one prays correctly (paragraph 18).

Prior to grace we have no merit by which we can earn grace, since grace produces in us all our good merits, and in crowning our merits God crowns his own gifts (paragraph 19). Augustine points out how Paul taught that even eternal life, which scripture often calls a recompense, is grace (paragraphs 20 and 21).

Augustine answers those who try to excuse themselves for living sinful lives on the grounds that they did not receive grace to live good lives, for, if they live sinful lives, they do so because of sin, either original sin alone or original sin along with personal sins (paragraph 22). Augustine turns against them the words of the apostle who asks who they are to answer back to God (paragraph 23). Of adults one can say that they refuse to understand or refuse to obey so that they are without excuse (paragraph 24). Those who know the law and do not carry it out are especially without excuse (paragraph 25). The Jews who rejected Christ would not have had that sin if Christ had not come, but they would still have had other sins (paragraph 26). Every sinner is without excuse either because of the guilt of original sin or because of the guilt of personal sin as well (paragraph 27). Knowledge of the law without grace is useless (paragraph 28). For those who are set free from the bondage of sin are set free only by grace (paragraph 29). No one is set free from sin, whether original sin or personal sin, except by the grace of Jesus Christ (paragraph 30).

Those who think that God shows favoritism have to face the fact that many infants die without baptism, though God is not unjust (paragraph 31). The lot of infants, some of whom die without baptism while others die after having been baptized, proves the gratuity of grace (paragraph 32). One can, when confronted with their different ends, only exclaim over the inscrutable judgment of God (paragraph 33).

Augustine appeals to the twin sons of Isaac, who did nothing either good or bad before they were born, in order to show that God's choice of Jacob was a gift of grace, while his rejection of Esau was just in view of original sin (paragraph 34). He rejects the idea that God foresaw their future works in choosing Jacob over Esau (paragraph 35). Paul used the example of these twins to teach the gratuity of grace (paragraph 36). He emphasized their conception from a single act of intercourse in order to exclude any difference in merits on their part or on the part of their parents (paragraph 37). Paul wanted to teach that Jacob had no reason to boast except in the Lord (paragraph 38). His choice had no preceding merits and involved no injustice on the part of God (paragraph 39). Again, Augustine asks those who excuse themselves Paul's question about who they think they are to answer back to God (paragraph 40).

Even if God did foresee the future works of Isaac's twin sons who grew up, he could not foresee the future works of infants who were going to die in infancy, because there were not going to be any (paragraph 41). If the Pelagians appeal to God's foreknowledge of what such infants would have done if they had lived, they are faced with even worse problems (paragraph 42).

The Pelagians are confronted with the authority of scripture and with the practice of infant baptism, which includes the rites of exorcism and exsufflation (paragraph 43). Augustine appeals to the example of the wild and domesticated olive trees to show that the child of baptized parents still needs to be baptized for the removal of original sin (paragraph 44). Baptism truly brings about the forgiveness of sin even in infants (paragraph 45), just as it truly drives out the devil who has dominion over them only because of sin (paragraph 46). Finally, Augustine urges Sixtus to exercise pastoral vigilance in the face of the restlessness of the Pelagian heretics (paragraph 47).

To his lord who is most beloved in the Lord of lords, his holy brother and fellow priest Sixtus, Augustine sends greetings in the Lord.

1, 1. In the letter that I sent by means of our dearest brother, the acolyte Albinus, I promised that I would send a lengthier one by means of our holy brother and fellow priest Firmus, who brought us the letter of Your Holiness full of the purity of your faith, which provided us with such great joy that we can more easily possess it than we can express it. For I must admit to Your Charity that we were very sad when rumor spread it about that you sided with the enemies of the grace of Christ. But in order that this sadness might be wiped from our hearts, first of all, that same rumor was not silent about the fact that you first declared them anathema in a large crowd of people; secondly, along with the letter of the Apostolic See sent to Africa concerning their condemnation,[1] your letter also was delivered to the primate, Aurelius. Although it was short, it sufficiently indicated the strength of your opposition to their error. But now in your letter the very faith of the Roman church states more openly and more at length what you hold about and in opposition to that teaching along with us. For it was especially to that church that the blessed apostle Paul said many things in many ways about *the grace of God through Jesus Christ our Lord* (Rom 7:25). Hence, not only has all that cloud of sadness fled from our hearts, but such a great light of joy has also flowed into them that that sadness and fear seem to have had no effect on us apart from increasing the flame of the joys that were to follow.

2. And so, my dearest brother, though we do not see you with the eyes of the flesh, yet with our spirit we hold you, embrace you, and kiss you with the heart in the faith of Christ, in the grace of Christ, and in the members of Christ. And I now reply to your letter as the most holy and reliable courier, whom you wanted to serve for us not merely as a carrier of your letter but also as someone to recount and to bear witness to your actions, goes back from us to you. And we converse with you at somewhat greater length, advising you to press on to teach those people whom you have, as we learned, begun to cause to have some fear. For there are certain people who think that they should still quite freely defend those impious teachings that have been justly condemned, and there are some who

---

1. That is, the *Tractoria* of Pope Zosimus, issued in the summer of 418. The work is no longer extant.

secretly enter homes[2] and do not cease to spread in secret what they are afraid to proclaim in the open. But there are some who are completely silent, over-whelmed by great fear, but who still hold in their heart what they do not dare now to utter with their lips. Yet they may be very well known to the brethren because of their previous defense of this teaching. Hence, some should be subjected to stronger means of coercion, others should be more carefully watched, and still others should be dealt with more gently, but they should be not taught in a half-hearted manner. For, if we do not fear that they may cause others to perish, we still should not neglect them lest they themselves perish.

2, 3. For, when they suppose that free choice is taken away if they agree that a human being cannot have a good will without the help of God, they do not under-stand that they do not strengthen human choice but inflate it with pride so that it is carried off amid vanities rather than set down upon the Lord as if upon solid rock. For *the will is prepared by the Lord* (Prv 8:35 LXX).

4. But when they think that they believe that God shows favoritism if they believe that without any preceding merits *he shows mercy to whom he wills* (Rom 9:18; 2 Thes 1:11), calls whom he wills, and makes devout whom he wills, they do not pay enough attention to the fact that the one condemned is given the punishment that was deserved, while the one set free is given grace that was not deserved. Hence, the former cannot complain that he did not deserve it, nor can the latter boast that he did deserve it. And there is no favoritism present where one and the same mass of condemnation and sin includes that the one set free learns from the one not set free what punishment would be appropriate for him if grace had not come to the rescue. But if it is grace, it is certainly not repay-ment for any merits but given out of gratuitous goodness.

5. "But it is unjust," they say, "that in one and the same situation the one is set free and the other is punished." It is just, therefore, that both be punished. Who would deny this? Let us, then, give thanks to the savior since we see in the condemnation of those like us that we have not received what we recognize that we also deserved. For, if both were set free, what was owed to sin through justice would certainly remain hidden; if no one were set free, what grace bestows would remain hidden. Instead, in this most difficult question we use the words of the apostle, *Wanting to display his anger and to demonstrate his power, God endured with much patience the vessels of anger that were made for destruction and in order to make known the riches of his glory toward the vessels of mercy* (Rom 9:22-23). The clay pot cannot say to him, *Why have you made me so?* since he has *the power to make from the same lump of clay one vessel for honor and another for dishonor* (Rom 9:20-21). And because this whole lump has

---

2. See 2 Tm 3:6.

deservedly been condemned, justice gives the dishonor that was deserved and grace gives the honor that was not deserved, not because of a title to merits, not because of the necessity of fate, not because of the fickleness of fortune, but because of *the depth of the riches of the wisdom and knowledge of God* (Rom 11:33). The apostle does not explain this but stands in awe at its hiddenness when he cries out, *O the depth of the riches of the wisdom and knowledge of God! How inscrutable are his judgments and unsearchable his ways! For who has known the mind of the Lord? Or who has been his counselor? Or who first gave to him and will be repaid? For from him and through him and in him are all things; to him be glory for age upon age! Amen.* (Rom 11:33-36)

3, 6. But they do not want him to receive glory for justifying sinners by gratu-itous grace since, not knowing his righteousness, they want to establish their own.[3] Or, when they are pressured by the outcries of religious and pious people who protest, they admit that they are helped by God to have or to produce righ-teousness in such a way that some merit of theirs comes first, as if they wanted first to give in order to be paid back by him of whom scripture says, *Who first gave to him and will be repaid by him?* (Rom 11:35) And they believe that their own merits anticipate him of whom they hear, or rather refuse to hear, *For from him and through him and in him are all things* (Rom 11:36). From the depth of the riches of his wisdom and knowledge[4] there pour forth the riches of his glory toward the vessels of mercy, which he calls to be his adopted children.[5] He wants to make known these riches even through the vessels of anger, which were made for destruction. And what are his unsearchable ways but those of which the psalm sings, *All the ways of the Lord are mercy and truth* (Ps 25:10)? And so, his mercy and truth are unsearchable, because *he shows mercy to whom he wills*, not out of justice but out of the grace of mercy, and *he hardens whom he wills* (Rom 9:18), not out of injustice, but out of the truth of punishment. Yet, because it says in scripture, *Mercy and truth have met each other* (Ps 85:11), this mercy and truth meet in such a way that mercy does not impede the truth by which one who deserves it is punished, nor does the truth impede the mercy by which one who does not deserve it is set free. Of what merits of his own is the one set free going to boast? For, if his merits received their due recompense, he would only be condemned. Are there, then, no merits of the righteous? Clearly there are because they are righteous. But they had no merits in order to become righteous. For they were made righteous when they were justified. But, as the apostle says, *They were justified gratuitously by his grace* (Rom 3:24).

---

3. See Rom 10:3.
4. See Rom 11:33.
5. See Rom 9:22-23.

7. Though these people, then, are bitter enemies of this grace, yet Pelagius anathematized in the Palestinian court those who say that the grace of God is given in accord with merits, for otherwise he would not have left that court without punishment.[6] But nothing else is found even in their later arguments than that this grace is given in accord with merits, the grace that the apostle's Letter to the Romans especially commends in order that its proclamation might spread out to the whole world from there as if from the capital of the world. For this is the grace by which the sinner is justified, that is, by which someone who was first a sinner is made righteous. And no merits precede the reception of this grace because to the merits of a sinner there is due not grace but punishment. Nor would this grace be grace if it were not given gratuitously but as a recompense that was owed.

8. But when these people are asked what grace Pelagius thought was given without any preceding merits when he condemned those who say that the grace of God is given in accord with our merits, they reply that the grace without any preceding merits is the human nature in which we are created. For, before we existed, we could not merit to be anything. This fallacy should be banished from the hearts of Christians. The apostle certainly does not refer to the grace by which we were created so that we might be human beings. For this is *the grace through Jesus Christ our Lord.* For Christ did not die for human beings in order that they might be created but for sinful human beings in order that they might be justified. The man, of course, already existed who said. *Wretched man that I am! Who will set me free from the body of this death? The grace of God through Jesus Christ our Lord.* (Rom 7:24-25)

9. They can surely say that the forgiveness of sins is a grace that is not given because of any preceding merits. For what good merit can sinners have? But not even the forgiveness of sins is without any merit if faith wins it. Nor does faith lack all merit, for with faith that man said, *O God, be merciful to me, a sinner,* and *he returned justified* (Lk 18:13-14) by the merit of his faithful humility, *because one who humbles himself will be exalted* (Lk 14:11; Mt 23:12). It remains, then, that the very faith from which all righteousness takes its beginning, because of which it is said to the Church in the Song of Songs, *You will come and pass from the beginning of faith* (Sg 4:8 LXX)—it remains, I repeat, that we not attribute faith itself to human choice, which they extol, or to any preceding merits, because any good merits there are begin from faith, but rather that we admit that it is a gratuitous gift of God, if we have in mind true grace, that is, without any merits. For, as we read in the same letter, *God imparts to each a measure of faith* (Rom 12:3). Good works are, to be sure, produced by a human

---

6. That is, at the Council of Diospolis held in December of 415. See *The Deeds of Pelagius* for Augustine's account and interpretation of that council, which found Pelagius innocent.

being, but faith is produced in a human being, and without it no good works are produced by any human being. For *whatever does not come from faith is sin* (Rom 14:23).

10. Hence, in order that a man at prayer might not extol himself or the merit of his prayer, even if help is given to him as he prays in order to conquer the desires for temporal goods and in order to love eternal goods and God, the source of all good things, the faith prays that was given to him when he did not pray, and unless it had been given, he could not pray. For *how will they call upon him in whom they have not believed? Or how will they believe in him of whom they have not heard? How will they hear without someone to preach? And so, faith comes from hearing, and hearing come through the word of Christ.* (Rom 10:14,17) Hence the minister of Christ, the preacher of this faith, plants and waters in accord with the grace that was given him.[7] And yet *neither the one who plants nor the one who waters is anything, but only God who gives the increase* (1 Cor 3:7,6), God *who imparts to each a measure of faith* (Rom 12:3). For this reason it is said elsewhere, *Peace to the brothers and love along with faith* and, in order that they would not attribute this to themselves, he immediately added, *from God the Father and our Lord Jesus Christ* (Eph 6:23). For not all who hear the word have the faith, but only those to whom God imparts a measure of faith, just as not every seed that is planted and watered sprouts but only that seed to which God gives the increase. But why one person believes and another does not, when they both hear the same word and when, if a miracle occurs before their eyes, they both see it, pertains to *the depth of the riches of the wisdom and knowledge of God* (Rom 11:33), whose *judgments are inscrutable* (Rom 9:14), and in whom there is no injustice when *he shows mercy to whom he wills and hardens whom he wills* (Rom 9:18). Nor are these judgments unjust because they are hidden.

11. Then, after the forgiveness of sins, unless the Holy Spirit has a house that has been cleansed, will not the unclean spirit return with seven others *and the last condition of that man be worse than the first* (Mt 12:45)? But in order that the Holy Spirit might dwell there, does he not breathe where he wills?[8] And is not the love of God, without which no one lives a good life, *poured out in our hearts* not by us but *through the Holy Spirit who has been given to us* (Rom 5:5)? The apostle described this faith when he said, *Neither circumcision nor the lack of circumcision counts for anything, but the faith that works through love* (Gal 5:6). This indeed is the faith of Christians, not of demons, for even *the demons believe and tremble* (Jas 2:19). But do they also have love? After all, if they did not believe, they would not say, *You are God's Holy One* (Lk 4:41), or, *You are the*

---

7. See Rom 15:16.15; 1 Cor 3:5-6; Rom 12:3.
8. See Jn 3:8.

Son of God (Mk 3:11). But if they had love, they would not say, *What do we have to do with you?* (Mt 8:29)

12. Faith, then, draws us to Christ, and unless it were given to us from above as a gratuitous gift, he would not say, *No one can come to me unless the Father, who sent me, draws him* (Jn 6:44). For this reason he also says a little later, *The words that I have spoken to you are spirit and life. But there are some among you who do not believe.* Then the evangelist adds, *For Jesus knew from the beginning who was going to believe and who was going to betray him* (Jn 6:64-65). And so that no one would suppose that those who believe come under his foreknowledge in the same way as those who do not believe, that is, not insofar as faith is given them from above, but only insofar as their future will is foreknown, he immediately goes on to say, *And he said, For this reason I told you that no one can come to me unless it has been given to him by my Father* (Jn 6:66). This is why some of those who heard him speaking of his flesh and blood went away scandalized, but some remained because they believed, because no one can come to him unless it has been given to him by the Father and, hence, by the Son and by the Holy Spirit. For the gifts and works of the inseparable Trinity are not separate. But, in honoring the Father in that way, the Son does not introduce a proof of any distance between them but offers a great example of humility.

13. Here again, what else are these defenders of free choice—or rather these deceivers of it because they inflate it with pride, and they inflate it with pride because they put their trust in it—going to say, not against us but against the gospel? What else are they going to say but what the apostle said as an objection to himself, as if such people said it? *And so you say to me: Why does he still blame us? For who resists his will?* (Rom 9:19) He raised this objection for himself as if coming from someone else, as if coming from the mouth of those who refused to accept what he had said previously, *And so, he shows mercy to whom he wills and he hardens whom he wills* (Rom 9:18). To such people, then, let us say with the apostle, for we cannot find anything to say better than: *Who are you, a human being, to answer back to God?* (Rom 9:20)

14. We look for what merits this hardening, and we find it. For the whole mass was condemned as punishment for sin, and God does not harden by imparting malice but by not imparting mercy. For those to whom he does not impart it do not deserve it, nor do they merit it. Rather, they deserve and merit that he not impart mercy. This is what they deserve; this is what they merit. But we look for what merits mercy, and we do not find it, because there is nothing. Otherwise, grace is done away with if it is not given gratuitously but as recompense for merits.[9]

---

9. See Rom 11:6.

15. For if we say that faith, by which one would merit grace, came first, what merit did a human being have before faith in order to receive faith? For what did he have that he did not receive? But if he received, why does he boast as if he had not received?[10] For, just as a human being would not have wisdom, understanding, counsel, fortitude, knowledge, piety, and fear of the Lord if he had not, in accord with the words of the prophet, received the Spirit *of wisdom and understanding, of counsel and fortitude, of knowledge, piety, and fear of the Lord* (Is 11:2-3), neither would he have courage, love, and continence if he had not received the Holy Spirit, of whom the apostle says, *You have not received a spirit of fear, but of courage, love, and continence* (2 Tm 1:7). So too, he would not have faith if he had not received the Spirit of faith, of which the same apostle says, *But having the same Spirit of faith in accord with what scripture says: I believed, and for this reason I spoke, we also believe and for this reason we speak* (2 Cor 4:13; Ps 116:10). But he shows most clearly that he did not receive faith by merit but by the mercy of him who *shows mercy to whom he wills* (Rom 9:18), when he says of himself, *I obtained mercy in order that I might be a believer* (1 Cor 7:25).

4, 16. If we say that the merit of prayer comes first in order to obtain the gift of grace, prayer shows by its very petitions that whatever it obtains by petition is a gift of God, lest a human being think that it comes from himself. For, if it were within his own power, he would certainly not ask for it. But so that it would not be thought that at least the merits of prayer come first and that grace is given to those merits not as gratuitous (and then it would not be grace since it would be paid as something owed) even prayer is found among the gifts of grace. The teacher of the nations[11] says, *We do not know what we should pray for in the proper manner, but the Spirit himself pleads for us with indescribable groans* (Rom 8:26). But what does *pleads* mean but "makes us plead"? For to plead with groans is a most certain sign of someone in need. But it is not right to believe that the Holy Spirit is in need of anything. Rather, it was said that he pleads because he makes us plead and inspires us with the desire to plead and to groan. In the same sense it was said in the gospel, *For it is not you who speak, but the Spirit of your Father who speaks in you* (Mt 10:20). For this does not come about in our regard while we, so to speak, do nothing. The help of the Holy Spirit is described in such a way, therefore, that he is said to do what he makes us do.

17. For the apostle himself shows clearly enough that we should not understand our spirit to be the one of which it was said that he *pleads for us with indescribable groans* but the Holy Spirit who helps our weakness. For he began in this way: *The Spirit,* he said, *helps our weakness,* and then he added as follows:

---

10. See 1 Cor 4:7.
11. See 1 Tm 2:7.

For we do not know what we should pray for in the proper manner (Rom 8:26), and so on. Elsewhere he says more clearly about this Spirit, *For you have not received the spirit of slavery once again in fear, but you have received the Spirit of adoption as children in whom we cry out, Abba, Father* (Rom 8:15). See, he does not say here that the Spirit himself cries out in praying but, *in whom we cry out, Abba, Father.* In another passage, nonetheless, he says, *Because you are children of God, God has sent the Spirit of his Son into your hearts crying out, Abba, Father* (Gal 4:6). Here he did not say, *in whom we cry out,* but preferred to say that the Spirit himself cries out who makes us cry out. In the same way we should understand the words, *The Spirit pleads for us with indescribable groans* (Rom 8:26), and, *It is the Spirit of your Father who speaks in you* (Mt 10:20).

18. Just as no one, then, is truly wise, truly understanding, truly endowed with counsel and fortitude, just as no one is knowledgeably pious or piously knowledgeable, just as one fears God with a chaste fear, unless he has received the Spirit *of wisdom and understanding, of counsel and fortitude, of knowledge, piety, and fear of the Lord* (Is 11:2-3), so no one has any true courage, sincere love, or religious continence except through *the Spirit of courage, love, and continence* (2 Tm 1:7). And in the same way no one is truly going to believe anything without the Spirit of faith or to pray in a salutary manner without the Spirit of prayer. It is not that there are so many spirits, *but one and the same Spirit produces all these things, distributing the appropriate gifts to each one, as he wills* (1 Cor 12:11), because *the Spirit breathes where he wills* (Jn 3:8). But we must confess that he helps in one way before he dwells in a person and in another way when he dwells in a person. For, when he does not yet dwell in a person, he helps him to become a believer, and when he dwells in a person, he helps a person who is already a believer.

5, 19. What merit, then, does a human being have before grace so that by that merit he may receive grace, since only grace produces in us every good merit of ours and since, when God crowns our merits, he only crowns his own gifts? For, just as we have obtained mercy from the very beginning of faith, not because we were believers but in order that we might be believers, so in the end, when there will be eternal life, he will crown us, as scripture says, *in compassion and mercy* (Ps 103:4). It is not in vain, therefore, that we sing to God, *And his mercy will come before me* (Ps 59:11), and, *His mercy will follow after me* (Ps 23:6). For this reason even eternal life itself, which we shall certainly have in the end without end, is given as recompense for preceding merits, but because the same merits to which it is given as recompense were not produced by us through our own abilities but were produced in us through grace, it too is called grace for no other reason than that it is given gratuitously, not because it is not given to our merits but because even the very merits to which it is given were given to us. But in the place where we find that eternal life is also called grace, we have in the same magnificent defender of grace, the apostle Paul, the words, *The wages of sin is death, but the grace of God is eternal life in Christ Jesus our Lord* (Rom 6:23).

20. See, I beg you, the great brevity with which he vigilantly sets down his words, and, if they are examined carefully, the obscurity of this question is somewhat cleared up. For, when he said, *The wages of sin is death*, who would not judge that he would go on most properly and logically if he said, "But the wages of righteousness is eternal life, and it is true that, just as death is paid as wages to the merit of sin, so eternal life is paid as wages to the merit of righteousness." Or, if he did not want to say, "of righteousness," he would say, "of faith," because *the righteous person lives from faith* (Rom 1:17; Gal 3:11; Heb 10:38; Hb 2:4). For this reason it is also called a recompense in many passages of the sacred scriptures, but righteousness or faith is never called a recompense, because a recompense is given to righteousness or faith. But what a recompense is for a worker, wages are for a soldier.

21. But pride tries so much to come upon great persons unawares that the blessed apostle said that an angel of Satan was given to him to strike him lest he raise up his head in presumption.[12] Against this plague of pride, then, he fought most vigilantly, saying, *The wages of sin is death* (Rom 6:23). It is correctly called *wages* because it is owed, because it is deservedly given, because it is recompense for merit. Then, lest righteosness extol itself over human good merit, just as human bad merit is undoubtedly sin, he did not say by way of contrast, "The wages of righteousness is eternal life," but, *The grace of God is eternal life*. And so that we would seek no other way apart from the mediator, he added, *in Christ Jesus our Lord* (Rom 6:23), as if to say, "Having heard that the wages of sin is death, why do you try to extol yourself, O human pride—not righteousness, but clearly pride under the name of righteousness? Why do you try to extol yourself and demand eternal life, the very opposite of death, as if it were the wages you deserved? It is true righteousness to which eternal life is owed. But if it is true righteousness, it does not come from you, but *it is from above, coming down from the Father of lights* (Jas 1:17). In order to have it, if in fact you have it, you have certainly received; *for what* good *do you have that you have not received?* (1 Cor 4:7) Hence, if you, a human being, are going to receive eternal life, it is the wages of righteousness, but it is grace for you, since righteousness itself is grace for you. For it would be given to you as a recompense owed to you, if you had from yourself the righteousness to which it is owed. But now *we have received from his fullness* not only the grace by which we are now living righteously in the midst of our labors up to the end but also *grace in return for this grace* (Jn 1:16) , so that we might afterward live in rest without end." Faith

---

12. See 2 Cor 12:7.

believes nothing more salutary than this, because the intellect finds nothing truer, and we should listen to the prophet as he says, *Unless you believe, you will not understand* (Is 7:9 LXX).

6, 22. "But," he says, "human beings excused themselves who did not want to live a good and faithful life, saying: 'What did we do who are living a bad life since we did not receive the grace by which we might live a good life?'" They cannot truthfully say that they do no evil because they live a bad life. For, if they do no evil, they are living a good life. But if they are living a bad life, they live a bad life because of their own sin—either that which they contracted from their origin or that which they added to it. But if they are *vessels of anger that were made for destruction* (Rom 9:22), which is given them as their recompense, they should ascribe this to themselves, because they were made from that lump of clay[13] which God rightly and justly condemned on account of the one sin in which all sinned.[14] But if they are *vessels of mercy* (Rom 9:23) made from that same lump, to whom he chose not to give the punishment due to them, they should not puff themselves up but glorify him who showed them the mercy they did not deserve, and if they think otherwise, he will perhaps reveal this to them as well.[15]

23. Finally, how will these people excuse themselves? They will undoubtedly do so by that brief question which the apostle raised for himself as an objection, as if coming from their lips, so that they say, *Why does he still blame us? For who can resist his will?* (Rom 9:19) For this is to say, "Why is there a complaint about us because we offend God by living bad lives, since no one can resist the will of him who hardened our hearts by not showing us mercy?" If, then, they are not ashamed to contradict not us but the apostle with this excuse, why should we be ashamed to say the very same thing that the apostle said, *Who are you, a human being, to answer back to God? Does the clay pot say to the potter: Why did you make me so? Does not the potter of the clay have power to make from the same lump*, which was, of course, justly and deservedly condemned, *one vessel for honor*, which it did not deserve, on account of gratuitous mercy, *and another vessel for dishonor*, which it deserved, on account of righteous anger, *and in order to make known the riches of his glory toward the vessels of mercy* (Rom 9:20-21,23)? In that way he shows what he gives to these latter when the vessels of anger receive the punishment that all equally deserved. For the time being it is enough for a Christian, who is still living by faith and does not yet see what is perfect but knows only in part, to know or to believe that God sets no one free except out of gratuitous mercy through our Lord Jesus Christ and condemns no one except in accordance with the most just truth through the same

---

13. See Rom 9:21.
14. See Rom 5:12.
15. See Phil 3:15.

Lord of ours, Jesus Christ.[16] But as to why he sets free or does not set free one person rather than another, let him who is able search out the great depth of his judgments, but let him beware of falling off the cliff.[17] For *is there injustice in God? Heaven forbid!* (Rom 9:12) But *his judgments are inscrutable, and his ways unsearchable* (Rom 11:33).

24. On the other hand, it can with reason be said of those of an adult age: These people refused to understand in order that they might do good.[18] And, what is worse, these others understood and did not obey because, as scripture says, *A stubborn servant will not be corrected by words. For, even if he understands, he will not obey.* (Prv 29:19 LXX) Why will he not obey except because of his most evil will? And he deserves a more severe condemnation from God's justice. For more will be demanded of one to whom more is given.[19] Scripture, of course, says that they are without excuse who are not ignorant of the truth, and in them wickedness persists. *For the anger of God is being revealed from heaven,* the apostle says, *against all the impiety and injustice of those human beings who hold the truth in their iniquity, since what is known about God is obvious to them. For God has shown it to them. For from the creation of the world the invisible reality of God is seen, having been understood through those things that have been made, even his everlasting power and divinity, so that they are without excuse.* (Rom 1:18-20)

25. The apostle says that they are without excuse who were able to see his invisible reality, which had been understood through the things that have been made, and who still did not obey the truth but remained unjust and sinful. For they did not lack knowledge, but *knowing God,* he says, *they did not glorify him as God or give him thanks* (Rom 1:21). How much more, then, are they without excuse who, instructed by his law, presume to be leaders of the blind and, though teaching others, do not teach themselves, who preach that one should not steal, and they steal, and all the other things of which the apostle speaks! To them he says, indeed, *For this reason you are inexcusable, every one of you who judge. After all, in judging another you condemn yourself. For you do the same acts that you condemn.* (Rom 2:1)

26. The Lord himself also says in the gospel, *If I had not come and spoken to them, they would have no sin. But now they do not have an excuse for their sin.* (Jn 15:22) He certainly did not mean that those people would have no sin who were filled with many other and great sins. Rather, he meant that, if he had not come, they would not have had the sin of not believing in him when they heard him. He says that they do not have an excuse to say, "We did not hear him, and

---

16. See Rom 1:17; Gal 3:11; Heb 10:38; Hab 2:4.
17. See 1 Cor 13:9.10.12; Rom 9:14.
18. See Ps 36:4.
19. See Lk 12:47-48.

for that reason we did not believe in him." Human pride, of course, as if presuming upon the strength of free choice, thinks that it has an excuse when the fact that it sins seems to be due to ignorance and not to the will.

27. In terms of this excuse the divine scripture says that they are all without excuse whom it proves guilty of sinning knowingly. And yet the just judgment of God does not spare those either who did not hear him, *For whoever have sinned without the law will perish without the law* (Rom 2:12). And although they think that they have an excuse, he does not accept this excuse who knows that he made man righteous[20] and gave him the command to obey and that the sin which was also passed on to his descendants stemmed only from the choice of his will, which he used wrongly. For those who have not sinned are not condemned, since that sin was passed on to all from the one in whom all sinned in common prior to any personal sins in their individual lives.[21] And for this reason every sinner is without excuse either because of the guilt of origin or because of what is added by one's own will, whether or not one has knowledge, whether or not one judges.[22] For ignorance itself in those who refuse to understand is undoubtedly a sin, but in those who could not understand it is the punishment of sin. In neither, then, is there a just excuse but only just condemnation.

28. For this reason the words of God declare that they are without excuse who sin not in ignorance but with knowledge; thus they may see that they are without excuse in terms of the condemnation of the pride by which they presume too much upon the strength of their own will. For they do not have an excuse because of their ignorance, and they do not as yet have the righteousness for which they were presuming that their own will was sufficient. But that man to whom the Lord gave the grace of both knowing and obeying said, *Knowledge of sin came through the law* (Rom 3:20), and, *I knew sin only through the law, for I would not have known concupiscence if the law had not said: You shall not desire* (Rom 7:7; Ex 20:17; Dt 5:21; 7:25). Nor does he want us to understand someone ignorant of the law with its commands but lacking the deliverance of grace when he says, *I take delight in the law of God in accord with my inner self* (Rom 7:22). And not only with this knowledge of the law but also with delight in it he afterward says, *Wretched man that I am! Who will set me free from the body of this death? The grace of God through Jesus Christ our Lord!* (Rom 7:24-25) No one, therefore, sets anyone free from the wounds of that butcher except the grace of the one savior. No one sets free those sold into subjection to sin from the chains of the jailer except the grace of the redeemer.

29. And for this reason all who want themselves to be excused for wickedness and sinfulness are punished with full justice because those who are set free are

---

20. See Eccl 7:30.
21. See Rom 5:12.
22. See Rom 2:1.

set free only by grace. For, if their excuse were just, it would not be grace but justice that set them free from punishment. But since only grace sets one free, it finds nothing righteous in the one it sets free: no will, no action, not even an excuse. For, if this excuse were just, whoever uses it would be set free by merit, not by grace. For we know that certain people are set free by the grace of Christ, even from among those who say, *Why does he still complain? For who can resist his will?* (Rom 9:19) If this excuse is just, then grace is no longer gratuitous, but they are set free on account of the justice of this excuse. But if it is grace by which they are set free, this excuse is by no means just. For it is true grace by which one is set free when one does not receive this as a debt of justice. Nothing else, then, happens in those who say, *Why does he still complain? For who can resist his will?* but what we read in the book of Solomon, *The stupidity of a man corrupts his ways, but in his heart he makes God his excuse* (Prv 18:22).

30. God, therefore, makes *the vessels of anger for destruction* in order to show his anger and to demonstrate his power, by which he makes good use even of evil, and *in order to make known the riches of his glory toward the vessels of mercy* (Rom 9:21-23), which he makes for an honor not owed to the mass that deserves damnation but given by the generosity of his grace. And yet in those same vessels of anger made for dishonor, which they deserved on account of what the mass merited, that is, in human beings created on account of the good-ness of their nature but destined for punishment on account of their sins, God himself could condemn but not produce the sinfulness that the truth blames with full justice.[23] For, just as human nature, which is undoubtedly worthy of praise, is attributed to his will, so sin, which deserves condemnation without anyone's objecting to this, is attributed to the will of the man. This will of the man either passed on hereditary sin to his descendants, whom he contained in himself when he sinned, or in addition it acquired other sins when each human being lived wickedly in his own life. But neither from the sin contracted from our origin nor from the sins that each person accumulates in his own life, whether by not under-standing or by refusing to understand, or that, after having also learned of the law, one increases by adding transgression, is anyone set free and justified except by *the grace of God through Jesus Christ our Lord* (Rom 7:25). One is set free not merely by the forgiveness of sins but also, first, by the infusion of faith and fear of God and by the salutary gift of love for prayer and its practice, until God heals all our illness, redeems our life from corruption, and crowns us in compassion and mercy.[24]

7, 31. But the people who think that God shows partiality,[25] if in one and the same situation his mercy descends upon some while his anger remains over

---

23. See Ps 45:8; Heb 1:9.
24. See Ps 103:3-4.
25. See Acts 10:34.

others, lose all the force of their human arguments when it comes to infants. For I want to pass over for the moment the punishment that includes even the infants, however recently born from their mothers' wombs, of which the apostle says, *Through the sin of the one all human beings entered into condemnation*, a condemnation from which only he sets us free of whom the same apostle says, *Through the righteousness of one all human beings come to the righteousness of life* (Rom 5:18). I will pass over this for the moment, then, and will say only that, frightened by the authority of the gospel or rather crushed by the completely unanimous agreement of the Christian peoples in the faith, the Pelagians also concede without the least opposition that no infant enters the kingdom of the heaven without having been reborn of water and the Spirit.[26] What reason, I ask, will they give as to why one is cared for so that it leaves this life after being baptized, while another expires after being entrusted to the hands of non-believers or even of believers before being presented by them for baptism? Are they going to ascribe this to fate or to fortune? I do not think that they will plunge into such great madness if they want to hold onto the name of Christians to some slight degree.

32. Why, then, will no infant enter the kingdom of the heavens without having received the bath of rebirth?[27] Has an infant chosen for himself non-believing or negligent parents to be born from? What shall I say of the countless unexpected and sudden deaths by which the infants of even pious Christians are overtaken and snatched away from baptism, while, on the other hand, the children of sacrilegious folks and enemies of Christ somehow come into the hands of Christians and leave this world with the sacrament of rebirth? What will those people say at this point who maintain that some human merits come first in order that grace may be given lest God show favoritism?[28] What merits, finally, came first in this case? If you have in mind the merits of the same infants, they have none of their own, and both in common belong to that mass of condemnation. If you look to the merits of the parents, those whose children perished by sudden deaths without Christ's baptism had good merits, while those whose children came to the sacraments of the Church though the intervention of Christians had evil merits. And yet the providence of God, for whom the hairs of our head are numbered and without whose will not even a sparrow falls to the earth,[29] is not subject to fate, nor is it impeded by chance events or defiled by any injustice. Yet his providence does not take care of all the infants of his own children so that they may be reborn for the heavenly kingdom but does take care of the infants of some unbelievers. This infant, born of believing parents

---

26. See Jn 3:5.
27. See Ti 3:5.
28. See Acts 10:34.
29. See Mt 10:30.29.

and welcomed with the joy of parents, suffocated by the sleepiness of its mother or nurse, becomes a stranger to and is excluded from the faith of his parents; that infant is born of wicked adultery, exposed by the cruel fear of its mother, taken up by the merciful goodness of strangers, baptized out of their Christian concern, and becomes a member and partaker of the eternal kingdom. Let them think of these examples; let them ponder them; let them dare at this point to say that God either shows favoritism with his grace or rewards preceding merits.

33. For, though they try to find some merits, either good or bad, at a later age, what will they say about these infants, since one of them could not merit the violence of suffocation for any evil merits of its own and the other could not merit the care of the one who baptized it? They are filled with excessive folly and blindness if, after considering these examples, they still do not agree to cry out with us, *O the depth of the riches of the wisdom and knowledge of God! How inscrutable are his judgments and unsearchable his ways!* (Rom 11:33) Let them not, then, oppose the gratuitous mercy of God with a most stubborn insanity. Let them allow the Son of Man *to seek and save* at any age *what was lost* (Lk 19:10; Mt 18:11). And let them not dare to judge about his inscrutable judgments why in one and the same situation his mercy descends upon one and his anger remains over another.

8, 34. For who are these people that they should answer back to God?[30] For Rebekah was carrying twins from a single union with Isaac, our father. Though, when they were not yet born, they had not done anything good or bad, in order that the plan of God might remain in accord with his choice, a choice based on grace, not on a debt, a choice by which he made, not found, those worthy of being chosen not because of their works but because of God's call, he said that the older would serve the younger.[31] The blessed apostle also used in support of this statement the testimony of a much later prophet, *I loved Jacob, but I hated Esau* (Rom 9:13; Mal 1:2-3), in order that what was present in the predestination of God through grace before they were born might be understood clearly afterward through the prophet. For what did he love in Jacob before he was born and had done anything good or bad but the gratuitous gift of his own mercy? And what did he hate in Esau before he was born and had done anything bad but original sin? For in the former he would not love righteousness that he had not made, nor would he hate in the latter the nature that he made good.

35. But it is surprising to see the steep cliffs they hurl themselves over when they are trapped by these difficulties and fear the nets of the truth. They say, "He hated one and loved the other of those not yet born because he foresaw their future works." Who would not be surprised that the apostle lacked this very clever idea? He certainly did not see this when, as if the question were raised as

---

30. See Rom 9:20.
31. See Rom 9:10-12; Gn 25:21-23.

an objection for him by an opponent, he did not instead give this reply that is so short, so clear, and—as they suppose—so absolutely true. For, when he proposed an awesome question, namely, how it could be correctly said of those who were not yet born and had not done anything either good or bad that God loved the one and hated the other, after having posed the question for himself and expressed the concern of his hearer with the words, *What then shall we say?* He replied, *Is there injustice in God? Heaven forbid!* (Rom 9:14) This, then, was the place for him to say what these people think, "For God foresaw their future works when he said that the older would serve the younger." Yet the apostle did not say this but rather, so that no one would be able to boast of the merits of his own works, he wanted what he said to be able to emphasize the grace and glory of God. For, when he said, "*Heaven forbid* that there should be *injustice in God*," it was as if we said to him, "How do you explain this since you say that it is not because of works but because of God's call that it was said, *The older will serve the younger?*" (Rom 9:11-12; Gn 25:23) The apostle said that God *said to Moses: I will show pity to whom I will show pity, and I will be merciful to whom I will be merciful. Therefore, it does not depend on the one who wills or the one who runs, but upon God who shows mercy* (Rom 9:15-16; Ex 33:19). Where now are the merits, where are the works either past or future, carried out or to be carried out, by the strength of free choice? Did not the apostle make a clear statement of his endorsement of gratuitous grace, that is, of true grace? *Has not God made foolish the wisdom* (1 Cor 1:20) of the heretics?

36. But what was at issue that the apostle should say this when he mentioned the example of the twins? What was he trying to persuade them of? What did he want to teach? It was what their madness opposed, what the proud do not grasp, what they refuse to believe who, *not knowing the righteousness of God and wanting to establish their own righteousness, are not subject to the righteousness of God* (Rom 10:4). The apostle was, of course, concerned with grace, and for this reason he mentioned the children of the promise. For only God does what God promises, for it is reasonable and true that a human being makes a promise and God carries it out, but it is a sign of proud impiety and a wicked idea that a human being should say that he does what God promises.

37. Emphasizing the children of the promise, then, he showed that this was first symbolized by Isaac, the son of Abraham. For the work of God is seen more clearly in him who was born contrary to the usual order of nature from a sterile womb worn out with old age so that, in the children of God who were foretold to be coming, this would be a sign of the work of God, not of human beings. *From Isaac*, he says, *your descendants will take their name. That is, it is not children of the flesh who are children of God; but the children of the promise will be counted as offspring. For this is the word of the promise: At that time I shall come, and Sarah will have a son. And not only that, but Rebecca also conceived*

twins from one union with Isaac, our father. (Rom 9:7-10) What did it mean that he added *from one union* except to prevent Jacob from boasting not only of his own merits or of the merits of other ancestors but even of the will of that one father, which was perhaps changed for the better? It meant to prevent him from saying that the creator loved him because, when his father begot him, he was more praiseworthy for his better conduct. He said *from one union* because their father had at that point the same merit in fathering them and their mother had the same merit in conceiving them. For, even if their mother carried them enclosed in her womb until she gave birth to them and perhaps changed in her desire and loves, she of course changed not regarding one but regarding both, whom she bore equally in her womb.

38. We must, then, look to the intention of the apostle to see how, in order to emphasize grace, he did not want the one of whom it was said, *I loved Jacob* (Mal 1:2), to boast except in the Lord. For, before they did anything good or bad, God loves the one and hates the other, though they were from the same father, from the same mother, and from the same union. In that way Jacob could understand that only by grace could he have been set apart from that mass of original sinfulness when he sees that his brother, with whom he shared a common situation, merited to be condemned. He says, *When they were not yet born and had not done anything good or bad, in order that the plan of God might remain in accord with his choice, not because of works but because of God's call it was said to him: The older will serve the younger* (Rom 9:11-12; Gn 25:23).

39. In another passage the apostle shows most clearly that God's choice is made by grace without any preceding merits from works. He says, *In that way a remnant was saved also at that time according to a choice that was grace. But if it is by grace, it is no longer by works; otherwise, grace is no longer grace.* (Rom 11:5-6) In accord with this grace he also logically makes use of the testimony of the prophet; he says, *As scripture says, I loved Jacob, but I hated Esau,* and he immediately adds, *What then shall we say? Is there injustice in God? Heaven forbid!* But why should heaven forbid this? Is it on account of the future works of both of them that God foresaw? On the contrary; heaven forbid this as well! *For he said to Moses: I will show pity to whom I will show pity, and I will be merciful to whom I will be merciful. Therefore, it does not depend on the one who wills or the one who runs, but upon God who shows mercy.* (Rom 9:13-18; Mal 1:2-3; Ex 33:19; 9:16) And in order that in the vessels that were made for the destruction that was owed to the condemned mass the vessels that were made from the same mass for honor might recognize what the divine mercy has given them, he says, *For scripture said to Pharaoh: I have raised you up in order that I may reveal my power in you and in order that my name may be glorified in the whole world.* Finally, he concludes with regard to both, *Therefore, he shows mercy to whom he wills and he hardens whom he wills.* (Rom 9:13-18) He in whom there

is no injustice does this. He shows mercy, therefore, by a gratuitous gift, but he hardens by most just punishment.

40. But the unbelieving presumption of the proud and the damnable excuse of someone punished may still say, *Why does he still blame us? For who resists his will?* Let him say this, and let them hear what answer is appropriate for such a human being, *Who are you, a human being, to answer back to God?* (Rom 9:19-20) and the rest that I have already discussed often enough to the extent that I could. Let him hear this and not scorn it. But if he does scorn it, let him realize that his heart has been hardened in order to scorn it. If, however, he does not scorn it, let him believe that he too has been helped in order not to scorn it—but hardened as he deserved and helped by grace.

9, 41. For, even if God foresaw the future works of the twin sons of the patriarch Isaac, for they both lived and reached old age, and for this reason loved Jacob but hated Esau—an idea whose great blindness we have already made clear—one cannot say that God foresees the works of infants who are going to die so that he may take care that one receives baptism and not take care of the other. For how can we call those works future works since there will not be any?

42. "But," they object, "God foresees in those whom he takes from this life how each one would live if he were going to live and for this reason he also causes to die without baptism one who he knows was going to live sinfully. And in that way he punishes in him evil works, not those he did but those he was going to do." If, then, God also punishes evil actions that were not done, let them first notice how false is their promise that infants who die without baptism will not enter into condemnation. For, if they were not baptized because they were going to live bad lives if they lived, they will undoubtedly be condemned on account of this bad life, if even those sins that were not going to be committed are condemned. Secondly, if God takes care that they receive the sacrament of baptism who he knows were going to live good lives if they lived, why does he not keep in this life all those who he knows will adorn it with good works? Why do some of those who are baptized also live long and very bad lives and at times even go as far as apostasy? If even sins that are not yet committed are justly punished, why did God not throw out of paradise beforehand that first pair of sinners, who he certainly knew were going to sin, in order that they might not commit in paradise a sin that was so inappropriate to so holy a place? Then, what does God give to one who is carried off *so that malice does not change his mind and so that deception does not mislead his soul* (Wis 4:11), if those sins are also punished that, though he did not commit them, he was nonetheless, going to commit if he continued to live? Finally, why does God not provide better for a person about to die, so that he might receive the bath of rebirth[32] if he was going

---

32. See Ti 3:5

to live a bad life if he lived? For in that way the sins he was going to commit would be forgiven in baptism. For who is so stupid as to deny that those sins can be forgiven in baptism that he says can be punished without baptism?

10, 43. But in arguing against those people who, though they have been completely refuted, try to persuade others that God punishes even sins that have not been committed, we have to fear that we may be thought to have made up these charges against them. They may in no way be believed so foolish as either to hold these views or to try to convince anyone of them. And yet, if I had not heard them say these things, I would not think that they had to be refuted. For they are bound by the authority of the divine scriptures and by the rite of the Church handed down from of old and held firmly in the baptism of infants. There it is most clearly shown that infants are set free from the dominion of the devil when they undergo exorcism and when they reply through those who present them that they renounce the devil. And since these heretics find nowhere to go, they continue on headlong into stupidity as long as they refuse to change their mind.

44. They certainly think that it is with great insight that they say, "How is sin passed on to the children of believers, since we have no doubt that it was forgiven in the parents through baptism?" They imply that carnal generation cannot have what only spiritual regeneration takes away or that in true baptism the weakness stemming from concupiscence of the flesh is immediately healed, just as its guilt is immediately abolished, but by the grace of being reborn, not by the condition of being born. Hence, if anyone is born through this concupiscence, even from someone reborn, it will undoubtedly harm him when he is born, unless he himself is likewise reborn. But whatever difficulty there is regarding this question, the workers in Christ's field are not kept from baptizing infants for the forgiveness of sins, whether they are born from believers or non-believers, just as farmers are not kept from turning wild olive trees into domesticated olive trees through the practice of grafting, whether they arise from wild olive trees or domesticated ones. For, if a farmer is asked why, though a domesticated olive tree is different from a wild olive tree, only a wild olive tree comes from the seed of both of them,[33] the farmer does not stop the work of grafting, even if he cannot answer the question. Otherwise, while thinking that the saplings sprung from the seed of the domesticated olive tree are domesticated olive trees, his stupid laziness causes that whole field to fill up with harsh barrenness.

45. Now when they were pressed by the weight of the truth, they thought up another idea. But *the Lord is faithful in his words* (Ps 145:13), and for this reason his Church in no way falsely baptizes infants for the forgiveness of sins, but, if the rite is performed with faith, there certainly takes place what the words say. What Christian, then, would not laugh at the idea they thought up when the most obvious weight of the truth was crushing them, no matter how clever he might find it? For

---

33. See Rom 11:24.

they say, "Infants in fact respond truthfully by the lips of those who present them that they believe in the forgiveness of sins, yet not because their sins are forgiven but because they believe that sins are forgiven in the Church or in baptism in those people in whom they are found, not in those who have none." And for this reason they deny that "infants are baptized for the forgiveness of sins in the sense that this forgiveness is produced in them, since they maintain that infants have no sin but that, though they are without sin, they are still baptized in that baptism by which the forgiveness of sins is produced in certain sinners."

46. It is certainly possible for this slippery sophism to be refuted with greater subtlety and cleverness at leisure. Given all their cunning they still do not find anything to say to the fact that infants undergo exorcism and exsufflation. For these rites are undoubtedly not carried out truthfully if the devil does not have dominion over them. If, however, he does have dominion over them and they truly undergo exorcism and exsufflation, how does he, who is of course the prince of sinners, have dominion over them except through sin? Hence, if they now blush with shame and do not dare to say that these rites are carried out in the Church as lies, they should admit that even in infants Christ seeks what had been lost. For only through sin had there been lost what can only be sought and can only be found through grace. But thanks be to God that, though they argue against the forgiveness of sins so that people will not believe that it takes place in infants, they at least still admit that infants already believe, though they do so through the hearts and the lips of adults. Just as, then, they hear the Lord who says, *Whoever is not reborn of water and of the Spirit will not enter the kingdom of heaven* (Jn 3:5), for which reason they grant that the infants must be baptized, so let them hear the same Lord when he says, *One who does not believe will be condemned* (Mk 16:16). For, just as they admit that they are reborn by the ministry of those who baptize them, so they admit that they also believe through the hearts and lips of those who make the responses. If, then, infants are not bound by any chain of original sin, let them dare to say that the just God will condemn them in their innocence.

47. If this letter is long and adds a burden to your work, pardon me, because I forcibly interrupted my work in order to write to you and discuss these topics with you, after your letter invited me to do so by the signs of your good will toward us. If you know of any other argument that they think up against the Catholic faith, and whatever you teach in opposition to them out of a faithful and clearly pastoral love so that they do not ravage the weak among the Lord's flock, inform us of this. The restlessness of the heretics certainly rouses us as if out of a lazy sleep to search the scriptures with great watchfulness in order to confront the heretics so that they do not harm the flock of Christ. In that way, by the manifold grace of the savior, God transforms what the enemy devises for our destruction into a help for us, *because for those who love God all things work together for the good* (Rom 5:28). My dearest brother, may you always live for God and be mindful of us.

Letter 195

Probably in 418 Jerome wrote from Bethlehem to Augustine in Hippo in order to congratulate him on his conquering the Pelagians and other heretics. On this account Catholics recognize Augustine, Jerome says, as the second founder of the faith, while all heretics depise him.

To Augustine, his holy lord and blessed bishop, Jerome sends greetings.

At no time have I failed to show reverence for Your Beatitude with all due honor, and I have loved the Lord, our savior, who dwells in you. But now, if it is possible, we add something to that and fill out what is already full so that we do not allow even one hour to pass without mention of your name. For you have stood firm with the ardor of faith against the blasts of the winds, and you have preferred, to the extent that it depended upon you, to be set free by yourself from Sodom rather than to dally with those who are perishing.[1] Your Wisdom knows what I mean. Well done! You are famous throughout the world. Catholics revere and embrace you as the second founder of the ancient faith. And, what is a sign of greater glory, all the heretics despise you, and they persecute me with like hatred in order to slay with their desire those whom they cannot slay with swords. May the mercy of Christ the Lord keep you safe and sound and mindful of me, my venerable lord and most blessed bishop.

---

1. See Gn 19:14.

Letter 196

At the end of 418 Augustine wrote to Asellicus, bishop of Tusuros in Byzacena, who had written to the primate of Byzacena, Donatian, with regard to a group of Christians who were living according to the Jewish law and called themselves Jews and Israelites. Donatian forwarded Asellicus' letter to Augustine and asked him to reply to him (paragraph 1). Augustine quotes Paul's Letter to the Galatians, in which he forbids Christians to live like Jews (paragraph 2) and explains that Christians do not observe the works of the law and holds that even the commandments, which Christians do observe, do not justify anyone apart from faith in Christ and without the grace of God (paragraph 3). For without the help of the Spirit the letter of the law spells death (paragraph 4). The benefit of the law lies in showing human beings to themselves so that they realize that they cannot fulfill the law without the help of grace (paragraph 5). We are not justified by the commandments of the law but by the gift of grace (paragraph 6). The Pelagian heretics who suppose that they can fulfill the law by their own strength are like those who Paul said wanted to establish their own righteousness and were not subject to the righteousness of God (paragraph 7). A true Christian, therefore, must not only refrain from living according to the Jewish law but must attribute any progress or success in obeying the commandments to the grace of God (paragraph 8).

Augustine turns to the question of whether a true Christian should be called a Jew or an Israelite and quotes Saint Paul at length on the distinction between a Jew according to the flesh and a Jew according to the spirit (paragraphs 9 and 10). Christians, then, are the true children of Abraham and Israel, not by carnal birth but by spiritual rebirth (paragraph 11). Ishmael symbolized the Jews according to the flesh, while Isaac symbolized the Jews according to the spirit (paragraph 12). So, too, Esau symbolized Israel according to the flesh, while Jacob symbolized Israel according to the spirit (paragraph 13).

Despite this spiritual meaning, Christians should not be called Jews in ordinary conversation (paragraph 14). Saint Paul clearly distinguished the Christians from the Jews, as Augustine shows from many passages (paragraph 15). Hence, when Aptus, about whom Asellicus had written to his primate, teaches Christians to live as Jews and carry out all the observances of the Jewish law, he is urging Christians to be Jews not spiritually and inwardly but carnally and outwardly (paragraph 16).

To his most blessed lord and fellow bishop, Asellicus, Augustine sends greetings in the Lord.

1, 1. The primate Donatian[1] was so good as to forward to me the letter that Your Holiness sent to that venerable man concerning the avoidance of Judaism,

---

1. Donatian was the bishop of Telepte and primate of the Province of Byzacena.

and by his highly insistent request he compelled me to answer it. Since I do not want to show him disrespect, I am replying as best I can with the help of the Lord. And I think that it is also pleasing to Your Charity that in writing to you I have not refused to obey the command of that man whom we both respect for his merits.

2. Paul the apostle teaches that Christians, especially those coming from the Gentiles, ought not to live like Jews when he says, *I said to Peter in the presence of all: If you, though you are a Jew, live like a Gentile and not like a Jew, why do you force the Gentiles to live like Jews?* And he went on to say, *We are Jews by birth and not sinners from the Gentiles. But knowing that a person is not justified by the works of the law but only through faith in Jesus Christ, we too have believed in Jesus Christ in order that we might be justified through faith in Christ and not because of the works of the law, for no flesh will be justified by the works of the law.* (Gal 2:14-16)

3. But it is not only the works of the law that are contained in the old sacraments and that are not now observed by Christians after the revelation of the New Testament, such as the circumcision of the foreskin, bodily rest on the Sabbath, abstinence from certain foods, the offering of animals in the sacrifices, the feasts of the new moon and unleavened bread, and other things of this sort, but not even the commandment that we read in the law, *You shall not desire* (Ex 20:17; Dt 5:21; 7:25), which no one doubts must apply to Christians, justifies anyone *except through faith in Jesus Christ* (Gal 2:16) and through the grace *of God through Jesus Christ our Lord* (Rom 7:25). The same apostle says, to be sure, *What then shall we say? That the law is sin? Heaven forbid! But I did not know sin except through the law. For I would not know concupiscence if the law had not said, You shall not desire. But given the opportunity, through the commandment sin produced in me every desire. For without the law sin was dead. But I was living at one time without the law. When, however, the commandment came, sin came back to life, but I died, and this commandment that was meant for life was found in my case to lead to death. For, given the opportunity, sin deceived me through the commandment and killed me through it. And so the law is holy, and the commandment is holy and just and good. Did that which is good therefore become death for me? Heaven forbid! But in order that sin might be seen as sin, it produced death for me through what is good in order that through the commandment sin might become sinful beyond all measure. For we know that the law is spiritual, but I am carnal, sold as a slave to sin. For I do not know what I do, for I do not do what I will, but I do that which I hate. But if I do what I do not will, I agree that the law is good.* (Rom 7:7-16)

4. And so we see in these words of the apostle that the law is not only not sin but is even holy, and *the commandment is holy and just and good* that says, *You shall not desire* (Ex 20:17). But sin deceives through what is good and kills

through it those who, since they are carnal, think that they can fulfill the spiritual law by their own strength. And for this reason they become not only sinners, as they would be even if they had not received the law, but also transgressors, as they would not have been if they had not received the law. Thus he says in another passage, *Where there is no law, there is also no transgression* (Rom 4:15). *The law*, therefore, *entered in*, as he testifies elsewhere, *in order that sin might abound. But where sin abounded, there grace was also superabundant.* (Rom 5:20)

2, 5. This, then, is the benefit of the law, namely, that it reveals us to ourselves in order that we may know our weakness and see how the prohibition increases carnal concupiscence rather than heals it. For what is forbidden is desired more intensely as long as we are forced to obey carnally what we are commanded spiritually. But it is not the law but grace that makes us spiritual so that we may fulfill the law. That is, it is not an order but a gift; it is not the letter that commands but the Spirit that helps. A human being begins to be renewed in his interior self in accord with grace[2] in order that he may do in his mind what he loves and may not consent to the flesh that does what he hates,[3] that is, not in order that he may have no desire at all but in order that he may not pursue his desires.[4] This is in fact so great a good that, if it were fully realized and if, even though sinful desires are present while we are *in the body of this death* (Rom 7:24), we still did not give our assent to any of them, there would be no reason why we should say to our Father, who is in heaven, *Forgive us our debts* (Mt 6:12 and Lk 11:4). And yet we would not for this reason be the sort of persons we will be *when this mortal body puts on immortality* (1 Cor 15:54). For then we will not only not obey any sinful desire but there will be no desires of the sort that we are commanded not to obey.

6. Now, then, when the apostle says, *It is now not I who do that, but the sin that dwells in me* (Rom 7:17,20), he speaks of the concupiscence of the flesh that produces in us its impulses, even when we do not obey them, provided that sin does not reign in our mortal body so that we obey its desires and provided that we do not offer our members to sin as weapons of iniquity.[5] By making progress perseveringly in righteousness that has not yet been brought to perfection, we shall at some time come to its perfection when sinful concupiscence does not have to be held in check and reined in but when it does not exist at all. By saying, *You shall not desire* (Ex 20:17), the law did not set forth something we can achieve in this life but something toward which we should tend by making progress. But this is not achieved by the law that commands it but by the Spirit who

2. See 2 Cor 4:16.
3. See Rom 7:15.
4. See Sir 18:30.
5. See Rom 6:12-13.

gives it. It is not, then, due to the merits of a human being who works but to the grace of the savior who bestows it. The benefit of the law, then, is that it convinces human beings of their weakness and compels them to beg for the medicine of grace, which is found in Christ. For *everyone who calls upon the name of the Lord will be saved. How, then, will they call upon him in whom they have not believed? How will they believe in him of whom they have not heard?* (Rom 10:13-14) For this reason he says a little later, *And so, faith comes from hearing, but hearing is made possible though the word of Christ* (Rom 10:17).

7. Since this is so, those who boast that they are Israelites according to the flesh and apart from the grace of Christ boast in the law; they are the ones of whom the apostle also says that, *not knowing the righteousness of God and wanting to establish their own, they are not subject to the righteousness of God* (Rom 10:3). He does indeed call the righteousness of God that which a human being has from God, but he calls their own righteousness that which they suppose is sufficient for them to carry out the commandments without the help and the gift of God, who gave the law. Those who, though they profess that they are Christians, are so opposed to the grace of Christ that they think they can fulfill the commandments of God by their human strength are like these Jews. And so they too, *not knowing the righteousness of God and wanting to establish their own, are not subject to the righteousness of God*, and they live like Jews—not, of course, with that name but nonetheless with the error. Persons of this sort found as their leaders Pelagius and Caelestius, the fiercest defenders of this impiety; they were even removed from the Catholic communion by the recent judgment of God through his careful and faithful servants, but on account of their unrepentant heart they still continue under this condemnation.

8. Whoever wants to have nothing to do with this carnal and natural and hence blameworthy and damnable Judaism must keep himself from those ancient practices that, with the revelation of the New Testament after the arrival of those realities that were prefigured by those practices, ceased without a doubt to be necessary. As a result, no one is judged *over food and drink or over a feast day or the new moon or the Sabbath, which are shadows of what was to come* (Col 2:16-17). But besides that there are the things that the law commanded in order to be able to transform the conduct of the faithful, that is, *so that, rejecting impiety and worldly desires, we may live temperately, justly, and piously in this world* (Ti 2:12). Among these there is also that commandment from the law that the apostle chose to emphasize, *You shall not desire* (Rom 7:7; Ex 20:17), and whatever else is commanded in the law about loving God and neighbor apart from any figures of the sacraments. For upon these two commandments even Christ the Lord himself says that the whole law and the prophets depend.[6] Let the

---

6. See Mt 22:37-40; Mk 12:30-31; Lk 10:27; Dt 6:5; Lv 19:18.

Christian accept, embrace, and have no doubt that he should observe all these in such a way that whatever progress he makes in them he ascribes not to himself but to *the grace of God through Jesus Christ our Lord* (Rom 7:25).

3, 9. But it is reasonable to ask whether whoever is in this way a true and genuine Christian should also be called a Jew or an Israelite. Even if this is not understood in a carnal but in a spiritual sense, we should not give ourselves that name in ordinary conversation but should retain it only in its spiritual meaning lest, on account of the ambiguity of the word, which our daily speech does not distinguish, it be thought to express something inimical to the name of Christ. But the same blessed apostle clarifies and resolves for us this question, namely, whether one who is a Christian can also be understood to be a Jew or an Israelite , when he says, *Circumcision is indeed useful if you keep the law, but if you are a transgressor of the law, your circumcision has been turned into a lack of circumcision. If, then, someone uncircumcised keeps the precepts of the law, will not his lack of circumcision be counted as circumcision? And will not someone naturally uncircumcised who keeps the law judge you who are a transgressor of the law regarding its letter and circumcision? For he is not a real Jew who is one outwardly, nor is that real circumcision that is seen in the flesh, but he is a real Jew who is one inwardly and by the circumcision of the heart, by the Spirit, not by the letter, whose praise comes not from human beings, but from God.* (Rom 2:25-29) When, therefore, we hear the apostle of Christ commending to us the Jew inwardly, not by the circumcision of the flesh but by that of the heart, by the spirit, not by the letter, who is this but a Christian?

10. And so we are Jews not according to the flesh but spiritually, just as we are the offspring of Abraham not according to the flesh, like those who boast of that name with pride in their flesh, but according to the spirit of faith, which they do not have. For we know that we were promised to Abraham when God said to him, *I have made you the father of many nations* (Gn 17:5). And we know how much the apostle said about this. *For we say*, he said, *that Abraham's faith was credited to him as righteousness. How was it credited to him? When he was circumcised or when he was still uncircumcised? Not when he was circumcised, but when he was uncircumcised. And he received circumcision as a sign or seal of the righteousness of faith that he had when uncircumcised in order that he might be the father of all believers from the uncircumcised in order that their faith might be credited to them as righteousness. Thus he would be the father of the circumcised not only for those who come from the circumcised but also for those who follow the path of faith that our father Abraham had when he was uncircumcised.* (Rom 4:9-12) And a little later he said, *That is why it comes from faith, in order that the promise might be solid for all the offspring according to grace, not only for the offspring that come from the law but also for those that come from the faith of Abraham, who is the father of us all, as scripture says, I*

have made you the father of many nations. (Rom 4:16-17; Gn 17:5) Likewise he says to the Galatians, *In that way Abraham believed, and it was credited to him as righteousness. Understand, then, that those who have faith are the children of Abraham. Foreseeing, however, that God justifies the nations by faith, scripture foretold to Abraham, All the nations will be blessed in you. Thus those who have faith are blessed along with Abraham who had faith.* (Gal 3:6-9; Gn 15:6 ; 22:18) Then a little later in the same letter he says, *Brothers, I speak in human terms: No one cancels or overrides a person's testament which has been ratified. The promises were made to Abraham and his seed. He does not say: To his seeds, as if to many, but as if to one: And to your seed, who is Christ.* (Gal 3:15-16)[7] A little later he says, *For all of you are one in Christ Jesus. But if you belong to Christ, you are therefore Abraham's seed, heirs according to the promise.* (Gal 3:28-29)

11. In accordance with this interpretation by the apostle, then, we find that the Jews who are not Christians are not children of Abraham, though they take their origin from the flesh of Abraham. For, when he says, *Understand, then, that those who come from faith are the children of Abraham* (Gal 3:7), he certainly means that those who do not come from faith are not children of Abraham. And for this reason, unless Abraham is the father for the Jews as he is for us, what good does it do them that they have come into existence from his flesh and borne his name without his virtue? But when they cross over to Christ and begin to be children of Abraham because of faith, then they will be Jews, not outwardly but inwardly, by the circumcision of their heart, by the Spirit, not by the letter, and their praise will come not from human beings but from God.[8] But, separated from this faith, they will be reckoned among the branches broken off from the domesticated olive tree, onto whose root the same apostle says the wild olive branch is grafted,[9] that is, the Gentiles. This is done, of course, not by means of the flesh, but by means of faith, not through the law but through the spirit, by the circumcision not of the flesh but of the heart, not outwardly but inwardly, with praise not from human beings but from God. In that way, just as each Christian is not a carnal but a spiritual child of Abraham, so each Christian is not a carnal but a spiritual Jew, not a carnal but a spiritual Israelite. For the apostle speaks as follows concerning this name, *For not all who come from Israel are Israel, nor are all who are the offspring of Abraham his children. But from Isaac your offspring will take its name. That is, it is not the children of the flesh who are children of God, but the children of the promise will be counted as offspring.* (Rom 9:6-8; Gn 21:12) Are these not great wonders and is it not a deep mystery that many born from Israel are not Israel and many are not the children of Abraham

---

7. See Gn 13:15; 17:8.
8. See Rom 2:28-29.
9. See Rom 11:17-24.

though they are his offspring? How is it that they are not and that we are, if it is not that they are not the children of the promise who belong to the grace of Christ but the children of the flesh who bear the name empty of meaning? And for this reason they are not Israel in the sense that we are, nor are we Israel in the sense that they are. For we are Israel in accordance with spiritual rebirth, while they are Israel in accordance with carnal birth.

12. We must, of course, consider and distinguish the one Israel that received its name on account of the flesh from the other that obtained the reality signified by that name on account of the Spirit. For were they children of Israel who were born from Hagar, the servant of Sarah? Was not Ishmael born from her, and was he not the father of the people, not of the Israelites but of the Ishmaelites? But Israel came from Sarah by means of Isaac, who was born according to the promise made to Abraham.[10] And yet, though that is the way things stand in terms of the propagation of the flesh, we come to a spiritual interpretation and find that the Israelites according to the flesh, who take the origin of their flesh from her, do not belong to Sarah, but that instead the Christians belong to her, who are not children of the flesh from Ishmael but children of the promise from Isaac, belonging not to the carnal offspring but to the spiritual mystery of Isaac. It is in this vein that the apostle speaks to the Galatians, *Tell me, you who want to be under the law, have you not heard the law? For it is written that Abraham had two sons, one from the slave girl and one from the free woman. But the one who was born of the slave girl was born according to the flesh, and the one who was born of the free woman was born through the promise. These events are an allegory. For they are the two testaments. The one, of course, was given on Mount Sinai, giving birth into slavery; that is Hagar. For Sinai is a mountain in Arabia that is compared to the Jerusalem that presently exists, for she is in slavery along with her children. But the Jerusalem from above is free; she is our mother. For scripture says: Rejoice, O barren one, you who do not bear children; burst forth and cry out, you who do not give birth. For the children of the abandoned woman are many more than those of the one with a husband. But we, brothers, are children of the promise like Isaac. But just as then the one who was born according to the flesh persecuted the one born according to the Spirit, so it is now as well. But what does scripture say? Cast out the slave girl and her son, for the son of the slave girl will not be an heir along with the son of the free woman. But we, brothers, are not children of the slave girl but of the free woman, because Christ has set us free with this freedom.* (Gal 4:21-5:1)

13. See, in accord with this spiritual and apostolic interpretation we who do not take from her the propagation of our flesh rather belong to the free Sarah, but the Jews who do take from her the propagation of their flesh are shown to belong

---

10. See Gn 18:10.

rather to Hagar, from whom they do not take the propagation of their flesh. In the grandchildren of Abraham and Sarah, that is, in the sons of Isaac and Rebecca, the twins Esau and Jacob, who was later called Israel, we find this great and deep mystery. When, in speaking of it, the same apostle had recalled the children of the promise who belong to the grace of Christ, he said, *And not only that, but Rebecca was pregnant from one union with our father, Isaac. For, when they were not yet born and had not done anything either good or bad, in order that God's plan might remain in accord with his choice, she was told, not because of works but because of God's call, The older will serve the younger. As scripture says, I have loved Jacob, but I have hated Esau* (Rom 9:10-13; Mal 1:2-3). This apostolic and Catholic teaching certainly shows us quite clearly that in terms of the origin of their flesh the Jews, that is, the children of Isaac, belong to Sarah, but the children of Ishmael belong to Hagar. But in terms of the mystery of the Spirit the Christians belong to Sarah and the Jews to Hagar. Likewise, in terms of the origin of the flesh the people of the Edomites belong to Esau, who was also called Edom, but the people of the Jews belong to Jacob, who was also called Israel.[11] But in terms of the mystery of the Spirit the Jews belong to Esau, and the Christians belong to Israel. In that way, of course, the scripture is fulfilled: *The older will serve the younger* (Gn 25:23), that is, the older people of the Jews will serve the younger people of the Christians. See how we are Israel, boasting of our adoption by God, not of our human parentage, Jews not outwardly but inwardly, not by the letter but by the Spirit, by circumcision not of the flesh but of the heart.[12]

4, 14. Though this is how things stand, we should still not confuse the usual manner of human speaking by an inappropriate terminology, and in drawing distinctions we should not introduce familiar words with a different meaning so that by an unusual use of the term someone wants to call Jews those people who are Christians and who have "Christian" as their most usual name. Nor, when one is and is called a Christian, should one prefer instead the name "Israelite." We should not decide to use in our everyday language with an insolence that is quite out of place and, if one can say this, with an ignorant learnedness something that should always be understand as a mystery and rarely uttered by our lips. For did the apostles through whom we learned these things not know them, that is, how we are rather the offspring of Abraham, heirs to the promise made concerning Isaac,[13] and Jews by the Spirit, not by the letter, through circumcision of the heart, not of flesh,[14] not Israel according to the flesh but the Israel of God? Of course they knew this with much more wisdom and certitude than we

---

11. See Gn 32:28.
12. See Rom 2:28-29.
13. See Gal 3:29; 4:28.
14. See Rom 2:28-29.

do, and yet in their usual manner of speaking they called Jews and Israelites those people who come from the family of Abraham according to the flesh and are called by those names by everyone.

15. The apostle Paul says, *The Jews look for signs, and the Greeks seek wisdom, but we preach Christ crucified, a scandal to the Jews and folly to the Gentiles, but to those who are called, both Jews and Greeks, Christ the power of God and the wisdom of God* (1 Cor 1:22-24). Those whom he called Greeks he also referred to by the term "Gentiles," because the Greek language was the most common among the Gentiles, but he calls Jews those whom everyone calls by that name. For, if Christians are Jews, then Christ crucified is also a scandal to Christians. After all, Paul said of him that he was *a scandal to the Jews*. Who but someone completely out of his mind would think that? Likewise he says, *Do not give scandal to the Jews or the Greeks or to the Church of God* (1 Cor 10:32). How could he distinguish these if he ought to call the Church of God the Jews in the everyday manner of speaking? Likewise he said, *He also called us not only from the Jews but also from the Gentiles* (Rom 9:24). How did he call them from the Jews if he did not call them from the Jews but rather called them to be Jews? Likewise he says concerning the Israelites, *What, then, shall we say? That the Gentiles who had not pursued righteousness have attained righteousness, the righteousness that comes from faith. But Israel, which pursued the law of righteousness, did not attain the law of righteousness. Why? Because they sought it not from faith, but as if from works. For they stumbled upon the stumbling block.* (Rom 9:30-32) Likewise he says, *But what does he say to Israel? All the day I stretched out my hands to a people that does not believe and rebels* (Rom 10:21). And he went on to say, *I say, then: Has God rejected his people? Heaven forbid! For I too am an Israelite, from the offspring of Abraham, from the tribe of Benjamin. God has not rejected his people that he foreknew.* (Rom 11:1-2) How could the apostle here call Israel *a people that does not believe and rebels* if Christians are Israel, or how could he call himself an Israelite? Was it because he had become a Christian? Certainly not! But because in terms of the flesh he came *from the offspring of Abraham, from the tribe of Benjamin*, which we are not in terms of the flesh, though in terms of faith we are the offspring of Abraham and, for that reason, are also Israel. But what he acknowledged by an understanding of a more profound mystery is different from what the everyday usage of the word demands.

16. Finally there is the fellow Aptus, whoever he is who you wrote teaches Christians to live like Jews, calls himself a Jew and an Israelite, as Your Holiness had intimated, in the sense that he forbids those foods that the law given through the holy servant of God, Moses, forbade in accord with what was appropriate to that time,[15] and encourages the other practices of that time, which have now been

---

15. See Lv 11:1-42; Dt 14:3-21.

abolished and done away with among Christians. The apostle calls these observances foreshadowings of what was to come[16] so that we might understand the
prophecy contained in them and see that their observance has now been emptied
of value. From this it is clear that this Aptus wants to be called an Israelite and a
Jew not in a spiritual but in an altogether carnal sense. But we are not held bound
by those observances that were done away with when the New Testament was
revealed. And we have learned and we teach that the commandments of the law
that are also necessary for the present time, such as, *You shall not commit adultery. You shall not commit murder. You shall not desire* (Rom 13:9; Ex
20:14,13-17), and any other commandment that is summed up in the words, *You
shall love your neighbor as yourself* (Lk 10:27; Gal 5:14; Jas 2:8), are to be
observed not by human strength, as if we were establishing our own righteousness,[17] but *by the grace of God through Jesus Christ our Lord*, in the righteousness that we have from him. And yet we do not for this reason deny that we are
the offspring of Abraham, to whom the apostle says, *You, then, are the offspring
of Abraham* (Gal 3:29). Nor do we deny being inwardly Jews of the sort to whom
he says, *For he is not a real Jew who is one outwardly, nor is that real circumcision that is seen in the flesh, but he is a real Jew who is one inwardly and by the
circumcision of the heart, by the Spirit, not by the letter, whose praise comes not
from human beings, but from God* (Rom 2:28-29). Nor do we deny that we are
spiritual children of Israel, meaning that we pertain to that younger son, whom it
was foretold the older would serve.[18] But we do not give ourselves these names
in an improper way, and we confine them within the understanding of the
mysteries, not bandying them about in insolent language.

---

16. See Col 2:16-17.
17. See Rom 10:3.
18. See Gn 25:23; Rom 9:12.

Letter 197

At the end of 419 or the beginning of 420 Augustine wrote to Hesychius, the bishop of Salona, near Split, who was metropolitan of the church of Dalmatia. Augustine tells Hesychius that he thought it better to send him some writings of Jerome on the weeks in the prophecies of Daniel and tells him that he thinks that they refer to past events rather than to the future coming of Christ (paragraph 1). Scripture clearly states that no one can know the time of the end of the world (paragraph 2). To calculate the time of the end of the world is nothing else than to try to know what Christ said could not be known (paragraph 3). We can know that the gospel will be preached to all nations throughout the world before the end of the world, but we cannot know how soon the end will come after that (paragraph 4). Augustine asks Hesychius to share with him anything that the Lord may have revealed to him on these questions but claims for himself a cautious ignorance rather than a false knowledge (paragraph 5).

To his most blessed lord, Hesychius, Augustine sends greetings.

1. Since your son and our fellow priest Cornutus, from whom I received the letter of Your Reverence by which you were so kind as to visit my lowly self, is returning to Your Holiness, I am by my reply fulfilling my duty of greeting you in turn, while strongly commending myself to your prayers, which are most acceptable to the Lord, my lord and most blessed brother. Concerning the prophetic statements or predictions about which you wanted me to write something, I thought it better to send to Your Beatitude explanations of the same words by the holy Jerome, a most learned man, taken from his works, in case you do not have them. If you have them, however, and they do not satisfy your questions, I ask you not to hesitate to write back to me what you think of them and how you yourself understand those prophetic utterances. For I think that the one about the weeks of Daniel in particular should be understood in terms of time that is already past. For I do not dare to calculate the time of the coming of the savior that is expected in the end, nor do I think that any prophet has determined ahead of time the number of years before that event but rather that what the Lord said holds true, *No one can know the times that the Father determined by his own authority* (Acts 1:7).

2. As for what he says in another passage, *Concerning that day and hour, however, no one knows* (Mt 4:36; Mk 13:32), there are some who interpret this so that they think that they can calculate the times; it is only the exact day and hour that no one can know. I omit here the way the scriptures are also accustomed to use "day" or "hour" in place of "time." But surely what was said about not knowing the times was spoken with perfect clarity. For, when the Lord was questioned about this by his disciples, he said, *No one can know the times that*

the Father has established by his own authority (Acts 1:7). For he did not say "day" or "hour" but *times,* which usually does not refer to a short stretch, like "day" or "hour," especially if we look at the Greek words. For we know that the same book in which this was written was translated into ours from that language, even though it could not be exactly expressed in Latin. For in Greek we read at this point, χρόνους ἢ καιρούς. Our books translate both χρόνους and καιρούς as "times," though these two words have a significant difference between them. The Greeks call καιρούς certain times, not the times that pass in the course of events but the times in events that are felt to be auspicious or inauspicious for something, for example, the harvest, vintage, heat, cold, peace, war, and any like these. But they call stretches of time χρόνους.

3. And the apostles certainly did not ask this in the sense that they wanted to know the one last day or hour, that is, a small part of the day, but whether it was now the auspicious time for the kingdom of Israel to be restored. At that point they heard, *No one can know the times that the Father has determined by his own authority,* that is, χρόνους ἢ καιρούς. But if in Latin we said "times and auspicious moments," we would not express in that way what was said. For, whether the times are auspicious or inauspicious, they are called καιροί, but to calculate the times, that is, χρόνους, in order to know when the end of this world or the coming of Christ will be, seems to me to be nothing else than to want to know what he himself said that no one can know.

4. But the occasion for that time will certainly not occur before the gospel is preached in the whole world as a testimony to all nations. For we read the perfectly clear statement of the savior on this matter, when he says, *And this gospel of the kingdom will be preached in the whole world as a testimony to all nations, and then the end will come* (Mt 24:14). What does *then the end will come* mean but "it will not come before that"? When it will come after that is uncertain for us. But we certainly ought to have no doubt that it will not come before that. If, then, the servants of God undertook this labor so that they roamed the world and gathered as best they could what remained of the nations where the gospel was not yet preached, we could from this observe to some extent how far the present time is from the end of the world. If because of some inaccessible and inhospitable places it does not seem possible for the servants of God to roam the whole world and to provide reliable reports about the many great nations that are still without the gospel of Christ, still less do I think that we can grasp from the scriptures how much time there will be before the end, since we read in them, *No one can know the times that the Father has established by his own authority* (Acts 1:7). Hence, if we already had absolutely certain reports that the gospel was being preached in all nations, we still could not say how much time remained before the end, but we would be correct to say that it is now coming closer and closer. Perhaps someone might reply that the Roman peoples and

many barbarians came to hear the preaching of the gospel with such great speed and that some of them have been converted to the faith of Christ, not gradually but so suddenly, that it is not incredible that in a few years, even if not in the life of those of us who are already old, but surely in that of the young who will reach old age, all the remaining nations can have the gospel preached to them. But if it is to be so, it will be easier to prove it by experience after it has happened than to be able to show it from reading the scriptures before it happens.

5. The opinion of a certain person, whom the priest Jerome also accuses of rashness,[1] forces me to say this, because he dared to explain the weeks of Daniel as referring to the future, not to the coming of Christ in the past. But if the Lord has revealed or will reveal something better to your holy and humble heart in accord with your greater merits, I beg you to be so good as to share it with us and to receive this reply of ours as that of a man who would prefer to have knowledge rather than ignorance regarding the questions that you asked me. But since I was not yet capable of it, I choose to admit cautious ignorance rather than to profess false knowledge.

---

1. See Jerome, *Commentary on Daniel (Commentarium in Danielem)* 9, 24.

Letter 198

Shortly after receiving the previous letter, Hesychius, the bishop of Salona in Dalmatia, wrote to Augustine. Hesychius thanks Augustine for his letter and explains that he has taken Augustine up on his request to put his thoughts in writing (paragraph 1). He argues that it would be surprising if the prophets fore-told what human beings could not come to know (paragraph 2). Furthermore, scripture repeatedly warns us about the need to know the times (paragraph 3) and teaches us that those who await the Lord's coming are blessed (paragraph 4). Though no one can know the day or the hour of the Lord's coming, signs bear witness that his coming is near at hand (paragraph 5). After the emperors became Christian, the gospel spread through the world rapidly in a short time (paragraph 6). What Jerome wrote about the prophecy of Daniel leaves his readers with problems. Hence, Hesychius asks Augustine for further help (paragraph 7).

To his most blessed lord Augustine, his brother who should be venerated with most sincere love and his fellow bishop, Hesychius sends greetings in the Lord.

1. Our holy fellow priest Cornutus brought me the letter of Your Beatitude that I desired and awaited. It brought me joy because you were so good as to have a favorable memory of us, for you explained to me in a few words of your own in passing the thoughts of your holy mind on the matters that I asked about. But you added some things from the works of our holy fellow priest Jerome in order that I might be able to resolve my question by the reading of his work on the holy scrip-tures. And since you were so kind as to ask us to convey to Your Most Sincere Charity by letter what we think on these questions, I have written below what I learned about those points from the writings I read, insofar as my small mind with its middling ability could grasp or understand.

2. Since all things, both those that have been made and those that will be made, are governed by the will and power of almighty God, the creator of the whole world, we know those events that have occurred or even those that will occur from the words of the holy prophets who, by God's will, foretold to human beings those things that were going to be before they came about. Hence it would be quite surprising if God decreed that the events that God wanted to be foretold could never enter the minds of human beings in accordance with the words that the Lord spoke to the blessed apostles when he said, *No one can know the times that the Father has established by his own authority* (Acts 1:7). For, first of all, in the most ancient books of the churches it does not say, *No one can*, but, *It is not for you to know the times or moments that the Father has established by his own authority.* And this manner of expression is correctly complemented by the words that follow when he says, *But you will be witnesses to me in Jerusalem and in Judea and in Samaria and to the end of the world* (Acts 1:8). He did not,

therefore, want us to understand that the apostles were witnesses to the end of the world but to his name and resurrection.

3. For the Lord himself warns about knowledge of the times, *Who is the faithful and prudent servant whom the master has set over his servants to give them food at the proper time? Blessed is that servant whom, when he comes, the Lord finds doing this.* (Mt 24:45-46; Lk 12:45-46) The family of Christ is fed by the word of preaching, and a servant is found to be faithful who offers at the proper time the food that the faithful need to those who are waiting for the Lord. For a bad servant is criticized as follows, *But if the bad servant says, My master is slow in coming, his master will come on a day he does not know and at an hour of which he is ignorant* (Mt 24:48,50; Lk 12:45-46), and so on. Similarly, he blames them because they do not know the time when he says, *You hypocrites, you know how to read the appearance of the sky. Why do you not recognize this time?* (Lk 12:56) So, too, the apostle says, *In the last days perilous times will come upon us* (2 Tm 3:1), and so on. Similarly, the apostle says, *But regarding times and moments we do not have to write to you, for you yourselves know quite well that the day of the Lord will come like a thief in the night. When they say, Peace and security, then sudden destruction will overtake them like the pains of a woman in childbirth, and they will not escape.* (1 Thes 5:1-3) Likewise, the apostle says, *Do you not recall that, when I was with you, I told you these things? And you now know what is holding him back in order that he may be revealed at his proper time. For the mystery of iniquity is already at work. Only let him who is holding it back hold it back now until he is removed from our midst, and then the man of iniquity will be revealed whom the Lord Jesus will slay with the Spirit of his lips.* (2 Thes 2:5-8; Is 11:4) Likewise, the Lord chides the Jews in the gospel, *And if you had known the time of your visitation, you would perhaps have remained, but now it has been hidden from your eyes* (Lk 19:42,44). And the Lord preached to the Jews in this way, *Do penance; the times are completed; believe the gospel* (Mk 1:15). He was correct to tell the Jews that the times were completed, because their times came to an end thirty-five or forty years after he preached.[1] And in Daniel we read, *Until the beast has been slain and has perished and its body has been given to be burned and the reign of the other beasts has been ended, and they are given a duration of life up to a time and a time,* which in Greek says: ἕως χρόνου καὶ καιροῦ. And there follows, *And behold with the clouds of heaven there comes one like the son of man* (Dan 7:11-13). The mystery of the beast and of the other beasts is clear for those with understanding from the figurative meaning of scripture.

4. We should long for and await the coming of the Lord. For it is great happiness for those who long for his coming, as the blessed apostle Paul bears witness.

---

1. That is, with the destruction of the temple in 70 A.D.

He says, *Henceforth there is stored up for me a crown of righteousness that the Lord, the just judge, will give to me on that day, but not to me alone but also to those who long for the coming of the Lord* (2 Tm 4:8). And the Lord says in the gospel, *Then the righteous will shine like the sun in the kingdom of their Father* (Mt 13:43). Similarly, the prophet says, *For, behold, darkness and clouds will cover the earth above the nations, but the Lord will appear in you, and his majesty will be seen in you* (Is 60:2). Likewise, the prophet says, *Those who wait for the Lord will exult with might; they will grow wings like eagles; they will run without effort; they will walk and not grow hungry* (Is 40:31). And we find many other such things that pertain to the happiness of those who long for the coming of the Lord.

5. But it is clear that no one can calculate the periods of times. The gospel certainly says, *No one knows the day or the hour* (Mt 24:36; Mk 13:32). But, taking into account the inability of my intellect, I say that neither the day nor the month nor the year of his coming can be known. But by seeing and believing signs of his coming it is right that I wait for it and distribute this food to believers so that they may await and long for his coming. For he said, *When you see all these things, know that he is near the gates* (Mt 24:33). Hence the signs in the gospel and in the prophets that have been fulfilled among us reveal the coming of the Lord. For in vain do either those who seek them or those who criticize them seek to calculate the days and the years, because scripture says, *And if those days were not cut short, no flesh would be saved, but those days will be shortened on account of the elect* (Mt 24:22; Mk 13: 20). It is certain that the time cannot be calculated that the Lord, who has established all times, will shorten, but it is certain his coming has drawn near. For we see from events that have occurred that some signs of his coming have been realized. And again, he says, *But when these events begin to come about, you will take a breath and lift up your heads, because your redemption has drawn near* (Lk 21:28). What signs he said that they would see are clear in the Gospel of Saint Luke, *And Jerusalem will be trod upon by the Gentiles until the time of the Gentiles has been completed* (Lk 21:24). This has been done, and no one doubts that it is being done. And there follows, *And there will be signs in the sun and the moon and in the stars, and on earth the consternation of the nations* (Lk 21:25). The sufferings and chastisement that we endure compels us to admit it, even if the will perhaps does not want to. For it is clear that at the same time people saw signs in the sky and endured the consternation of the nations on earth. And there follows, *As human beings wither away out of fear and in expectation of what is coming upon the whole world* (Lk 21:26). It is certain that no country, no place is not afflicted and brought low in our times, as scripture says, *out of fear and in expectation of what is coming upon the whole world*, and all the signs that the gospel discloses above to its readers have been for the most part realized.

6. But it is said, *And this gospel will be preached in all the world, and then the end will come* (Mt 24:14), first, because it was the promise of the Lord himself that the apostles would be his witnesses *in Jerusalem and in Judea and in Samaria and to the end of the world* (Acts 1:8), and the apostle teaches on the basis of this authority, *But I say, Have they not heard? Their voice has gone out to the whole world, and their words to the ends of the earth.* (Rom 10:18; Ps 19:5) He likewise teaches, *On account of the hope that has been stored up for you, of which you heard before in the word of the truth, that is, of the gospel that has come to you, bearing fruit and increasing, as it is in all the world* (Col 1:5-6). But the faith preached among the nations by the apostles had many persecutors so that it was held back and grew strong slowly; thus the words of scripture were fulfilled, *Before all these things, they will first lay hands upon you and persecute you and hand you over to their synagogues and prisons, taking you before kings and governors, on account of my name* (Lk 21:12). Thus were these words also fulfilled, "And you will quickly be rebuilt by those who destroyed you."[2] For from the time when the most merciful emperors became Christian by God's will, however slowly the faith grew in the world on account of persecution, once the emperors became Christian the gospel of Christ spread everywhere in a short time.

7. Though the saintly Jerome, our fellow priest, has explained the interpretation of blessed Daniel concerning the weeks,[3] as the teachers of the Church have handed it down, it leaves the reader perplexed.[4] For, if that most learned man, our fellow priest, says that "it is dangerous to pass judgment on the opinion of the teachers of the churches and to prefer one to another,"[5] how much less is a reader able to do what a teacher has hesitated to do! But we believe that the Lord said, *Heaven and earth will pass away, but not one iota or one little mark will disappear from the law until all of it has come about* (Mt 5:18). I wonder, therefore, how the mystery of the weeks has been fulfilled before the birth and passion of Christ, since in the middle of a week the prophet said this, *In the middle of the week my sacrifice and supplication will be taken away, and the abomination of desolation will take the place of sacrifice* (Dn 9:27). If this abomination had already been realized, then, how does the Lord warn us when he says, *When you see the abomination of desolation, as was predicted by the prophet Daniel, standing in the holy place, let the reader understand* (Mt 24:15; Mk 13:14; Dn 9:27). But lest I be someone who scorns the request of Your Beatitude, I have written to Your Charity what I thought. But be so good as to teach us and bring us joy by writing back with the word of Your Grace.

---

2. The sentence is not found in scripture.
3. See Dn 9:24-27.
4. See Jerome, *Commentary on Daniel the Prophet* (*Commentarium in Danielem prophetam*) 9, 24.
5. Ibid.

Letter 199

Soon after receiving the previous letter, Augustine replied to Hesychius, the bishop of Salona, with this long letter, which Augustine mentions in *The City of God* 20, 5, 4, where he gave it the title *The End of the World*. Augustine begins his reply to Hesychius' questions by indicating the disposition that a Christian ought to have in awaiting the second coming of the Lord. Those who long for his coming find delays difficult to bear (paragraph 1). Our good actions will prepare us for this event, and he will find us at his coming as he finds each of us at our death (paragraph 2). Hence, we must be watchful and ready (paragraph 3).

Hesychius interpreted the Lord's words to his disciples, *It is not yours to know the times or moments that the Father established by his own authority* (Acts 1:7) in the sense that the Lord did not want them to be witnesses to the end of the world but to his resurrection. Augustine express his uncertainty about how to interpret Hesychius' statement and points out that the Lord spoke of what was not theirs to know, not of what was not theirs to preach (paragraph 4). God did not want the apostles to preach what he knew was not useful for them to know (paragraph 5). Christ did not admonish the Jews about their not knowing the times because they did not know the time of his second coming at the end of the world but because they did not recognize the time of his first coming (paragraph 6).

It was long ago when John wrote that *it is the last hour* (1 Jn 2:18), and the end is still not here (paragraph 7). Paul's warning that the day of the Lord would come like a thief in the night would seem to preclude the Lord's coming in these times, when no one is confident of peace and security (paragraph 8). Paul is warning us lest the coming of the Lord find us unprepared (paragraph 9). What Paul said about the mystery of iniquity does not indicate when this mystery will be revealed or when the Antichrist will appear (paragraphs 10 and 11).

Christ rebuked the people of Jerusalem about not knowing the time of their visitation because they did not recognize the time of his first coming (paragraph 12). Augustine asks Hesychius to explain how the passages of scripture that he cites have to do with knowing the time of the Savior's second coming (paragraph 13). The coming of the Lord should certainly be loved (paragraph 14), but a true love of his coming does not entail a belief that he will come soon (paragraph 15).

Augustine asks Hesychius to explain what he said about calculating the times of the Lord's coming, since it may be that they are in agreement (paragraph 16). He turns to an explanation of the sense in which scripture speaks of years, days, and hours (paragraph 17). He suggests that in speaking of the present as the last hour John probably used "hour" for "time" and left the length of that time undetermined (paragraph 18).

Hesychius had cited the Lord's promise about the shortening of the last days on account of the elect and tied it to the weeks of the prophet Daniel. Augustine points to difficulties with this interpretation if the weeks of Daniel really refer to

Christ's second coming (paragraphs 19 and 20). Augustine indicates that the weeks of Daniel might refer to Christ's first coming, to his second coming, or to both (paragraph 21).

Augustine turns to other signs indicative of the end of the world and points to scripture's use of the present tense in describing them (paragraphs 22 and 23). Though the final days began at the time of the apostles, we do no know how long they will last (paragraph 24).

Augustine begins to examine the Lord's eschatological discourse, in which he spoke of the destruction of Jerusalem, of his coming in his members in the Church, and of his coming at the end of the world (paragraph 25). Hence, one has to consider carefully which signs refer to which events (paragraph 26). Luke's account makes it clear that the Lord's words about the shortening of the days refer to the time of the destruction of Jerusalem (paragraph 27). Unlike Matthew and Mark, Luke shows that the abomination of desolation predicted by Daniel was realized at the destruction of Jerusalem (paragraph 28). At the time of the city's destruction there were some of the elect in it on whose account those days were shortened, however that shortening is to be understood (paragraphs 29 and 30). At any rate, there is no need to suppose that the shortening of the days disturbed the count of the weeks in Daniel or that those weeks have not already come but will come at the end of the world (paragraph 31). Augustine suggests a spiritual interpretation of the passage warning a person on the roof not to come down and a person in the field not to return to his house for his coat (paragraph 32). He also indicates some of the problems that arise if the weeks of Daniel are to be fulfilled at the end of the world (paragraph 33).

Regarding the signs in the heavens and on earth, Augustine notes that the eclipse of the sun that occurred at the crucifixion was unparalleled (paragraph 34). He suggests that the wars that were predicted should be interpreted in relation to the conflict between the people of Christ and the people of the devil (paragraph 35). Furthermore, he argues that, if the evils people are suffering at present are certain signs of the Lord's coming, we are still left with Paul's statement that people will be saying at his coming, "Peace and security," which no one is now saying (paragraph 36). Such evils can be better interpreted as applicable to the Church (paragraph 37). Though Paul said that the time is short, he also described in the same letter how people should live in this world as they await the Lord's coming (paragraph 38). Augustine warns that it is safer to interpret the signs in the sun and the moon as referring to the Church (paragraph 39). Luke's words about the affliction of the nations should be interpreted as referring to the nations that will stand on Christ's left (paragraph 40). Christ's coming on the cloud can be interpreted either as his coming in the Church or as his coming in his own risen body at the last judgment (paragraph 41). When Christ appears, the kingdom of God will still not be here, though it will be near (paragaph 42). The parable of the fig tree also warns only that the end is near (paragraph 43). Matthew makes explicit that all the events mentioned refer to Christ's coming (paragraph 44). But it still remains possible that all the signs found in the three evangelists refer to Christ's coming in his members in the Church—except for those passages clearly referring to his coming for the last judgment (paragraph 45).

Before the end of the world the gospel must be preached to the whole world, and there are still many nations that have not heard the gospel (paragraph 46). The Lord promised that all the nations, not just the Romans, would be the offspring of Abraham (paragraph 47). Hence, the Church must spread to all the nations in order that such prophecies may be fulfilled (paragraph 48). When the Lord said that his disciples would be his witnesses to the ends of the world, he did not mean only those disciples to whom he was then speaking (paragraph 49). Both in the Old and in the New Testament the past tense is often used for events that lie in the future (paragraphs 50 and 51).

Augustine uses a parable of three good servants, one of whom believes that the Lord will come sooner, another that he will come later, while the third admits his ignorance of this. All of them are in harmony with the gospel (paragraph 52). Augustine points out, however, that it is more dangerous to hold the view of the first servant, since, if the Lord comes later, those who believe otherwise may be subjected to insults and mockery (paragraph 53). The view of the second servant is not dangerous, but may be erroneous, while the view of the third servant avoids both danger and error (paragraph 54).

The End of the World

To his most blessed lord, his brother and fellow bishop to be embraced with reverence, Hesychius, Augustine sends greetings in the Lord.

1, 1. I received the letter of Your Reverence by which you urge us in a very salutary way to long for and desire the coming of our savior. You do this as a good servant of the same master, eager for the gains of your Lord and wanting to have very many companions in the love with which you yourself are most of all and constantly aflame. Seeing, therefore, that you have recalled from the apostle that he said that the Lord would give a crown of righteousness not only to him but to all who long for his revelation,[1] we accordingly live correctly and act like pilgrims in this world when our heart is stretched out more and more in this love, whether he whose manifestion we long for with faithful love and desire with pious affection comes more quickly or more slowly than we think. Certainly the servant who says, *My master is slow in coming* (Mt 24:48-49; Lk 12:45), strikes his fellow servants, eats and drinks with drunkards, does not at all long for his manifestation. For his frame of mind is apparent from his conduct. And so the good master took care to describe his conduct, though briefly, that is, his pride and dissoluteness, in such a way that his words, *My master is slow in coming*, would not be thought to be said out of a desire for his lord, the desire with which the psalmist was ablaze who said, *My soul is thirsting for the living God. When shall I come and appear before the face of God?* (Ps 42:3) For, by asking, *When shall I come?* he shows that he bears

---

1. See 2 Tm 4:8.

up under the delays with difficulty, because even what is speeded up in time seems slow for his desire. But how is his coming slow or how will it be far in the future if even the apostles at the time when they were still in the flesh said, *It is the last hour* (1 Jn 2:18), though they heard from the Lord, *It is not yours to know the times*? They, then, did not know what we do not know either—I speak for myself and for those who with me do not know. And yet those to whom he said, *It is not yours to know the times that the Father has established by his own authority* (Acts 1:7), longed for his revelation and gave their fellow servants food at the proper time, and they did not strike them by lording it over them, nor did they behave dissolutely with the lovers of this world, saying, *My master is slow in coming.*

2. Not knowing the times is one thing; quite another is the deterioration of morals and the love of sins. For, when the apostle Paul said, *Do not readily change your mind, and do not be frightened whether by word or by a letter supposedly sent by us, as if the day of the Lord were upon us* (2 Thes 2:2), he certanly did not want them to believe those who thought that the coming of the Lord was already approaching, and yet he did not want them to say like that servant, *My master is slow in coming,* and to give themselves to pride and dissoluteness for their destruction. Rather, he did not want them to listen to false rumors about the last day's approach, and yet he wanted them to await the coming of the Lord with loins girded and lamps lit.[2] For he said to them, *But, brothers, you are not in the darkness so that that day may catch you like a thief. For you are all children of the light and children of the day; we are not children of the night and of darkness.* (1 Thes 5:4-5) But that fellow who says, *My master is slow in coming,* so that he strikes his fellow servants and feasts with drunkards, is not a child of the light but of the darkness. And for this reason that day will catch him like a thief because each of us ought to fear for the last day of our lives. For, as the last day of each of us catches us, so the last day of the world will catch each of us. For, as each of us is at death on our last day, so each of us will be when we are judged on the last day of the world.

3. The words in the Gospel according to Mark are pertinent here, *Watch, then, because you do not know when the master of the house may come, late, in the middle of the night, at the cock's crow, or in the morning, so that, when he comes suddenly, he does not find you sleeping. But I say to all what I say to you: Watch!* (Mk 13:35-37) Who are the *all* to whom he says *Watch!* but his chosen and beloved ones who belong to his body, which is the Church?[3] Hence he did not say this only to those who heard him when he was speaking but also to those who came after them before us and to us and to those who will come after us up to his last coming. But is that day going to find all in this life, or is anyone going to say that the words, *Watch so that, when he comes suddenly, he does not find you*

---

2. See Lk 12:35-36.
3. See Col 1:24.

sleeping, also apply to the dead? Why, then, does he say to all what pertains only to those who existed then except because it pertains to all in the way I said? For that day will come for each of us when the day comes for us to leave this life as we will be when we are judged on the last day. And for this reason every Christian ought to watch so that the coming of the Lord does not find him unprepared. But that day will find him unprepared whom the last day of this life of his finds unprepared. Certainly it was clear at least to the apostles that the Lord was not going to come in their time, when they were still living in the flesh. Yet who would doubt that they were most watchful and observed what he said to all so that he would not come suddenly and find them unprepared?

2, 4. I do not yet understand how we ought to interpret what Your Holiness wrote, namely, that the Lord said to the apostles, *It is not yours to know the times and moments that the Father has established by his own authority*, because he went on to say, *But you will be witnesses to me in Jerusalem and in Judea and in Samaria and to the end of the earth* (Act 1:7-8). You explain the meaning of the scripture by saying, "He did not, therefore, want us to understand that the apostles were witnesses to the end of the world but to his name and resurrection."[4] He certainly did not say, "It is not yours to preach the times," but, *It is not yours to know the times*. But if you want us to understand his words, *It is not yours to know*, as if he had said, "It is not yours to make known," that is, "It is not yours to teach this," who of us would dare to teach or presume to know what that teacher, God, did not teach his disciples who questioned him when he was present and what such holy and great teachers could not teach the Church?

5. Or will someone reply that it was not the apostles but the prophets who taught this? For you said this, and it is true that "we know the events that will occur from the words of the holy prophets who, by God's will, foretold to human beings those things that were going to be before they came about."[5] But if Your Reverence says that it is "quite surprising if God decreed that the events that God wanted to be foretold could never enter the mind of human beings,"[6] how much more surprising it is that the apostles were kept from knowing or teaching what the prophets foretold to human beings! But how could the apostles fail to understand the prophets whom we are discussing when they taught about the times if *we* understand them? Or, if the apostles understood them when they prophesied about this computation of time, how would they fail to teach what they understood when their preaching made known the very prophets who taught these things in their books? And so, from the same writings from which they themselves learned those things others also could have learned them in the nations in which the apostles commended the authority of the prophets. Why, then, was it

---

4. Letter 198, 2.
5. *Ibid.*
6. *Ibid.*

said to them, *It is not yours to know*—or if we should understand, "It is not yours to teach"—*the times that the Father has established by his own authority*? For they were teaching those things when they made known these prophets in whose writings they learned them. Hence it is more believable not that God did not want to be known what he wanted to be preached but that he did not want to be preached what he saw it would be useless to know.

6. Why, then, you ask, does the Lord himself warn us about knowledge of times when he says, *Who is the faithful and prudent servants whom the master has set over his servants to give them food at the proper time?*[7] and so on? He truly does warn not that a good servant should know the end of time but that one should be watchful at every time and in every good work. He does not warn that we should know better than the apostles *the times that the Father has established by his own authority*, but he warns that, since we do not know when the Lord is coming, we should imitate the apostles in having our hearts ready. I have already said enough on this previously. But he blames the Jews for not recognizing the time, when he says, *You hypocrites, you know how to interpret the appearance of the sky* (Lk 12:56), and so on, because they did not recognize the time that he wanted them to recognize, that is, the time of his first coming so that they would believe in him and want to await his second coming vigilantly, whenever that would be. For one who does not know the first coming of the Lord will not be able to prepare for the second by believing in him and by watching faithfully so that it does not catch him like a thief in the darkness, whether he comes more slowly or more quickly than we hope.

3, 7. The apostle Paul says, as you remind us,[8] *In the last days perilous times will come upon us* (2 Tm 3:1) and so on. But does he for this reason teach us *the times that the Father established by his own authority* (Acts 1:7)? Or does anyone for this reason know how long or short those same times will be that we must admit are the last? We, of course, ought to bear in mind how long ago it was said, *My little children, it is the last hour* (1 Jn 2:18).

8. Again, you mention that the apostle said, *But regarding the times and moments we do not have to write to you, for you yourselves know quite well that the day of the Lord will come like a thief in the night. When they say, Peace and security, then sudden destruction will overtake them like the pains of a woman in childbirth, and they will not escape.* (1 Thes 5:1-3) Here too he did not say after how much time this would come about but only how it would come about. That is, he did not say how short or long the time would be but, however great the interval or stretch of time might be, this last evil would only overtake them when they said, *Peace and security*. By these words the apostle seems to remove either the hope or the fear of this last day from our own time. For we do not see those

---

7. See Letter 198, 3.
8. See Letter 198, 3.

lovers of this world, whom sudden destruction will overtake, now saying, *Peace and security.*

9. The apostle shows clearly enough, then, what it is sufficient to know when he says, *Regarding the times and moments we do not have to write to you,* or as other codices have, *You do not need us to write to you.* Nor did he go on to add: "For you yourselves well know how much time remains," but, *For you yourselves well know that the hour of the Lord will come like a thief in the night* (1 Thes 5:2). This, then, is what it is necessary to know so that they may take care to be children of the light and to watch with their hearts ready if they do not want to be caught by that hour as if by a thief in the night. For, if in order to avoid this evil, that is, in order that the hour of the Lord might not, like a thief, find them unprepared, it was necessary to know the lengths of the times, the apostle would not have said that there was no need for him to write this but rather that he should write this to them as a most provident teacher would judge. But now he showed that this was not necessary for them for whom it was enough to know that the Lord would come like a thief for those who were unprepared and sleeping and that, by knowing this, they would be vigilantly ready however much later he came.[9] And in that way he would stay within his limits and would not, though an apostle, presume to teach others what he knew that the Lord told the apostles, *It is not yours to know* (Act 1:7).

10. You also quote the words of the same apostle, *Do you not recall that, when I was with you, I told you this? And you now know what is holding him back in order that he may be revealed at his proper time. For the mystery of iniquity is already at work. Only let him who is holding it back hold it back now until he is removed from our midst, and then the man of iniquity will be revealed whom the Lord Jesus will slay with the Spirit of his lips.* (2 Thes 2:5-8) I wish that you had not merely quoted but also explained these words of the apostle. They are certainly obscure and uttered in a mystical sense, yet in such a way that it is clear that he said nothing about the times that have been set and that he did not disclose any interval or length of time. For he says, *In order that he may be revealed at his proper time,* nor did he say after how much time this would be. Next he added, *For the mystery of iniquity is already at work.* As much as this *mystery of iniquity* may be understood by one person in one way and by another in another way, it is hidden how long it will be at work. And the apostle did not express this as if he were someone from among those to whom it was said, *It is not yours to know the times* (Acts 1:7). For, though he was not among those apostles when the Lord said this to them, we have no doubt that he also belonged to their community and company.

11. Likewise, the words that follow, *Only let him who is now holding it back hold it back until he is removed from our midst, and then the man of iniquity will*

---

9. See Lk 12:36-39; Jn 12: 36.

be revealed whom the Lord Jesus will slay by the Spirit of his lips (2 Thes 2:7-8), teach us that the Antichrist will be revealed, since he seems to have emphasized with a somewhat clearer meaning that he will be slain by the Spirit of the lips of the Lord Jesus Christ. But he did not say even obscurely after how much time this would be. For anyone can strain to understand or to get some inkling of who it is who is now holding back or what he is holding back or what the apostle meant by *is removed from our midst*, since, however one reads what is written, the text is completely silent about how long he is holding back and about the length of time after which he will be removed from our midst.

4, 12. You say, "Likewise, the Lord chides the Jews in the gospel when he says, *And if you had known the time of your visitation, you would perhaps have remained, but now it has been hidden from your eyes*" (Lk 19:42.44).[10] But this refers to the time of the Lord's first coming, not to that of his second, which is now at issue. Regarding his second coming, not his first, he said, *It is not yours to know the times*. For his disciples were asking him about the coming that they were hoping for, not about the first coming that they already saw. *For if the Jews recognized* his first coming, *they would never have crucified the Lord of glory* (1 Cor 2:8). And for this reason they could have not been overthrown but could have remained. But his words to them, *Do penance; the times are completed; believe the gospel* (Mk 1:15), you yourself have maintained were said of the times of the Jews that were going to come to an end after a few years, and we now know that those times have passed, that is, when the city was destroyed in which their kingdom was established.

13. Next, you said that what Your Reverence quoted from Daniel concerning the beast that was slain and the kingdom of the other beasts and, between these, concerning the coming of the Son of Man on the clouds of heaven is evident for those who understand scripture. But if you would be so good as to explain how this pertains to knowing the length of time after which the Lord will come, so that we may discover this clearly and without any ambiguity, I myself would also admit with much gratefulness that the words of the Lord, *It is not yours to know the times* (Acts 1:7), were said only to the apostles and not to their successors, who were going to know them.

5, 14. We ought to long for and await the coming of the Lord, then, as you exhort us to in a holy fashion, when you say that his coming is great happiness for those who long for it and when you use the testimony of the apostle whose words you quote as follows, *Henceforth there is stored up for me a crown of righteousness that the Lord, the just judge, will give to me on that day, but not only to me, but also to those who long for the coming of the Lord* (2 Tm 4:8). For then, as you mention from the gospel, *The righteous will shine like the sun in the kingdom of their Father* (Mt 13:43). And as the prophet says, *For, behold,*

---

10. *Ibid.*

clouds and darkness will cover the earth above the nations, but the Lord will
appear in you, and his majesty will be seen in you (Is 60:2). Likewise, scripture
says, *But those who await the Lord will exult with might; they will grow wings*
like eagles; they will run without effort; they will walk and not grow hungry (Is
40:31).

15. You say this clearly and with great piety and truth, commending the
happiness of those who long for the coming of the Lord. But those to whom the
apostle said, *Do not be easily upset in your mind, as though the day of the Lord*
were upon us (2 Thes 2:2), were certainly longing for the day of the Lord, nor by
saying this did the teacher of the nations tear them away from that longing with
which he wanted them to be afire. And for this reason he did not want them to
believe the people from whom they heard that the day of the Lord was upon
them. Otherwise, when the time when they believed that he would come had
passed and they saw that he had not come, they would think that other false
promises had been made to them, and they would give up hope about the reward
of faith. The person who longs for his coming, then, is not the person who claims
that the coming of the Lord is drawing near or the person who claims that it is not
drawing near. It is, rather, the person who awaits his coming, whether it is near or
far off, with the sincerity of faith, the firmness of hope, and the ardor of love. For,
if the Lord is love more to the extent that one believes more and preaches more
that he will come more quickly, they loved him more who said that his coming
was already upon them than did those whom the apostle forbade to believe it or
than did the apostle himself who certainly did not believe it.

6, 16. But if my weakness is not burdensome to Your Holiness, I ask that you
not hesitate to explain more clearly the sense in which you said, "No one can
calculate the lengths of the times."[11] Otherwise I may have the same ideas that
Your Charity does, and either of us may wait in vain to be taught by the other.
For, after you had said this, you then went on to add, "The gospel certainly says,
No one knows the day or the hour (Mt 24:36). But, taking into consideration the
inability of my intellect, I say that neither the month nor the year of his coming
can be known."[12] For this sounds as though one cannot know in what year he will
come, but one can know in what period of seven or ten years he will come, as if
one can state definitely that he will come within this or that period of seven years
or within this or that period of ten years. But if not even this can be grasped, I ask
whether the time of his coming can at least be determined so that we may say that
he will come within these fifty or one hundred years or within any number of
years, however large or small, but that we do not know in which of them. If you
have already grasped this, it is a great deal that you have been able to grasp. But
this is what I ask that you kindly reveal to us, using suitable proofs by which you

11. Letter 198, 5.
12. *Ibid.*

were able to discover this. But if you are not confident that you have grasped even this, you hold what I do.

17. For all of us who believe them see from the appearance of many signs, which we read the Lord foretold, that these are the last times. But even the time of a thousand years, if their end would be the end of the world, could as a whole be called the last time, or even the last day, since scripture says, *A thousand years are in your eyes like one day* (Ps 90:4; 2 Pt 3:8). In that way whatever might be done during those same thousand years would be said to be done in the last time or on the last day. For I say again what in this area must be said often; let us consider how many years ago the blessed evangelist John said, *It is the last hour* (1 Jn 2:18). For, if we lived at that time and had heard this, would we have thought that so many years were going to pass afterwards, and would we not rather hope that the Lord would come while John himself was still living? Nor did he say, "It is the last time," or, "the last year," or, "month," or, "day," but, *It is the last hour*. And see how long this hour is! Still, he did not lie; rather, we must understand that he used *hour* in place of "time." Some interpret this in the sense that six thousand years supposedly make up one day, so that they divide it into parts like the twelve hours of a day. In that way the last hour is seen to have the last five hundred years. And John, they say, was speaking of these years when he said that it was the last hour.

18. But it is one thing to know something and another to suspect it. For, if one day is to be counted as six thousand years, why is a twelfth part and not a twenty-fourth part one hour, that is, not five hundred but two hundred and fifty years? For the whole revolution of the sun, not from the east to the west but from the east to the east, is more correctly called a whole day. In that way, when a whole day has passed, that is, twenty-four hours, it starts over again. And thus we find that the last hour from the time at which John was speaking already ended almost seventy years ago, at least, and the end of the world has not yet come. In addition, if we carefully examine the history of the Church, we find that the apostle John died long before five thousand five hundred years had passed from the beginning of the human race. And so it was not yet the last hour, if a twelfth part of six thousand years, that is, five hundred years, is counted as the length of even one hour. But if according to the scripture we make one day a thousand years,[13] for much better reasons the last hour of so long a day already passed long ago. I do not mean if a twenty-fourth part of it, which amounts to a few more than forty years, but if a twelfth part of it is counted, which has twice that number of years. Hence it is better to believe that the apostle used *hour* for "time," and we do not know how long that hour is because it is not ours *to know the time that the Father established by his own authority* (Acts 1:7). And yet that

---

13. See Ps 90:4 and 2 Pt 3:8.

it is the last hour we certainly know for much better reasons than those who lived before us from the time when it began to be or to be called the last hour.

7, 19. But I do not at all understand the idea of Your Reverence that we cannot grasp the lengths of the times in order to determine the year when the end will come because, according to the Lord's promise, the days will be shortened. For, if they will be shortened in order to become fewer instead of more, I ask in what sense it is true that there were going to be more if they were not shortened. For the weeks of holy Daniel do not pertain to the first coming of the Lord, as many suppose, but rather to the second coming, as you think. Will those years, then, be shortened so that there will be one fewer of those weeks, and the prophecy will be false that took care to determine the number of weeks with such exactness that it said that a certain event would be accomplished in half of a week? I am stunned if the prophecy of Daniel is destroyed by the prophecy of Christ. Next, what sort of idea is it that Daniel, or rather the angel from whom he learned these things, did not know that the Lord was going to shorten those days and was mistaken when he said this or actually knew this but lied to the one whom he instructed? But if that is absurd, why do we not rather believe that the prophet Daniel foretold so many weeks in accord with the way the Lord was going to shorten those days, at least if that number of years refers to the second coming of the Lord, though I do not know how that can be proved?

20. Finally, it is much more certain and safe to say that the coming of the Lord will take place within seventy or at most one hundred years if those weeks foretell it. For there are four hundred and ninety in seventy sevens. But today marks almost four hundred and twenty years from the birth of the Lord; from his resurrection or ascension, however, there are more or less three hundred and ninety. And for this reason, if we count from the time when he was born, seventy years remain; if we count from the time when he suffered, approximately one hundred remain, within which all the weeks of Daniel will be completed if they were a prophecy concerning Christ's last coming. Someone, then, who says, "He will come within so many years," says something false if he comes later. But because the years will be shortened, there can be fewer, not more. It will, then, be correct to say, "He will come within these years," because, however much they are shortened, it will be true. For, if this shortening is to be understood so that there are fewer years, it does not permit the day of the Lord to come after them but always to come within those years, no matter how much they are shortened. This shortening, then, does not disturb the calculator who figured it out, so that he says that the day of the Lord will come within so many years, but rather helps him. For the more those days are reduced in number, the more the Lord's coming will fall within those fewer years and will not be able to come after them, and in that way what he figured out, so that he said, "He will come within so many years," will be true, though he does not know in which year he will come.

21. Hence the whole question comes down to whether the prophecy about the weeks of Daniel was fulfilled at the first coming of the Lord or referred to the end of the world or refers to both. For there were some who also held this last view, saying that the prophecy was fulfilled at the time of the first coming of Christ and will be fulfilled all over again from then until the end of the world. I myself see that, if his first coming did not fulfill the prophecy, his second coming must fulfill it, because that prophecy cannot be false. If it was fulfilled at the time of the first coming, we do not have to understand that it will also be fulfilled regarding the end of the world. And for this reason it is uncertain, even if it is true. We certainly should not deny that it will be, but neither should we presume that it will be. The upshot is that one who wants to insist that we believe that this prophecy is about the end of the world should strive as well as he can and show, if he can, that it was not fulfilled by the first coming of the Lord in opposition to so many commentators on the words of God who show not only by the computation of the time but also by the events themselves that this prophecy was fulfilled, especially because it is written there, *And the holy of holies will be anointed*, or because of what the Hebrew manuscripts have more explicitly in the same prophecy, *And the Christ will be killed, and he will not belong to it any more* (Dn 9:24, 26), that is, he will not belong to that city, because he became a stranger to the Jews who did not believe that he was their savior and redeemer, since they could kill him. For Christ is not going to be anointed or killed at the end of the world so that we should expect this prophecy of Daniel to be fulfilled then and believe that it has not already been fulfilled.

8, 22. But who would deny that we should hope that the coming of the Lord is near because of the signs from the gospels and the prophets that we see are taking place? Every day his coming is closer and closer. But as to how close it is, it is said, *It is not yours to know* (Acts 1:7). Notice when the apostle said, *For our salvation is now closer than when we began to believe. The night has passed, but the day has drawn near.* (Rom 13:11-12) And see how many years have passed! Nor is what he said false. With what better reason should we now say that the coming of the Lord is drawing near when we have advanced so far toward the end! The apostle certainly said, *The Spirit clearly says that in the last times certain persons will withdraw from the faith* (1 Tm 4:1). The times of heretics and of the sort of people he described had not yet come, but they have come now. And for this reason we seem to be warned in these last times even by those people about the end of the world. He likewise says elsewhere, *But bear in mind that in the last days dreadful times will come upon us* (2 Tm 3:1), or as other manuscripts have, *perilous times*. Then he describes the sort of times they will be, *There will be people who love themselves, who love money, puffed up, proud, blasphemous, disobedient to their parents, ungrateful, impious, without religion, without feeling, slanderers, without self-control, cruel, lacking kindness, traitors, rash, blind, loving pleasure more than God, having a semblance of piety, but denying its power* (2 Tm 3:2-5). It would be surprising if such persons never existed. Finally, because they already did exist, he goes on to say, *And avoid them. For there are some among them who work their way into homes.* He does not say, "Who will work their way," as if foretelling that this will take place, as he said above, *Perilous times will come upon us*; rather he says, *They work their way into homes, and they captivate poor women.* (2 Tm 3:5-6) He does not say, "They will captivate," or, "They are going to captivate," but, *They captivate.*

23. Nor should you think that in this passage he uses verbs in the present tense in place of verbs in the future tense, for he was warning the man to whom he wrote to avoid those people. And yet he did not say for no reason, *In the last days perilous times will come upon us* (1 Tm 3:1). And in showing that there will be perilous times, he foretold that there would be such persons but that they will be more in number and more prevalent the nearer the end is. We see, then, that such persons even now abound. But what if they will be even more abundant after us and most abundant of all when at last the end is upon us, though no one knows how far off it will be? To be sure, the days were said to be the last even in the first days of the apostles, when the ascension of the Lord into heaven had just occurred, when on the day of Pentecost he sent the Holy Spirit he had promised and some people were astounded, amazed at them for speaking in languages that they had not learned, though others mocked them and said that they had too much wine.[14] On that day, when speaking to those who reacted in different ways to this, Peter said, For *these men are not drunk, as you suppose. For it is only the third hour of the day. Rather, pay attention because this is what the prophet foretold: In the last days it shall be, says the Lord, I shall pour out my Spirit over all flesh* (Acts 2:15-17; Jl 3:1), and so on.

24. Even then those days were the last. How much more are they now, even if as many days remain up to the end as have passed from the ascension of the Lord until now or if there remains more or less time? This, of course, we do not know because it is not ours *to know the times that the Father has established by his own authority* (Acts 1:7), though we know, nonetheless, that we are living in the last times, in the last days, in the last hour, just as the apostles were. But those who lived after them and before us were living in the last times even more, and we ourselves are yet more, and still more than us will be those who will live after us up to those days that will be, if we can say this, the last of the last and until that very last day of all, which the Lord wants us to understand when he says, *And I will raise him up on the last day* (Jn 6:40), and how far off that day is cannot be known.

---

14. See Acts 2:1-14.

9, 25. The signs that were foretold in the Gospel according to Luke,[15] as Your Holiness mentioned, are the same in the Gospels according to Matthew[16] and according to Mark.[17] For the three of them report what the Lord said when his disciples asked him when the things he had foretold about the destruction of the temple were going to take place and what would be the sign of his coming and of the end of the world.[18] For there is no discrepancy about events if one says something that another omits or expresses it in another way. But when they are compared, they help to guide the understanding of the reader. But it would take a long time to discuss them all. For the Lord gave those replies to the disciples who asked him what was going to follow after that time, whether about the destruction of Jerusalem, the topic that occasioned the questions, or about his coming through the Church, in which he does not cease to come until the end. For we recognize him as he comes in his own members when they are daily born. Of this coming he said, *Soon you will see the Son of Man coming in the clouds* (Mt 26:64). Of these clouds the prophet said, *I shall order my clouds to produce rain over the earth* (Is 5:6). And they asked him about the end, when he will appear *to judge the living and the dead* (2 Tm 4:1).

26. Since, then, he mentions signs that refer to these three, that is, to the destruction of that city, to his coming in his own body, which is the Church,[19] and to his coming as head of the Church, which he is himself, we must distinguish through careful consideration which of those signs refers to which of those three events. Otherwise we might suppose that what pertains to the destruction of Jerusalem refers to the end of the world. Or just the opposite, we might state that what pertains to the end of the world refers to the destruction of that city. Or we might say that what pertains to his coming in his body, because he is the Church, refers to his last coming in his body, which is the head of the Church. Or again, we might claim that what pertains to his last coming by himself refers to his coming through the Church. In all these there are some points that are clear, but there are others so obscure that it is difficult to decide or rash to say something definite about them as long as we do not understand them.

27. For who can fail to see that the words, *But when you see Jerusalem surrounded by an army, know that its desolation has then drawn near* (Lk 21:20), pertain to that city? Likewise, who can fail to see that the words, *When you see these events take place, know that the kingdom of God is near* (Lk 21:31), pertain to the last coming of the Lord? But his words, *Woe to those who are pregnant or nursing in those days. But pray that your flight may not be in winter or on the Sabbath. For then there will be great tribulation such as there has not been from*

---

15. See Lk 21:7-33.
16. See Mt 24:4-33.
17. See Mk 13:5-29.
18. See Mt 24:1-3, Mk 13:1-4; Lk 21:5-7.
19. See Eph 1:22-23; Col 1:24.18.

the beginning of the world and will not be afterwards (Mt 24:19-21), are written in such a way in Matthew and in Mark that it is uncertain whether they ought to be understood of the destruction of the city or of the end of the world. For we read this in Mark as follows, *But woe to those who are pregnant or nursing in those days. Pray that they do not come about in winter. For those days will be days of tribulation such as there have not been from the beginning of the creation, which God made, up to now, and such as there will not be afterwards. And if God had not shortened those days, no flesh would have survived. But on account of the elect, whom he has chosen, he shortened those days.* (Mk 13:17-20) Matthew said it similarly. But Luke expressed this so that it is clear that it pertains to the destruction of the city. For in him we read as follows, *But woe to those who are pregnant and nursing in those days. For there will be great difficulty on the earth and wrath for this people, and they will fall at the point of the sword and will be led captive into all the nations. And Jerusalem will be trampled upon by the nations until the time of the nations is completed.* (Lk 21:23-24)

28. But in coming to this point, Matthew writes this way, *Therefore, when you see the abomination of desolation, which was predicted by Daniel the prophet, standing in the holy place, let the reader understand. Then those who are in Judea should flee to the mountains, and he who is on the roof should not come down to take something from his house. And one is in the field should not return to take a coat. But woe to those who are pregnant and nursing in those days* (Mt 24:15-19), and so on. But Mark puts it this way, *But when you see the abomination of desolation standing where it ought not to be, let the reader understand. Then let those who are in Judea flee to the mountains, and him who is on the roof not come down to the house and enter to take something from his house. And let him who is in the field not return to take his cloak. But woe to those who are pregnant or nursing in those days* (Mk 13:14-17), and so on. But in order to show that the abomination of desolation, which was predicted by Daniel, came about when Jerusalem was stormed, Luke mentions in the same passage the words of the Lord, *But when you see Jerusalem surrounded by an army, know that its desolation has then drawn near* (Lk 21:20). It is clear, therefore, that the abomination of desolation, of which those two evangelists spoke, was at that time established there. Then this evangelist likewise continues, *Then let those who are in Judea flee to the mountains* (Lk 21:21). And instead of what the others said, *And let him who is on the roof not come down to the house and enter to take something from his house* (Mt 24:17), he says, *And let those who are in its midst leave* (Lk 21:21), in order to show that those words quoted by the other evangelists commanded haste in flight. And instead of what they had, *And let him who is in the field not return to take his garment* (Mt 24:18), Luke says more clearly, *And let those who are in the surrounding regions should not enter it because these are days of punishment, in order that all the things that have been written may be fulfilled* (Lk 21:21-22). Then he continues in similar fashion

in order to make it very clear that this passage of the gospel is about this one event of all three, *But woe to those who are pregnant and nursing in those days* (Lk 21:23), and the other things that pertain to this, which I have already mentioned above.

29. Luke, then, makes it clear that what might have been uncertain, namely, the statement about the abomination of desolation and the statement about the shortening of days for the sake of the elect, refers not to the end of the world but to the storming of Jerusalem. For, though he himself did not speak of those events, he nonetheless said more clearly other things concerning this by which he showed that these referred to it. For we ought not to have any doubt that, when Jerusalem was destroyed, there were in that people God's chosen ones who came to believe from the circumcision or were going to come to believe, people chosen before the creation of the world, for whose sake those days were shortened so that the evils might be more tolerable. For it seems to me that some people did better in understanding that those evils were themselves signified by the term *days,* just as other passages of the divine scripture speak of evil days.[20] For days themselves are not evil, but the things that happen on them. They are said to be shortened, then, in the sense that, because God granted people endurance, they felt them less, and in that way evils that were lengthy became short.

30. But whether that shortening of the days should be understood in this way either because they were reduced to a few or because they were shortened by a quicker revolution of the sun—for there are some who also have this idea, namely, that it was said that the days would be shorter just as the day was longer when Joshua the son of Nun prayed[21]—Luke the evangelist nonetheless taught that this shortening of the days and the abomination of desolation pertain to the destruction of Jerusalem. Luke did not mention these two events himself, though Matthew and Mark did, but along with them he said more clearly other things concerning the same topic that they expressed more obscurely. For Josephus who wrote the history of the Jews, says that such evils befell that people at that time that they scarcely seemed credible.[22] Hence, it was not said without reason that there had not been such tribulation from the beginning of creation and that there would not be afterwards. But even if there is such tribulation or worse at the time of the Antichrist, we should understand that it was said of that people that they will not have such tribulation any more. For, if they first of all and most of all welcomed the Antichrist, the same people will then cause rather than suffer tribulation.

31. There is, therefore, no reason why we should think that the weeks of the prophet Daniel were either disrupted on account of the shortening of the days or

---

20. See Ps 41:2; 49:6; Eph 5:16.
21. See Jos 10:12-14.
22. See Flavius Josephus, *The War of the Jews* (*De bello Judaico*) 6, 3, 3.

were not completed at that time but are going to be completed at the end of the world. For they were not completed before the passion of the Lord, and those who think that they were are most correctly refuted by your statement, in which you said, "If this abomination had already been realized, then, how does the Lord warn us when he says, *When you see the abomination of desolation, as was predicted by the prophet Daniel, standing in the holy place, let the reader understand*" (Mt 24:15).[23] It is right that these words of Your Beatitude should correct those who say that, though the Lord said this, that abomination took place even before his passion and resurrection. But those who say, as Luke the evangelist also most clearly testifies, that it took place when Jerusalem was destroyed ought to see what answer they might give to those who think that these events will happen at the end of the world or near the end of the world, although on account of the obscurity of the expression this abomination of desolation need not be understood by everyone in one way.

32. And the words, *Let him who is on the roof not come down to take something from his house, and let him who is in the field not return to take his cloak* (Mt 24:17-18; Mk 13:15-16), can be better understood in a spiritual sense, because in all tribulations we must beware lest anyone be conquered and descend to the life of the flesh from a spiritual height or lest one who has made progress, reaching out to what is ahead, look backwards by giving up. But if this is true in every tribulation, how much more ought we to be commanded to beware of it in the tribulation that was predicted for that city, which would be *such as there has not been from the beginning and will not be afterwards* (Mt 24:21; Mk 13:19). And if it is true of this day, how much more will it be true of the day that will be the last for the whole world, that is, for the Church spread throughout the whole world! For Luke himself, not in fact when the Lord was asked by his disciples about his coming, where Matthew and Mark mention this,[24] but in another passage where the Pharisees asked him when the kingdom of God would come,[25] reports that he said something of the sort. He said, *In that hour let him who is on the roof and whose possessions are in the house not come down to take them, and likewise let him who is in the field not come back* (Lk 17:31).

33. But now we are dealing with the weeks of Daniel because of the calculation of the times, and if they were not completed around the time of the first coming of the Lord and are to be completed in the end, who would believe that the apostles did not know this or that they in fact knew it but were forbidden to teach it? And yet, if this is the case, it is useful for the nations not to know what the Lord forbade those men, whom he wanted to be teachers of the nations, to

---

23. Letter 198, 7.
24. See Mt 24:3; Mk 13:3.
25. See Lk 17:20.

teach. But if they have been completed, because the Holy of Holies has already been anointed,[26] Christ has already been slain so that he does not belong to that city, sacrifice has already been removed from that temple, and the anointing has aready been abolished, it was right that this response was made to the apostles when they asked about the end, *It is not yours to know the times that the Father has established by his own authority* (Acts 1:7). For the times that they were able to know by means of the prophet Daniel did not pertain to the end of the world, about which they were asking.

10, 34. But as for the signs in heaven and on earth, have we seen greater ones than they saw who lived before us? If we read the history of the nations, do we not find that such great wonders were produced in heaven and on earth that some of them are not even believed? But to omit many examples, which it would take long to pursue, when have we seen two suns? Those who lived at that time, before the Lord had come in the flesh, set down in writing that they saw two suns. When have we seen the sun darkened as it was darkened when the light of the world hung upon the cross?[27] Or perhaps we will count the eclipses of the sun and the moon, which astronomers frequently observe and predict, among the miracles in the heavens, because we have seen the full moon fairly often in eclipse, but the sun only rarely, though we have seen it in eclipse in the final phase of the moon according to their calculations. The eclipse of the sun when Christ was crucified was not of that sort, and for this reason it was truly miraculous and wondrous. It was, of course, the Passover of the Jews, which is celebrated only at the full moon. According to the calculations of the astronomers it is certain that the sun cannot be in eclipse when the moon is full, but according to those calculations it is in eclipse when the moon is in its final phase—not always, but never at other times. From the time the Lord foretold them, what does anyone remember to have appeared in the heavens of the sort that appeared when he suffered? Hence, if such prodigies will appear—if we should not rather understand them in a spiritual sense—they will appear at the point when the end will draw near so that they ought to appear.

35. When, however, has the earth not been devastated by wars at different times and in different places? For, to pass over the most ancient wars, under the emperor Gallienus,[28] when the barbarians spread everywhere through the Roman provinces, how many of our brothers living in the flesh at that time do we suppose could have believed that the end was near, because that occurred long after the ascension of the Lord! And for this reason we do not know what sorts of wars there will be when the end is immediately imminent, unless they were foretold in such a way that we ought to understand them of the Church. There are, of

---

26. See Dn 9:24.26-27.
27. See Mk 13:8; Mt 24:7; Lk 21:10.
28. Gallienus was Roman emperor from 253 to 268.

course, two peoples and two kingdoms, that is, one of Christ, the other of the devil, of which it could have been said, *People will rise up against people, and kingdom against kingdom* (Mk 13:8; Mt 24:7; Lk 21:10). This does not cease happening since the Lord said, *Do penance; for the kingdom of heaven has drawn near* (Mt 3:2; 4:17). See when he said this, and see how many years have passed since then, and yet he spoke the absolute truth. For in the last days the Lord was born of a Virgin, nor would this be called the last hour[29] unless the kingdom of heaven were drawing near, and during the course of this whole hour there are taking place the events that the Lord foretold would take place at the approach of his kingdom. But if in regard to how long this hour will last the apostles were told, *It is not yours to know the times* (Acts 1:7) how much more should an ordinary human being, such as I am, recognize his limits so that he does not think more of himself than he ought![30]

11, 36. "But," you say, "our punishment compels us to admit that the end is already here since there is being realized what was foretold, *Human beings wither away out of fear and in expectation of what is coming upon the whole world* (Lk 21:26). It is certain," you say, "that no country, no place is not afflicted and brought low in our times, as scripture says, *out of fear and in expectation of what is coming upon the whole world.*"[31] If, then, the evils that the human race is now suffering are certain indications that the Lord will come, what do the words of the apostle mean, *When they say, Peace and security* (1 Thes 5:3)? For, when the gospel said, *Human beings wither away out of fear and expectation*, it immediately added, *For the powers of the heavens will be disturbed, and then they will see the Son of Man coming on a cloud with great power and majesty* (Lk 21:26-27).

37. Let us see, then, whether it is not perhaps better to understand that the events that were foretold by those words are not now being fulfilled but will rather come when the whole world has tribulation, so that it pertains to the Church, which suffers tribuation in the whole world, and not to those who cause it tribulation. For the latter are going to say, *Peace and security* (1 Thes 5:3), so that sudden destruction will overtake them and the coming of the Lord will catch them like a thief in the night, while they, on the contrary, will rejoice and exult who long for the revelation of the Lord.[32] But now we see that the evils that people believe to be the greatest and the last are common to both peoples and to both kingdoms, that is, to Christ's and to the devil's. Both the good and the evil are without any doubt equally afflicted by these. Nor is there anyone who says, *Peace and security*, wherever they occur or there is fear that they may not occur.

---

29. See 1 Jn 2:18.
30. See Rom 12:3.
31. Letter 198, 5.
32. See 2 Tm 4:8.

Yet amid these evils people everywhere throng to luxurious banquets; drunkenness is widespread; greed thrives; there is the sound of salacious singing, organs,
flutes, lyres, harps, dice, and many and various kinds of music and games. Is this
to wither away because of fear or rather to be soaked in lust?[33] But the children
of darkness will have and enjoy these in greater abundance when they say, *Peace
and security.*

38. What about *the children of the light and the children of the day* who *are
not in darkness* so that *that day will catch them like a thief* (1 Thes 5:4-5)? Do
they not still *use this world as if they were not using it* (1 Cor 7:31)? For, though it
was said many years ago at the time of the apostles, they still weigh with care the
words, *The time is short* (1 Cor 7:29). Do not the greater part of them still plant,
build, buy, own, pursue careers, and take wives? I am speaking of those who,
though waiting for *their master when he will come back from the wedding* (Lk
12:36), yet do not refrain from carnal marriage but hear with most obedient love
the apostle commanding how wives ought to live with their husbands and
husbands with their wives, children with their parents and parents with their
children, servants with their masters and masters with their servants.[34] Do not all
these use this world in all these ways? They plow, sail, do business, beget children, and act as soldiers and administrators. I think that they will not be like that
when *there will be*, as the gospel predicted, *signs in the sun and in the moon and
in the stars, and on earth the anguish of peoples because of confusion over the
sound of the sea and its waves. Human beings will wither away out of that fear
and in expectation of what is coming upon the whole world. For the powers of
heaven will be thrown into confusion.* (Lk 21:25-26)

39. I think that it is better to understand these predictions as applying to the
Church, lest the Lord Jesus seem to have foretold as something important, as his
second coming approaches, events that have often happened in this world even
before his first coming. And then we would be mocked by those who have read
in the history of the nations more and much greater events than those that we
dread as the last and greatest of all. For the Church is the sun and the moon and
the stars, to which it was said, *Beautiful as the moon, chosen as the sun* (Sg 6:9).
This moon prostrated herself before our Joseph in this world, as if in Egypt,
where he had been raised up to power from the lowest position. For Joseph's
mother certainly could not prostrate herself before him, for she had already died
before Jacob had come to his son[35] so that the truth of the prophetic dream that
was to be realized by Christ the Lord might be preserved.[36] For, when *the sun is
darkened, and the moon does not give its light, and the stars fall from heaven,*

---

33. See Lk 21:26.
34. See Eph 5:22-6:9; Col 3:18-22.
35. See Gn 35:19; 46:1-7.
36. See Gn 37:9-11.

and the powers of the heavens are thrown into confusion (Mt 24:29; Mk 13:24-25), as this passage is expressed by the other two evangelists, the Church will not be seen. At that time, when the wicked persecutors rage beyond all limit and without any fear, as if the happiness of the world were smiling upon them, they say, *Peace and security* (1 Thes 5:3), *stars will fall from the heavens, and the powers of the heavens will be thrown into confusion*, because many who seemed to be resplendent with grace will yield to the persecutors and fall, and some very firm believers will be thrown into confusion. For this reason, however, in the Gospels of Matthew and Mark it is said that this will occur *after the tribulation of those days* (Mt 24:29; Mk 13:24-25), not because these things will happen after that whole persecution has passed, but because tribulation will come first so that the apostasy of some may follow, and because it will happen in that way through all those days. And for this reason it will happen *after the tribulation of those days*, but it will still happen in those same days.

40. The statement in Luke, *and on earth the affliction of the nations* (Lk 21:25), meant for us to understand the nations which do not belong to the offspring of Abraham, in whom all the nations will be blessed,[37] but the nations that will stand on the left when all the nations will be gathered before the judge of the living and the dead.[38] For both groups will be found in all the nations, the one that persecutes, the other that suffers persecution, the one that says, *Peace and security* (1 Thes 5:3), the other in which the sun will be darkened and the moon will not give its light, from which the stars will fall, and in which the powers of the heavens will be thrown into confusion.[39]

41. *And then they will see the Son of Man coming on a cloud with great power and majesty* (Lk 21:27; Mt 24:30; Mk 13:26). I see that this can be interpreted in two ways. In one way it will be understood of the Church coming, as it were, on the cloud, just as even now it does not cease to come in accordance with the words, *Now you will see that Son of Man sitting at the right hand of power and coming on the clouds of the sky*, but then *with great power and majesty* (Mt 26:64), because his greater power and majesty will be seen by the saints to whom he will give great courage so that they are not overcome by such a great persecution. Or in another way it will be understood of his body, in which he sits at the right hand of the Father, in which he also died, rose, and ascended into heaven,[40] in accordance with what we read in the Acts of the Apostles, *When he had said this, a cloud carried him off, and he was taken up from them.* And because the angels also said there, *He will come as you saw him going into heaven* (Acts 1:9,11), it is right to believe that he will not only come in the same body but also

---

37. See Gn 22:18; 26:4.
38. See Mt 25:33.32; Acts 10:42.
39. See Mt 24:29; Mk 13:24-25.
40. See Rom 8:34; Mk 16:19; Col 3:1.

on a cloud, because he will come just as he went away, and a cloud received him as he went away.

42. But it is difficult to judge which of these two it is better to choose. The more obvious sense, of course, is that, when someone hears or reads, *And then they will see the Son of Man coming on a cloud with great power and majesty* (Lk 21:27), he will interpret this precisely as his coming not through the Church but by himself, when he comes to judge the living and the dead.[41] But the scriptures need to be examined carefully, and we ought not to be content with their surface meaning, since they were composed to exercise our minds and hence demand to be penetrated more deeply. For this reason we must carefully study what follows. For, after he had said, *And then they will see the Son of Man coming on a cloud with great power and majesty,* he went on to say, *But when these things begin to happen, look up, and raise up your heads, for your redemption is drawing near. And he told them a parable. Look at the fig tree and all the other trees. When they are already producing their fruit, you know that summer is near. So too, when you see these things happen, know that the kingdom of God is near.* (Lk 21:28-31) When, therefore, he says, *When you see these things happen,* what events can we understand save those that were mentioned above? Among these words, however, is the statement, *And then they will see the Son of Man coming on a cloud with great power and majesty* (Lk 21:27). Hence, even when this is seen, the kingdom of God will not be already here, but it will be near.

43. We see that the other two evangelists keep this same order. For, in Mark, after it had been said, *And the powers that are in the heavens will be thrown into confusion,* he says, *and then they will see the Son of Man coming in the clouds with much power and glory.* Then he adds what Luke did not say, *And then he will send his angels, and he will gather his chosen ones from the four winds, from the ends of the earth to the ends of heaven.* (Mk 13:25-26) Then what Luke said about the fig tree and the other trees Mark says about the fig tree alone. He says, *Learn a parable from the fig tree. When its branch is already supple and its leaves have sprouted, you know that summer is at hand. So too, when you see these things happen, know that he is at hand, right at the door.* (Mk 13:27-29) What does, *When you see these things happen,* refer to but to those events he already mentioned? Among them there is also the one where he says, *And then they will see the Son of Man coming on the clouds with much power and glory, and then he will send his angels, and then he will gather his chosen ones* (Mk 13:27). The end, therefore, will not be then, but then it will be near.

44. Or should we say that we are not to understand all the events that were mentioned when he says, *When you see these things happen* (Mk 13:29; Lk 21:31), but only some of them, that is, with the exclusion of this event that was mentioned, *And then they will see the Son of Man coming* (Mk 13:26; Lk 21:27),

41. See 2 Tm 4:1.

and so on? That will certainly be the end; then it will not be near. But Matthew shows that the words, *When you see these things happen,* are to be taken without any exceptions; for in him it was said, *And the powers of the heavens will be thrown into confusion, and then the sign of the Son of Man will be seen in heaven and then all the tribes of the earth will mourn, and they will see the Son of Man coming in the clouds of heaven with much power and majesty, and he will send his angels with a trumpet and a loud cry, and they will gather his chosen ones from the four winds, from one end of the heavens to the other. But learn a parable from the fig tree. When its branch is already supple and its leaves have sprouted, you know that summer is near. So too, when you see these things happen, know that he is near, right at the door.* (Mt 24:29-33)

45. We know that he is near, then, when we see not some of those signs but all of them, among which there is also this sign: the Son of Man will be seen coming, and he will send his angels, and from the four corners of the world, that is, from the whole world, he will gather his chosen ones. He does this in the whole last hour,[42] coming in his members[43] as if on the clouds, or in the whole Church, which is his body,[44] as if on a great cloud bearing fruit and increasing in the whole world,[45] from the time he began to preach and say, *Repent; for the kingdom of the heavens has drawn near* (Mt 3:2; 4:17). In that way perhaps, if all the statements of the three evangelists about this coming are gathered together and more carefully examined, they might be found to have to do with the fact that he comes daily in his body, which is the Church. Regarding this coming of his he said, *Now you will see the Son of Man sitting at the right hand of the power and coming on the clouds of heaven* (Mt 26:6; Mk 14:62). From this interpretation are excluded the passages in which he promises his last coming in himself *to judge the living and the dead* (2 Tm 4:1) so that he is said to draw near, as well as the last part of the discourse in Matthew where there is expressed in a perfectly obvious way the coming whose nearness is shown above to be understood from certain signs. In Matthew the discourse, to be sure, concludes with a reference to this; he says, *But when the Son of Man comes in his majesty and all the angels with him, he will be seated upon the throne of majesty, and all the nations will be gathered before him* (Mt 25:31-32) and the rest until where he says, *And these will enter into eternal punishment, but the righteous will enter into eternal life* (Mt 25:46). For no one has any doubt that this was foretold concerning the last coming of Christ and the end of the world. For there were some people who wanted to teach by a respectable line of argument that even those two pairs of five virgins[46] pertain to this coming of Christ that is now taking place through the

---

42. See 1 Jn 2:18.
43. See 1 Cor 6:15.
44. See Col 1:24.
45. See Col 1:6.
46. See Mt 25:1-12.

Church. But such statements should not be rashly made for fear that something may turn up that flatly contradicts them, especially since in such obscurities of the divine scriptures, by which God has chosen to exercise our minds, of those who comment on the scriptures in a manner that is not unintelligent, not only is one person more keenly inspired than another, but also any given one of them understands less well at one time and better at another.

12, 46. I do not know yet whether in regard to this present question we could discern something more certain, if we were able to use reason or ability, than what I already quoted in the earlier letter about when the whole world will have the gospel preached to it.[47] For I have established by certain proofs that what Your Reverence thinks was already accomplished by the apostles is not the case. For there are among us, that is, in Africa, countless barbarian nations where the gospel has not yet been preached; it is easy for us to learn this every day from those who are taken captive from them and are now among the slaves of the Romans. Yet it was only a few years ago that certain of them, very exceptional ones and few in number, were pacified and became part of the Roman territories, so that they do not have their own kings but have governors set over them by the Roman empire, and they and their governors began to be Christian. But those who are further inland and are not under Roman power have no contact with the Christian religion in any of their people, and yet it is by no means correct to say that God's promise does not pertain to them.

47. For by means of an oath the Lord also promised not the Romans but all nations to the offspring of Abraham.[48] Because of that promise it has already come about that some nations that are not subject to Roman rule have received the gospel and have been united to the Church, which is bearing fruit and increasing in the whole world.[49] For it still has room to increase until it becomes what was foretold of Christ through Solomon, who symbolized him, *He will have dominion from sea to sea and from the river to the ends of the earth* (Ps 72:8)—*from the river*, that is, where he was baptized because he began to preach the gospel from there,[50] but *from sea to sea* there is spread out the whole world with all the nations, because the world is girded by the sea called Ocean. But how will that prophecy otherwise be fulfilled, *All the nations whom you have made will come and worship before you, O Lord* (Ps 86:9)? For they will not come by migrating from their own places but by believing in their own places. The Lord, to be sure, said of believers, *No one can come to me unless it has been given him by my Father* (Jn 6:66). The prophet, however, says, *And they will worship him, each from his own place, all the islands of the nations* (Zep 2:11). He said *all the*

---

47. See Mt 24:14.
48. See Gn 22:16-18; 26:3-4.
49. See Col 1:6.
50. Set Mt 3:13-16; Mk 1:9; Lk 3:21.

islands as if to say "even all the islands," showing from this that there will be no land left where the Church does not exist, since no island will be left. Some of them are located even in Ocean, and we have learned that some of them have already received the gospel. And so even in each individual island there are being fulfilled the words, *He will have dominion from sea to sea* (Ps 72:8), the sea by which each island is girt. It is the same way in the whole world, which is in a sense like the largest island of all because Ocean girds it. And we know that the Church has arrived in the East at its shores, and to whatever shores of it she has not come, she will come as she bears fruit and increases.[51]

48. If, then, since the prophecy coming from the truth cannot lie, all the nations that God has made must worship him,[52] how will they worship him if they do not call upon him? But *how will they call upon him in whom they have not believed? Or how will they believe in him of whom they have not heard? But how will they hear without someone to preach? Or how will they preach unless they are sent?* (Rom 10:14-15) For he sends his angels and gathers his chosen ones from the four winds,[53] that is, from the whole world. In the nations in which the Church does not yet exist it must come to be—not in order that all who live there may believe, for God promised all the nations, but not all the human beings of all the nations. *For not all have the faith* (2 Thes 3:2). Every nation, therefore, believes in all those that were chosen *before the creation of the world*,[54] and every nation does not believe in the others but hates those who believe. For how will that prophecy also be fulfilled, *You will be hated by all nations on account of my name* (Mt 24:9; 10:22; Mk 13:13; Lk 21:17), if there are not in all the nations both those who hate and those whom they hate?

49. How, then, was this preaching completed by the apostles since there are still nations—and this is completely certain for us—in which it is now beginning and in which it has not yet begun to be completed? And so it was not said to the apostles, *You will be my witnesses in Jerusalem and in all of Judea and Samaria and to the end of the earth* (Acts 1:8), as if they alone to whom he was then speaking were going to complete so great a task. Rather, who can fail to understand that, just as he seems to have said to them alone, *See, I am with you up to the end of the world* (Mt 28:20), he nonetheless promised it to the whole Church, which, as some die and others are born, will last here *until the end of the world*. In the same way he said to them what does not at all pertain to them, and yet it was said to them as if it even pertained to them alone, *When you see all these things, know that he is near, right at the door* (Mt 24:33; Mk 13:29). For to whom does this pertain but to those who will be living in the body when all these things will

---

51. See Col 1:6.
52. See Ps 86:9.
53. See Mt 24:31; Mk 13:27.
54. See Eph 1:4.

be accomplished? How much more does that hold for what was largely to be done by them, though the same action was continued also by their successors?

50. The apostle said, *Have they not heard? Their voice has gone out through the whole earth, and their words have reached the ends of the world.* (Rom 10:18; Ps 19:5) Though he used verbs in the past tense, yet he said what was going to be, not what was already done and completed. In the same way the prophet, whom he used as a witness, did not say, "It will go out through the whole earth," but, *Their voice has gone out*, though of course this had not yet happened. In the same way scripture said, *They have pierced my hands and feet* (Ps 22:17), which we know happened long afterward. But so that we do not suppose that these ways of speaking are found only in the prophets and not also in the apostles, did not the same apostle say, *It is the Church of the living God, a pillar and foundation of the truth. And undoubtedly it is a great sacrament of piety that has been revealed in the flesh, has been justified in the spirit, was seen by the angels, preached to the nations, believed throughout the world, and assumed into glory* (1 Tm 3:15-16)? It is evident, of course, that what he put in the last place has not yet been realized. How much less was that the case when he said these things? The Church will indeed be assumed into glory when it will be said, *Come, blessed ones of my Father, receive the kingdom* (Mt 25:34), and yet the apostle spoke as if what he certainly knew lay in the future had already been done.

51. Much less should we be surprised that he also used verbs of the present tense in the statement, which you likewise mentioned that he made, *On account of the hope that has been stored away for us, of which you have heard before in the word of the truth, that is, of the gospel that has come among you, as it is also bearing fruit and increasing in all the world* (Col 1:5-6), although the gospel had not yet taken hold of the whole world. But he said that it was bearing fruit and increasing in the whole world in order to signify how far it would go by bearing fruit and increasing. If, then, we do not know when, as the Church bears fruit and increases, the whole world will be absolutely filled *from sea to sea*,[55] we undoubtedly do not know when the end will be; it will, of course, not be before that.

13, 52. But in order to disclose to you as a holy man of God and a most sincere brother what I hold on this question, we must avoid error in both respects, as far as it is possible for a human being to avoid it —by believing, in other words, that the Lord will come either more quickly or more slowly than is going to be the case. But a person does not seem to me to be in error when he knows that he does not know something, but when he thinks that he knows what he does not know. Let us, therefore, get rid of that bad servant who says in his heart, *The master is slow in coming* (Mt 24:48-49; Lk 12:45), lords it over his fellow servants, and associates with drunkards in carousing. He certainly and without a doubt hates the coming of his master. With that bad servant out of the way, let us set before our eyes the three

---

55. See Ps 72:8; Sir 44:23; Amos 8:12.

good servants who carefully and soberly manage their master's household, desiring ardently the coming of their master, awaiting him with vigilance, and loving him faithfully, even if one of them thinks that the master will come sooner and another that he will come later, while the third admits his ignorance about this. And though they are all in accord with the gospel, because they all long for the coming of the Lord, desire it, and vigilantly await it,[56] let us still see which of them is more fully in accord with the gospel.

53. One says, "Let us watch and pray because the Lord is going to come sooner." The second says, "Let us watch and pray because this life is both short and uncertain, though the Lord is going to come later." The third says, "Let us watch and pray, because this life is both short and uncertain, and we do not know the time when the Lord will come." The gospel says, *Pay attention; watch and pray, for you do not know when the time may be* (Mt 13:3). I ask you, what else do we hear this third person say but what we hear the gospel say? All, in fact, because of their desire for the kingdom of God, want what the first one said to be true, but the second denies this, while the third does not deny either of them but admits that he does not know which of them is speaking the truth. Hence, if what the first one predicted comes about, the second and third will rejoice with him. For all of them long for the coming of the Lord.[57] And so they will exult because what they long for has come sooner. But if this does not happen and what the second said instead begins to appear to be true, we would have to fear that, amid these delays, those who believed what the first one said may be disturbed and begin to think that the coming of the Lord will not be late but will not be at all. And you see what great harm that is for souls. But if they are people of such great faith that they change their views to the predictions of the second person and faithfully and patiently await the Lord, even though he is slow in coming, there will nonetheless be an abundance of reproaches, insults, and scorn from their enemies, who will turn many weak persons away from the Christian faith, saying that the promise of the kingdom is as false as the promise that it was going to come quickly. But if those who believe what the second one says, namely, that the Lord is going to come more slowly, find out that this is false when the Lord comes sooner, those who believed him will by no means be disturbed in their faith but will rejoice over their unexpected joy.

54. Hence, one who says that the Lord will come sooner says what is more desirable but is in danger if mistaken. Would, then, that it be true, because it will cause trouble if it is not. But the one who says that the Lord will come later, and yet believes, hopes, and loves his coming, even if he is mistaken about his slowness, is of course mistaken, though happily so. For he will have greater patience if this is the case and greater joy if it is not. And for this reason the first one is

---

56. See 2 Tm 4:8.
57. See 2 Tm 4:8.

listened to with more pleasure by those who long for the coming of the Lord[58] but the second one is listened to with greater safety. But the one who admits that he does not know which of these is true hopes for the former, endures the latter, and is mistaken in nothing, because he does not either affirm or deny any of them. I beg you not to look down on me for being such a person, because I love you for affirming what I want to be true, and the more I desire what you promise, the more I want you not to be mistaken, and the more I see danger if you are mistaken. Pardon me if I have been a burden to your holy eyes and ears. For the more rarely it comes about, the more it has delighted me to converse at greater length with you at least by letter.

---

58. See 2 Tm 4:8.

Letter 200

At the end of 418 or the beginning of 419 Augustine wrote to Count Valerius, a Catholic layman and high official at the imperial court in Ravenna. He thanks Valerius for his three letters and tells the count of the high praise for Valerius that Augustine has heard from Firmus (paragraph 1). Augustine expresses his joy over Valerius' virtues (paragraph 2), and especially over his marital chastity. Finally, Augustine hopes that Valerius will be pleased by *Marriage and Desire*, which he has written for him and sent along with the letter (paragraph 3). At the time of this letter Augustine did not, of course, know that he would add a second book to the work after Valerius sent him a set of excerpts from Julian of Eclanum's *To Turbantius*.

Augustine sends greetings in the Lord to Valerius, his illustrious and truly most excellent lord and dearest son in the love of Christ.

1. I was long annoyed because I had written several times and had not merited any reply from Your Highness. Then I suddenly received three letters from Your Grace. One, which was not for me alone, was delivered by my fellow bishop Vindemialis, and not long afterwards I received two from the hands of my fellow priest Firmus. That holy man, as you were able to learn from him, is united to us in the closest love; he conversed with us at length about Your Excellency and truthfully conveyed the sort of man he knew you to be in the heart of Christ.[1] In that way he outdid not only the letters brought by the aforementioned bishop or those that he himself brought but even those that we complained of not having received. And his report concerning you was more pleasing to us precisely because he said things that you yourself could not have written in reply, even at my request, lest you become the herald of your own praises—which holy scripture forbids.[2] Perhaps I should be afraid to write this to you for fear of being suspected of flattering you, my illustrious lord and my deservedly most excellent and most dear son in the love of Christ.

2. See what a delight and joy it was for me to hear the praises of you in Christ or, rather, the praises of Christ in you, from that man who could neither deceive me because of his trustworthiness nor fail to know them because of his friendship with you. We have also heard other reports from other persons, though not so many or such reliable ones, about your sound Catholic faith, your pious expectation of things to come, your love for God and the brethren, and your humble attitude amid your high honors. We have heard of how you do not place your hope in the uncertainty of riches but in the living God and of how you are

---

1. See Phil 1:8.
2. See Prv 27:3.

rich in good works,[3] of how your home is a place of rest and solace for holy persons and a place of terror for unbelievers, of how great your concern is that no one, whether among his old or his more recent enemies, should under the guise of Christ's name set ambushes for the members of Christ, and of how you look out for the salvation of these same enemies but are opposed to their error. As I said, we are accustomed to hear these and similar reports from other persons, but now from the aforementioned brother we have come to know them in more detail and with greater certitude.

3. But how would we have heard of your chastity in marriage except from some intimate friend who knew your life not superficially but in depth, so that we can also praise and love that in you? Regarding this virtue of yours, a gift of God, I am delighted to speak with you in a more familiar fashion and somewhat more at length. I know I will not be a burden to you if I send you a lengthy work so that by reading it you may be with us for a longer time. For I have also learned that amid your many great concerns you readily and gladly find time to read and that you are pleased by our little works, even those written for others, if any have been able to come into your hands. How much more attentively and gratefully will you give your attention to something written for you, in which I may speak to you as if you were present! Go from this letter to the book I sent along with it;[4] by its beginning it will more adequately convey to Your Reverence both why I wrote it and why I sent it to you in particular.

---

3. See 1 Tm 6:17-18.
4. Augustine wrote the first book of *Marriage and Desire* for Valerius after he had heard that some Pelagians had written to Valerius and had claimed that Augustine was condemning marriage in defending original sin. See *Revisions* 2, 53 (80). Valerius later sent Augustine various excerpts from Julian of Eclanum's work, *To Turbantius*, which Julian wrote against the first book of *Marriage and Desire*. The excerpts caused Augustine to write the second book of *Marriage and Desire*.

Letter 201

On 9 June 419 the emperors Honorius and Theodosius wrote to Aurelius, the bishop of Carthage and primate of Africa. They announce a new edict against Pelagius and Caelestius as well as anyone who offers them shelter or support anywhere in the provinces (paragraph 1). The emperors inform Aurelius that he is to use his authority to correct the stubborn obstinacy of any bishops who defend the Pelagian teaching or do not publicly attack it (paragraph 2).

The emperors Honorius and Theodosius, Augusti, send greetings to Bishop Aurelius.

1. It had already been determined some time ago that Pelagius and Caelestius, the authors of a wicked doctrine, should be banished from the city of Rome as being a kind of contamination of Catholic truth so that they would not pervert the minds of the ignorant with their deadly persuasion.[1] In this matter our clemency has followed the verdict of Your Holiness, by which it is established that they have been condemned by all after an impartial examination of their view. But because the persistent evil of their obstinate error demanded the renewal of the decree, we have also ordered by a recent edict that, if anyone who knows that they are hiding in any part of the provinces delays either to drive them off or to report them, he should be subject to the prescribed penalty as a participant in their crime.

2. It will be helpful, however, our dearest and most beloved father, if the authority of Your Holiness presses on, especially to correct the obstinacy of certain bishops who either support the wicked arguments of the Pelagians by tacit consent or do not destroy them by public attack, since Christian devotion on the part of all is in agreement on the abolition of this absurd heresy. Your Reverence, therefore, will warn all by appropriate letters and notify them that this directive has been enjoined upon them by the decree of Your Holiness, namely, that whoever out of impious obstinacy fails to subscribe to the condemnation of the aforementioned persons, by which they may prove their own innocence, will be punished by the mandatory loss of the episcopacy, permanently expelled from the cities, and excommunicated. For, since in accord with the Council of Nicaea we venerate with a sincere confession God, the creator of all things and

---

1. On 30 April 418 Emperor Honorius condemned and exiled Pelagius and Caelestius; on 1 May the Council of Carthage condemned in nine canons the principal doctrines of Pelagius and Caelestius, and in June or July of that year Pope Zosimus issued his *Tractoria,* in which he too condemned the teaching of Pelagius and Caelestius. Julian of Eclanum and eighteen other bishops refused to assent to the condemnation of Pelagius and Caelestius and continued to promote the Pelagian teachings.

the source of our empire, Your Holiness will not permit that persons adhering to this detestable heresy, who are devising new and unheard-of ideas to the injury of religion, conceal in remote regions their sacrilege, which has now been condemned by public authority. For, dearest and most beloved father, they commit one and the same sin who either connive at this error by feigning ignorance of it or offer it harmful support by not condemning it. [In another hand:] May the divinity keep you safe and sound for many years. Given on 9 June at Ravenna during the consulate of Monaxius and Plinta. Also sent with the same content to the holy bishop Augustine.

Letter 202

At the end of 419 Jerome wrote to Alypius, the bishop of Thagaste, and to Augustine. He congratulates them on their victory over the Caelestian, that is, the Pelagian, heresy (paragraph 1). Jerome explains why he has not replied concerning the books of a certain Annianus and conveys the greetings of various other persons to Alypius and Augustine (paragraph 2).

To his truly holy lords, Alypius and Augustine, bishops who are to be venerated with all affection and by every right, Jerome sends greetings in the Lord.

1. The holy priest Innocent, the bearer of this letter, did not take with him my letter to Your Reverence last year, on the grounds he was not going to return to Africa. But we thank God that it turned out that you overcame our silence by your letters. For every occasion on which I write to Your Reverence is most pleasant for me. I call upon God as my witness that, if it were possible, I would take up the wings of a dove and wrap myself in your embraces. This would always be in accord with the merits of your virtues, but it is so now especially because the Caelestian heresy[1] has been slain by your cooperation and initiative. It had so infected the hearts of many that, though they perceive that they have been defeated and condemned, they still do not give up their poisonous ideas. And they hate us—the only thing they can do—because they think that through us they lost the freedom to teach heresy.

2. But you ask[2] whether I replied to the books of Annianus,[3] the fake deacon of Celeda, who dines most lavishly in order that he may serve up the frivolous words of a strange blasphemy. You should know that I received not long ago on little scraps of parchment those books sent to me by my holy brother, the priest Eusebius, and then, because of either the worsening illnesses or the death of your holy and venerable daughter, Eustochium,[4] I was so saddened that I almost thought that they should be ignored. For he is stuck in the same mud,[5] and apart from some ringing and borrowed words he says nothing else. Still we worked hard in order that, when he tries to reply to our letter, he may reveal himself more

---

1. Caelestius was am ally of Pelagius; he was condemned at the Council of Carthage in 411. Augustine wrote *The Perfection of Human Righteousness* against a work of Caelestius entitled *Definitions*.
2. The letter of Augustine to Jerome is not extant.
3. Annianus was a lesser-known follower of Pelagius.
4. Eustochium, the daughter of Paula, was the first young lady of the Roman nobility to consecrate her life to God as a virgin. Paula and Eustochium followed Jerome to Bethlehem. Eustochium assumed direction of the monastery after the death of her mother; Eustochium herself died in 418 or 419.
5. See Terence, *Phormio* 780.

openly and disclose his blasphemies to everyone. For whatever he denies that he said in that wretched synod of Diospolis he openly admits in this work, and it is nothing grand to reply to utterly inept nonsense. But if the Lord grants me life and if we have an abundance of secretaries, we will reply with a few ideas not to refute a heresy that is already dead but to lay bare by our words his ignorance and blasphemies. Your Holiness would do this better so that we would not be forced to praise our own work in opposition to a heretic. Albinus, Pinian, and Melania, the holy son and daughters whom we share, greet you.[6] I have entrusted to the holy priest Innocent this short letter from holy Bethlehem to be delivered to you. Your daughter Paula[7] humbly begs that you keep her in mind and heartily greets you. May the clemency of Our Lord Jesus Christ keep you safe and sound and mindful of me, my truly holy lords and fathers who are venerable with all affection.

---

6. For Albina, her daughter, Melania, and her son-in-law, Pinian, see Letters 124, 125, and 126. They had passed through Africa after the fall of Rome and then moved on to Palestine. Augustine wrote for these wealthy members of the nobility *The Grace of Christ and Original Sin* after they wrote to Augustine that they believed that Pelagius had admitted the correct view on grace.

7. This Paula is obviously not the mother of Eustochium, but it is not clear who she may be.

Letter 202A

At the beginning of 420 Augustine wrote to Optatus, the bishop of Milevis, who had written against the Donatists and to whom Augustine had written Letter 190. Augustine explains that he cannot send Optatus the answer he had hoped to have received from Jerome since Jerome has not answered his question (paragraph 1). Furthermore, he does not want to publish his letter to Jerome without Jerome's answer (paragraph 2). He quotes from Jerome's letter to show that Jerome had excused himself from replying because of various problems (paragraph 3). Jerome had not, however, refused to reply at some later time, and Augustine remains hopeful that he will (paragraph 4). Augustine also does not want others who might read his letter to Jerome to think that they are quarreling (paragraph 5). If Jerome never replies and Augustine's letter becomes public, those who read it will at least be able to learn how one should not rashly affirm what one does not know, and Augustine admits that he has not discovered how the soul derives original sin from Adam if the soul itself is not derived from Adam (paragraph 6).

Augustine asks Optatus to explain an apparent contradiction in the letter that he sent to Caesarea and to defend the view that he said was full of the truth (paragraph 7). Optatus had criticized those who hold the propagation of souls on the ground that God creates human souls. Augustine asks him to prove that God creates souls apart from propagation (paragraph 8). Augustine also asks Optatus to send him a copy of his profession of faith and to indicate the testimonies in favor of creationism (paragraph 9). The reason Optatus gives for rejecting the propagation of souls is insufficient (paragraph 10).

Augustine again cites the alternatives that Optatus proposed and insists that they are not mutually exclusive and that he accepts both of them (paragraph 11). Just as God is the creator of human bodies, though they are procreated by parents, so he is the creator of human souls, even if they are propagated by parents (paragraph 12). Augustine urges Optatus to defend the position that God is the creator of all things, including human souls, against anyone who denies this (paragraph 13). But whether God creates human souls by means of propagation or apart from propagation is quite another question (paragraph 14).

Augustine points out that there are things about which it is permissible to doubt, just as the apostle did not know whether or not he was in the body when he was rapt to the third heaven (paragraph 15). If it were possible, Augustine would rather know when Christ will come again than know the origin of human souls (paragraph 16). He lists the truths that he knows about the soul, including the fact that every infant is born with original sin contracted from Adam that can only be removed by baptism (paragraph 17). Augustine asks Optatus to inform him, if he knows, how the soul of an infant contracts sin from its origin if it does not take its origin from Adam. If Optatus does not know the answer to this question, Augustine asks him to be patient with his inability to answer Optatus' question about the soul's origin (paragraph 18). Augustine adds that he has written to Optatus as to someone who rejected the propagation of souls with certitude, but that he would have written something different in reply to those who defend this view (paragraph 19). Finally, Augustine warns Optatus that he should be wary of the Pelagian heresy in thinking about or discussing the origin of the soul (paragraph 20).

To Optatus, his most blessed and sincerely most dear lord, most beloved brother and fellow bishop, Augustine sends greetings in the Lord.

1, 1. I received by means of the pious priest Saturninus the letter of Your Reverence; you ask of me with great desire something that I do not yet have. But you explained to me the reason why you did this, namely, because you believe that I consulted someone on this matter and have already received a response. Would that it were so! Heaven forbid that I should deprive you, who I know are awaiting it so eagerly, of a share in this gift. But if you believe me at all, look, almost five years have passed from the time I sent to the East my book, filled not with presumptions but with questions.[1] And I have not yet merited to receive a reply that might resolve for me this question, on which you desire that I deliver to you my definitive opinion. I would have sent both of these if I had both of them.

2. It does not seem right that I should now send or publish what I have without the other that I do not yet have. Otherwise, that man, who is perhaps going to reply to me, as I desire, may rightly become angry at seeing that my questions, which were developed with laborious argumentation, were circulating in people's hands and minds without his response, for which I should not give up hope. For he might think that I did this more out of pride than out of usefulness, as if I could pose questions that he could not resolve, though he perhaps can, and he might think that I should wait until he does. For I know that he is more occupied with other tasks that cannot be postponed and that are more important.

3. But in order that Your Holiness may know this as well, attend briefly to what he wrote to me the other year through the return of the same courier by whom I had written to him. For I have copied this from his letter. "A most difficult time," he says, "has come upon us when it is better for me to be silent than to speak. As a result our studies have ceased for fear—to use the words of Appius—that our eloquence may be that of a dog.[2] And so I could not reply to the two books of yours that you dedicated to me,[3] books full of learning and resplendent with every sparkle of eloquence, not because I found anything blameworthy in them but because in the words of the blessed apostle, *Each person abounds in his own ideas* (Rom 14:5), *one in this way, another in that* (1 Cor 7:7). Certainly you have stated and discussed whatever could be said and drawn

1. Augustine refers to Letter 166 to Jerome, which is also called *The Origin of the Soul*.
2. See Sallust, *History*, fragment 2, 37.
3. That is, Letters 166 and 167, also called *The Origin of the Soul* and *The Opinion of James*.

from the sources of the holy scriptures by your lofty mind. But I ask Your Reverence to allow me to praise your talent a little. For we converse among ourselves for the sake of gaining knowledge. But if enemies, and especially heretics, see differences of opinion between us, they will slander us by saying that they stem from rancor of the heart. Yet I have decided to love you, to cherish you, to honor you, to admire you, and to defend your statements like my own. To be sure, even in the dialogue that I recently published,[4] I was mindful, as was proper, of Your Beatitude. Let us make a greater effort to remove from the churches the very destructive heresy that constantly feigns repentance in order to have the possibility of teaching in the churches and of avoiding being expelled and dying outside, if it is seen in full daylight."[5]

2, 4. You surely see, my venerable brother, that these words of my very dear friend in reply to my question did not refuse to give a response but only gave an excuse for the time being, because he is forced to devote his attention to other more urgent matters. You also see what a benevolent attitude he has toward me and what warning he gives so that enemies, and especially heretics, may not slander us by saying that what we do between ourselves for the sake of gaining knowledge, without any harm to love and to the sincerity of friendship, stems from rancor of the heart. Hence, if people read both of our works, the one in which I asked my questions and the one in which he responds to my questions, there will be no small benefit when this comes to the knowledge of many. For I must be grateful for having received instruction if the same question has been sufficiently explained in accord with his view. And in that way our juniors will not only know what they ought to hold on this matter, which has been discussed between us in careful debate, but will also learn by our example through God's mercy and kindness how there may exist between dearest brothers a mutual discussion for the purpose of gaining knowledge, while love nonetheless remains inviolate.

5. But if my letter, in which this most obscure question is merely posed, is released and spread about more widely without his reply, in which the answer may perhaps be found, it may also come into the hands of those who, as the apostle says, *comparing themselves with one another* (2 Cor 10:12), do not understand the spirit with which we are acting, because they do not know how to act with that spirit. And they will interpret my attitude toward my very beloved friend, who is worthy of honor for his great achievements, not as they see it, since they do not see it, but as they want and suspect at the prompting of their hatred. This is something that we certainly ought to avoid as much as we can.

6. But if what we do not want to become known through us should perhaps become known, even against our will, to those by whom we did not want it to

---

4. That is, *The Dialogue against the Pelagians* (*Dialogi adversus Pelagianos*).
5. Letter 172, 1.

become known, what will remain but to accept the will of the Lord calmly? For I ought not to write to anyone what I wanted to remain unknown forever. For, if—God forbid!—by some chance or necessity that man never replies, our questions that we sent to him will undoubtedly at some point become known. Nor will they be read without benefit because, though people will not find the answers they sought, they will certainly find how they should ask questions and how they should not rashly affirm what they do not know, and in accord with what they read there, they themselves will take care to consult those whom they can with zealous love, not with a rivalry full of discord, until they either find what they want or exercise the keenness of their mind by investigation so that they realize that they should not pursue their questions any further. But now I think that I have convinced Your Charity that, as long as we should not give up hope of a response from the friend who has already been consulted, I should not, insofar as it is up to us, publish our questions, though you also did not request my questions alone but wanted us to send you the response of the man whom I consulted attached to my questions. And I would certainly do this if I had his response. But if I may use the words of Your Holiness that you wrote in your letter, when you say, "a clear proof of my wisdom, which the source of light has given to me, in accord with the merit of my life," you are not referring to my questions and inquiry. Rather, you suppose that the solution of the matter about which I asked has already come to me, and you are asking that I send it to you. I would do so if the facts were as you suppose. But I confess that I still have not found out how the soul derives sin from Adam—a point that we may not doubt—while the soul itself is not derived from Adam. I must investigate this carefully rather than assert something thoughtlessly.

3, 7. Your letter speaks of the countless elders and men taught by learned priests whom you could not win over to the idea of your modest capacity and to your statement utterly filled with the truth. Yet you do not say what is the statement utterly filled with the truth to which you could not win over the elders and men taught by learned priests. For if these elders held or hold what they received from learned priests, how has the ordinary and less educated mass of clerics caused difficulties for you in these matters in which they were taught by learned priests? But if these elders or the mass of clerics have by their sinfulness departed from what they received from learned priests, they should rather have been corrected by the authority of those priests and restrained from their most contentious uproar. But again, when you say that as a new and inexperienced teacher you were afraid to undermine the teachings of such great and good bishops and feared to bring people to a better position on account of injury to those who have died, what do you leave us to understand but that those whom you wanted to correct have, by refusing to abandon the teachings of learned and great dead bishops, refused to yield to a new and inexperienced teacher? In this matter I remain silent for the present concerning them. But I strongly desire to know the statement of yours that you say is utterly filled with the truth. I do not mean just the opinion but its defense.

4, 8. You have sufficiently brought it to our knowledge that you disapprove of those who maintain that all souls are propagated and passed on by the succession of generations from the one soul that was given to the first human being. But we do not know, because your letter does not contain it, the argument or the testimonies of the divine scriptures by which you showed that it is false. Second, as I read your letter that you sent earlier to the brothers at Caesarea and that you most recently sent to me, I do not clearly see what you yourself hold in place of the view you reject, except that I see that you believe, as you write, that "God made, is making, and will make human beings, nor is there anything in heaven or on earth that has not come to be and does not continue to be with him as its author." This is, of course, so true that no one ought to have any doubt about it. But you still need to state out of what God makes souls, which you deny are made by propagation. Is it from something else? And if so, what is that something? Or is it from absolutely nothing? For God forbid that you should hold the view of Origen and of Priscillian[6] and of anyone else who might hold something of the sort, namely, that souls are given to mortal and earthly bodies in accord with the merits of a previous life. The authority of the apostle contradicts this opinion when he says that, when they were as yet not born, Esau and Jacob had done nothing either good or bad.[7] Hence your view on this question is not entirely but only partially known to us. But its defense, that is, how you show that what you hold is true, is completely hidden from us.

9. On this account I had asked in my previous letter if you would be so good as to send me the profession of faith that you mention you wrote and to which you complain some priest or other had falsely added his signature. I also ask for this now as well as for the divine testimonies that you were able to use to resolve this issue. For you say in the letter to the brothers at Caesarea that you "decided that for the full testing of the truth even secular judges should hear the case, and by an outpouring of his mercy," as you write, "the divinity has granted to those who sat in judgment at the request of all and examined everything regarding the faith that they might produce a stronger statement and defense of it in accord with their minds than" your "modest abilities maintained regarding them by the authorities

---

6. Origen, the great theologian of the Eastern church, was accused of holding the preexistence of human souls and their fall into bodies as a punishment for sins committed before their embodiment. Whether he actually held such a doctrine is debated among Origen scholars. Priscillian, a Spanish priest, was accused of all sorts of heretical teaching, though he was usually accused of holding that the soul was divine, as the Manichees did , rather than of holding the preexistence and fall of the soul into bodies. See Augustine, *To Orosius in Refutation of the Origenists and Priscillianists.*

7. See Rom 9:11.

of important testimonies." I desire to know, therefore, these "authorities of important testimonies."

10. You seem to have followed only one line of argument to refute your opponents, namely, that they deny that our souls are the work of God. If that is what they hold, it is right that their opinion be judged worthy of condemnation. For, if they said this about bodies, they undoubtedly ought to have been either corrected or detested. For what Christian would deny that the bodies of individual newborn infants are the work of God? And yet we do not for this reason deny that they are born from their parents because we say that they are made by God. When, therefore, it is said that a certain special kind of incorporeal seeds of our souls are in that way derived from our parents and yet that souls are made from them by the work of God, you have to use as a witness to refute this not human conjecture but divine scripture. For a wealth of testimonies from the books of canonical authority are available to us by which it is proven that God makes souls. Those testimonies refute those who deny that each individual soul in newborn infants is a work of God, but not those who admit this and still maintain that they are formed like bodies by the work of God but through propagation from their parents. In order to refute these people you must seek out certain divine testimonies. Or, if you have already found them, we ask with as much urgency as we can that they be sent out of mutual love to us who have not yet found them.

5, 11. Your brief and final question in the letter that you sent to the brothers at Caesarea reads as follows: "I beg," you say, "that you teach me, your son and disciple, who with the help of God has come only quite recently to these mysteries. Give me the instruction that you ought and that is proper, with which it is suitable for prudent priests to respond. Should we rather hold the view that says that the soul comes by propagation and that the other souls flow through some hidden origin and secret order into the whole human race by transmission from Adam, who was formed first? Or should we instead choose the position that all your brothers and the priests stationed here hold and affirm, and should we retain the belief that testifies and holds that God was, is, and will be the author of all things and of all human beings?" Of these two that you proposed as questions, then, you want me to choose one of the two and to give it to you as the answer, which those with knowledge would have to do if these two were so opposed to each other that, if one were chosen, the other would have to be rejected.

12. But now, if anyone does not choose one of these two but replies that each of them is true, that is, that the other souls flow into the whole race of human beings by transmission from Adam, who was formed first, and still believes and says that God was, is, and will be the author of all things and of all human beings, what do you suppose should be said against this? Are we going to say, "If souls are propagated from parents, God is not the author of all things because he does

not make souls"? For, if we say that, we will receive the answer, "Then, because bodies are propagated from parents, God is not the author of all things, if on this account he must be said not to make bodies." But who would deny that God is the author of all human bodies and would say that he is the author only of the one that he formed from the earth in the beginning, or at least of his wife's as well, since he himself formed her from his side, but not the author of other bodies, because we cannot deny that the other bodies flowed from these?

6, 13. And for this reason, if those with whom you are in conflict on this question claim that souls are propagated by derivation from that one soul so that they deny that God now acts and forms them, continue to attack, refute, and correct them to the extent that you can with the help of the Lord. But if they say that souls took their beginning from that one man and thereafter were derived from parents while still affirming that individual souls in individual human beings are created and formed by God, the author of all things, search especially the holy scriptures for what you might reply to them that is not ambiguous and that cannot be understood in some other way. Or, if you have already found something, send it to us as well, as I have already asked above. But if you still do not know it as I do not, by all means continue with all your strength to refute those who say that "souls do not come from God's work," for you said in your first letter that they murmured this amid their esoteric myths and then withdrew from your company and from the service of the Church on account of this stupid and wicked view. And against them defend and protect in every way what you said in that same letter: "God made, and is making, and will make souls, and there is nothing in existence in the heavens or on earth that has come to be and is without him as its author." For it is perfectly true and perfectly correct to believe, say, defend, and approve this with regard to absolutely every kind of creature. For God was, is, and will be the author of all things and of all human beings. You put this in the last part of your letter to our fellow bishops of the province of Caesarea, and in some way you urged them rather to choose and to hold onto that view by means of the example of all their brothers and fellow priests who are among you.

14. But it is one thing to ask whether God is the author and maker of all souls and bodies, which the truth maintains, or whether some nature comes into existence that he does not make, an opinion that is of course erroneous. It is another thing to ask, however, whether God makes human souls through propagation or without propagation, though it is still not permissible to doubt that he does make them. On this question I want you to be sober and vigilant. And do not reject the propagation of souls in such a way that you fall into the Pelagian heresy. For, if we say, and say truthfully, that God is the creator of human bodies, which everyone knows are propagated, not merely of the first human being or of the first couple but of all those propagated from them, I think that it is easy to understand that we do not have the intention of refuting those who defend the propagation of souls when we state that God makes souls, since he also makes bodies,

which we cannot deny come from propagation. But we have to look for other proofs by which to refute these people who think that souls are propagated if the truth says that they are in error. On this topic those deceased persons rather should have been questioned, if it were possible, since, as you write in the last letter you sent to me, you were afraid to convert people to a better view for fear of injury to them. For you said that "those deceased bishops were such good, great, and learned men, that, as a new and inexperienced teacher, you were afraid to aim at undermining their teachings." And so, if I could know the arguments or testimonies by which such good, great, and learned men have defended this view on the propagation of souls,[8] . . . in the letter sent to the bishops of Caesarea, showing no regard for their authority, you said that it "is a novel invention and unheard-of teaching," though, even if it is an error, we still know that it is not novel but old and ancient.

7, 15. But when some reasons compel us not without good reason to have doubts about some question, we ought not also for this reason to have doubts about whether we ought to doubt. About dubious matters we of course should undoubtedly have doubts. You see how the apostle did not hesitate to doubt about himself whether he was carried off to the third heaven *in the body or out of the body*; whether this or that was the case, he says, *I do not know; God knows* (2 Cor 12:2-3). Why, then, would I not be permitted to doubt as long as I do not know whether my soul has entered this life through propagation or without propagation, since I do not doubt that in either way it was made by the sovereign and true God? Why am I not permitted to say, "I know that my soul subsists as the result of God's work and is certainly the work of God, but whether it comes from propagation like the body or apart from propagation like the soul that was given to the first human being, *I do not know; God knows?*" You want me to affirm one of these. I could do so if I had knowledge. If you know this, look, you have in me someone more desirous to learn what I do not know than to teach what I know. But if like me you do not know, also pray like me that the teacher, who said to his disciples, *Do not desire that people call you, Rabbi. You have one teacher: Christ* (Mt 23:8.10), may teach us either through some servant of his or by himself, but only if that teacher, who knows not only what he should teach, but also what is beneficial to teach us, knows that it will benefit us also to know such things.

16. For I admit to Your Charity my desire. I certainly desire to know what you are seeking, but I would desire much more to know, if it were possible, when *the desired of all nations* (Hg 2:8) will make his appearance and when the kingdom of the saints will come to be than to know how I began to come to this earth, and yet, when his disciples, our apostles, asked that of him who knows

---

8. The CSEL edition indicates a lacuna at this point.

everything, they received the answer, *It is not yours to know the times that the Father established by his own authority* (Acts 1:7). Suppose he, who certainly knows what it is useful for us to know, also knows that it is not ours to know this. And of course I know through the apostle that it is not ours *to know the times that the Father has established by his own authority.* But whether it is ours to know the origin of our souls, which I do not yet know, that is, whether it belongs to us to know this, I certainly do not know. For, if I at least knew that it was not ours to know this, I would not only not make any affirmation, as long as I do not know, but I would also cease doing any investigation. But now, although this question is so obscure and deep that I avoid rashness in teaching anything on it more than I desire to learn something, I still would also like to know this, if I could. And though what that holy man said is much more necessary, *Make known to me, O Lord, my end* (Ps 39:5)—he did not, after all, say, "my beginning"—I wish that my beginning, insofar as it relates to this question, were not hidden from me.

8, 17. I am not, however, ungrateful to my teacher even about my beginning, because I know that the human soul is a spirit, not a body, and that it is rational or intellectual. I also know that it is not the nature of God but rather a creature. It is in some respect mortal insofar as it can change for the worse and be separated from the life of God, by partaking of which it becomes happy, and it is in some respect immortal because it cannot lose the consciousness by which after this life it will be either happy or unhappy. I also know that it did not merit to be enclosed in flesh in return for actions it did before being in the flesh. And I also know that the soul does not for this reason exist in a human being without the filth of sin, *even if,* as scripture says, *his life has lasted a single day on earth* (Job 14:4-5 LXX). And for this reason I know that no one is born from Adam through the process of generation without the sin on whose account it is necessary even for infants to be reborn in Christ through the grace of rebirth. I am grateful that I have learned, and I affirm that I know, these many and not unimportant points concerning the beginning or origin of our souls. Among them more things pertain to that knowledge that rests upon faith. Hence, if regarding the origin of souls I do not know whether God makes them for human beings through propagation or without propagation, though I still have no doubt that he does make them, I prefer to know this also rather than not to know it. But as long as I cannot, I do better to doubt this than to dare to affirm something as certain that might perhaps be opposed to some point about which I ought not to have any doubt.

18. And so, my good brother, since you are consulting me and want me to decide on one of these: whether the other souls come from that one man by propagation as bodies do or whether without propagation individual souls are made by the creator for individual human beings as that one soul was made (or we do not deny that those souls are made by him, whether in this way or in that) permit me to consult you as well. How does a soul contract sin from an origin from

which the soul itself does not derive its origin? For we do not deny that all souls are alike in contracting original sin from Adam, lest we fall into the despicable Pelagian heresy. If you yourself do not know what I ask you, be patient in allowing me to be ignorant of both what you ask and what I ask. But if you already know what I ask, when you have taught me this, I will then answer the question that you want me to answer, now having no fear about it. I ask, therefore, that you not be angry because I could not give a firm answer to your question, but I could show you the question you are asking. And when you find the answer, you should not hesitate to support the answer to the question you were asking.

19. I thought that I should write this to Your Holiness, for you think that the propagation of souls should be rejected, as if you had certitude about it. On the other hand, if I had to reply to those who maintain this, I would perhaps have shown how they do not know what they think they know and for what reason they ought to fear being so daring as to maintain this.

20. In the letter of reply from my friend, which I inserted in this letter, do not at all let it upset you that he mentioned that I had sent two books to which he replied that he did not have the free time to respond. There is one on this question, not two. But in the other I asked him something else by way of consultation and commentary. When he warns and exhorts "that we make a greater effort to remove the very destructive heresy from the churches,"[9] he refers to the Pelagian heresy, and I warn you, my brother, as much as I can, to avoid it most carefully, when you either think or argue concerning the origin of souls, so that the idea does not enter your mind that we should believe that any soul, except that of the one mediator, did not contract from Adam original sin, which is acquired by birth and must be removed by rebirth.

---

9. Letter 172, 1.

Letter 203

Probably in 418 to 420 Augustine wrote to Largus, a Catholic layman, possibly the Largus who was proconsul of Africa in 418-419. Augustine urges him to scorn the things of earth and to turn his hopes to the world to come. He consoles Largus on account of what he has suffered and urges him to benefit from his sufferings by improving his life.

To his illustrious and most excellent lord and most beloved son, Largus, Augustine sends greetings in the Lord.

I received the letter of Your Excellency in which you asked me to write to you. You would certainly not desire this unless you regarded as gratifying and pleasing what you thought that I might be able to write. But this is it: You should scorn the vanity of this world now that you have experienced it, if you desired it before you experienced it. For in it pleasure is deceiving, labor without fruit, fear constant, and success dangerous. It begins without a plan and ends with regret. Such are all those things that we seek with more desire than wisdom in these pains of our mortality. Quite different is the hope of believers, different the fruit of their labor, different the reward of their perils. For in this world it is impossible not to fear, not to grieve, not to labor, not to face danger. But it makes a great difference for what reason, with what expectation, and with what outcome one suffers these things. I myself, when I gaze upon the lovers of this world, do not know when wisdom could have the chance to heal their minds. For, when they have prosperity, they reject with scorn salutary warnings and regard them as an old wife's refrain. But when they are faced with adversity, they think more of how to escape from their present difficulties than of receiving the means of their being cured and of how they may arrive where they will not have any troubles at all. At times, however, some of them use the ears of their heart and apply them to the truth, more rarely amid prosperity, more often amid adversity, but they are nonetheless few, for it was foretold that they would be few.[1] I desire that you be among them, because I truly love you, my illustrious and most excellent lord and most beloved son. Let this admonition be my reply to your greeting, because, though I do not want you to suffer hereafter the sort of things you have endured, I am yet more saddened that you have suffered such difficulties without some reformation of your life for the better.

---

1. See Mt 20:16 and 22:14.

Letter 204

In the summer of 418 Augustine wrote to Dulcitius, a tribune and imperial commissioner in charge of implementing the imperial edicts. Dulcitius's brother Laurentius was a Roman priest for whom Augustine wrote his *Handbook on Faith, Hope, and Charity*. In *Revisions* 2, 59, Augustine states that Dulcitius wrote to Gaudentius, the Donatist bishop of Thamugadi, "urging him to Catholic unity and dissuading him from the fire by which he was threatening to destroy himself and his people in his church." Dulcitius also persuaded Augustine to produce his *Answer to Gaudentius* in reply to two letters Gaudentius had sent to Dulcitius, justifying his plan of suicide. In the present letter Augustine acknowledges Dulcitius' request that Augustine instruct him in how to refute the Donatist heretics (paragraph 1). He insists that the threat on the part of some Donatists to kill themselves ought not to deter the Catholics from trying to bring others into the unity of the Catholic Church (paragraph 2). Augustine points out that the Donatists of the town of Thamugadi have misunderstood Dulcitius' words to them about their deserving death (paragraph 3). Augustine points out that he is very busy and that he has responded in many other writings to the claims of the Donatists (paragraph 4). He nonetheless argues from scripture that it is wrong to kill an innocent human being, even one who is dying and wants to be killed (paragraph 5). The Donatists have appealed to the example of death that Razis inflicted upon himself according to the Books of the Maccabees (paragraph 6). But, Augustine points out, his death is reported, not praised; it is proposed for our judgment, not for our imitation (paragraph 7). Razis' death was noble and manly but not wise, a great act but not a good one (paragraph 8). Finally, Augustine acknowledges his debt of love to the people of Thamugadi, namely, that he should reply to the two letters of Gaudentius which the Donatist bishop had written in defense of his actions and had sent to Dulcitius (paragraph 9).

To his excellent lord and honorable son, Dulcitius, Augustine sends greetings in the Lord.

1. I ought not to disregard your request when you want to be instructed about how you ought to reply to the heretics, for you are also seeking their salvation in the mercy of the Lord by the insistence of your zeal. For, though great numbers of them—for which we are very grateful—understand what a benefit they receive, some of them, nonetheless, who are ungrateful to God and to men under the wretched impulse of their madness, believe that they strike terror into us by their own destruction when they cannot wreak havoc upon us with their butchery. Thus they seek either their own joy from our deaths or our sorrow from their deaths. But the mad error of a few human beings ought not to prevent the salvation of so many and such numerous peoples. Not only God and wise human beings but also they themselves, though they are most hostile to us, realize what

372

we want for them. For, when they suppose that they ought to strike terror into us by their own destruction, they do not doubt that we fear that they may perish.

2. But what should we do, seeing that by the help of the Lord many find the path to peace through the opportunity you provide? Can we or should we keep you from this insistence upon unity because we fear that certain people who are very hardhearted and cruel toward themselves might destroy themselves not by our choice but by their own? We should certainly want all those who bear the standard of Christ in opposition to Christ and who boast of the gospel, which they do not understand, in opposition to the gospel, to abandon their perversity and to rejoice along with us in the unity of Christ. But since by his deeply hidden but still just providence God has predestined some of them to the direst punishments, it is undoubtedly better that some of them perish in their own fires rather than that all of them burn in the everlasting fires of hell as a punishment for their sacrilegious schism.[1] For incomparably more in number have been reunited and gathered from that pestilential schism and division. For the Church mourns these people when they perish, just as holy David mourned his rebellious son, for preserving whose safety he had issued commands out of anxious love. For he grieved over him as even his tear-filled voice bore witness, when his son deserved to be slain as a punishment for his wicked impiety. Nonetheless, when the proud and wicked son departed for the place he deserved, the people of God, who were divided by his revolt, acknowledged their king, and the achievement of unity consoled the father's grief over the loss of his son.[2]

3. We do not, therefore, my excellent lord and honorable son, blame you because you thought that such persons should first be warned at Thamugadi by a decree. But because you said in it, "Know that you will be handed over to the death you deserve," they thought, as their replies show, that you had made this threat because you were going to kill them when they were arrested. They did not understand that you were speaking about the death that they themselves want to inflict upon themselves. For you have not received the power of life and death over them by any laws, nor have any imperial decrees, with whose execution you have been charged, commanded that they be put to death. By the second decree of Your Charity you certainly made more clear what you intended. But since you thought that you should also address their bishop by letter, you revealed in a most friendly manner the great gentleness that restrains those in the Catholic Church whom the power of the emperor has placed in charge of correcting errors, either by injecting terror or by imposing penalties, except that you addressed him with more respectful language than it was fitting to address a heretic.

---

1. See Mt 5:22; 18:19.
2. See 2 Sm 18-19.

4. Since you wanted me to answer his reply, I believe that you thought that I should also offer the people of Thamugadi a refutation in somewhat greater detail of the false teaching of the man who led them astray. But we are both very busy and have already refuted this sort of nonsense in many other works of ours. For I have no idea how many times we have shown in speech and by the written word that they cannot have the death of martyrs because they do not have the life of Christians. For it is not the punishment but the reason for it that makes a martyr. We have also taught that human beings were given free choice in such a way that it is still entirely correct that penalties are established by divine and human laws for serious sins, that it is the task of the religious rulers of the earth to restrain by due severity not only adulteries, murders, and other such crimes or outrages but also sacrileges, and that they are very mistaken who think that we receive such persons as they are because we do not rebaptize them. For how do we receive them as they are, since they are heretics and, by coming over to us, become Catholics? It is not forbidden to correct hearts that have fallen into error because it is forbidden to repeat sacraments that have been conferred once.

5. Concerning the insane deaths that some of them inflict upon themselves, because of which they are often despicable and abominable even to many of their own people whose minds have not been taken over by such great madness, we have often replied to them in accordance with the scriptures and the reasonings of Christians. For scripture says, *To whom will one be good who is bad to himself?* (Sir 14:5) Or surely, if he thinks it good and permissible to kill himself, he should also kill his neighbor when he finds him in the same trials and wanting to die, since scripture says, *Love your neighbor as yourself* (Mt 22:39; Mk 12:31; Lk 10:27; Lv 19:18). The Books of Kings indicate clearly enough that it is not permitted without the command of any laws or legitimate authorities to kill another person, even a person who wants and asks to be killed and is no longer able to live. There King David ordered that the man who killed Saul be put to death, though he had said that Saul, who was wounded and half-dead, had asked him to do this and to release his soul from those torments by one blow of the sword, since it was struggling with its ties to the body and desired to be set free.[3] Hence, because everyone who kills a human being without any authority from a legitimate power is a murderer, whoever kills himself is not a murderer only if he is not a human being. We have said all these things in numerous ways in many of our other discourses and letters.

6. But I recall—I must admit—that I have never as yet replied to them with regard to the elderly Razis. Having found themselves with a complete dearth of examples, they boast that they just barely found him at long last in the Books of the Maccabees,[4] after having examined all the authorities of the Church as

---

3. See 2 Sam 1:1-16.
4. See 2 Mc 14:37-46.

authorization for the crime by which they destroy themselves. But here is what ought to suffice for Your Charity and any wise persons for refuting them: If they are ready to apply to the life of the Christian people as examples all the actions from the Jewish people and those writings, then let them apply this as well. In them there are many actions of those persons who are praised by the truth of those writings, but they are either not suitable to the present time or were not correctly done even at that time. Such is the act that this Razis committed upon himself. He was a noble man among his own people and had made much progress in Judaism, which the apostle says is loss and rubbish in comparison with Christian righteousness,[5] and for this reason the same Razis is called "Father of the Jews." Yet why is it surprising if proud thoughts took possession of him as a man so that he preferred to die by his own hand rather than to endure shameful slavery at the hand of enemies after being so elevated in the eyes of his own people?

7. These actions are often praised in the books of the pagans. But though this man was praised in the Books of the Maccabees, his action was reported, not praised, and it was set before our eyes, as if it were, for judgment rather than for imitation. We should certainly not judge it by our own judgment, which we could also have as human beings, but by the judgment of sober teaching that is clear even in the old books. This Razis was certainly far removed from those words where we read: *Accept whatever is done to you, and endure it in sorrow, and have patience in your humiliation* (Sir 2:4). This man, then, was not wise in choosing death but impatient in bearing humiliation.

8. Scripture says that he wanted *to die nobly and manfully* (2 Mc 14:42). But did he, therefore, do so wisely? He wanted to die nobly in order that as a captive he would not lose the freedom of his people and manfully because he had such strength of mind that he was able to take his own life, and, when he could not accomplish this by the sword, he threw himself headlong from the wall. And so, while still alive, he ran to a steep rock, and there, now drained of blood, he tore out his intestines, which he spread about and scattered over the people with both hands, and after that he died exhausted.[6] These are great acts, but not good ones. After all, not everything that is great is good, since there are also great sins. God said, *Do not kill the innocent and righteous* (Ex 23:7). If, then, he was not innocent and righteous, why is he proposed for imitation? If, however, he is innocent and righteous, why is he, a killer of someone innocent and righteous, that is, of Razis himself, also to be thought worthy of praise?

9. For the time being these ideas are enough for completing this letter so that it does not become too long. But because they have been highly commended to me both by your desire and by my honorable and most dear son, Eleusinus, who

---

5. See Phil 3:8.
6. See 2 Mc 14:42-46.

serves as tribune among them, I owe to the people of Thamugadi a service of love, namely, that I reply to the two letters of Gaudentius, the bishop of the Donatists, especially to his most recent one, which he thinks that he has produced in accordance with the holy scriptures. Otherwise he might think that something has been passed over.

Letter 205

Probably in 419 or 420 Augustine wrote to Consentius, a Catholic layman from the Balearic Islands, who was enthusiastically interested in various theological questions. Besides the present letter, Augustine wrote Letter 120 to Consentius, and Consentius wrote Letters 119, 11*, and 12* to Augustine. Moreover, Augustine dedicated to Consentius his work, *Against Lying*. In the present letter Augustine tells Consentius how much he would like to see him (paragraph 1) and goes on to answer Consentius' question about whether Christ's body in heaven has bones and blood, insisting that it certainly does. He points to the clothes and sandals of the people of Israel that lasted for forty years in the desert as evidence that God can make bodily things incorruptible (paragraph 2). The Lord's body is now incorruptible, even if it has blood and the other humors of our corruptible bodies (paragraph 3). The three young men in the fiery furnace show that God can protect bodies from corruption (paragraph 4).

When the apostle said that flesh and blood would not possess the kingdom of God, he meant that corruptibility would not possess it (paragraph 5). To explain Paul's meaning, Augustine does a line-by-line exegesis of the pertinent verses of chapter fifteen of the First Letter to the Corinthians, in which he stresses the differences in various kinds of bodies and points out that our risen body will be free from corruption and will be spiritual and glorious, just as Christ's body is now (paragraphs 6 through 9). He rejects the idea that our body will be turned into a spirit so that it will no longer be a body (paragraph 10). Christ, the new Adam, is a life-giving spirit who will give our risen bodies life and make them spiritual (paragraph 11). He continues his exegesis of the chapter, explaining that Christ became mortal in order to make us immortal (paragraph 12). Hence, the expression *flesh and blood* in this passage means the corruptibility of flesh and blood (paragraph 13). Both the just and the unjust will rise incorrupt, but only the just will be transformed to full incorruptibility (paragraph 14). The wicked will rise incorrupt in terms of the integrity of their members but will suffer the pain of punishment (paragraph 15). As "flesh" can have two senses, so both God and the devil can be said to tempt, though in different senses (paragraph 16).

Consentius had asked whether God forms the features of our bodies, and Augustine points to scripture texts that show that he does (paragraph 17). With regard to his question about whether all the baptized will be saved, Augustine refers him to his work, *Faith and Works* (paragraph 18). Finally, he answers Consentius' question about whether the breath God breathed into Adam was or was not his soul (paragraph 19).

To Consentius, his most beloved brother, Augustine sends greetings.

1, 1. In terms of the eyes of the body we see certain people and do not know them, since we do not know their interests and life. Others we know, though we do not see them, since their love and affection has become well known to us, and

377

among these we count you. And for this reason we desire to see you more in order that you may be among those whom we both see and know. For those who are thrust before our eyes without being known are not only not desired but are hardly tolerable, unless from some signs we see the beauty of the inner person in them. But we already know those whose mind, like yours, we know through understanding before seeing their body. But we desire to see them also in order that, through what we see by the eyes, we may enjoy with much more delight and familiarity that inner friend whom we already know. But God will perhaps grant us this as well in your case, when human affairs have become more quiet and peaceful, as we hope, in order that this may be the result of sincere love rather than painful necessity. Now let me reply, as well as I can with the Lord's help, to the questions that you asked me, which you sent on a separate sheet apart from the letter.

2. You ask whether the body of the Lord now has flesh and blood or the other features of the flesh. What if you added whether he also has clothes? Would the question not be broadened? For what reason except that we can scarcely imagine to be without corruption those things we know are corruptible in the course of this life of ours, though we have already been given some proofs of divine miracles from which we may conjecture greater ones? For, if the clothing of the Israelites could last for so many years in the desert without wearing out, if the leather of their sandals lasted so long with decay,[1] God can certainly prolong the incorruptible character of any bodies for as long as he wants. Hence I believe that the body of the Lord is in heaven as it was on earth when he ascended into heaven. But he said to his disciples, as we read in the gospel, when they were doubtful about his resurrection[2] and thought that what they were seeing was not a body but a spirit, *Look at my hands and feet; touch and see, because a spirit does not have bones and flesh, as you see that I have* (Lk 24:39). Just as he was touched by their hands when he was on earth, so he was followed by their eyes when he went into heaven. Then the voice of the angel sounded, *He will come just as you saw him going into heaven* (Acts 1:11). Let faith be present, and no question will remain.

3. Or perhaps we should ask about blood because, when he said, *Touch and see, because a spirit does not have flesh and bones* (Lk 24:39), he did not add "and blood." We ourselves, then, should not add a question about what he did not add in his words, and the question should be quickly ended, if you please. For some more troublesome investigator may perhaps use blood as an occasion and press us, saying, "If blood, why not phlegm as well; why not yellow bile and black bile, by which four humors the science of medicine also tells us that the nature of the flesh is held in balance?" But whatever anyone adds, let him be

---

1. See Dt 29:4.
2. See Lk 24:37.

careful not to add corruption so that he does not corrupt the soundness and purity of his own faith.

4. Human weakness measures the works of God that it has not experienced by its familiarity with the things that it has experienced, and it supposes that it chatters on cleverly when it says, "If there is flesh, there is also blood; if there is blood, there are also the other humors; if there are the other humors, there is therefore corruption." And in that way this weakness would say, "If there is a flame, it also burns; if it burns, it also consumes; if it consumes, then it burned up the bodies of the three men thrown into the fiery furnace by the wicked king."[3] But if whoever thinks correctly regarding God's works does not doubt that this miracle took place in the case of the three men, why should we not believe that he who made those bodies unable to be corrupted by fire made Christ's body unable to be corrupted by fire, hunger, disease, old age, or by any other force by which corruption usually destroys human bodies? And if anyone says that incorruptibility was not added to the flesh of those men in the face of the fire but that the ability to corrupt was taken from the fire, why should we fear that God could not make the flesh unable to be corrupted if he could make the fire unable to corrupt? For, if the case of the three men is understood in terms of a change not of the flesh but of the fire, it is much more marvelous; for, at the same time it did not burn the human bodies lest it harm them, it burned the wood in the furnace so that it was ablaze. But those who do not believe even these miracles are too dubious about God's power, nor is our conversation now with them or directed to them. Those, however, who believe these miracles may also conjecture from them the one that they investigate with faith. God's power, then, is able to remove from this visible and tangible nature of bodies the qualities he chooses to remove, while others remain. And for this reason it can also endow mortal members with unwavering strength, while the shape of their features remains, though the corruption of their mortality is gone. Thus decay is gone, but the features are present. And motion is present, but fatigue is gone. The power of eating is present, but the need to eat is gone.

2, 5. When, therefore, we read in the apostle, *Flesh and blood will not inherit the kingdom of God* (1 Cor 15:50), the question is, of course, also answered in the way you mentioned. That is, by the terms *flesh and blood* we understand the works of flesh and blood. But since the apostle was not speaking of works but of the manner of resurrection and was weighing that question in his argument, *flesh and blood* are better understood in that passage as meaning "the corruption of flesh and blood." For, if the term "flesh" signifies an activity, why should it not also signify "corruption" in the way scripture says, *All flesh is grass*? For here too corruptibility was signified. For there follows, *And all the beauty of the flesh*

---

3. See Dn 3:19-24.

is like the flower of the field; the grass dries up, and the flower falls. (Is 40:6-8)
Does this also belong to that flesh of which Christ said, *Touch and see, because
a spirit does not have bones and flesh* (Lk 24:39)? For how would it dry up and
fall, since scripture says that *Christ rising from the dead now no longer dies, and
death will no more have dominion over him* (Rom 6:9).

6. Hence, look at that statement of the apostle above, and consider the whole
of it. Since he wanted to convince those who were saying that there is no resurrection of the dead, after he set forth Christ's resurrection as an example among
the other things that he discussed there, he posed for himself a question and
asked, *But someone will say: How will the dead rise? In what body will they
come?* that is, in what sort of body? Then, using seeds as proof, he said, *You fool!
What you sow does not come to life until it first dies, and when you sow, you do
not sow the body that will come to be, but the mere seed, for example, of wheat or
of some other kind. But God gives it a body as he wishes, and to each of the seeds
its own body.* (1 Cor 15:35-38) In this sense he had said, *You do not sow the body
that will come to be.* For it is not that wheat will not come from wheat but that no
one sows grass or straw or the many sheaves of the grain in the straw, though the
seeds spring up with these. For this reason he said, *but the mere seed,* wanting to
show from this that, if God can add what was not present in the mere seed, he can
for even better reasons repair what was present in the human body.

7. Now what he adds pertains to the difference of those who rise, on account
of the differences in glory of the faithful and the saints. He says, *Not all flesh is
the same flesh; the flesh of humans is different from the flesh of cattle, from the
flesh of birds, and from the flesh of fishes. There are both heavenly bodies and
earthly bodies. But the glory of heavenly bodies is different from the glory of
earthly ones. And the glory of the sun is different from the glory of the moon and
from the glory of the stars. For star differs from star in glory. The resurrection of
the dead will be like that.* (1 Cor 15:39-43) In all of this the sense is this: If,
though the kinds of flesh are all mortal, they nonetheless differ among themselves in accordance with the differences of the animals, and if, though all bodies
are visible, they nonetheless differ in accordance with the differences of their
places so that *the glory of heavenly bodies is different from that of earthly ones,*
and if, though all heavenly bodies are in places above, they themselves differ in
the brightness of their light, it is no surprise that, in the resurrection of the dead,
the glory of the merits of the saints will differ.

8. From here he now comes to what all flesh that rises to eternal life has in
common, and he says, *It is sown in corruption, but it rises in incorruptibility; it is
sown in ignominy, but it rises in glory; it is sown in weakness, but it rises in
power; a natural body is sown, but a spiritual body rises* (1 Cor 15:42-44). From
these words of the apostle may we suppose that our bodies will rise in a better
condition than Christ's, though he was set before us as an example that we ought

to aim at with faith and to hope for through grace? And for this reason Christ's body could in no way rise with corruptibility if we are promised that ours will rise in incorruptibility, nor could his body rise without glory if ours will rise in glory. But what glory is present where there is still corruption? It is much too absurd for us to believe, therefore, that his body was both sown, that is, put to death, in weakness and will rise in weakness, though our body is sown in weakness but will rise in power. And the same apostle says of Christ, *Even though he was crucified because of weakness, yet he lives because of the power of God* (2 Cor 13:4). But who would think so absurdly as to believe that his body was sown as natural and raised up as natural if our body is sown as natural but rises as spiritual?

9. It is certain and in no way to be doubted, therefore, that though the body of Christ did not see the corruption of decay in the tomb, for which reason scripture said, *Nor will you allow your holy one to see corruption* (Ps 16:10), it could still be pierced by nails and a lance. And though it was sown in the ignominy of suffering and death, it is now in the glory of eternal life. Though it could be crucified because of weakness, it now reigns in power. And that which was a natural body, because it was taken from Adam, is now spiritual since it has been inseparably united to the spirit. For, when the apostle wanted to use the testimony of the scriptures about the natural body, he quoted what we read in Genesis. He said, *If there is a natural body, there is also a spiritual body. For scripture says, The first Adam was made into a living soul*, or, *into a live soul.* (1 Cor 15:44-45) You recall, of course, how scripture said, *And God breathed into his face the breath of life, and the man was made into a live soul* (Gn 2:7). But it was also said of the animals, *Let the earth bring forth a live soul* (Gn 1:24). It is therefore understood that the natural body is said to be like the rest of the animals on account of the dissolution and corruption of death, which is daily repaired by food, and afterward the structure of the living being is overcome and destroyed. But a body is called spiritual because it is now immortal with its spirit.

10. Some people think that the body will become spiritual when the body itself is changed into a spirit and that, though a human being was composed of body and spirit, the two of them will be entirely spirit, as if the apostle had said, "A body is sown, but a spirit will rise." But he said, *A natural body is sown, but a spiritual body will rise* (1 Cor 15:44). Hence, just as a natural body is not a soul but a body, so we ought to think that a spiritual body is not a spirit but a body. Besides, who would dare to suppose either that Christ's body did not rise as spiritual or, if it rose as spiritual, was then not a body but a spirit? For he refutes this opinion of his disciples where, when they saw him and thought they saw a spirit,[4] he said, *Touch and see, because a spirit does not have bones and flesh, as you see that I have* (Lk

---

4. See Lk 24:37.

24:39). That flesh, then, was already a spiritual body, and yet it was not a spirit but a body no longer to be torn or separated from the soul by death. In the same way a natural body of the sort that was given to the soul by the breath of God, when *the man was made into a live soul* (Gn 2:7), would have become spiritual from natural without the intervention of death if the transgression of the commandment had not imposed its penalty for the sin that was committed before God gave the crown of glory for the righteousness that was preserved.[5]

11. For this reason the Lord Christ came to us by means of us when, as righteous, he found sinners through the pathway, so to speak, of our lowliness but not with the disease of our sinfulness. For he was seen by us through a natural, that is, through a mortal body, though he certainly would have come for the first time with an immortal body if he had chosen to. But, because we had to be healed by the lowliness of the Son of God, he came down to our weakness and revealed by the power of his resurrection the merit and reward of our faith. And so the apostle went on and said, *The last Adam became a life-giving spirit* (1 Cor 15:45). Whether we understand the first Adam as the one who was long ago formed out of dust and the last Adam as the one born of a Virgin, or whether both of these are realized in each human being, so that the first Adam is a human being in a mortal body and the last Adam the same human being in an immortal body, yet he wanted there to be this difference between a living soul and a life-giving spirit—that there is a natural body but here a spiritual body. The soul, of course, is living in a natural body but does not give life to the point of taking away corruptibility. But in a spiritual body, because by clinging completely to the Lord the soul becomes one spirit,[6] it gives life so that it produces a spiritual body, consuming all corruptibility and fearing no separation from the body.

12. Hence there follows, *But first there was not what is spiritual, but what is natural. Afterward there was what is spiritual. The first man from the earth was earthly; the second man from heaven was heavenly. As the earthly man, so also are those who are earthly, and as the heavenly man, so also are those who are heavenly. Just as we have borne the image of the earthly man, let us also bear the image of the man who is from heaven.* (1 Cor 15:46-49) What does it mean, *As the earthly man, so also are those who are earthly*, but that they are mortal because they come from a mortal man? And what does it mean, *As the heavenly man, so also are those who are heavenly*, but that they are immortal through the immortal one? Mortal through Adam, immortal through Christ. For the Lord became earthly, though he was heavenly, in order that he might make heavenly those who were earthly. That is, he become mortal from immortal *by taking on the form of the servant* (Phil 2:7), not by changing the nature of the Lord, in order

---

5. See 2 Tm 4:8.
6. See 1 Cor 6:17.

that by imparting the grace of the Lord, not by retaining the mistreatment of a slave, he might make immortal those who were mortal.

13. Since, therefore, when discussing the resurrection of the body, the apostle taught that our bodies will become incorruptible from corruptible, glorious from ignominious, strong from weak, and spiritual from natural, that is, immortal from mortal, he adds the words that we are concerned with and says, *But I say this, brothers: Flesh and blood cannot possess the kingdom of God*. And lest anyone think that the apostle stated this in terms of the substance of the flesh, he disclosed what he was saying by adding, *Nor will corruption possess incorruptibility* (1 Cor 15:50). It is as if he said: "I said, *Flesh and blood will not possess the kingdom of God*, because *corruption will not possess incorruptibility*." In this passage, therefore, he wanted us to understand by the terms *flesh and blood* the corruption of mortality.

14. Next, suppose that someone said to him, "How will it both be flesh and not be flesh? It will certainly be flesh, since after the resurrection the Lord said, *Touch and see, because a spirit does not have bones and flesh as you see that I have* (Lk 24:39). It will not be flesh, since *flesh and blood will not possess the kingdom of God* (1 Cor 15:50)." As if someone had said this, he explains what he said and adds, *See, I am telling you a mystery. All of us will indeed rise*—or as some Greek manuscripts have, *All of us will indeed fall asleep*—*but not all of us will be transformed*. The following shows whether he wanted us to understand this transformation for the worse or for the better. He says, *in an instant*, that is, in a moment of time that cannot be divided, *in the blink of an eye*, that is, at the highest speed, *at the last trumpet*, that is, at the last sign that will be given for these events to take place, *the trumpet will sound, and the dead will rise as incorrupt, and we will be transformed* (1 Cor 15:50-51). Hence we undoubtedly ought to understand this as a transformation for the better, because all, both the just and the unjust, will rise, but, as the Lord says in the gospel, *Those whose actions were good will rise for life, but those whose actions were bad will rise for judgment* (Jn 5:29). Here he calls eternal punishment a judgment, just as in another passage he says, *One who does not believe has already been judged* (Jn 3:18). Hence those who will rise for judgment will not be transformed into that incorruptibility that cannot experience the corruption of pain. For that belongs to the faithful and the holy, but these will be tortured by endless corruption, because *their fire will not be extinguished, and their worm will not die* (Is 66:24).

15. What, then, does this distinction mean, *And the dead will rise as incorrupt, and we will be transformed* (1 Cor 15:52), but that all will rise as incorruptible, and from these the just will also be transformed into that incorruptibility which absolutely no corruption can harm? And for this reason those who will not be transformed into it will indeed rise as incorrupt in the integrity of their members but will nonetheless be corrupted by the pain of punishment,

when they hear, *Go, you accursed ones, into the eternal fire that was prepared for the devil and his angels* (Mt 25:41). *Of that bad news the righteous will have no fear* (Ps 112:7). But after he had said concerning that transformation of the just, *We will be transformed*, as if we had asked how this will take place, he goes on to say, *For this corruptible body must put on incorruptibility and this mortal body must put on immortality* (1 Cor 15:52-53). We should not, as I think, doubt that *flesh and blood will not possess the kingdom of God* (1 Cor 15:50) was said in the sense that the corruption and mortality of flesh and blood will not exist there. For in this passage he used *flesh and blood* to refer to these qualities.

16. Hence, in order to quote by way of example something that comes to mind in the meanwhile, scripture says, *For fear that the tempter might tempt you and our labor be in vain* (1 Thes 3:5), and here the devil is understood, as if God does not tempt at all, since scripture says of him in another passage, *But he tempts no one* (Jas 1:13). Nor is this statement opposed to the one that says, *The Lord your God is tempting you* (Dt 13:4). But the matter is resolved because the word "tempt" has different meanings, since temptation to lead astray is one thing, and temptation to test is another. In accordance with the first meaning the tempter is only the devil, but in accordance with the second meaning God tempts. In the same way, when we say, "Flesh will possess the kingdom of God," and, "Flesh will not possess the kingdom of God," the meaning of this term is also distinguished, and the matter is resolved. For "flesh" in the sense of its substance, in accordance with the words, *A spirit does not have flesh and blood, as you see that I have* (Lk 24:39), will possess the kingdom of God, but "flesh" when understood in the sense of its corruption will not possess it. For this was explained when, after it said, *Flesh and blood will not possess the kingdom of God*, there was immediately added, *Nor will corruption possess incorruptibility* (1 Cor 15:50), as I think we have discussed sufficiently.

3, 17. But your question as to whether God the creator forms the features of each body will not trouble you if you understand, to the extent the human mind can, the power of God's action. For how will we be able to deny that God even now makes everything that is created, since the Lord says, *My Father is at work even now* (Jn 5:17). Hence we should understand that on the seventh day he ceased from creating natures, not from governing those that were said to have been created. Since, then, the nature of things is governed by the creator and since all things come to be in their order at set places and times, God is even now at work. For, if God does not now form them, how is it that we read, *Before I formed you in the womb, I knew you* (Jer 5:17)? And how can we interpret, *If God so clothes the grass of the field that is today and tomorrow will be thrown into the furnace* (Mt 6:30)? Are we supposed to believe that God clothes the grass and does not form our bodies? For, when he said *clothes*, he shows clearly enough that he was speaking not of God's past action but of his present activity. In the same sense there is also that statement of the apostle about seeds, which we mentioned above. He says, *You do not sow the body that will be, but the mere seed of, for example, wheat or any of the rest. But God gives it a body as he wants.* (1 Cor 15:37-38) He did not say, "He gave," or, "He arranged," but, "He gives," in order that you might understand that the creator applies the power of his wisdom to the creation of things that come to be each day at their proper times. Of that wisdom scripture said, *It stretches from end to end mightily and*—it did not say "disposed" but—*disposes all things gently* (Wis 8:1). But it is a great task to have even a slight grasp of how changeable and temporal things are created not by changing and temporal actions of the creator but by his eternal and unchanging power.

4, 18. On the point on which you thought that you should question me, namely, whether all the baptized are at any time going to obtain pardon if they left their body without doing penance while ensnared in various sins, I have written a book of no small size,[7] and if you take care to read it, you will perhaps have no further question for me.

19. You also want to know from me whether that breath of God in Adam is the same as the soul. To respond briefly: Either it is the soul or the soul was made by it. But if it is the soul, it was made. It is certainly of the soul that God speaks through Isaiah the prophet when he says, *I made every breath,* as the following words indicate clearly enough. For there follows, *I saddened it,* that is, the breath, *a little on account of sin* (Is 57:16-17 LXX), and other things that can only be understood of the human soul. For on this question one must especially avoid believing that the soul is not a nature made by God but the very substance of God like the only-begotten Son, that is, his Word, or some particle of him, as if that nature and substance, whatever it is, by which he is God, could be subject to change, something that no one who knows that he has a soul fails to know that the soul is. While I was dictating this, the courier, who was already waiting for the wind, was strongly pressing me in order that he might set sail. And so, if you read something expressed clumsily or without refinement or if you find the whole of it to be such, pay attention to my teaching but pardon my expression. [In another hand:] May you live for God, my most beloved son!

---

7. *Faith and Works* written in 413, shortly after *The Spirit and the Letter.*

Letter 206

In approximately 420 Augustine wrote to Valerius, a Catholic layman and a high official at the imperial court in Ravenna, to recommend to his care Felix, a fellow bishop from North Africa. See Letter 200, which Augustine sent to Valerius along with the first book of *Marriage and Desire*, which Augustine wrote after having received reports from Valerius that Julian of Eclanum was claiming that Augustine's teaching on original sin amounted to a denunciation of marriage.

To Valerius, his rightly illustrious lord and most excellent son who is most dear in Christ, Augustine sends greetings in the Lord.

As often as people ask me that I recommend them to your goodness and trustworthiness, if I do not do so, I think that I do not judge correctly either about your mercy toward those in need of help or about your good will toward us. And so I am doing so, and I do not hesitate, my rightly illustrious lord and son who are most dear in Christ, to recommend especially the ministers of Christ who have charge of the Church, of which we rejoice that you are a coheir and son. When, therefore, our holy brother and fellow bishop Felix asked this of me, I certainly ought not to have refused. Hence I recommend to you a bishop of Christ who needs the help of a lofty personage. Do, therefore, what you can, because the Lord has given you great power, and we know that you deeply desire his riches.

Letter 207

Perhaps in 421 or 422 Augustine wrote to Claudius, an Italian bishop from whom he had received a copy of Julian of Eclanum's *To Turbantius*. Augustine now sends Claudius his *Answer to Julian* and explains how in his two books on *Marriage and Desire* he had not been able to reply to the text of Julian since he had only the reports of others and excerpts made from Julian's work by someone else.

Augustine sends greetings in the Lord to Claudius, his blessed brother and fellow bishop.

Because you were stirred by brotherly love for me and sent to me the four books of Julian that he wrote against my one book,[1] I thought that I could do nothing better than to have you in particular read what I wrote in answer and judge whether I answered correctly and appropriately. For someone or other had written some excerpts from these four books for Count Valerius, an illustrious and religious man, in opposition to that same book of mine, which he knew I had written for him.[2] When those excerpts came into my hands thanks to that same lofty person, I did not delay in adding a second volume to that first one in which I refuted all those points as best I could. But now, when I inspected those books more carefully, I found that the man who made some excerpts from them did not cite everything as it is to be found in those books.

Hence Julian or anyone else of those people could think that I had not spoken truthfully, since I was not able to come to know those four books as I was able to know the passages that were excerpted from them and sent to the count whom I mentioned. Whoever, then, reads that second book of mine which, like the first book, was written for the same Count Valerius, will recognize that in some places I did not answer Julian but rather the person who selected those statements from his books and did not cite them as he found them but thought that he should change them somewhat, perhaps in order in that way to make his own what is clearly the work of another. But now, relying on the more accurate copies that Your Holiness sent, I see that I ought to answer the author himself. He boasts that he has refuted my one book by his four and does not cease from spreading venom against the faith. I have, then, undertaken this work with the

---

1. Julian wrote the four books of *To Turbantius* in reply to the first book of Augustine's *Marriage and Desire*.
2. Augustine wrote the first book of *Marriage and Desire* for Count Valerius, a high official at the imperial court in Ravenna. See Letter 200. After Augustine received the excerpts from Julian's work, he wrote the second book of *Marriage and Desire*. Finally, after he received from Claudius a copy of Julian's work, Augustine wrote his *Answer to Julian*.

help of the savior of infants and of adults, and I know that you have prayed for me so that I might complete it and for the people whom we believe and hope that these labors of ours will benefit. Give your attention, then, to my answer. Its beginning follows this letter. May you enjoy good health in the Lord, my blessed brother, and keep us in your thoughts.

Letter 208

Toward 423 Augustine wrote to Felicia, a consecrated virgin and recent convert from Donatism, who was scandalized by the actions of certain bad pastors in the Catholic Church. Augustine expresses his concern over Felicia's disappointment with scandals in the Church (paragraph 1). He points out that Christ himself had predicted that there would be scandals and distinguished the good shepherds from the bad ones (paragraph 2). But only Christ can separate the good from the bad and only at the end of the world (paragraph 3). In no case should one leave the Church on account of scandals in it (paragraph 4). Even the bad shepherds can teach sound doctrine, and we should listen to what they say without acting as they do (paragraph 5). We should place our hope in our one shepherd, Christ, rather than in human shepherds (paragraph 6). Finally, Augustine exhorts Felicia to love Christ and the Church. Though she was compelled to enter the unity of the Church by Christ's ministers, she should not place her hope in them but in Christ (paragraph 7).

To Felicia, his rightly respected lady and honorable daughter among Christ's members, Augustine sends greetings in the Lord.

1. I have no doubt that your heart was troubled both for your own faith and for the weakness or sinfulness of others, since the holy apostle, full of deep feelings of love, admits and says, *Who is weak and I am not weak? Who is scandalized and I do not burn?* (2 Cor 11:29) For that reason I too was saddened and concerned for your salvation in Christ, and I thought that I should send this letter of either consolation or exhortation to Your Holiness, because in the body of Christ, which is his Church and the unity of his members,[1] you have become for us a most true sister who are loved like an honorable member in his body and live along with us by his Holy Spirit.

2. Hence I counsel you not to be so seriously troubled by these scandals. It was predicted that they were going to come so that, when they came, we would recall that they were predicted and not be deeply upset by them. For the Lord himself predicted them in the gospel in this way: *Woe to the world because of scandals! It is necessary that scandals come, but woe to the person through whom scandal comes!* (Mt 18:7; Lk 17:1) Who are these people but those of whom the apostle says, *Seeking their own interests, not those of Jesus Christ* (Phil 2:21). There are, therefore, some men who occupy the chairs of shepherds in order to take care of the flocks of Christ, but there are others who sit in them in order to enjoy their own temporal honors and worldly advantages. It is necessary that these two kinds of shepherds continue to exist in the Catholic Church, as

---

1. See Col 1:24.

some die and others take their place, until the end of the world and until the judgment by the Lord. For, if at the time of the apostles there were such men among the false brethren whom the apostle lamented when he said, *Perils from false brethren* (2 Cor 11:26), and whom he did not expel through pride but endured through patience, how much more is it necessary that they exist in our own time, since the Lord says most clearly concerning the time of this world that is drawing to its end, *Because wickedness will abound, the love of many will grow cold* (Mt 24:12). But what follows ought to console and encourage us. *Whoever perseveres*, he says, *until the end will be saved* (Mt 24:13; 10:22; Mk 13:13).

3. Just as there are good and bad shepherds, so there are also good and bad persons in the flocks. The good are referred to as sheep but the bad are called goats. But they graze, mixed together until *the prince of shepherds*, who is called *the one shepherd* (1 Pt 5:4; Jn 10:16), comes and, as he promised, separates *like a shepherd the sheep from the goats* (Mt 25:32). For he entrusted to us the flock but reserved for himself the separation of the sheep from the goats, because he who cannot make a mistake ought to separate them. For those proud servants who were quick to dare to separate them ahead of time, an action that the Lord reserved for himself, were instead separated themselves from the Catholic unity.[2] For, if they were impure because of their schism, how could they keep their flock pure?

4. In order, therefore, that we may remain in unity and not abandon the threshing floor of the Lord when we are offended by scandals from the chaff but may rather remain as grain until the end of the winnowing and endure the straw that is crushed by the strong weight of love, our shepherd himself warns us about good shepherds in the gospel. He warns us that we should not place our hope even in them because of their good works but that we should glorify our Father who is in heaven,[3] the one who made them such, and he warns us about bad shepherds, whom he chose to indicate by the terms "scribes" and "Pharisees," those who teach what is right but do what is wrong.[4]

5. For he speaks in this way about good shepherds, *You are the light of the world. A city set upon a mountain cannot be hidden, nor do they light a lamp and put it under a bushel but on a lampstand in order that it may give light for all who are in the house. In that way let your light shine before men in order that they may see your good works and glorify your Father who is in heaven.* (Mt 15:14-16) But concerning the bad shepherds he warns the sheep when he says, *They sit in the chair of Moses. Do what they say, but do not do what they do. For they talk, but they do not act.* (Mt 23:2-3) After having heard this, the sheep of

---

2. Augustine refers to the Donatists who wanted to separate themselves from what they regarded as the church of sinners.
3. See Mt 15:16.
4. See Mt 23:2-3.

Christ hear his voice even through the bad teachers and do not abandon his unity, because the good that they hear them speak does not come from them but from him. And for this reason the sheep graze in security because even under bad shepherds they are fed in the pastures of the Lord. But they do not do the bad actions of the bad shepherds because such actions are not his but theirs. With those whom they see are good, they not merely listen to the good words that they speak, but they also imitate the good actions that they do. The apostle was one of these; he said, *Be imitators of me, as I too am of Christ* (1 Cor 11:1; 4:16). He was a light enlightened by the everlasting light, the Lord Jesus Christ, and he was set upon the lampstand because he gloried in the cross of Christ. For this reason he said, *God forbid that I should glory save in the cross of our Lord Jesus Christ* (Gal 6:14). And because he did not seek his own interests but those of Jesus Christ, though he exhorted those to whom he gave birth through the gospel to the imitation of himself, he nonetheless severely rebuked those who created schisms over the names of the apostles and reprimanded those who said, *I belong to Paul.* He asked, *Was Paul crucified for you? Or were you baptized in the name of Paul?* (1 Cor 1:12-13; 3:4)

6. From this we understand that good shepherds do not seek their own interests but those of Jesus Christ[5] and that, though good sheep imitate the actions of their good shepherds, they nonetheless do not put their hope in those by whose ministry they were gathered into the flock[6] but rather in the Lord by whose blood they were redeemed. In that way, when they happen to come upon bad shepherds preaching Christ's doctrine but doing their own evil deeds, they do what the bad shepherds say, but they do not do what they do.[7] And they do not abandon the pastures of unity on account of the children of iniquity. For, in the Catholic Church, which does not exist only in Africa like the sect of Donatus, but, as was promised, expands and spreads out through all the nations, as the apostle says, *bearing fruit and increasing* (Col 1:6), there are both good and bad people. But people separated from her cannot be good as long as their thoughts are opposed to her. For, though a seemingly praiseworthy manner of life is thought to prove that some of them are good, their very division makes them bad, as the Lord says, *Whoever is not with me is against me, and whoever does not gather with me scatters* (Mt 12:30).

7. For this reason I also exhort you, my rightly respected lady and honorable daughter among the members of Christ, to hold faithfully onto what the Lord has given you and love him and his Church with your whole heart, for he has not permitted you to lose the fruit of your virginity or to perish with the wicked.[8] For,

---

5. See Phil 2:21.
6. See Ps 78:7.
7. See Mt 23:3.
8. See Dt 6:5; Mt 22:37; Mk 12:30; Lk 10:27.

if you left this world separated from the unity of the body of Christ, the preservation of your body's integrity would do you no good. But *God who is rich in mercy* (Eph 2:4) has done with you what is written in the gospel. When those invited to the dinner by the head of the house excused themselves, he said to his servants , among other things, *Go out into the roads and pathways, and whomever you find, force them to come in* (Lk 14:18,23). Although, then, you owe a most sincere love to his good servants by whose ministry you were forced to come in, you ought nonetheless to put your hope in him who prepared the banquet, about which you too are concerned out of a desire for eternal life and happiness. Entrusting to him your heart, your plan of life, your holy virginity, your faith, hope, and charity, you will not be upset by the scandals that will abound until the end, but you will be safe with solid strength and will be glorious in the Lord through persevering in his unity until the end.[9] But inform me by your reply how you have received this concern of mine for you, which I have taken care to convey to you by what words I could. May God's mercy and grace always protect you.

---

9. See 1 Cor 13:13.

Letter 209

Probably in the beginning of 423 Augustine wrote to Celestine, who became pope after the death of Boniface on 4 September 422 and died on 27 July 432. Augustine congratulates Celestine on his peaceful election to the papacy (paragraph 1). He explains to the pope how it came about that Antonius was ordained bishop of Fussala when the man whom Augustine wanted to be ordained refused to be ordained at the last minute (paragraphs 2 and 3). Augustine explains to Celestine that Antonius was accused of serious crimes by the people of Fussala (paragraph 4). When brought to trial, Antonius was required to make restitution to the people from whom he had stolen property and was allowed to retain the dignity of the episcopacy, though not over the people whom he had mistreated (paragraph 5). Augustine pleads for Celestine's help and calls his attention to how Antonius had induced the primate of Numidia to intercede on his behalf with Pope Boniface (paragraph 6). Antonius is now insisting that he should be bishop over the people of Fussala or should not be a bishop at all (paragraph 7). Augustine points to examples of penalties imposed on other bishops similar to that imposed on Antonius (paragraph 8). Augustine begs the pope for his help in order that Antonius may not do further harm to the people of Fussala or to himself (paragraph 9). Augustine tells Celestine of his sorrow and fear over the whole affair, which has brought him to consider resigning from the episcopacy (paragraph 10). In Letter 20* to Fabiola, a Roman laywoman, Augustine presents further details about the problems that Antonius had caused.

To Celestine, his most blessed lord and holy father to be venerated with due love, Augustine sends greetings in the Lord.

1. First, I congratulate you for your merits because the Lord our God has placed you in that great see without, as we have heard, any division among his people.[1] Secondly, I report to Your Holiness our situation in order that you may help us not only by praying for us but also by counseling us and bringing us relief. Finding myself in great trouble, I have sent this letter to Your Beatitude, because, though I wanted to do good to certain members of Christ in our neighborhood, I inadvertently and carelessly caused them a great loss.

2. A town bordering on the territory of Hippo bears the name Fussala; previously there was never a bishop there, but it belonged to the diocese of the church of Hippo along with the adjoining region. The country had few Catholics; the error of the Donatists held in wretched captivity the remaining people there, who were very great in number, so that in the same town there was no Catholic at all. It came about through the mercy of God that all these places were brought to the

---

1. The election of Celestine's predecessor, Boniface, had been disputed, with one part of the people favoring Boniface and another favoring Eulalius. Zosimus died in December 418, but Boniface was not recognized as the sole bishop of Rome until Easter of 419.

unity of the Church. It would take a long time to explain the many labors and perils of ours by which this was accomplished. The priests who were first sent there by us to bring back the people were robbed, beaten, injured, blinded, and killed. Yet their sufferings were not useless and without fruit since unity was securely attained. But the town I mentioned is at a distance of forty miles from Hippo. Since for governing the faithful and bringing back those few persons of both sexes who were still in schism, no longer in a threatening way but in flight, I saw that I was extended further than I ought to be and that I was unable to give them the attention that I realized with most certain evidence needed to be given them, I arranged to ordain and establish a bishop there.

3. In order to achieve that goal, I looked for someone apt and suitable for that place, who was also trained in the Punic language. And I had a priest in mind who was prepared, and to ordain him I got the holy old man who was then the primate of Numidia[2] to come from a distance, pleading with him by letter. And when he was already present and the hearts of all were eagerly awaiting so important an event, the man who I thought was suited backed down at the last minute, absolutely refusing. Of course I ought to have postponed things rather than to have rushed into such a dangerous action, as the outcome has proved. But since I did not want the most reverend and holy primate, who was so exhausted in coming to us, to return home without accomplishing the purpose for which he had come so far, I presented a certain youth, Antonius, who was with me at that time, though the people had not asked for him. He had been raised by us in the monastery from an early age, but apart from the office of lector[3] he had not attained any level or functions of the clergy. But those poor people most obediently obeyed me when I offered him to them, for they did not know what was going to happen. Why should I say more? He was ordained; he began to be their bishop.

4. What am I to do? I do not want to worsen in the eyes of Your Reverence a man whom I undertook to raise to the episcopacy, and I do not want to abandon those people whom I have brought to birth in Christ, gathering them to the Church amid fear and sorrow. And I cannot find a way to do both. The situation has developed into so great a scandal that the people who obeyed us by accepting him as bishop, thinking that they were looking out for their interests, presented their accusations against him here before us. But since in those accusations they could not prove capital charges of sexual misconduct, which were raised not by people of whom he was bishop but by certain others, and since he seemed to have been acquitted of those charges that were so hatefully spread about, he became so pitiful in our eyes and those of others that, whatever accusations were made

---

2. This was probably Silvanus of Zumma, the predecessor of Valentine of Baia, who was primate by 419.

3. The office of lector was one of the minor orders.

by the people of the town and of that region concerning his unbearable domination of them, concerning robberies, various acts of oppression, and harassment, they did not seem to us such that we thought that he should, for this reason or for all of them put together, be removed from the episcopacy. But we determined that he should restore the things that it was proven that he stole.

5. Finally, we tempered our verdicts so that, while he retained the episcopacy, those actions nonetheless were not left entirely unpunished that ought not to have been proposed either for him to repeat in the future or for others to imitate. And so we preserved the full episcopal dignity of the young man who was to be corrected, but in correcting him we diminished his power, that is, so that he did not preside over those people with whom he had behaved in such a way that with just resentment they absolutely could not bear his being over them and showed that their impatience would perhaps burst forth into some crime with danger to themselves and to him. Their frame of mind was also clearly seen to be such when the bishops dealt with them concerning him, though Celer,[4] a respected man about whose use of excessive power against him Antonius had complained, no longer holds any position of power either in Africa or anywhere.

6. But why should I delay over the many details? Work together with us, I beg you, my most blessed lord, who are venerable for piety and worthy of reverence with due love, O holy father, and command that everything that has been sent to you be read out. See how he has exercised the episcopacy, how he was in such agreement with our verdict that he would be excommunicated unless he first restored everything to the people of Fussala and how afterward, once the proceedings were over, he set aside a sum of gold for the estimated value of the property in order that he might be restored to communion. Consider how with a cunning argument he induced the holy old man, our primate, a highly respected man, to commend him to the venerable Pope Boniface as completely exculpated. What need is there for me to recall all the other things since the venerable old man I mentioned has reported all of them to Your Holiness?

7. But in those many records which contain our judgment about him, I would have to fear more that we may be thought to have pronounced judgment less severely than we ought to have, if I did not know that you were so inclined toward mercy that you would think that you should spare not only us because we spared him but also the man himself. But that man is trying to turn what we did out of kindness or negligence into a precedent in his favor and to use it as such. He cries out, "I either ought to sit upon my episcopal throne or I ought not to be a bishop," as if he now sits on any throne but his own. For on this account those places over which he was previously a bishop were left and entrusted to the same man lest he be said to have been illicitly transferred to another see contrary to the

---

4. For Celer, see perhaps Letters 56 and 57.

statutes of our predecessors.[5] Ought anyone to be a judge of such severity or of such leniency that either those who he decides should not be deprived of the dignity of the episcopacy should not be punished in any way or those who he decides deserve any punishment should be deprived of the dignity of the episcopacy?

8. There exist cases in which the Apostolic See judged or upheld the judgment of others that for certain sins certain men were neither to be stripped of their episcopal dignity nor to be left entirely unpunished. In order not to seek out examples far removed from our times, I shall mention recent ones. Let Priscus, a bishop of the province of Caesarea, cry out, "Either access to the primacy ought also to be open to me as it is to the others or the episcopacy ought not to remain mine." Let Victor, another bishop of the same province, who was left in the same punishment Priscus was and who was in communion with no bishop anywhere but in his own diocese, cry out. Let him cry out, I say, "Either I ought to be in communion with bishops everywhere, or I ought not to be in communion with them in my own area." Let Lawrence, a third bishop of the same province, cry out even in the words of Antonius, "Either I ought to sit on the episcopal throne for which I was ordained or I ought not to be a bishop." But who would find fault with these punishments except someone who does not pay enough attention to the fact that not all wrongdoing should be left unpunished nor all wrongdoing be punished in the same way?

9. Since, therefore, with the vigilant caution of a shepherd Pope Boniface stated in his letter when speaking of the bishop Antonius, "If he has honestly revealed to us the sequence of events," be informed now of the sequence of events that Antonius did not mention in his report and then of what was done after the letter of that man of holy memory was read in Africa. Then come to the aid of the people who are asking for your help through the mercy of Christ much more eagerly than Antonius, from whose disruptiveness they long to be set free. He himself or very frequent rumors threaten those people with legal proceedings, public officials, and attacks by the military as if they were charged with carrying out the judgment of the Apostolic See. As a result poor Catholic Christian people fear worse things from a Catholic bishop than they feared from the laws of the Catholic emperors for having been heretics. Do not allow this to go on, I beg you by the blood of Christ, by the memory of Peter the apostle, who warned the leaders of Christian peoples not to lord it over brethren with violence.[6] I commend to the kindness and love of Your Holiness both the people of Fussala, my Catholic children in Christ, and Bishop Antonius, my son in Christ, because I love them both. I am not angry at the people of Fussala for

---

5. That is, the particpants of the councils of Nicaea, Sardica, and Antioch, who had forbidden that a bishop move from one see to another.
6. See 1 Pt 5:3.

having brought a just complaint about me to your hearing because I afflicted them with a man by whom they were so mistreated, who was not yet tested by me and not yet grown strong with age. Nor do I want Antonius to be harmed, for the more I resist his evil desire the more sincerely I love him. Both of them deserve your mercy—the people in order that they may not suffer wrongs, Antonius in order that he may not cause them; they in order that they may not hate the Catholic Church if they do not receive help from Catholic bishops, especially from the Apostolic See itself, against a Catholic bishop, but he in order that he may not involve himself in such a great crime that he alienates from Christ those whom he wants to make his own against their will.

10. Amid this danger to both of them so great a fear and sorrow torments me, as I must confess to Your Goodness, that I would consider withdrawing from the office of administering the episcopacy and devoting myself to lamentations suited to my mistake if I saw that the Church was being ravaged by that man whose episcopacy I supported through imprudence and that it was even perishing—may God prevent this!—along with the destruction of the one who was ravaging it. For, recalling the words of the apostle, *If we would judge ourselves, we would not be judged by the Lord* (1 Cor 11:31), I will judge myself so that he may spare me, *who will judge the living and the dead* (2 Tm 4:1). But if you also want to revive the members of Christ in that area from their deadly fear and sadness and console my old age with this merciful justice, may God who comes to our aid through you in this tribulation and who has established you in that great see, reward you in the present life and also in the life to come.

Letter 210

In approximately 423 Augustine wrote to Felicity, the superior of the women's monastery at Hippo, who had taken the place of Augustine's sister at the latter's death, and to Rusticus, the superior of the men's monastery at Hippo, who was also the chaplain to the women's monastery. Augustine points out that among God's great acts of mercy is the tribulation that he occasionally sends to sinners as a warning that they should bring their lives into harmony with the word of God and thus avoid the wrath to come (paragraph 1). He insists that a rebuke is usually felt to be painful when it is received but often brings much good to the person who receives it. He tells them that one who gives a rebuke ought never to do so in order to repay evil with evil and urges the two to put more effort into achieving harmony than into giving rebukes (paragraph 2).

To his most beloved and most holy mother, Felicity, to his brother, Rusticus, and to the sisters who are with you, Augustine and those with me send greetings in the Lord.

1. *The Lord is good* (Lm 3:25), and his mercy is poured out everywhere, consoling us in his heart by your love. For he shows how much he loves those who believe and hope in him and love him and one another and what he reserves for them hereafter. He does this especially insofar as, though he threatens with eternal fire and with the devil[1] the wicked who are without faith and without hope if they persevere in their bad will up to the end, yet he bestows great blessings upon them in this world. For he *makes his sun rise over the good and the bad and sends rain upon the just and the unjust* (Mt 5:45). For he said this in a few words in order that we might think of more gifts. For who is able to count how many blessings and gratuitous gifts the wicked have in this life from him whom they hold in contempt? Among these there is this great gift: Through examples of occasional tribulations, which like a good doctor he blends in with the sweetness of this world, he warns them, if they are willing to pay attention, to flee from the wrath to come,[2] and, while they are on the road, that is, in this life, to bring themselves into harmony with the word of God, which they make into their enemy by living bad lives.[3] What, then, does the Lord God not give to human beings out of mercy when even tribulation is a benefit from him? For prosperity is a gift from the God who consoles us, but adversity is a gift from the God who warns us. And if he gives this, as I said, even to the evil, what does he prepare for those who are awaiting him in patience? Rejoice that you have been gathered by

---

1. See Mt 25:41.
2. See Mt 3:7; Lk 3:7.
3. See 1 Pt 4:11.

his grace into their number, *supporting one another in love, striving to preserve the unity of the Spirit in the bond of peace* (Eph 4:2-3). For you will not lack something to tolerate in one another except when the Lord has purified you, after death has been swallowed by victory, so that God may be all in all.[4]

2. We should, however, never love disagreements, but at times they arise, nonetheless, from love and are a test of love. For can we easily find anyone who is willing to be rebuked? And where is that wise person of whom scripture says, *Rebuke a wise man, and he will love you* (Prv 9:8)? Should we not, then, rebuke and correct a brother in order that he may head toward death without a worry? For it is likely to happen, and it often does happen, that, at the time when he is rebuked, a person becomes sad, resists, and objects. And yet afterwards he considers the rebuke alone in silence, where there is only God and he himself and where he does not fear the displeasure of human beings because he is rebuked but fears the displeasure of God because he is not corrected. And afterwards he will avoid committing the sin for which he was rightly rebuked. And to the extent he hates his sin, he loves his brother who he saw was opposed to his sin. But if he belongs to that number of people of whom scripture said, *Rebuke a fool, and it will cause him to hate you* (Prv 9:8 LXX), then the disagreement of that person does not arise from love, but it still actualizes and tests the love of the one who gives a rebuke. For he does not display hatred toward him, but the love that leads him to give the rebuke continues undisturbed, even when the one rebuked hates it. If, however, the one giving the rebuke wants to return evil for evil to someone who is angered at the person giving the rebuke, he was not worthy to give the rebuke but clearly deserves to be rebuked himself. Do this so that cases of anger either do not exist among you or so that they are done away with by a most speedy reconciliation as soon as they arise. Put more effort into establishing harmony among yourselves than into rebuking one another. For, just as vinegar spoils a container if it is kept there too long, so anger ruins a heart if it lasts until the next day. *Do this, then, and the God of peace will be with you* (Phil 4:9), and at the same time pray for us also that we may quickly carry out the good admonitions we give.

---

4. See 1 Cor 15:57.54.28.

Index of Scripture

(prepared by Michael Dolan)

(The numbers after the scriptural reference refer to the section of the work)

Old Testament

Genesis

1:22	184A, 1, 3
1:24	205, 2, 9
2:2	166, 5, 11
2:7	205, 2, 9; 205, 2, 10
2:23	190, 5, 18
15:6	196, 3, 10
16:12	165, 2, 2
17:5	196, 3, 10
21:12	196, 3, 11
22:18	185, 1, 5; 196, 3, 10
25:23	194, 8, 35; 194, 8, 38; 196, 3, 13
26:4	185, 1, 5
46:26 LXX	190, 5, 18

Exodus

3:15	157, 4, 24
9:16	186, 6, 17; 194, 8, 39
20:14. 13-17	196, 4, 16
20:17	157, 2, 6; 157, 2, 9; 177, 10; 194, 6, 28; 196, 1, 3; 196, 1, 4; 196, 2, 6; 196, 2, 8
23:7	204, 8
28:3	157, 1, 2
33:19	186, 6, 16; 186, 9, 33; 194, 8, 35; 194, 8, 39
34:4	173, 3

Leviticus

19:18	177, 10; 189, 2
26:12	187, 12, 35

Deuteronomy

5:21	157, 2, 6; 194, 6, 28; 196, 1, 3
6:5	189, 2
6:13	170, 2
7:25	157, 2, 6; 194, 6, 28; 196, 1, 3
13:3	162, 7
13:4	205, 2, 16

Job

7:1	187, 8, 28; 189, 8
14:1 LXX	190, 3, 10; 193, 2, 3
14:4-5 LXX	166, 3, 6; 202A, 8, 17
14:5 LXX	193, 2, 3
28:28 LXX	167, 3, 11

Psalms

2:1-2	185, 5, 19
2:7	185, 1, 3
2:8	185, 1, 3
2:10-11	185, 5, 19
3:3	177, 1
4:4	188, 3, 9
7:3	186, 10, 34
7:4	186, 10, 34
9:5	186, 10, 36
13:1	184A, 3, 6
16:10	164, 2, 3; 164, 3, 8; 187, 2, 5; 205, 2, 9
18:37	185, 2, 11
19:5	198, 6; 199, 12, 50
22:7	161, 1
22:17	199, 12, 50
22:17-19	185, 1, 3
22:28-29	185, 1, 3
23:5	158, 2
23:6	194, 5, 19
25:10	186, 4, 12; 194, 3, 6
27:9	157, 2, 10; 180, 6; 182, 3
29:10	187, 13, 38
30:8	188, 2, 7
32:9	177, 5; 185, 2, 7

401

General Index

(prepared by Kathleen Strattan)

The first number in the Index is the Letter number.
The number after the colon is a paragraph number.